P9-AQM-485

David Glenn Hunt
Memorial Library
Galveston College

In Memory Of

Mr. A. B. Wisrodt

BAY ST. LOUIS
SOCIETATIS VERBI DIVINI

EX LIBRIS
FATHERS' LIBRARY
BAY ST. LOUIS, MISS.
SOCIETATIS VERBI DIVINI

THE LION RAMPANT

THE STORY OF HOLLAND'S RESISTANCE TO THE NAZIS

mod. Hist.
EX LIBRIS
FATHERS' LIBRARY
BAY ST. LOUIS, MISS.
SOCIETATIS VERBI DIVINI

949.207
De J

Copyright, 1943
by L. de Jong and Joseph W. F. Stoppelman

All rights reserved, including the rights to reproduce this book or portions thereof in any form, except for the purpose of reviews in newspapers, or magazines

FIRST PRINTING

This book is based upon L. de Jong's "Je Maintiendrai, I & II" written in Dutch and printed in London. It has been translated, adapted and brought up to date by Joseph W. F. Stoppelman

THE LION RAMPANT

THE STORY OF HOLLAND'S RESISTANCE TO THE NAZIS

By L. de JONG
AND
JOSEPH W. F. STOPPELMAN

DAVID GLENN HUNT
MEMORIAL LIBRARY
GALVESTON COLLEGE

QUERIDO • NEW YORK

D
802
.N4
J452

PRINTED IN THE UNITED STATES OF AMERICA

CONTENTS

PAGE

Foreword i

Introduction iii

CHAPTER

1 The Debacle—Self-Reliance Regained 1

2 In the German Web 31

3 The Locusts Settle Down 50

4 The Specter of Malnutrition 72

5 Labor's Downfall and Enslavement 89

6 Plight of the Peasants 109

7 Mussert's School for Traitors 128

8 Unholy Crusades 153

9 "A Mighty Fortress . . ." 186

10 Slaughter of the Innocents 209

11 A Rallying Cry 234

12 Youth under Siege 248

13 "Kultur" Infusions 271

14 Charity at Pistol Point 306

15 Tragedy in the Far East 319

16 Triumph of the Spirit 331

Appendix I—Text of General Winkelman's Declaration (June 27, 1940) 347

Appendix II—The Peace Courts in Action 349

Appendix III—Texts of, and Excerpts from, Several Pastoral Letters 354

Bibliography 364

Index 366

H. M. QUEEN WILHELMINA OF THE NETHERLANDS

Foreword

Seventy years ago a distinguished American scholar, John Lothrop Motley, visited Holland. He buried himself in the archives of the sixteenth and seventeenth centuries and before his mind's eye there rose the picture of a nation which, united and undaunted, struggled for freedom political and religious.

Our knowledge of conditions and events in occupied Holland is, alas, far from complete. Thus the time has not yet come for a second John Lothrop Motley to write a logical sequence to "The Rise of the Dutch Republic." This is, however, certain: the trials which the people of the Netherlands are now facing can only be compared with those of the famous Eighty Years' War of Liberation against Spain. What they lack in duration, they make up for in intensity. The tyranny of Seyss-Inquart and Himmler is worse than that of the Duke of Alva. But the spiritual courage and perseverance of Dutch men and women in the twentieth century equal those of their ancestors. Since the day when Germany treacherously attacked the Dutch, an epic chapter is being added to Holland's history. It is written with the life blood of the nation.

The Dutch are an industrious people. Their standard of living was one of the highest in Europe. Now millions of them are starving. Hundreds of thousands are mercilessly exploited in German factories. Families have been broken up. The wealth of a nation is being destroyed. The forced mass migration of one-third of the entire population threatens the Dutch like the sword of Damocles.

Worse than the material pillage of the Germans is their spiritual tyranny. Churches are robbed of their freedom—the press and radio, the arts and education have been or are being nazified. The noblest sons of the Dutch people suffer in concentration camps. Those Netherlanders who are of Jewish descent are herded together, and transported to the slaughterhouse.

It is with a sense of gratitude and humility that I can record here that in spite of their unspeakable sufferings the Dutch have not merely kept up their will to active resistance, but their spirits have deepened. Truly apostolic virtues have grown in this people. Innumerable Dutchmen have risked their lives so as to protect their fellow men. Innumerable others have refused to betray their conscience even when they knew this refusal meant imprisonment in a concentration camp. Time and again the Protestant churches courageously protested against German injustice. The Catholic Church of Holland defends its spiritual heritage in a way which is, perhaps, unequalled in all other countries that have been overrun by the Nazis. Stronger than ever are the ties which, with the sad exception of a handful of traitors, bind all Dutchmen together to indissoluble unity. Stronger than ever are the ties which bind the Dutch nation in Europe to their brothers, Dutch and Indonesian, in the Netherlands East Indies who suffer under the yoke of another tyranny.

There is not one Dutchman who doubts that the Allies will win the war.

There are some, however, who doubt whether the war will be won in time. In time before irreparable damage has been done to the nation of William the Silent, Grotius and Rembrandt, which in the future might no doubt add valuable treasures to mankind's civilization. Darkness grows deeper every day over the quiet towns and pastures of Holland. If we, together with the United Nations, win the war in time, collaboration with the peoples of Indonesia, Surinam, and Curaçao—within the frame of the new commonwealth based upon the complete partnership of which Queen Wilhelmina spoke in her memorable speech of December 6, 1942—will create that renewed kingdom which will be able to fulfill its honorable task among the free nations. The shadows of henchmen are multiplied. Hunger gnaws at a shivering people.

For the Dutch, for their great Queen, for their government the winning of this war is not measured in years, but in months, in weeks, even in days.

PIETER S. GERBRANDY,
Prime Minister of The Netherlands

Introduction

The story of Holland's occupation is one of ever-growing suffering. If during the first twelve months of Nazi subjugation existence was still bearable, the situation changed swiftly for the worse after the weary winter months of 1940-1941. Each day brought new measures, restricting still further the normal scope of life. The Germans no longer endeavored to hide their greed and arrogance. Robbing the Netherlands of all its material wealth had failed to satisfy their claim to blind obedience and recognition as Europe's one and only "Herrenvolk." In their usual deliberate, methodical manner they now concentrated on the disintegration of Holland's spiritual heritage. The last vestiges of their would-be "friendly attitude" were thrown to the winds.

From the spring of 1941 the people of the Netherlands have led an existence of nerve-shattering tension. There is boundless terror to be faced; every hour may hold fresh, completely incalculable acts of tyranny. The freedom of body and mind, which was a Dutchman's birthright, has utterly disappeared. Each action and utterance, and almost every thought, are carefully "regulated" by the enemy.

Gradually chaos is taking the place of order and progressive action. The individual is made to obey orders by the foulest of tricks; his livelihood, and his belongings—even his personal safety—are of no consequence. It is the National-Socialist State, and more especially the unquestioned servitude to Nazi Germany, which comes first, last and always. Whatever in such circumstances there is left to enjoy, must be adequately appreciated and thankfully acknowledged. Even those last pitiable scraps of freedom may soon be lost.

Not a single Dutch citizen, immaterial of sex or creed, knows whether next week, tomorrow or even the next few minutes will bring his arrest by the Gestapo and his removal to the fearful tortures of a German prison, or concentration camp. In a country where home-life was highly developed and intensely respected, families are now torn asunder without so much as an excuse. A defenseless minority of Dutch Jews has been badgered and brow-beaten for two long years and is now being exterminated with a display of unbelievable bestiality. Thousands of others whose "Aryan" qualifications cannot be doubted, are none the less up-rooted from the soil on which they lived for countless generations, and deported to far-off lands with which their mental make-up has little or nothing in common.

The bitter contrast between what is now and what was only three years ago, is particularly tragic because of the very genuine prosperity Holland knew before the coming of the Nazis. Where "enough for everyone" was taken for granted, where timely social measures had done much to cope with the problems of unemployment, ill health and old age, there are hunger, forced labor and the persecution of masses of workers who steadfastly refuse to be nazified. Where the dietetic care of babies embraced all classes of the community so that the death rate had been greatly reduced, the health of children and adolescents is impaired and undermined through the chronic lack of the most essential nourishment. Where food was cheap and good, where vegetables were produced in such abundance that even the poorest could make their choice and have their fill, there is only left the empty promise of easily-printed rationing cards. Acorns, thistles and the leaves of wild plants, things once hardly considered fit for cattle fodder, are now eagerly gathered to "complete" the daily diet of millions of Netherlanders.

And as if such undeserved privations were not enough, nature made the winter of 1941-1942 one of the severest experienced within living memory. From October to the middle of March the country was covered with snow; across the land the storms blew wilder and more implacable than ever. There was little solace in the fact that for more than four consecutive months many of Holland's lakes lay frozen, ready to carry the throngs of skaters. Not a single home had sufficient fuel. Throughout the entire nation the cold brought additional hardship. And in the midst of these material sufferings came the terrible shock of the loss of the Netherlands East Indies.

The occupying powers might well have expected that such atrocious months would mellow the proud spirit of Dutch recalcitrancy, the obstinacy which thus far had made things so difficult for them. They may conceivably have hoped that the people of the Netherlands would, at last, decide to become tractable. But in expecting such things to happen, the Germans simply repeated their common error of underestimating the rallying power of a "subjugated" nation.

The longer the occupation lasted, the better the Dutch people realized that no compromise could be possible with their enemies. The struggle for an independent existence, a battle for life or death, had to be fought to the end—no matter the cost. The more terrible and heartrending their privations, the stronger grew their conviction that the slightest rapprochement between them and the enemy would be an irreparable mistake. Proportionately the general hatred for Anton Mussert's Dutch Nazi movement grew in intensity. These traitors had ample reasons for complaint, in their papers and on the nazified radio, of their compatriots' stupidity. Wherever loyal Netherlanders saw their chance, they made the lives of those 100,000 Dutch Nazis most uncomfortable.

During that entire winter, and throughout 1942, sabotage increased apace—in a thousand different manners, at a thousand different risks. Not even the harshest Nazi punishment could stem this tide. Hundreds of brave compatriots fell victims to the German firing squads; immediately their empty places were filled by others. It is the glory of the Netherlands that German tyranny has not been able to exterminate its preparedness to stake everything on the grim fight against nazification. The people of Holland realized that, exposed as they were to slow but certain impoverishment, the moment was near in which there would be "nothing to lose but their chains."

Today the struggle continues. It is a harsh and relentless fight, not only for a mere sustenance but also to protect the spiritual values of life. There are few in the occupied territory who have not at some time during those many months felt the pangs of despair and utter weariness. In those hours most of them must have derived support from their beliefs. For even if before the German invasion, religious life in the Netherlands tended to become rather stagnant and colorless, now—in common vicissitudes

—it underwent a miraculous rebirth. It turned into something deeper, much more akin to its original concept. Hundreds of thousands suddenly recognized in the time-hallowed words of the Bible a profound and significant mirror of their own tribulations. Thus the Church became one of the most important places in which the people of Holland could demonstrate their strong decision never to yield the freedom of spirit which had been theirs for so many centuries.

There were, undeniably, periods of disappointment and depression, during and after the second year of German occupation. So much had, for instance, been expected of Colonel Briton's "V" campaign which promised to be such a splendid weapon. But the enemy, with uncanny astuteness, knew how to wrest it from the Allied grasp, applying it deftly to its own purposes. There were, moreover, the ever-repeated prophecies of optimists who "foresaw a speedy end to the war." There was the surge of hope when Rudolph Hess made his mysterious flight to England. There was the jubilant expectation of an early German defeat when the Nazi radio, forced to stop its usual boast, admitted sadly that the winter campaign in Soviet Russia was no longer "progressing according to plan."

So great was the enemy's pressure, so burning the desire for liberation that often the wish turned possibilities into "reality," or blew up small happenings to events of primary importance. But perhaps this wishful thinking was an indispensable ingredient in the mixture of staunch belief in ultimate victory, confidence in the future and courage to cope with present miseries. For however deep the inevitable disappointments, Dutch buoyancy proved so great and indestructible that it easily survived each successive blow. The evidence provided by refugees from the Netherlands—men who escaped as late as the early autumn of 1942—is conclusive; the Dutch have not changed. Their hope of early liberation is natural enough; for the longer the occupation lasts, the greater and more serious will be the damage done to the national structure, both materially and spiritually.

However deeply loathed and hated, however fiercely obstructed, a system which punishes the good and innocent and rewards the bad and cruel, must needs have devastating results in the long run—if not on the adult population then certainly on the country's adolescents, the hundreds of thousands whose moral consciousness still undergoes the process of formation.

INTRODUCTION

Every new day is a long and weary fight against the heaviest of odds, a struggle more difficult because it cannot be fought out in the open. The enemy is holding a splendid card; it is with ruse and subterfuge alone that his attention can be diverted from his invidious game. Danger lurks in every corner; the Nazi execution squads are indefatigable. Perfidy and rascality have taken the place of law and order; but in his heart every loyal Dutchman knows that ultimately justice will be done. One day the Germans will discover how weak were the foundations of their power; it is the anticipation of that day which fires Dutch resistance. To hasten the coming of that hour every patriot wants to do something, be it listening to prohibited broadcasts, the stealthy reading of an underground newspaper or the act of sabotage which he may have to pay for with his life—and perhaps with the lives of many hostages.

The story of that bravery is the story of millions of Dutch soldiers in the front ranks of battle against the iron-fisted Nazi robot. It is the story of Holland's war, a war which did not end with the subjugation of its regular armies, but will continue until the glorious moment has come of a decisive Allied victory.

JOSEPH W. F. STOPPELMAN

New York, June, 1943.

1

THE DEBACLE—SELF-RELIANCE REGAINED

> ". . . After the first few weeks of occupation, romancing—in the worst sense of the word—made its re-appearance. It began with Prince Bernhard carnations, orange-colored chicken rings, etc. Soon it took to more serious manifestations, the destruction of sign posts and cutting of wires and cables. Not to mention the most immoral utterances of mental degeneration in revolutionary times, such as the threat of assassination held out against National-Socialist compatriots . . ."
>
> *National-Socialist leader Anton Adriaan Mussert, in his weekly 'Volk en Vaderland' of March 7, 1941.*

At 7 p.m. on Tuesday May 14, 1940, the Dutch radio which had been ominously silent almost all day, asked attention for an important statement. The tired voice was heard of the Commander-in-Chief of all Dutch defense forces. In a few sentences General Winkelman told the people of Holland that their army—after an heroic struggle in which it had suffered bloody losses—had been forced to capitulate. Only in the province of Zeeland, that southwestern island corner of the Kingdom, the battle against the Nazi hordes was still progressing. This announcement made an overwhelming impression; it was the heaviest blow yet experienced since the start of the invasion on Friday, May 10, at dawn.

The five days of war had been filled with emotion. And on this very afternoon of May 14 the people had been told that their Queen, obliged to leave the country, had proceeded to London. The Government, too, had departed for a "safer place"; and now —as a culminating blow—came this announcement of the capitulation. The Netherlands had lost its independence; it had fallen victim to the cruelest aggression of all time.

Seven p.m.; the shadows were growing longer. The fertile fields of Holland lay bathed in golden light; in a short while the sun would set and the dark of night descend upon immeasurable suffering and painful confusion. All over the country desperate people were asking themselves: "Why this fateful decision? Why did we not fight on?"

General Winkelman knew why. His defense plan had been that of giving up the northern and eastern parts of the Netherlands and retiring within the fortress of Holland—behind the double protection of the Grebbe and Water Lines. With the help of the British and the French, via the provinces of Brabant and Zeeland, that fortress was to be made into an impregnable bastion. But this plan had come to nought.

In the north the Dutch troops supported by Dutch gunboats had been able to retire across the Zuider Zee dyke, a magnificent piece of Dutch engineering which had turned a part of the sea into new territory ready to receive and feed thousands of citizens. With French and British assistance it had been possible to prevent the Germans from crossing the Zuider Zee in boats to attack the heart of Holland; but in the center and south of the country the enemy had got all he wanted—though with considerable delay. He broke the Grebbe Line first of all, so that in the afternoon of May 14 Nazi troops were rapidly approaching the city of Utrecht. In the south the German panzer divisions had crushed their way through the defense lines of the Peel, in North Brabant province, and though fighting heroically, the Dutch troops and their French comrades were thrown back towards Antwerp. On the Monday night the German troops, after a fierce battle near Dordrecht and the Moerdijk Bridge, had reached Rotterdam. Here Nazi parachutists who had based themselves upon the Waalhaven airdrome, were fiercely battling against attacks of the R.A.F. and answering the fire of the Dutch who were holding the northern bank of the Maas river. Throughout Tuesday, May 14, these fights continued, without success for the Germans. Yet, it was evident that resistance near Rotterdam had sooner or later to come to an end, as all contact with the fortress of Holland had been cut off. Simultaneously every chance of receiving assistance from the South had been destroyed.

But the German High Command was in a hurry. Its efforts to take the heart of Holland by surprise, to land paratroops on the airfields around The Hague so as to imprison the Queen and her Government, had come to nothing thanks to the decisive and courageous behavior of the Netherlands Reserve troops. At the Belgian-French border German mechanized divisions were fighting fiercely. The Belgian Army, as well as the northern French divisions and the British Expeditionary Force, were almost encircled; but hundreds of thousands of Germans now engaged in subjugating Holland were urgently needed to help annihilate those allied armies by pushing them into the sea.

And still the defenses of Rotterdam held out.

At 1:20 that Tuesday afternoon fifty-four German Stukas, in exemplary formation, appeared above the center of the town. No longer did the Dutch have any fighters to assist in the defense and it was, therefore, an easy matter for the Germans to silence the few anti-aircraft guns which were trying to shoot the gigantic Nazi bombers out of the sky.

The Stukas made a thorough job of it. A rain of heavy caliber bombs came down upon the streets and squares of the city. Against this monstrous onslaught there was not the slightest chance of defense. The Rotterdam fire brigade, doing its heroic best, was powerless as almost immediately after the start of the attack the water mains had burst. Fires started here, there and everywhere and in less than twenty minutes more than two square miles of city blocks were turned into a blazing hell of death and devastation. The compact columns of black smoke arising from these ruins could be seen for miles around; in fact—throughout the province of South Holland the destruction of its capital was visible.

Inside the city the scene was a veritable shambles. Thousands of people were torn to shreds by the concussion of the heavy German bombs; and thousands more who had desperately run to shelters for some sort of protection, were choked to death in the fumes, or burned alive. All roads leading out of the town were crowded with dazed or hysterical refugees, carrying children or objects—generally of the most insignificant kind. They pushed and crushed each other in a mad scramble to get out of this man-made inferno. The insatiable flames devoured one street after the other. The venerable tower of the ancient St. Laurens Church burned like a torch, and above the roaring of the flames could be heard the thundering noise of crumbling houses and the shrieking and exploding of more and more Nazi bombs, coming down with clockwork regularity.

At 10:30 that same morning General Winkelman who, with his staff, was staying in the vicinity of Rotterdam, had been served with an ultimatum to halt the defense of Rotterdam immediately, as otherwise the severest measures would be taken. That ultimatum expired at 12:30 p.m., . . . but the General had been unable to act upon it. It was unsigned, so that in view of Fifth Column treachery already experienced by army and civilians alike, the possibility of a hoax was by no means excluded.

General Winkelman, therefore, answered that a proposal of this kind could only be taken into consideration "if it were duly authenticated and signed by a German Commander." The answer to this written request arrived at 12:15 p.m.—one-quarter of an hour before the original ultimatum expired. Immediately the Dutch Commander-in-Chief took the necessary measures to have one of his Staff meet a German officer at a certain point of Rotterdam's outer defenses. To this officer a new ultimatum was handed at 1:20 p.m. It was valid for a further period of three hours; but before the Dutch messenger could return to Winkelman's Headquarters, the wanton bombardment of Rotterdam had already commenced and was approaching the height of its monstrous fury. Had General Winkelman remained adamant, unwilling even to discuss the matter of surrender, the destruction of Rotterdam would have been followed up by similar cowardly attacks on the thickly-populated centers of Amsterdam, The Hague and Utrecht. Before the Government left for London it had given the General complete authority to act as he thought fit. No doubt, to take the decision to capitulate was an exceedingly grave responsibility—but there was no other way out. If a continuance of the unequal battle could have been of any advantage to the Allied cause, General Winkelman would have been the first to ignore the German ultimatum. But continued resistance would only have meant the useless sacrifice of hundreds of thousands more innocent lives. That this decision confused the Dutch masses, however, was nothing to wonder at. The people of Holland were filled with indignation at the treacherous German attack, the use of parachutists and the appearance of a thoroughly-loathed Fifth Column. It was hard to realize that the fight against the hated Hun had suddenly collapsed.

Nine million people saw themselves suddenly placed under the German yoke. In five days a struggle which had been expected to last five months had come to its end. It seemed ages ago that life had been peaceful and unharassed; and the near future was a dark, impenetrable abyss. Town and country were in a state of chaos. Family existence was broken up. Here a town would lie abandoned; there a city would be overcrowded with thousands of refugees. Jewels of architecture, lovely age-old bell-towers, had been turned into heaps of smoking rubble. In Zeeland province the guns were still speaking. Across the North Sea a few small vessels were gingerly "feeling" their way through the mine fields: poor fugitives, not knowing what tomorrow would hold in store for them. All ports were blocked and the gasoline storage tanks beside the North Sea Canal were burning away like furnaces.

In Amsterdam the situation was particularly tragic, for here thousands of German refugees had found a haven, ofttimes after endless vicissitudes and suffering under Hitler domination. Once again they were caught in the Nazi net—but hundreds of them felt incapable of shouldering anew the terrible burden of persecution. The number of suicides that day was so great that the municipal Health Department was incapable of gathering the bodies of all the unfortunates with its ambulances. Large trucks were hired, and these lumbering vehicles drove incessantly in and out of the hospital gates. Among those who took their lives were many Netherlanders who preferred death to suffering under German tyranny. Not only in Amsterdam, but also at The Hague and in numerous smaller towns, men and women who had attained honorable places in the ranks of Holland's intellectuals, administrators, scholars and creative artists, killed themselves.

That same evening the Dutch authorities were ordered to release all members of the Dutch Nazi Movement—the N. S. B.'ers as they were generally called—who had been imprisoned during the days of war. They swarmed into the open from all sorts of real and makeshift prisons . . . six thousand Hollanders who had proved themselves fully unworthy of that name. They had conspired with the enemy, betrayed their own country; and only ten of them had paid for those crimes with their lives. Their leader, the ex-engineer Anton Adriaan Mussert, thoroughly shaken by the hostile attitude of the large majority of patriots, did not dare to show himself as yet. He remained in hiding somewhere east of Amsterdam.

The next day came and the fires of Rotterdam were still burning with undiminished fierceness. Tens of thousands of homeless had been forced to spend the night in the open. And amidst this utter misery, while Holland was still bleeding from a thousand wounds, the capitulation was formally signed in the village school of Rijsoord, under the smoke of devastated Rotterdam.

But in Zeeland the valiant Dutch were still fighting and

neither the Netherlands navy nor the powerful Merchant Marine had fallen into the enemy's hands.

*

Without loss of time the German military authorities started to "regulate" things their way. For the while they left in office the various Secretaries-General of the governmental departments who—now that the Ministers had gone to London—formed a sort of Cabinet ad interim. A price ceiling was announced for nearly all commodities, and private transportation with motorcars and -cycles was made dependent on special permits. The German High Command in the occupied Netherlands had already started to requisition all Dutch stocks of gasoline and transportation material, mainly for the transfer of troops and arms to Belgium and Northern France. Payment was made in strange-looking banknotes, the like of which Holland had never seen before. They were the so-called "Reichskreditkassenscheine," Reich's credit bills.

In an incessant stream German columns marched through Haarlem and Amsterdam to Utrecht. But the Dutch paid little attention to these "victorious" troops. Only a handful of Mussert's followers came out to "welcome their German brothers" with flowers, chocolates and cigarettes. For the rest Amsterdam was like a dead city; its inhabitants stayed at home.

But when the next few days went by without tidings of murder or pillaging, the people seemed to regain their equilibrium. And, strange to say, gradually life began to follow its normal course again. Once more the newspapers appeared, all of them carrying an announcement in bold lettering that "publication was resumed *without censorship* of the German High Command." But the risibility of this announcement was clear from the sentence immediately following: that the printing of any news item detrimental to German interests must be strictly avoided . . . Theatres and cinemas reopened their doors and even the bars were allowed to resume business. But simultaneously all sorts of "prohibitions" were announced. The distribution of pamphlets in which resistance against the Germans was recommended, became a punishable act. Strikes, too, were "verboten." Netherlands and German soldiers must from now on salute each other. On Saturday, May 18 a decree from Adolf Hitler himself outlined the authority of those Germans who were to be placed at the head of the occupation troops. A Reich's Commissioner was to be appointed, with The

Hague for his domicile. It would be up to him to "protect" all German interests and to head civil authority in the country. As to military power, this would be wielded by the Commander of the German troops within the occupied Netherlands.

The Reich's Commissioner would be assisted by the so-called "Green" or German police for the execution of his instructions. The same police would be at the disposal of the German Military Commander in Holland whenever he might be in need of it. Finally, the Reich's Commissioner *might* also avail himself of the services of Dutch administrators. Dutch law would remain in force, as far as feasible under the occupation. All decrees would be printed in a new official journal, to appear under the name of "Verordeningenblad voor het bezette Nederlandsche gebied."*

And finally the name was revealed of the new Reich's Commissioner . . . He was the Austrian arch-traitor Dr. Arthur Seyss-Inquart! "An Austrian," the Germans said significantly, hoping that this would awaken memories in the Dutch of Tyrolese yodeling and Viennese jollity. But the Netherlands' people were not so short of memory that they could not recall the name of Seyss-Inquart. Indeed—they knew him only too well, this Austrian rapscallion. So *he* was considered good enough to play boss over all Hollanders. What irony of fate!

Meanwhile more bad news seeped through from the outer world. The French lines had yielded. German panzer troops were blitzkrieging in the direction of Paris. And on May 19 the last stronghold of the Netherlands, the island of Walcheren, capitulated. Now the entire Netherlands lay under the heel of Nazism.

On May 25, less than a fortnight after the destruction of Rotterdam, Seyss-Inquart took full command of the country and on that occasion addressed the people of Holland in a speech which was an extraordinary mixture of flattery and blackmail. All over the country, people gathered before Government buildings and shop windows to read this peculiar document.

"From today," it began, "I have taken over the highest Civil authority in the Netherlands. The magnanimity of the Fuehrer and the force of German arms have made it possible that only a few days after the catastrophe which was brought about by the former leaders of the Netherlands, order is being restored to public life. Certain measures will be taken, but only in so far as the circumstances will make them necessary . . ."

---

*"Official Journal of Decrees for the occupied territory of the Netherlands."

Then came the flattery.

"The soldiers of the Netherlands have fought bravely, and the entire civilian population behaved orderly towards the fighting troops. There is nothing to prevent us from meeting each other now with full respect. The German people, under the command of its Fuehrer, fights a decisive battle for existence, a struggle forced upon it by the hatred and envy of its enemies. That struggle obliges the German nation to stake all its strength, and entitles it to use every means at its disposal. This, and the law of necessity, will influence the life of the Dutch people and their economy. I shall, however, strive to attain that the people of Holland, blood relatives of the German people, will not fall into less favorable circumstances than our common destiny and our enemies' lust for destruction will necessitate . . ."

No special perspicacity was required to read between the lines of this announcement. To be sure, the magnanimity of the German defense forces had been overwhelmingly experienced in Rotterdam, Middelburg or Rhenen . . . "The catastrophe which was brought about by the former leaders of the Netherlands" . . . , but not a soul believed in the German fairy tale of an Allied invasion of the Rhineland via Holland, a plan which—supposedly—had been frustrated by the German attack on the Netherlands.

Four days after the publication of this literary product, Seyss-Inquart appeared in person, and the Germans—despite their airs of friendliness—did not want to miss this chance to make it clear that the people of Holland had lost their sovereignty to the mighty Reich.

With specifically Teutonic absence of all tact the ancient Hall of the Knights (Ridderzaal) at The Hague, in which Queen Wilhelmina used to open the winter session of the States-General in solemn ceremony, was prepared for the inaugural rites of Reich's Commissioner Seyss-Inquart. In vain did the Nazis endeavor to hire a Netherlands orchestra for the occasion. In the end the orchestra of the Cologne Broadcasting System was commandeered and transported to The Hague, to produce the usual Wagnerian hullabaloo.

Seyss-Inquart's inaugural speech brought little news. He complained bitterly that the Dutch Government, "now cowardly taken to flight," had made common cause with the enemy, thus *forcing* the Germans to occupy Holland. "Rather would we have come here with our hand lifted in salute than with weapons in our

JUGGERNAUT OVER HOLLAND

(*top*:) Nazi soldiers inspect a Dutch machine gun in an abandoned pillbox; (*bottom, left*:) the assault on Maastricht. German soldiers mount a smashed bridge over the Maas River by means of ladders; (*right*:) more Nazi parachutists descend upon Holland's peaceful meadows.

JUGGERNAUT OVER HOLLAND

(*top*:) German planes burning on a main road near The Hague; (*bottom, left*:) the attack on Rotterdam. The city is already aflame; the river bridge in the background is blown up; (*right*:) members of a mechanized Nazi column crossing a heavily defended canal, under protection of their own machine guns.

THE WORK IS DONE! . . .

(*top:*) Remains of the beautiful, late-Gothic Town Hall of Middelburg, in Zeeland province; (*right:*) before the Nazi bombing; (*bottom:*) the ruins of Rotterdam's center—750 city blocks in ashes. The damaged tower of the devastated St. Lawrence Church dominates the general desolation.

THE WORK IS DONE! . . .

(*top, left*:) A child victim of the Nazi bombing of Rotterdam; the onlooker is dazed by the tragedy he witnessed; (*top, right*:) Nazi soldier trying to get information from taciturn inhabitants; (*bottom*:) inspection of Nazi troops in the courtyard of the Houses of Parliament, at The Hague.

fist . . . ," he said, and he continued:

"We Germans who go through life with an eye trained to discover the blood value of a nation, are glad to be in the Netherlands. We do not come here to suppress and annihilate a people, or to take away from it its liberty . . . The Germans do not wish to subjugate imperialistically this country and its population. Nor do they desire to force upon them their political convictions. Their activities will be limited by the necessities resulting from the state of war."

Common law was to be maintained as far as possible, Seyss-Inquart repeated reassuringly, and the standard of living was not to decline below the German level. His first deed would be that of founding a Reconstruction Fund. And the new Commissioner concluded:

"We are to build a new Europe based upon the foundations of honor and common labor. We all know that the ultimate purpose of our Fuehrer is: peace and order for all who are of good will."

In this ambiguous statement some Netherlanders found reasons for satisfaction. Whatever the Germans intended to do, they were, it seemed, not going to import their hated creed.

But those innocents were sadly mistaken. Had they asked any Dutch Nazi, they would soon have discovered the truth. For those privileged gentlemen knew that their chance had come at last. Had not those of them who were taken prisoners by the legal Dutch Government been quickly released by Hitler's henchmen? There even was the heartening case of twenty Dutch Nazis who, transferred to France during the days of battle with the intention of shipping them to Great Britain, had been extradited by the French and returned to The Hague.

On June 5 the first copy of the "Verordeningenblad" appeared and on the next day four General Commissioners were appointed as assistants to Seyss-Inquart and with the special task to supervise and direct the various government departments. The first threads of the German web had been spun.

*

Work had to be resumed. There was much to do—so much that many people were forced to forget their private worries. There were, as most urgent problems, the inundation and the chaos in Rotterdam.

For many months now large sections of the center of Holland had lain inundated and to these many more areas had been added during the invasion days. It had been necessary to evacuate tens of thousands of people. More than a hundred thousand head of cattle were grazing in strange pastures. All of these creatures—men as well as beasts—had to be returned from where they had come, and it took many weeks to accomplish this gigantic task. Bridges were to be repaired, traffic reinstated and a beginning was to be made with the reconstruction of devastated towns.

First of all came the draining of the flooded land. Pumping stations which had been inactive for decades, were put to work again—and in less than three weeks the entire inundated surface was drained. The peasantry could return to its soil, even though no trace was left of their farmsteads. Only where the land had been covered with brackish water more time would have to elapse before agricultural activities could be resumed. Undaunted, the farmers started out once more to tend to the soil, heartened perhaps by the promise that all damage done to their property would be indemnified . . . Not immediately—but as soon as a Special Commission had studied every separate case.

A far greater problem was the city of Rotterdam. The center of that busy town, once the greatest port of the European continent and the second city of the Netherlands, was a dismal ruin. The indignation about this wanton vandalism was general; all Holland mourned a town it had known so well and loved so deeply. As to the victims, weeks after the catastrophe innumerable families were still without news of missing relatives. Nonetheless, a month before clearance of the rubble had been completed the German authorities stated officially that 619 people had been killed in the bombardment of Rotterdam. But within a week these gentlemen were obliged to correct their ludicrous understatement; now they admitted that the number of victims was 740. This figure was published on August 7, 1940 and has never been corrected since. At present no one knows how many men, women and children were suffocated or burned alive during the holocaust. Figures as large as 20,000 dead and 30,000 wounded are still making the round—but only after the war will it be possible to reveal to a horrified world the exact size of this dastardly Nazi crime.

The fact remains that all of Rotterdam's hospitals were filled beyond capacity with the wounded and dying—in the end numbers of hospital ships were requisitioned and, anchoring on the River Maas, received their generous share of mangled Hitler victims.

More than 11,000 buildings, with a total of 26,000 apartments, had been destroyed. The wind blew clouds of dust throughout the desolate town and it was necessary to protect one's mouth with a kerchief when climbing across the ruins. Nevertheless, almost everybody in and around the theatre of destruction suffered from laryngitis.

Nearly 77,000 people had been robbed of their homes, and the majority of them had, moreover, lost all they ever possessed: furniture, clothing, offices, shops and industries. Where to find shelter for these refugees? Only ten thousand of them were able to pay for a hotel room, or find a hospitable roof elsewhere. The remainder was forced to rely on public charity. Every empty dwelling in or around Rotterdam was requisitioned; entire families were constrained to live in one room. But when every nook and corner had thus been filled, there were still forty thousand people to be taken care of—and to them were added 5,000 soldiers returning to the Netherlands after their demobilization.

In all surrounding towns, to a distance of more than 20 miles, municipal authorities and private enterprise tried to come to the rescue. But even then, with every house and public building in Gouda, Delft, The Hague, Schiedam and Vlaardingen filled to capacity, there were still twenty thousand people without homes. All around the city tent encampments sprang into existence, though most of these tents did not come up to military requirements. A few poles and across these a length of tarpaulin—and there you had another abode for one or more distracted families.

It was clear that this situation could not last, although the weather remained singularly good. The whole country had to help and so it happened that, ultimately, no less than 386 communities throughout Holland were giving shelter to fugitives from the Rotterdam hell. It is impossible to chronicle the share of every town and hamlet in the help to Rotterdam's victims. They vied with each other in their efforts to assuage the sufferings of their hard-hit compatriots. Yet, as long as ten months after the disaster almost 11,000 families were still "unsatisfactorily housed" —many of them living in shacks which had long ago been rejected as unfit for human habitation.*

But no help could make good the loss of Rotterdam's business quarter or of its picturesque inner ports. Streets once filled with life had been transformed into heart-breaking cemeteries. The

*See also page 62, last line.

skeletons of erstwhile houses stood black and smouldering. Heavy walls threatened to come down at any moment; it was clear that no reconstruction would be possible before the entire center of the inner town—a surface of more than two square miles—had been cleared. Towards the middle of this tragic summer, some twenty thousand laborers were busily engaged in this stony desert.

Rotterdam must arise from its ashes; no Hun was capable of destroying the spirit of energy and enterprise inherent in every Dutchman. On the morning after the German bombardment, one of the most important Rotterdam banks received visits from numerous people applying for credits to start upon the reconstruction of their lives and properties.

But it was not Rotterdam alone which had been badly damaged. In similar manner the heart of Middelburg, that shining pearl set in the loveliness of ancient Zeeland province, had been transformed into desolate rubble. On Friday, May 17, the Luftwaffe had effectively seen to that. Of course, the Germans never admitted this but, instead, tried to put the blame for the disaster on the British and the French. Even before the final destruction of Middelburg's historic treasures, its Town Hall, its Lange Jan Tower, its Abbey, the nazified Hilversum radio endeavored to make its listeners believe that the fires of Middelburg had been set by retreating English and French troops.

Several other towns in Zeeland and Brabant had suffered considerable damage, more especially Breda, Roosendaal, Boxtel and Zevenbergen. Besides all this, more than five hundred farms had been smashed to fragments all over the country. And right at the outset the work of reconstruction met with great difficulties. Thousands of factories had been cut off from their supply sources or had lost their outlets. What were they to do with their workers? To keep them in service meant using up large financial reserves; to dismiss them meant to throw those laborers upon the reserves of the State. The German authorities, aware of this dilemma, forbade the dismissal of all labor. They also ordered that no workman should be paid for less than 36 working hours per week. Work or no work—that was the minimum wage. Thus the Nazis forestalled the possibility of sudden general unemployment.

This sounded very good; but in reality it forced many enterprises to take up huge credits from their banks . . . , a fact which failed to upset the Germans. Life was to resume its normal course and so, to make sure of this, German officials had immediately been appointed to head all Labor Exchanges. Whoever was or became workless would find plenty of things to do in Germany! Meanwhile international rail connections were soon restored. Less than a month after the invasion it was once again possible to travel by train from The Hague to Berlin. Almost at the same time postal connections with whatever remained of neutral Europe were resumed, while on June 11 all telephones, throughout the country, could be used again without limitation.

Shortly afterwards the banking moratorium was lifted; Holland had attuned itself sufficiently to the great changes of the previous month to exclude the possibility of a run on the banks. During and immediately after war days, many communities had issued emergency money. The Department of Home Affairs now sent these towns a circular in which they were ordered to call back that self-made "money" instantly. But in the same breath the Germans insisted upon acceptance of their own token money, the so-called "Reichskreditkassenscheine," of which the German soldiers and officers seemed to possess inexhaustible supplies. The Nazi authorities found it necessary to warn the public via the radio that they were obliged to accept these bits of paper and added —for their reassurance—that they could be exchanged against Dutch money at any one of the "Reich's Credit Centers," which had hastily been established in various towns. What the announcer did not say, however, was that this Dutch money had been taken from the Netherlands Bank.

That is how the financial pillage of Holland began. Had the Germans requisitioned commodities and services without payment, there would of course have been a general outburst. Actually, the same thing was happening, but the semblance of normal transactions had been retained.

During the first weeks of the occupation the Germans attached great value to that semblance. For impeccable behavior had to gild the bitter pill of subjugation. If they made their soldiers give up their seats in a public vehicle to a lady or an older man, this kindness would—the Nazis thought—immediately convert to National-Socialism everyone privileged to witness the moving spectacle. Instead, these histrionics merely vexed the Dutch. This was only one of many ways in which the Germans tried to impress upon the Dutch that nothing had changed. The daily broadcasts over a certain radio station still ended with the playing of the national anthem, the "Wilhelmus." And the world-famous conductor Willem Mengelberg directed a jubilee concert of the Berlin Philharmonic two months after the invasion —just as if nothing out of the ordinary had happened.

It was a typically German policy displaying once again the Teutonic incompetence to understand the character of any other nation. But the people of Holland saw through it; they knew painfully well that their country was not now what it had always been. It was occupied; it had lost its independence. No longer did it have its own defense forces. It was, in fact, the demobilization of the Army and the Navy—in so far as they had been inside the Netherlands at the moment of surrender—which brought home to hundreds of thousands of Hollanders that their country was no free, self-dependent nation any more. The Dutch soldiers who had become Germany's prisoners of war, were gathered in camps in the neighborhood of Berlin, and even as deep down into Germany as Stettin. As a further "token of his good intentions" Hitler decided to send these men back to their country.

The first contingents passed the frontier on June 9. Their arrival had been looked forward to with tension by thousands who hoped to be reunited with a missing father, son or friend. Entire families traveled by train, on bicycles and even on foot to the frontier towns. The roads became clogged and there was a scarcity of foodstuffs. Finally, all entrance to the border towns was forbidden.

Slowly the transport trains rolled into the railroad station of Arnhem. A reporter from the nazified news agency ANP stood ready to receive the soldiers' testimonials of the splendid treatment they had met with in the Reich . . . But the reverse was only too evident from the ravenous way in which these newly-liberated prisoners attacked the food which was offered them.

What to do with those thousands of released war prisoners? As already related, the remnants of the Dutch Army and Navy within the Netherlands had been disarmed immediately after the surrender. The Royal Military Academy of Breda was discontinued and the Royal Institute for the Marine underwent the same fate, both institutions being amalgamated into a new semi-military body, which the Germans called the "School Breda of the Reconstruction Service." Every man released from military service had been forced to declare that he would "in no way be active against the interests of the German Reich"—an oath which many of them took whilst reserving the right to break it. As could have been expected, it soon became clear that there was great shortage of work for these demobilized soldiers. Some thousands of them returned to their former jobs, but labor conditions had already undergone such changes that it did not need prophetic qualities to foresee how a multitude of young men would soon belong to a new army: that of the unemployed.

The Germans tried to avoid this disaster. Five thousand demobilized soldiers were added to the State and Municipal Police corps. Each one of the three largest cities, Amsterdam, The Hague and Rotterdam, took three hundred "special" policemen in its service. The Military Police, or Marechaussee, was expanded from 1,250 to 4,000 men and the State Police, amounting to 1,000 men, was practically doubled. Large numbers of demobilized army men were, moreover, appointed to A.R.P. service. Amsterdam, for instance, used 800 soldiers for this purpose. In this way, the Nazis killed two birds with one stone: they found work for the unemployed and, at the same time, strongly reinforced the Dutch police . . . which they evidently considered a dire necessity.

Every man for whom no work of this kind had been found was inducted into the Reconstruction Service. On August 1, 1940 five thousand young men had thus been forced to don the Reconstruction Service uniform. Their duties, it was brought home to them, would be of a temporary nature only. As soon as they could find any kind of other work, the Reconstruction Service would automatically release them. Towards the end of September, however, no more men were accepted for the Reconstruction Service, and although its Commander had on various occasions lost himself in superlatives when describing the importance of his institution, it achieved very little indeed. The Dutch, with their indestructible sense of humor, aptly remarked of the triangle which was the emblem of the Reconstruction Service: "True enough, the Service is placed upon a broad base . . . ; but it all ends in nothing!"

While this attempt at "peaceful employment" of demobilized young soldiers had been progressing, their former Commander-in-Chief, General Winkelman, became a prisoner of the Nazis. Already on June 12, 1940 the puzzled nation was told that the General "had given many commands which, after June 3, did not form part of the task entrusted to him. He therefore recalls those orders which had, without exception, to do with Dutch industries."

After this incident and until July 6 no further remarks were publicly made. Apparently General Winkelman was continuing his work, "supported" by a high German officer, the Colonel Schwabedissen of General Christiansen's Staff. But on that 6th of July the news was aired that Winkelman had been transported to the Reich. In a long statement, the German General Christiansen "explained" that Dutch soldiers, by stubbornly refusing to salute German officers, had "shown a tasteless lack of discipline." General Winkelman, he asserted, had opposed this recalcitrancy most insufficiently, and he had thus "proved not to interpret his position the way every clear-thinking person would have imagined." That, and that alone, was the reason why he had been sent to a German camp, the statement insinuated.

But the citizens of Holland knew better.

The Nazis had continuously defended their attack upon the Netherlands by accusing the Dutch Government of having allowed the allies to use their country as a basis for operations against the Ruhr. This was a downright lie—and the German Government knew it. But in order to convince the stupid world at large, and perhaps also a few Doubting Thomases in Holland, the Foreign Department in Berlin published a White Book, towards the end of June. This pamphlet contained a number of documents in evidence of the German accusation, mainly detailed marching schedules for French and British troops, from Northern France to the center of Belgium. But in these statements there was nothing to prove that the troops concerned were to march through Belgium on their way to the Ruhr. On the contrary—it was clear to every unprejudiced reader that these troop movements would take place only *after* the Germans had attacked Belgium. The most "important" document was the one marked "No. 19." It was significantly headed :"Memorandum concerning collaboration between Dutch, Belgian, French and British Armies. Sent by the Commander-in-Chief of the Dutch Army and Navy."

What this pompous heading did not disclose, however, was that the message, though despatched by General Winkelman on March 23, 1940 to the Netherlands Ambassadors at Brussels, Paris and London, was sent under seal of secrecy. In a second letter all three diplomats had been requested to break the seals of the message only on reception of a certain code word. In the morning of May 10, 1940, after the Nazi attack had begun, this code word was flashed to Belgium, and the Brussels Ambassador read the following instructions:

"Your Excellency is requested, after reading this memorandum, to secure immediate contact with the Belgian Government so as to acquaint it with the contents of this Memorandum.

While awaiting the arrival of an authorized representative of the Dutch Commander-in-Chief of land and sea forces, Your Excellency may inform the Belgian Government that it will be the task of the Netherlands Army to delay the progress of the invading enemy as much as possible from the moment he passes our frontiers."

The memorandum further contained ample information concerning the disposition of the Dutch troops in the province of North Brabant. France was requested to send four divisions; England was asked to despatch one division to Zeeland, as well as bombers and fighter planes.

This was the "important memorandum" published in Germany's White Book. That the letter would never have been opened if Germany had not decided upon its vicious attack on the Lowlands was—curiously enough—left unmentioned. Von Ribbentrop must have believed that the people for whom this piece of propaganda was meant would, in any case, not be "smart" enough to understand the truth.

When this remarkable document was widely distributed throughout the Netherlands, General Winkelman thought it his duty to tell his people the actual sequence of affairs. That in doing so he ran the risk of being interned by the enemy, did not withhold him. He directed a dignified letter to all of his officers, and within a very few days the whole of Holland knew what had really happened.

This—and nothing else—was the reason of General Winkelman's imprisonment. (See Appendix I.)

*

The incidents with the White Book made it clear once again to the Nazis that it was not an easy matter to "convince" the people of the Netherlands. However, they did not give up. They had fostered great hopes that Seyss-Inquart's Austrian origin would make a deep impression, as the Dutch had always been more friendly disposed towards the easy-going Austrians than towards the harsh, brow-beating members of the Prussian tribe. They therefore decided to make good use of this sympathy for things "Austrian."

When Seyss-Inquart visited Rotterdam, on June 21, 1940, he announced that Austria was ready to receive thousands of Dutch children, "in gratitude for the good Holland did to hungry Austrian youngsters after the first World War." Free of all charge no less than twenty thousand children of Dutch parents were to travel to and stay on hospitable Austrian soil.

But the propaganda purposes of this sweetly-sentimental announcement were so obvious that every true Netherlander felt nothing but loathing for it. And so the joy-rides did not come off very smoothly. It took a full month before the first transport left the country . . . with no one less than the Reich's Commissioner in person to wave goodbye to the excited kiddies, and hand out bars of chocolate. All in all only six thousand of the promised twenty thousand youngsters—the majority of them belonging to Dutch Nazis' households—went abroad. Day upon day the newspapers brought lengthy and grateful reports on the splendid reception these children were having. The "Gauleiter" of Austria himself had gracefully consented to receive them! They were splendidly nourished and got on in an exemplary manner with their Austrian "comrades." A special correspondent was sent all the way to Austria to write moving articles and when—in late September—the children returned to their country, there was quite a crowd of radio reporters at the railroad station to "hear all about it."

As propaganda this vacation in Austria had been an absolute failure. The children, when interviewed during their vacation, did not show any undue enthusiasm. "Would you like to go back to Holland?", one of the reporters had asked; and the reply had been a doubtlessly unexpected but heartfelt, "Rather!"

But the return journey was even more disappointing. The children, in their honest and innocent fashion, talked a great deal—in fact they talked far too much to their hosts' liking. One child ventured to remark that the bread in Austria had been practically uneatable—"so sour!"—and the others were only too ready to uphold this frank opinion. Another child was asked how he had liked the return trip and he complained it had lasted too long as he had, practically speaking, not been able to sleep at all.

"Why not?" the reporter asked.

"There was no sleeping car on our train."

"Well—what did you expect? Did you want a first-class sleeper?"

"We had to sit on a very hard bench."

"How many of you?"

"Twelve of us—on one hard bench all night."

It was, indeed, a most discouraging bit of propaganda. The more so as all Netherlanders knew that their municipal councils had been forced to pay for this "free trip," and that most of the profits had gone into the pocket of Seyss-Inquart's brother, the owner of several Austrian Youth Shelters and similar institutions. It was obvious that something quite different must be tried next.

This time the R.A.F. furnished the "material."

On several occasions the British had attacked military objectives in the Netherlands, generally with great success. That during these raids the R.A.F. spared the citizens and all non-military objectives as much as possible, was proved by the fact that the German military took their living quarters by preference in civilian homes. Moreover, German military transports were as much as possible housed in the neighborhood of churches, while many public schools were converted into storage rooms for munitions.

But all this did not prevent the Germans from accusing the English of purposely bombing non-military objectives whenever homes or farms had been accidentally hit.

In June, 1940 a heavy British attack took place on the harbor of Den Helder. When the R.A.F. had returned to British shores and the searchlights had already been dimmed, all at once a new alarm was sounded. Strangely enough, the German anti-aircraft guns remained silent, nor did the searchlights shine forth again . . .

But the trick had been too transparent. "That was the Huns themselves!" said the understanding Dutch. Nevertheless, the same tactics were repeatedly applied—not only in Holland but also in Belgium. On several occasions radio Orange, the Free Dutch broadcasting station in London, was able to state on the authority of the British military that Dutch towns had been bombarded on nights *when no R.A.F. planes had been above the Netherlands.*

Once more a German propaganda plan had completely derailed. Instead of arousing indignation against England, the people of Holland were infuriated against the Germans themselves and particularly against the hypocrisy of certain local Nazi Commanders who made a habit of sending large wreaths, with conspicuous swastikas and "heroic" inscriptions, to the funerals of their own victims. More than once the nazified Dutch radio was forced to announce "indignant" contradictions; and on one occasion the speaker asserted: "He who in this moment still believes that German bombs are sowing death and destruction over our country, does not understand the portent of this hour. He fails to comprehend the greatness of this revolutionary time and is politically so superficial that he cannot well serve the interests of our people." When neither these broadcasts, nor the frequently repeated announcements in the gagged Dutch press seemed to bear any result, the Nazis printed a large poster which in the early autumn days was pasted upon the billboards and walls of every Dutch town and village. It showed a church and some homes caught in the rays of a searchlight. The headline read: "Dutchmen, take cover! English flyers know no mercy!" But the only effect worth chronicling was that an anonymous poet, in exquisite retaliation, made and distributed an ironic verse on the "mercy" of the German Luftwaffe as displayed during the bombardment of Rotterdam. In a close translation* this courageous poem reads:

Three score of airmen came on wings
Gentle as the dove and peaceful as the lamb
To carry a message of mercy and similar things
To the ancient Dutch town of Rotterdam.

With love and kindness all aglow
They dropped their load, bomb after bomb,
The airmen who the quality of mercy know
Gave Rotterdam its hetacomb.

There a hospital was set on fire,
Its sacred symbol wantonly defied;
There every law and decency was trampled in the murd'rous mire,
There a new feat of glory was written in the book of human fame
When the airmen who the quality of mercy know,
Turned Rotterdam into a hell of raging flame.

Then women, children, the aged and infirm,
All fleeing wildly and in vain,
Not knowing where for safety to turn,
In thousands by the falling bombs were slain.
For the airmen who the quality of mercy know,
Though at the sight of all this murder doubtless very pained
And loath to strike so foul a blow,
Knew also that the quality of mercy is not strained.

*Translation by J. H. Huizinga.

Wild and ferocious, a bitter cry
Out of the murdered city's ghastly ruins
Now rises to the shattered sky—
"Remember always, ne'er forget,
"Who us this fair example set."

Let that cry ring throughout our tortured land.
For then, as certain as *their* day will end
Our day will dawn, and all this gallant band
Of airmen who the quality of mercy know,
Shall learn that one must reap what one does sow.

It was copied, mimeographed and printed. It went from hand to hand. It was given to friends and acquaintances and surreptitiously slid into the pockets of strangers. It was broadcast by Radio Orange too, and all the Germans could do about it was to send people on whom one or more copies were found to jail for a period of six months "because they were in possession of a poem the contents of which are against the honor of the German Army."

Even less success was reserved for the extensive Nazi campaign to vilify the Queen, her Government and the British allies.

Though the Queen and government had left Holland on Monday, May 13, 1940, the people of the Netherlands had been advised of their safe arrival in London only on the next day. There had doubtlessly been excellent reasons for this reticence. First of all, there were grounds to believe that the immediate reaction, even from the side of the best patriots, would be an unfavorable one. Yet, the moment was most inappropriate for long and reasoned explanations. On the day of the capitulation it was the heart alone which spoke; and that heart could not coolly accept the fact that the country's Mother had left her children. The same applied to the Government. "Treason" and "flight" were the first words bound to well up from the depth of the people's consternation.

This reaction was as comprehensible as it was unjust.

For if ever a resolution of the Queen and her Government was worthy of praise, it certainly was the historical decision to continue the fight for Holland's freedom from British soil. The King of the Belgians who preferred to stay in his country is hardly more than a powerless prisoner of war. But Queen Wilhelmina encourages and leads her enslaved peoples from London. The difference is too obvious to require further elucidation and by now every true Netherlander understands and approves of an action which enabled the highest Dutch authority to escape from the enemy's grasp.

Indeed: "the enemy's grasp"—for it is now known that the German plan of conquest included the imprisonment of Queen, Government and Commander-in-Chief at the very outset of the attack. This shock would, the Nazis believed, mean the end to all Dutch resistance. General Von Sponeck, Commander-in-Chief of the German Air Division to whom had been entrusted the taking of the city of The Hague, had obtained minute maps of that town and its surroundings. The German Legation which many months before the invasion had been transformed into a thoroughly organized spy nest, provided Berlin with precise information regarding the abode of the royal family. Two months before the fatal tenth of May the German military attaché sent Berlin a most detailed chart of the royal palace at Soestdijk, and a month later he gave ample information concerning the guards on duty at the two palaces in and near The Hague. Thanks to the alertness and courage of the Dutch defense forces, this plan came to nought. One may rest assured that the announcement of the Queen's safe arrival in London was as bitter a disappointment to the Germans as—at that moment—it was for the Dutch.

It was equally bitter for the people of Holland to learn that without Queen or legal Government it had to continue its battle against the occupying forces. The Germans were clever enough to see the propagandistic possibilities of this circumstance. A large-scale whispering campaign was started to the effect that Queen and Government had left for mere reasons of personal safety. Time after time the Nazified Press Bureau did its utmost to throw mud upon Queen Wilhelmina. It even went so far as to imagine letters allegedly received from "indignant Hollanders" who one and all declared with great solemnity that from Orange-lovers they had become haters of the royal House. One Haarlem lady was reported to have written: "Surely, every civilized person understands that Adolf Hitler would never have made a martyr of our Queen who has always been so greatly respected a figure in Germany. And even if this had happened, I believe Her Majesty should not have taken to flight. At night when I hear the British bombers come over, I think: well, if it has to be, in God's name. And I am quite willing to admit that I never was half as religious as the Queen always told us *she* was . . ."

But all this hammering upon the sentiments of the Netherlanders was in vain, for by now everyone who mattered realized that the occupation of Holland's territory could not mean the exclusion of the country from the war against Hitler Germany. Besides, there were the East and West Indies, both free and independent, their more than seventy million people greatly in need of leadership.

And so, instead of the hatred desired by the Germans, there sprung into being a love for the House of Orange stronger than ever before. Even when the Germans, leaving the useless road of sentimentality, resorted to the Law and broadcast Article 21 of the Constitution: "In no case can the seat of the Government be outside the Kingdom," no one took the slightest notice. Nor did it seem to make any impression when another Article of the Constitution was chosen for public declamation. This time it was Article 57 which reads: "The King declares war only after preceding consent of the States-General." "Well," said the Germans, "as at the time of the invasion the States-General were not in session and have thus not voiced an opinion, the Netherlands is *not* at war with the German Reich!"

But the most ludicrous was the silly notion that if only the Dutch were forbidden to use the adjective "royal" they would slowly but surely forget the House of Orange. Hastily the Royal Library was renamed to "National Library" and the same "subtle" change was made for various institutions possessing the royal predicate. Even "Royal Dutch" Oil Shares were henceforth to be known as "Netherlands Oil Shares."

The work was badly done, however. And so even now, after two and a half years of Nazi occupation, there are quite a number of societies still proudly displaying the word "royal" in their nomenclature. And by a rather extraordinary 'oversight' the birthday of Queen Wilhelmina—August 31—is still mentioned as a legal holiday in the official "Manual of Labor Regulations in the Netherlands."

It was not only the Queen against whom the full force of German ire was constantly directed. Prince Bernhard, Prime Minister Pieter S. Gerbrandy, Foreign Minister Eelco N. van Kleffens, and several other authorities each got his share. And when it became known that the Colonial Minister of that moment, Mr. Charles J. I. M. Welter, was visiting the Indies, radio Bremen came with the not particularly original, though in this case completely unfounded, comment that "the rats were leaving the sinking ship."

As transparent as the action against Queen and Government, were the German efforts to arouse the Dutch against their British allies. Originally there appeared to be a fertile soil for this kind of propaganda; the fact that English help had failed to come in time created bitter disappointment among large groups of the populace. During the five days of war there had been fantastic rumors about enormous numbers of British war vessels and troops which were supposed to have been thrown into the fight for Holland. It was, for instance, "common knowledge" that no less than thirty British destroyers were ready for action at IJmuiden. When these stories turned out to be just another instance of wishful thinking, the disillusionment was, of course, very great.

With energy worthy of a better cause the Germans tried to utilize these facts in their propaganda against England. The English were accused of having sent the Dutch into the fire only to shield themselves, and the retreat of Dunkirk was fully exploited to "prove" this point.

As a matter of fact, though the British bombings did not call forth any vengeful feelings, it took many months before this deeply-rooted sentiment of deception turned to understanding. Only when the Hollanders saw how bravely the embattled people of England bore up under the atrocious bombardments of their towns and villages, did they recognize the true heroism of Britain's soldiers and citizens alike. No wonder that, with this thought prevailing, the Germans had little success with their broadcasts of assurances that "the avenging sword of German justice will soon come down on the guilty British. Those days will be sad and bitter ones for the English people. But it has not chosen otherwise and it will, therefore, have to suffer!" Unfortunately for the Nazis "the sad and bitter days" which followed appeared more sad and bitter for them than for the courageous English who, virtually alone, went through the holocaust undaunted, and came out of their tribulations more united, more ready to fight to the end than ever before.

*

Anton Adriaan Mussert, the podgy "Fuehrer" of the Nationaal-Socialistische Beweging (Dutch Nazi Party) had had a very thin time ever since he reappeared in public. During the worst of the battle against the invading Huns he had stayed in a safe hiding-place; but on his return, instead of finding a repentent Holland eager to kneel at his feet and drink of his Nazi wisdom, he met with distrust and disdain on every side.

The Netherlands had regained its self-confidence. There was not even the slightest display of a desire to hobnob with National-Socialists.

In the first days of July several leaders of Holland's political parties dared to voice their one ideal, that of an independent Holland under the rule of the House of Orange. The people began to be aware of an entirely new longing for real national unity. Old political and social differences were forgotten. Protestant, Catholic and Jew became one of purpose; they were, first of all, Netherlanders.

To disobey the occupying powers was going to be a hard struggle—but there was no choice. A people which had formed its own true character throughout a history of centuries, a nation that had fought for its independence and liberty as no other, could not become unfaithful to its ideals simply because the Germans wished this.

The N.S.B.'ers were no more than outcasts, creatures branded with the stamp of treachery. And if certain Netherlanders might have been inclined to forget and forgive, Mussert's well-known tactlessness saw to it that old political sores were torn open again and again. It was as if he could not often enough shout from the house tops his admiration for and agreement with the enemy. Six weeks after the invasion, when thousands of N.S.B.'ers imprisoned by the legal Government had been set free again by Hitler's troops, Mussert—in a public speech—tried to prove that the "treachery of the N.S.B. was only a myth. All the accusations ever made against Nazi Fifth Columnists were as unfounded as they were scandalous." He also expressed the hope that the Dutch Government would soon be forced to leave Great Britain and take refuge in Canada. "Holland," he continued, "must be free of Jewish influence, free of Walloons and free of the tyranny of the Church in matters of State."

Free of Jewish influence . . . but this same weak little man, at the start of his "political career" around 1931, had invited his Jewish compatriots to join his party freely. And subsequently, on more than one occasion, he had put himself out to explain that the N.S.B., though having adopted some planks of the German Nazi platform, did not agree with the Hitler-inspired persecutions.

In this same speech Mussert denied that Holland was at war with the Third Reich. "According to international law, maybe," he admitted, "but if that is so I do not care a hang about international law." (Applause) "Do you feel that you are at war with Germany?" "No!" yelled the gathered party members. Obviously encouraged by this astonishing unanimity, the great Mussert thereupon delivered a hymn of praise on the German aircraft "which would soon bring the war, forced upon the German nation, to a successful end." He also announced that the famous N.S.B. clock made of copper and tin and which in previous months had been dragged all over the country as a splendid show piece of Nazi artistry and achievement, would be presented to the creator of the German Luftwaffe, Herr Hermann Goering. (Tremendous applause!)

Homage to Goering's Luftwaffe . . . , and this less than six weeks after the wanton bombing of Rotterdam. Never will the people of Holland be able to forget this repugnant Mussert tribute of June 22, 1940.

*

A week later was Prince Bernhard's anniversary. The whispering campaign against Princess Juliana's husband had had a very poor result. On the contrary—many were the tales of heroic deeds done by this young Prince who battled to the last in the province of Zeeland and went to England only when the fall of the only remaining Dutch stronghold became inevitable.

Though the Germans realized that the Prince's birthday would not be allowed to pass unobserved, they did not take any special measures. The only "measure" had been an order under date of June 25 that "no national or orange-colored flags would be displayed from public buildings in the future. If public bodies thus give the example," the German comment ran, "it may be expected that the public in general will know how to conform."

But the public thought differently. On that 29th of June, 1940 all Holland with the exception of its N.S.B.'ers, wore an emblem of national allegiance: orange bows, or red, white and blue insignia. White carnations, which had been the Prince's favorite flower at all his public appearances, were readily sold and towards the end of the afternoon when the stocks began to run low, several guilders were gladly paid for one carnation. Thousands of people paraded silently through the streets of The Hague; it was a demonstration of indomitable belief and confidence.

Here and there members of the N.S.B. tried to tear carnations and insignia from the buttonholes of peaceful passers-by but these impertinences acted as boomerangs . . . Because later in the afternoon—when the story of these molestations had made the round—there were badly-cut Nazi fingers in The Hague. Fragments of sharp razor blades had been cunningly hidden in the innocent-looking carnations. Numerous were the brawls which resulted and the Dutch police seemed powerless to intervene.

But the demonstrations before the royal palace at the Noordeinde were the most impressive. Here a large congratulatory register had been deposited; it was signed with as much alacrity as if the royal family had been inside the palace rather than in far-away London. The faithful Burgomaster of The Hague, Mr. De Monchy, was the first to sign this register as his renewed oath of allegiance to the House of Orange. Untold thousands followed his example and other crowds demonstrated in front of various royal statues, in many districts of the town.

Soon the foot of the colossal statue of William the Silent, close to the royal palace, was literally covered with bunches and bouquets of multi-colored flowers. The churches held special services and were filled to overflowing.

In Amsterdam a large crowd filed patiently past the statue of Queen Emma, the beloved mother of Queen Wilhelmina, whose death, in 1934, was felt throughout the nation as a real loss. Times out of number the German police which had been "added" to the Dutch police force, dispersed the demonstrators but invariably they came back, singing the national anthem with courage and conviction.

In six weeks—only forty-two days—the Dutch people had discovered the true state of affairs. Neither the wily propaganda of Joseph Goebbels nor the honeyed promises of Seyss-Inquart had been able to blind them. Six weeks, during which not only Holland but also Belgium and even France, a few months ago considered impregnable, had been trampled down by the Nazi armies. The people of Holland did not ask how long it would be before this ruthless and seemingly invincible enemy would be beaten. It chose to be loyal to the House of Orange and it decided to demonstrate this devotion.

That is how on June 29, 1940 one of the mightiest displays of patriotic fervor in all of Holland's history was seen.

Several German measures followed. Burgomaster De Monchy

was dismissed and transported to Germany. The "Nationaal Jongeren Verbond" (National Youth League), which had been most active in planning the general display of Prince Bernhard carnations, had the honor of being the first organization to be disbanded by the invaders.

Soon afterwards many more symptoms proved how swiftly the hatred against the German oppressors was growing. On July 2, two local papers in the province of North Holland were suspended for two weeks because—so the official announcement explained—"they have been unable to keep away from their old time one-sided propaganda in favor of their friends."

Next followed the radio. Since the four independent Dutch stations had been throttled and replaced by one fully nazified broadcasting center, all of Holland was listening to the B.B.C. broadcasts from London. For a while the Germans had tolerated this but when the Dutch Minister of War, on that fateful June 29, addressed his oppressed fellow-countrymen from London in inspired and heartening words, they thought the moment had come to intervene. On July 6 another decree was published, under the hypocritical heading of "Measure for the Protection of the Dutch Population against Untrue Information." The gist of it was that in the future Netherlanders would only be allowed to listen to the 'coordinated' broadcasting stations of the Netherlands, Germany, Poland and Czecho-Slovakia. All other stations were henceforth "verboten"—also the neutral ones. Even the broadcasts from the Axis partner Italy must in no circumstances be listened to.

But it was of little avail. When on July 28, 1940 the official Dutch broadcasting station in London made its appearance under the name "Radio Orange" and when Queen Wilhelmina delivered the inaugural speech in a firm, resolute voice, practically every man, woman and child in Holland was listening.

A curious phenomenon could be observed as the hostile feelings against Germany increased. It was the slowly growing sympathy for the British. The continuous R.A.F. attacks on industrial targets in western Germany worked on the imagination of the populace. It was good to hear that the common foe got at least some of his own medicine. But the Nazi authorities were particularly concerned with the active support which, time and again, was given to British pilots and crews whose planes had been forced down over Dutch territory.

Towards the end of July, for instance, six workmen were

sentenced to three years in jail because they had assisted a British pilot, despite the warnings published from time to time by Nazi General Christiansen. Yet, only a few weeks afterwards Christiansen found himself constrained to publish a further warning: "No help of any kind must be given to members of the R.A.F." Two days later it was revealed that a British plane, with a crew of twelve men, had come down in the neighborhood of Breda, North Brabant province. The Nazis organized a veritable man-hunt which lasted for four days. Then they announced that the British air men "had been caught."

On July 11, 1940 it was reported to the German authorities that a heavy iron chest had been seen falling from a British plane. It was said to have come down in an Amsterdam backyard. Most probably the case contained a secret sender. The Nazis promptly promised a reward of five thousand guilders—more than $2700—to anyone giving sufficient clues to lead to the discovery of the chest. It was, however, never found.

These occurrences—trifling as they might be—did not fail to irritate the Germans who decided to show those stubborn Dutch how they would get things their way! And so they prohibited officially any kind of demonstration in favor of the House of Orange. No display of flags, insignia or anything of an orange color, including flowers which would be considered tokens of loyalty to the "run-away" royal house. This measure, coming on the first day of August, clearly betrayed the Nazis' fear of demonstrations on August 31 when Queen Wilhelmina would commemorate her sixtieth birthday. Had Holland been free the Dutch flag would have waved from every window, from every church tower and public building. Now even the display of a carnation was a "criminal act."

To avoid all misunderstanding the Nazis came with a further warning on the eve of the Queen's anniversary; and indeed, it remained comparatively quiet throughout the country on that August 31. But in the early morning hours the British, American and Orange flags could be seen fluttering side by side from the tower of the Amsterdam Municipal Theatre. And a few hours later R.A.F. planes appeared above the larger cities of Holland, throwing out orange-colored pamphlets and confetti. All Amsterdam was in the streets when this orange rain began, and the enthusiasm reached its zenith when, at night, the British allies gave a full-dress presentation of orange-colored fireworks high above the town. Immediately the Germans ordered the sounding of the air-raid alarm and in this petty way succeeded in clearing the streets.

But the events of that day provided ample evidence of the fact that German thrusts at the heart of Holland had failed completely. Only a few months of Nazi occupation sufficed to make the Dutch long nostalgically for their lost independence. More than that: it had strengthened their will to adhere firmly to their own democratic ways of life, no matter the cost.

No one doubted the relentlessness of this struggle. But it was a holy crusade in which perseverance only would count. Never say die. Never bend the knee. Show those Huns and Mussert-traitors how thoroughly you despise them. Orange first and last—always!

Those were the watchwords whispered, spoken, written, printed . . . The attitude of the Dutch reflected the strength of their self-confidence regained. German soldiers were passed by without a glance and every N.S.B.'er was a mere vacuum. Yes—the fight was on; and were it to last months, years, decades, it would be fought till victory.

The Dutch people, having recovered their equilibrium, were ready to shout defiantly at the German tyrants, as once did Luther at his opponents: "Here I stand; I can do no other. May God help me. Amen."

2

IN THE GERMAN WEB

The student of events marking the first year of Holland's occupation by the Nazis finds himself wading through a stream of decrees, measures, decisions of German instances and an equal, if not greater, number of rulings taken by Dutch authorities at the order of the invaders. More and more Dutch and German special Committees, officials galore and new titles in abundance. Only the faintest resemblance to the former administrative machine remains discernible.

Dutch Burgomasters are replaced by Commissars. In each of the eleven provinces the Queen's Commissioner is "relieved of his duties." Entire communities are robbed of their independence, and amalgamated. Secretaries-General are ousted, Prosecutors transferred, new departments formed overnight. German courts come into action.

Institutions and organizations are created for all sorts of purposes, but all of them known by ludicrously-ponderous German names such as the "Verkehrsueberwachungskommando." Advisors are appointed for the solution of numerous problems. A Dutch branch is founded of the German National-Socialist Labor Party; and even the Guilds of yore, but now rebaptized and introduced as "Fachgruppen" (professional groups), are resuscitated.

What is the meaning of all this?

It simply means that the Germans are quietly installing their own governmental apparatus, more or less successfully under cover of the authoritative institutions with which the average Dutchman has thus far been familiar. The Nazis have begun to spin the web in which the people of Holland are to be caught and sucked dry. Like a dozen other nations of devastated Europe, the Dutch are to become slaves in the service of the Herrenvolk.

But in those first months the Germans were most careful to avoid all mention of this ulterior aim. Under an avalanche of fine words and sweet promises, with repeated assurances of their brotherly intentions, they tried their best to camouflage the truth. Indeed—it cannot be denied that at this time the Nazi invaders gave themselves an amazing amount of trouble to reach their purposes without too public a use of the whip.

It is worth while examining the reasons for this German anxiety not to antagonize the Dutch masses; it is highly enlightening to find out why the Nazis spent their time and money lavishly to obtain "collaboration" rather than to impose their will by means of the fist.

Having built their superiority theory upon the basis of "Blood and Race," they could not deny that in neighboring countries peoples were living of approximately the same origin as the Germans themselves—and Holland belonged to those "blood-related" neighbors. Were not the Netherlanders a Nordic race, just like the Germans? Had not at some remote period in history the Netherlands been a part of the great German Reich?

True enough . . . but the Nazis wisely forgot to add when expounding this theory that the first German Reich, the so-called Holy Roman Reich of the German Nation, of which Holland had been a part, had never been more than an insecure edifice built by mediaeval German Kaisers—a building so badly constructed that for centuries it had to be artificially supported until it fell to pieces in Napoleon's day. In those Germanic structures the Kaiser's power had been less than feeble; his dukes and counts and vassal servants did what they liked. There never was any semblance of unity. If in those Middle Ages one had asked a Dutch peasant or citizen whether he considered himself a "Netherlander," he would in all probability have answered that he did not know the meaning of that word. But had he been asked whether he was a "German," his astonishment would have been even greater. For he undoubtedly considered himself a Hollander, a subject of the Count of Holland. To whom that Count was answerable was unknown to him and did not concern him in the least . . .

In the sixteenth century the Netherlands became Spanish territory, inherited as it was by the Spanish branch of the Habsburg family; and it was not before the end of the eighty years' struggle against Spanish tyranny that the free and independent state of the Netherlands was born. When this fact was admitted by the Treaty of Munster (1648), the first German Reich still existed—at least in name, and the Netherlands still formed part of it. But the Treaty broke this last vestige of Holland's dependency on German Kaisers, which had possessed no practical meaning anyhow.

Now the Netherlands entered upon a period of great prosperity and glory; it stood at the threshold of its Golden Century while the German Reich was on the downward path, through lack of unity and general disintegration.

This then is a true historical survey of all political connection there has ever been between the peoples of Holland and Germany. But the Nazis, with their usual facility to interpret events the most advantageous way, held quite a different opinion.

"The Dutch are a Germanic, an Aryan people!" they exclaimed. "For centuries they have been a part of the German Reich. If we ignore the Treaty of Munster—which we will for this particular purpose—they are a part of the German Reich even today!" Never mind whether this quaint logic plays havoc with historic facts. Anything will do to prove how Teutonic Holland actually is.

Of course, the most docile public for such tall stories is made up of children, poor victims who do not know better. That is why Nazi history books* describe the Treaty of Munster as a great crime by which the "Reich was cut off from the sea! The Netherlands separates itself and blocks the River Rhine!" "Germany," one writer sighs, "suffered an irreparable loss of valuable man power."** Through these extremely naive statements the Nazis thought they were proving conclusively how wilfully Holland had left Mother Germania. And now, three centuries after, it was simply invited to come home again—"everything forgiven and forgotten."

As a first step towards this return, the country would have to be occupied. Since this was done in May, 1940, the next move would be to flood the Netherlands with propaganda, to drench its people in Nazi ideologies. Once those ideas were accepted, a group of "privileged" Hollanders would be allowed to subsist, as active Nazis, on the sweat and blood of their compatriots.

From the beginning this policy was carefully disguised in a display of friendliness; the Dutch would be given a chance to show themselves "willing." They would not be crushed, like the Belgians, French and other subjugated nations. No Germans were to take over civil authority; even the postage stamps were not—as in

*These distortions are—with many others—to be found in a "History Book for the Youth of the Third Reich" (Geschichtsbuch fuer die Jugend des Dritten Reichs, by Schuette and Gade; pp. 43).

**"Deutsche Geschichte" (German History) of Heinrich Goebel, pp. 114.

other countries under German rule—imprinted with the words "Occupied Territory." On November 23, 1940 Anton Mussert who some weeks previously had been allowed to pay a visit to Hitler himself, announced reassuringly that the Fuehrer had the best intentions in regard to Holland. "We will be allowed to keep the Dutch East Indies!", he added and was thoroughly disappointed when this overwhelming concession seemed insufficient to move the Dutch to any display of gratitude. They merely shrugged their shoulders; they well knew what the Fuehrer's solemn promises are worth.

But meanwhile the mighty Mussert was not at all sure himself what was to happen to him and his party-members. Obviously, the Germans were using the Dutch Nazis as a lever to break up Dutch unity and it was equally clear that they were expected to perform assiduously as apostles of the Nazi cause. But would Herr Hitler elevate him, Anton Adriaan Mussert, to the same dazzling heights as had been climbed triumphantly by colleague Quisling of Norway? Would he become the political leader of the entire Dutch nation?

To these questions no answer was as yet forthcoming. The Germans advised Mussert to "get on with his propaganda work"—and be patient.

But Mussert's anxiety grew by the day. For things were further complicated by the fact that the N.S.B. was by no means the only National-Socialist movement in the Netherlands. For many years there had been two potent competitors, and as late as September, 1940 a new movement had been founded by some renegades of the Socialist Democratic Party, under the name of "Socialist Work Community." All these political groups were allowed to assemble, wear their own uniforms and live their own separate lives—yet, there was no gainsaying the fact that Mussert's party was the most numerous and the oldest.

During 1941, however, it became clear that the Germans had decided to weed out all of the smaller National-Socialist groups. The most insignificant were simply dissolved, the only exception being made for the N.S.N.A.P.* of Dr. Van Rappard which was "allowed" to recant its independence publicly and to declare that its members, voluntarily burying the hatchet, were "glad to join the party of Anton Adriaan Mussert."

*The N.S.N.A.P. under the leadership of Van Rappard was in almost continuous conflict with Mussert's movement—even so that Mussert's daily "Nationale Dagblad" repeatedly stressed the irreconcilability of Van Rappard's party with the N. S. B.

But in the early months after the occupation, Mussert was by no means treated by his German "colleagues" as a favorite. While on the one hand the Germans were using him and supporting the N.S.B., they did, on the other, not hesitate to attack him, be it in a secretive fashion—an attitude typical of the singularly changeable policy displayed by the Nazis during that period. To-day they would exercise ruthless pressure upon the Dutch to make them conform with Nazi ideologies; tomorrow again they would flatter and coax them as a truly-loving mother might scold her disobedient child.

Examples of these unbalanced tactics are manifold. Almost immediately after the first effort—the so-called "Dutch children to Austria free of charge"—had failed, a second action was started. In October, 1940 Seyss-Inquart founded a special organization to help Netherlanders who, through the war, had got into financial difficulties. It began in Rotterdam, where anyone in need of help was invited to ask for it. And although many Netherlanders refused to accept favors from the hands of the man who officially represented the German vandals, others reasoned: "Well—why not? We are paying for it ourselves anyhow." That is why during the winter of 1940-41 some 18,000 cases were taken in hand and support granted, varying from six to eighteen dollars per week. True enough, this assistance was paid for by the Dutch themselves as all the money came out of the coffers of the Netherlands Bank. But Seyss-Inquart carefully omitted to advertise this and the official report on the activities of the "Notstandsbeihilfe" proudly declared that "our action was swift and careful. We paid more than two million guilders to the people of Rotterdam alone" . . .

Repeatedly Seyss-Inquart returned to this more or less successful game of "playing Santa Claus." When appearing in public, he took good care to be photographed with laughing children. No playground could be opened in some out-of-the-way town—an event which normally would have passed by completely unnoticed—without Seyss-Inquart appearing and delivering a speech brimful of honeyed words and of expressions of gratitude toward the Fuehrer who "even in these difficult times does not forget the children, unwilling as he is to give up his firm belief in the Future."

Compare these sweet warblings with some of the speeches pronounced by the Reich's Commissioner in other circumstances, and no doubt is left as to the real policy of the German invaders.

It was, in short, a policy of pretended friendliness which might at any given moment be converted into bullying and suppression. In his inaugural speech of May 29, 1940 Seyss-Inquart had assured the Dutch that it was far from him to force German political beliefs upon them; but the sting immediately followed this reassurance. For this attitude, said he, would be ultimately "fixed by the circumstances of the war." Therefore, if those circumstances required the complete Nazification of Holland, what of it? Simple enough. The only thing to do would be to forget completely the originally announced policy of non-interference.

Time and again this same ambiguity could be observed in the official pronouncements of Seyss-Inquart and his henchmen. When the "Nederlandsche Unie" (Netherlands Union) was founded by three energetic Hollanders who at all costs wished to preserve the unity of a people bereft of its political parties, Seyss-Inquart stepped—for the first time—into the limelight with an unconcealed contradiction of his own former assurances. As representative of the occupying powers, he asserted, he could not reasonably be expected to acknowledge a new political movement. Such acknowledgement could only be obtained if that movement succeeded in "convincing the Dutch people of the righteousness of its policy."

However ambiguous this statement, it awakened the hope that, should the Union grow into a mass movement, it would automatically meet with the approval of the German authorities. But the reverse was bound to happen.

When within a short while the Union membership exceeded half a million, the Nazis deemed it expedient to frown upon this undesirable "rush." They began to shower greater favors upon the N.S.B. and for the first time since the invasion Mussert and his friends, Meinoud M. Rost van Tonningen and the deputy leader of the N.S.B., Van Geelkerken, were received by Hitler himself. This was followed up with a speech of Seyss-Inquart in which he made it clear that Holland would have to become a National-Socialist state. He did not say this straightforwardly; he still left the possibility to interpret his words in a friendly sense. "Whatever policy you will decide to follow is your own business," he said, "but we have to reserve our right to our own point of view. We want you to be a solidly-united people, a nation which will know how to respect, before all, Labor and the Purity of its Blood. We cannot tolerate a return to conditions such as existed before May 10, 1940. For the rest, do as you like . . ."

Slowly but surely the people of the Netherlands were being pushed toward the acceptance of Nazism. As yet the Netherlands Union was not disbanded but every opportunity was used to stress the fact that, to find favor in the eyes of the German overlords, its policy should resemble closely the creed of Adolf Hitler.

To mellow the Dutch and make them realize how unjust and unfounded were their virulent prejudices against the Great Fuehrer and his "ideals," Seyss-Inquart repeatedly pronounced a quaint sort of plea. Emphasizing the generous and beneficial intentions of the occupying powers, he made it a rule to end on a note of somewhat petulant reproach. "One thing we cannot forget," he would say, "and that is that your press has so long ridiculed our Fuehrer. We have been hurt by it, and we cannot tolerate it because we guarantee the integrity of our Fuehrer. But you have not been able to see the greatness of Adolf Hitler; and that is why I have had a pamphlet printed in which the Fuehrer is presented to you as he really is. All I desire with this booklet is to give you a true picture of the humane being the Fuehrer is—an inexpressibly great and magnanimous man who can be hard too, but only when necessary."

Indeed, during that period a profusely illustrated pamphlet was distributed throughout the Netherlands. It was called: "Do You Wish To Know The Truth?"* and contained very little text but a multitude of photographs of Adolf Hitler. There was Adolf, winsomely smiling, patting children's heads or stroking blond baby curls . . .; Adolf Hitler with his dog . . .; Adolf Hitler in front of his country house . . .; Adolf Hitler, a jovial friend of soldiers, laborers, housewives, artists and scholars. Adolf Hitler this and that—photographed from above, below, left and right . . .; Adolf Hitler speaking, smiling, grinning, lost in a brown study. And this remarkable collection of pictures—some of them fit for any Rogues' Gallery, was to convince the Dutch people once and for all that the man who only half a year ago had ordered the treacherous attack upon their country was a paragon of virtue.

To emphasize how malicious had been the slanderous gossip concerning this great philanthropist, the booklet also contained a few splendid cartoons by a well-known Dutch draftsman—powerful drawings which before the invasion had been published in the Netherlands. But, no doubt against the compiler's intentions,

*Several pages of this curious "build up" were reproduced in the weekly magazine "LOOK" of October 21, 1941. (See illustrations, opposite pages 38 and 39.)

they still managed to damage considerably the halo of saintliness which had been fastened with so much care around the egg-shaped, hypocritical head of the Great Fuehrer.

Thousands of Netherlanders felt no desire to keep this propaganda trash and returned it to Seyss-Inquart's personal address. As if by tacit arrangement, the majority of them forgot to attach the necessary postage.

The distribution of this strange "self-revelation" was only one of the many attempts made during those winter months of 1940 to convert the Dutch. "Our example," said Seyss-Inquart to an editor of Goebbels' Voelkischer Beobachter, "will teach the Dutch to accept a National-Socialist Commonwealth"—but the results did not seem to justify his confidence. The people of Holland, convinced of ultimate Nazi defeat, did not show the slightest anxiety to follow in the footsteps of their unwanted visitors.

As soon as the Germans noticed that the Dutch began to doubt their invincibility, Seyss-Inquart in his special New Year's Eve message reassured them emphatically, "During the year 1941 Germany will vanquish the British. There is no man in his right senses who can doubt the truth of this." And just in case there might be some such people around, nonetheless, the Reich's Commissioner added, "It is clear what is at stake. The problems requiring solution are plainly indicated. Now everyone can choose for himself: *with* us or *against* us!"

With us or against us. The Dutch Nazis eagerly greeted this marvelous new slogan and in February, 1941 an official propagandist of the Nazional-Sozialistische Deutsche Arbeiter Partei declared in a meeting of the German Nazi branch in the town of Haarlem, "The Netherlands has one chance only to be a free and independent country. And that is to become a National-Socialist State." But even such blunt assertions failed to influence the general attitude of the people; on the contrary, the Dutch found more than one chance to demonstrate their loathing of the various restrictive measures which had been and were being introduced—many of them directed against the Jewish population of the Netherlands. They even failed to hesitate when in February, 1941 the first physical attacks took place upon Dutch Jews in Amsterdam, The Hague and other cities. Immediately, with heartening spontaneity, a large portion of the gentile population declared a strike, paralyzing many public services and private enterprises and demonstrating with crystal clearness that the Christians of Holland fos-

HITLER EN DE VROUWEN

Zoo ongedwongen, als met boerinnen en arbeidsters, spreekt Hitler ook met de elegante artistes en de dames uit de Berlijnsche society.

ADOLF HITLER, PARAGON OF VIRTUE

These pages are reproduced from the booklet *"Do you wish to know the truth?"* which was generously distributed by the Nazis, in a desperate effort to "popularize" Adolf Hitler. The caption reads: *"HITLER AND THE WOMEN.* He is just as much at ease chatting with elegant artists and ladies of Berlin Society, as he is with peasants and working women."

DE JEUGD HEEFT HITLER

"YOUTH LOVES HITLER . . .

With the ballyhoo pictures reproduced on these two pages Joseph Goebbels tried to convince the unbelieving Dutch that Hitler is a true benefactor of the young and the adolescent.

BOVEN ALLES LIEF!

De kleinste kinderen openen voor hem hun hart. — De opgroeiende jeugd luistert naar zijn woord. — De geheele duitsche jeugd is een Hitler-jeugd. Wie de jeugd heeft, heeft de toekomst!

. . . ABOVE ALL"

"The smallest children open their hearts to him. . . . Adolescents listen to his words. . . . The entire German youth is Hitler's youth . . ." (And then, significantly:) "He who holds Youth, holds the future."

CAN HITLER BE BELIEVED?

"Does a liar look like *this?*" the booklet enquires. "Is this a man of war, or a man of peace?" . . . And again: "Hitler hates war . . .; he loves the peaceful mountains, children, animals, his home in the Alps. . . ." (*bottom, right:*) Hitler, meditating at the grave of his parents . . .

tered no wish to be instructed in the art of brow-beating successfully a group of defenseless Jews.

Once more Seyss-Inquart tried to "prove" that Germany and the Netherlands are blood-related nations. On March 12, 1941 a monster meeting was organized in Amsterdam's Concertgebouw, once the place where the strains of Holland's most famous Symphony Orchestra could be heard, uniting the music lovers of all creeds and parties, now given over to the bellowing voices of Nazi apostles, spreading the gospel of hate and destruction. By turning and twisting the history of Holland's growth, of its struggle for independence throughout the sixteenth and seventeenth centuries, the illustrious speaker managed to build up a very feeble case, culminating in the stock assertion that the Netherlands "had been torn from the body of the Reich in times past" . . . and that it was "now, at long last, returning into the family circle." Germanic blood guided by so "unique a phenomenon as Adolf Hitler" was engaged upon the construction of a new Europe. In this work the Netherlands must partake. Already it had yielded men and women eager to collaborate—the few thousand Mussert followers, known as N.S.B.'ers.

But how did Seyss-Inquart explain that in a period of nine years, from the founding of Mussert's party in 1931 until the invasion of 1940, the Nationaal-Socialistische Beweging had at no time been able to get the support of more than 1½ % of the entire populace? Very simple indeed. He merely accused the Dutch system of representative election of having been a "terror system," denying the Dutch Nazis a fair chance to get a justified numerical representation in the Upper and Lower Chambers of the country's government.

Naturally—the international, depraved spirit of liberalism under Jewish influence had been most guilty of this. "But the time had come," Seyss-Inquart howled, "to stop this nonsense." And obviously referring to the mushroom growth of the Netherlands Union, the Reich's Commissioner added:

"It seems as if at present another crowd of blind and irresponsible agitators is endeavoring to form the opinion of the Dutch for them and without them. If the people of Holland allow this, they will have to suffer for it in their entirety . . . . If during a duel for life or death an outsider takes the liberty of calling one of the fighting parties names and freely uttering his loathing and hatred, he should not be too surprised when the combatant in question, at a given moment, turns on him and sets him flying forever from the scene of the struggle . . ." This utterance was the first official threat of wholesale deportation; but unfortunately, there were few who understood the menace at that time.

Finally, in this same speech Seyss-Inquart addressed the laborers, peasantry and townspeople of the entire country. Among the workers, he suggested, there was sincere interest in National-Socialism and he hoped that many of them would find employment in the reconstruction of the devastated areas and (here came the sting) also in Germany! "As to the agriculturists," said Seyss-Inquart, they had "already adopted a positive standpoint and refused to be carried away by any emotionalism"—whatever this meant. But His Excellency was far less satisfied with the intellectual circles. From them had come the first protest against the persecution of Holland's Jews. In October it had been the Churches; in November the students of Leiden followed suit. February had brought the strikes and the revolt of Amsterdam. And so the Reich's Commissioner thought the time ripe to say something concerning the "Jewish problem."

"We do not consider the Jews a part of the Dutch people," he proclaimed. "They are the enemy with whom we neither wish to come to a truce, nor to a peace. The only thing we might be willing to talk about is the introduction of a bearable transition period."

And he continued, in a philosophic vein, "I have thought a great deal of the principle of Tolerance. I have now understood that the deeper sense and meaning of that principle was the desire of the people of Holland not to allow itself to be torn into factions. That is why tolerance in matters of religion was elevated to the rank of a principle, a precaution for the common good of the people as such. But tolerance for its own sake is only a by-product of the desire to reach the idyllic."

Should the Jews now "get back to the place they occupied at the time of William the Silent," Seyss-Inquart solemnly declared, he would think it a highly satisfactory solution.*

As a noble peroration to so outstanding a speech, Seyss-Inquart had a few words of reassurance to say regarding the inter-

*This status was more than the Jews could ever hope for under Nazi rule. It was William the Silent who actually confirmed their rather doubtful rights as citizens of the Dutch Republic and who, virtually speaking, inaugurated the period of tolerance and cooperation between Gentile and Jew which after more than three centuries of constant progress resulted in the perfect unity of both groups prevailing at the time of the German invasion.

national situation. First of all, let no one worry about a possible invasion of the European Continent, for the simple reason that such an attack is impossible. It was a pity, the Reich's Commissioner continued, that so many Netherlanders had been anxiously looking forward to such an invasion. They had seemingly failed to realize that the coming of the British would mean the almost certain and complete annihilation of the Dutch people! But the German army had proved invincible anyhow. The British air force seemed to believe that it was actually harming the Nazi war machine. As a matter of confidential fact, it had caused no damage to speak of. The morale in Germany was exceedingly good. The Nazi power to resist was "kolossal" and their determination terrible to behold. "Rather will Germany see the whole of Europe turned into one huge pile of rubble than to give up the righteous struggle . . . Heil dem Fuehrer!" (Stormy applause.)

For days afterwards the people of Holland were trying to get at the real meaning of this speech. Though not entirely devoid of the habitual "friendly approach," it contained an undeniable note of strong menace. For the first time a Nazi occupation official had openly declared that the senseless fight against the Jews was on in Holland, too. For the first time it had been stated coldly that all those opposing Nazi rule were in for a hard and not particularly healthy time. "Whoever refuses to be with us, is against us . . . !"

The challenge was made—and it did not take the Dutch long to show the enemy clearly that it had been accepted. With growing aversion and hatred they would continue to oppose all German efforts at co-ordination, regardless of the oppressor's overwhelming power, a force in which his Army played a predominant part.

Though the exact size of the Nazi Army of Occupation in the Netherlands, at that or any other time, was never published, it is conservative to say that a minimum of half a million German soldiers were constantly being fed, clothed and paid from Dutch resources. In every town and village of some importance a German force of some size could be found. It was invariably headed by the *Ortskommandant* who had readily taken upon himself the task of playing local dictator. In coastal towns this gentleman had the assistance of a special *Hafenkommandant* (port commander) whose duty it was to keep a sharp eye on all incoming and outgoing vessels. And finally, distributed across the whole country, was a net of semi-military *Verkehrsueberwachungskom-*

mando's (Traffic Guardian Troops) which had to keep all roads and canals open for German military movements. The entire set-up was placed under the leadership of the Nazi Air Force General Friedrich Christiansen who established his headquarters at The Hague.

Civil authority, however, was vested in a separate apparatus headed by Seyss-Inquart. Exactly a fortnight after the surrender a decree was published giving the detailed list of rights of this Hitler stooge. They were as sweeping as they were ill-defined. "The Reich's Commissioner," the first paragraph stated, "possesses every authority thus far, in accordance with the Constitution, due to the King and the Government." He was, however, to make use of the Dutch authorities in office at the time of surrender, except for the "German service branches under his leadership." Later paragraphs explained that to those "German service branches" belonged a number of Nazi General-Commissaries and "authorized persons" to be nominated by Seyss-Inquart at will, for the purpose of serving as his representatives in any one province, town or "special territory." Furthermore, the Netherlands' police force would henceforth be supervised by the "Deutsche Polizei" and would be obliged to act in accordance with the orders of the Germans.

But with this position Seyss-Inquart was not satisfied. It was not enough for him to possess both the law-giving and executive power in the Netherlands. On August 24, 1940, a further decree specified that the most important State functionaries were to be nominated by him personally. Among them were the Secretaries-General of all Government Departments; the Vice-President and members of the State Council; the President, Vice-President, Attorney-General and members of the Supreme Council; the Presidents and Attorneys-General of the five Dutch Courts; the Inspector of the State Police and Marechaussée; the Chiefs of Police, the Provincial Commissaries, formerly appointed by the ruling king or queen direct as his or her immediate representatives; the mayors of the eleven provincial capitals and the heads of all communities with more than 50,000 inhabitants. But this did not complete the list. There were, too, the President of the Netherlands Bank, the President of the Netherlands State Railroads, the Inspector-General of all Dutch merchant marine pilots, the Director of the State Artillery plant, the ship yards and, finally, the leader of the Post-war Reconstruction Service.

Thus the most important administrative and judicial posts

and all other functions in connection with "public safety," had been made subject to the will of the Austrian ex-lawyer. He could do with them as he pleased. He might give them to members of Mussert's movement exclusively; or he might hold them out as a bait to such obstreperous Dutchmen as were, at last, ready to promise to behave better in the future. And indeed—the N.S.B., home of most Dutch traitors, furnished within three months after the new decree no less than three Secretaries-General, two Attorneys-General, numerous Chiefs of Police, three provincial Commissaries, ten or more burgomasters and . . . the President of the Netherlands Bank. That was, for the time being, about all the intellectually poverty-stricken Dutch Nazi movement could possibly provide. Besides, it soon became evident that Seyss-Inquart had no intention of filling every vacancy occurring in town and provincial governments, or in other public bodies. Towards the end of June the Reich's Commissioner stated that he would consider each case on its own merits and take his decisions accordingly.

Obviously, the democratic system with its Parliament and free vote had, for the time being, been abolished. A decree was published on June 22, 1940 by which the activities of both the Lower and Upper Chambers were "postponed until further order." The State Council was, however, maintained and allowed to continue advising the various Departments, as it had done before the invasion. Unfortunately, there was not a single department left in a position to make its own decisions!

Each rule and every indication of attitude issued by the highest Berlin power reach the Offices of the Reich's Commissioner, except if they bear on military matters in which case General Christiansen is the chosen recipient. The right-hand men of Seyss-Inquart are his four General Commissaries. There is one for Law and Justice, a certain Dr. Wimmer who keeps a watchful eye on all municipal authorities for education, religion, culture in general, the people's health and the care of Holland's youth. His power is far-reaching indeed, and during the two-and-a-half years he has ruled the opportunity has never failed him to abuse his status and contribute generously to the suffering and misery of the Dutch people. General Commissary Number 2 is Leader of the Higher S.S. and of the Security Police, Rauter—who heads the German police divisions* in the occupied Netherlands and is, at the same time supreme ruler over all Dutch State and Municipal police. Col-

*His German title is: *Hoehere SS und Polizeifuehrer.*

league Number 3 is Dr. Hans von Fischboeck, former Austrian Finance Minister who is Seyss-Inquart's economic expert. The Finance Department is entrusted to this personage; but he also heads the departments of economics, waterways and social affairs. Even the postal services are placed in his sole power.

Number 4 is Dr. Schmidt, the Commissary-General for special events. This gentleman is to solve all problems concerning the "forming of public opinion" and those regarding non-economic societies. Thus far he has not done so very well, though his boss, on various occasions, gave him special assignments. To hide his lack of success in this particular field somewhat, Herr Schmidt has also been made the Fuehrer of the German Nazis in the Netherlands. In this capacity, having to do with well-drilled Germans free of those awkward characteristics which distinguish the recalcitrant Dutch, he has been reported considerably more successful.

Finally, there is the Reichs Commissioner's Press Department. It was until the late summer of 1942* headed by a certain Willy Janke who not so long before the invasion was deported from Dutch territory because of espionage. This noble journalist collaborated closely with the Dutch Nazi renegade Max Blokzijl who—from being a more or less respected Dutch correspondent in Berlin—has stooped low enough to become the willing stooge of Joseph Goebbels whose extraordinary characteristics he arduously tries to copy—though without much result. Day after day Blokzijl and half a score of Nazi press chiefs hold ponderous conferences in which they think of and discuss new schemes to make the free and highly individualistic press of the subjugated Netherlands conform to Nazi rules and praise the Fuehrer.

Needless to say that all these worthies have staffs of their own which, in some cases, have quite numerous . . . staffs of their own! There are "experts" and "advisers" galore, not to mention the "specially authorized" or otherwise endowed officials who crowd the streets and Government offices of The Hague, all of them being smartly dressed, well-fed and quite handsomely paid. The number of "Leiters" (leaders) who for some reason or other populate the various departments, is nothing less than confusing; and all their separate decrees and regulations are handed to the still-functioning department heads of the old regime, for early publication. Obviously, not all of them reach Seyss-Inquart's very

*Janke was "promoted" to the post of German Consul in Zuerich (Switzerland) in August, 1942.

own "Verordeningenblad";* but a few do and whenever this happens the Dutch Nazis jubilate. Another stone has been laid in the staunch and mighty edifice which will be their stronghold and support for all time.

But it is clear that those four high gentlemen do not represent the entire German infiltration. Nazi parasites have settled cozily in every civil service office and in every Court of the Netherlands. To begin with, the German Army has its own Military Courts. Next follow the Civil Courts, the so-called "Landesgerichte" topped by the High Court ("Obergericht") at The Hague. It is their duty to handle every "misdemeanor against the German Reich or against German officials"; they are also expected to deal out adequate punishment for plunder and robbery committed during air-raid alarms or blackout hours. With the exquisite taste characteristic of the Nazis, the building set aside for the first of these Landesgerichte was . . . the former palace of Princess Juliana at The Hague.

The next nation-wide institution to be ruled by German officials was that of the Labor Exchanges. On May 1, 1941 one hundred and eighty-five such Exchanges had been opened—all of them under the supervision of the Nazi-instituted Reich's Labor Bureau and an exact copy of the Labor Exchanges in Germany.

As time goes by the number of German institutions, inspections and control offices increases out of all proportion. Ever since the surrender of the Dutch armed forces a close check is being held on every movement in the Netherlands, social, cultural or economic. And striding high above it all, overseeing the enslaved people of Holland and ready to pounce upon anything or anybody, are the agents of the German secret police—the dreaded Gestapo—as choice a clique of spies, stool-pigeons and traitors as has ever been seen in the bloodiest periods of man's history. Yet, all this did not prevent Seyss-Inquart from declaring sanctimoniously in an interview with the German "Weltpressedienst" (World Press Service), published in the controlled Dutch newspapers of October 29, 1940: "The occupying power has, to tell the truth, been satisfied to place a staff of German leaders next to the central Dutch governmental bodies. It is their duty to look after the interests of the occupying power according to the needs of the moment. In other words: the people of the Netherlands are governed by their own authorities and Civil Servants."

*The Official Journal issued by the German occupying power to replace the erstwhile "Staatsblad" or State Journal.

At the present time, after two and a half years of German occupation, even such a professional hypocrite as Seyss-Inquart would hesitate to repeat such a statement. The list of loyal civil servants and other government authorities who have since been "relieved" of their duty, is long enough to occupy a score of pages. It is impossible to give even an adequate selection of them within the scope of this book. But one or two examples should be mentioned.

Before the first year of Nazi occupation had come to its close, the list of ousted authorities contained that of the President of the Netherlands Bank, Mr.* Trip who was also Secretary-General of the Finance Department. He was replaced by the "intellectual" Dutch Nazi Meinoud M. Rost van Tonningen, of whose remarkable conversion to Nazism more will be said in chapter seven. The Secretary-General of Social Affairs had also disappeared and the Department of Education, Culture and Sciences had been entrusted to the tender cares of the Fascist Professor Jan van Dam, long known for his totalitarian leanings and an editor of the semi-Fascist weekly "De Waag" (The Scales) many months before the invasion.

That most of these replacements were made in flagrant contradiction to International Law did not disturb the Germans in the least. They rubbed their hands, murmured something of Necessity being the "only true law-giver" and were particularly pleased when they found a Dutch traitor prepared to bear out the "legality" of their actions. The Dutch Nazi Professor J. J. Schrieke, successor to the loyal Secretary-General of Justice, Mr. J. C. Tenkink, said in a Hilversum broadcast on November 12, 1940:

"I know that some law authorities, basing their opinion on certain stipulations of International Law, think that an occupying power would exceed its authority were it to introduce such far-going reforms. But I also know that all of you will understand that the changes our Continent is undergoing at present are of such historical significance and depth, and are brought about by so strong a creative power that they cannot be held back by bits of printed paper." The greatest possible publicity was given to this extraordinary statement; the Nazis were only too happy to have Dutchmen do the dirty work for them.

The entire process of coordination was to be so slow that

*Mr. is a Dutch abbreviation of the title "Meester", being approximately the equivalent of the American Doctor of Law degree.

the average Dutchman would, as it were, fail to notice any change. The main idea was never to make too sweeping a reform. Step by step, through small quantitative changes, the final purpose was to be achieved. And while the majority of the Dutch were still inclined to believe that their old institutions had remained intact, the Nazis were changing their character completely.

Concentration and coordination were the underlying principles of every one of those changes. Long-existent societies and leagues were "permitted" to amalgamate. In July, 1940, for instance, the various ship-owners societies were "allowed to come together"; in mid-August the cigarette manufacturers of the entire Netherlands had to live up to this "good example" and September saw the innovation of a coordinated League of Insurance Brokers. During the autumn the Netherlands Football League followed suit and the next few months brought the coordination of many more craftsmen's leagues, including that of the Dutch fishermen and . . . of the police. This coordination rage reached a temporary lull with the unification of all Dutch mortician societies, a rather lugubrious finale but not entirely devoid of doubtlessly unintentional humor.

More serious than this typically Teutonic desire to "unify" all workers and their smaller or bigger societies, was the German effort to coordinate the entire economic life of the Netherlands and to paralyze it by putting National-Socialists in most of its key positions. As early as July, 1940 a "National Committee for Economic Collaboration" had been established. Its founder was a Dutchman who, although he had not officially belonged to the Dutch Nazi Party before the German attack, had been known to sympathize with Hitler's ideologies. This man, Dr. Fentener van Vlissingen, President of the Utrecht Chamber of Commerce, former President of the International Chamber of Commerce and President of the Board of Directors of the famous Utrecht Commercial Fairs, had formed a Committee in which several other Dutchmen of excellent repute had taken seats. The purpose of this Committee was stated to be the undefined "coordination of Holland's economic life." That was all the Dutch public was to hear for some months of this seemingly harmless institution.

But in November, 1941 Dutch industry and commerce were more than surprised to read that a so-called "Organizing Committee" had been formed to take all preparatory measures "fit and necessary to establish an independent organization for the development of Dutch industry and commerce." This Committee was "more especially authorized to found economic organizations"; but Fentener van Vlissingen was no longer mentioned in connection with it. Its President was a certain Mr. H. L. Woltersom, a director of a well-known banking concern. The same Committee, however, comprised three Dutch Nazis and a number of industrial, financial and economic experts whose political leanings were as yet not very clear. In fact, many Dutch observers outside the Dutch occupied territory believed that these men had accepted Woltersom's invitation only because they believed that, in so doing, they might be instrumental in the introduction of new features of permanent value to the Dutch economic system.

This Organizing Committee was supposed to coordinate every conceivable branch of commerce and industry, with the sole exceptions of agriculture, horticulture, cattle-breeding and river fisheries. A sub-division into six "main groups" was to be made, namely industry, crafts, commerce, banking, insurance and transportation. Each main group would in its turn be subdivided in industrial groups and every industrial group was to consist of certain "professional groups." Once again an intricate machinery would be established in close imitation of the German method. For a similar set-up had been introduced in the Reich in July, 1936; and at the time of the invasion of Holland that German organization possessed no less than 31 industrial groups, subdivided in 249 professional groups which comprised more than 350 professional sub-groups.

On the surface it all seemed a senseless by-product of the perverted Teutonic passion for organization. Actually, however, this highly complicated system plays a most important part in the war economy of the Nazis. It enables the labor chiefs to have at their disposal every figure wanted with regard to the production capacity of any given branch of commerce or industry. Decisions regarding the transfer of laborers from overstaffed to understaffed regions can be taken without any appreciable loss of time. Moreover, as each group is supervised by a Nazi of unchallenged loyalty, nothing can escape the eagle eye of the labor chiefs. In this way only is it possible to allow the principles of Nazism to penetrate into the smallest crevice of commercial and industrial life, and to prepare for a State governed in a truly National-Socialist sense.

It was obviously the task of the Woltersom Committee to reach something akin to that ideal State. Whether at that moment all of its members realized this or not, is difficult to say but the fact remains that six months after its initiation the Committee had achieved nothing more than the institution of one "main group," that of the leather industry with separate professional groups for leather shoes, leather goods and power transmission belts. Only in April, 1942—almost two years after its start—the Committee announced triumphantly that it had now completely "organized" industry, insurance and banking but admitted that transportation, commerce and crafts were still "to be taken in hand." Agriculture, horticulture, cattle-breeding and fisheries were also to be re-organized on the German model. But this work was entrusted to a completely different section of Holland's people; and subsequent Nazi efforts in this direction are related in chapter six (*Plight of the Peasants*).

While such complicated institutions are obviously meant to be permanent and form part of the "New Order" framework for post-war use, there are a host of German bureaus whose existence is admittedly only temporary. The bulk of them busy themselves with the distribution of raw materials and foodstuffs.

The series was headed by a General State Institution for the Distribution of Foodstuffs in Wartime. It was swiftly followed by special offices for coal, textiles, woollens, leather, hides, paper, metals, and a long list of other commodities. From month to month new centers were added to those already existing. Now it was a "State Bureau for Tobacco and Tobacco Products," then again a special center where all owners of hotels, cafés, restaurants and rooming houses were forced to register.

New titles, new jobs, new officials, new institutions, new bureaus . . . ; in less than one year the Nazis had fastened their tentacles firmly to every vital organ of the national body. Holland's riches and its labor could now be fully and undisturbedly exploited for the benefit of the German war machine. Gradually the Nazi net was closed; it would be foolish to deny that it had not been solidly and ingeniously constructed.

The Dutch nation was irrevocably caught—but the leading Nazi hypocrites still pointed at the result of their efforts with a sweet smile and a generous gesture. Their eyes brimful of emotion and goodwill, they declaimed with pathos: "Everyone can now see for himself how the Netherlands, though it lost the war against us, is still ruled by its own authorities and its own Civil Servants—thanks to the magnanimity of our Fuehrer! . . ."

3

THE LOCUSTS SETTLE DOWN

"The rich stores of raw materials gathered during a period of many years were voluntarily yielded by the Netherlands to our common economic needs."

Seyss-Inquart's declaration in the "Volkischer Beobachter," of December 5, 1940.

"The German authorities in the Netherlands do everything to promote, within the stipulated limits, the economic life of the Dutch people."

Dr. Hans Fischboeck, Commissary-General of Finance and Economy, on June 12, 1941.

Even before the Nazis sent Seyss-Inquart to take over civil authority in the occupied Netherlands, another German official had made his appearance. Ironically enough the name of this gentleman was Dr. Wohltat.* He was nominated Commissary to the Netherlands Bank and started his work on May 23, 1940 to leave it again towards the end of March, 1941 when he was sent to Japan. Within that short period of ten months he worked like a man possessed to organize and stimulate the German plunder of the Netherlands. The emptier the Dutch treasury chests became the more arduous grew the economy propaganda of the Nazis. The refrain to every instance of insolent robbery was the same: "The difficulties may be great today— but never forget that tomorrow will bear golden fruit."

By preference such promises were made through the medium of traitorous Dutchmen, without exception members of Mussert's movement. As a rule those gentlemen predicted that the future would bring a "Germanic Commonwealth" in which the people of the Netherlands would enjoy undreamt of economic advantages. In fact, they would be nothing less than astounding. Agriculture and horticulture would be endowed with immense new territories —not only because of greater buying power inside the Netherlands and Germany, but also because the exportation to erstwhile pov-

***Wohltat = Munificent action; good deed.**

erty-stricken regions of Central Europe—now of course transmuted into prosperous territories—would swiftly increase and reach such heights as were never known before. New railroads, new canals and an unparalleled net of motor highways would enable quicker delivery of Dutch produce to parts of the world as yet beyond its reach. And of course, by that time the British Empire would no longer exist, Britannia would no longer rule the waves . . . Once more the enterprising merchantmen of Holland would be given their chance, naturally within the framework of the above-mentioned "Germanic Commonwealth!"

Other trumpet-blowers added new flourishes to the same idyllic subject. With regard to the Netherlands East Indies no Hollander need have fear. Adolf Hitler himself had promised that "the people of Holland would be allowed to keep the Indies." They would, of course, also be "gleichgeschaltet" (coordinated) and conform in every respect to the requirements of the New Order.

For poor tortured Rotterdam, still bleeding from its thousands of gaping wounds, still a ghastly rubble heap, the Nazi prophets predicted a glorious future. Together with other North Sea ports it would, once and for all, take the place of London.

If now and again, amidst these high-sounding promises, a modest voice was heard, pointing out that "things had not been so bad before the war," the defenders of the New Order looked very knowingly and remarked, their eyes filled with human kindness, "Ah yes, but only for a few privileged people!" The truth, however, was that since the coming of the unwelcome German guests the entire Netherlands populace had been rapidly forced to accept an incomparably lower standard of living.

And if by any chance a daring listener would hesitantly remark that "things are not too good with us now, are they?", the standard reply would be, "What of it? You wait till the golden future comes!"

But unfortunately for the Nazis, very few people seemed to have much confidence in that splendor-to-be. It was, indeed, difficult to attain such heights of optimism in view of the looting and robbing carried out from day to day by the legions of Nazi invaders. Hardly had the last Dutch dead been buried before the first freight train, made up of an endless string of cars and heavily loaded with an astounding variety of stolen goods, rumbled across the plains of Holland, on its way to the Reich. On their return trip such trains were almost as long and as closely packed—but this time the cargo was composed of war materials for the use of the occupation troops. That those "exports" were paid for with Dutch money or with claims on the German Treasury, did not make the slightest difference. Whenever the necessary funds were not taken from the Netherlands Bank, payment was made with Nazi Treasury Bills, the so-called "Reichskreditkassenscheine." It is true that the seller could exchange these bills for Dutch paper money, but finally the German notes were presented to the Netherlands Bank and—with the benign consent of Dr. Wohltat—exchanged for . . . German marks, or other valuable German paper from the safes of that bank. Seyss-Inquart's solemn assurance, quoted at the head of this chapter, that "the rich stores of raw materials gathered during a period of many years were voluntarily yielded by the Netherlands to our common economic needs," may thus be safely ranked among the classic examples of perfidy.

It is impossible to give a list anywhere near complete of the immense wealth which was thus carried away from the subjugated Netherlands. To mention only a few stray examples: 6,000 tons of tea, 28,000 tons of coffee, at least 20,000 tons of cocoa, 1,000 tons of butter and more than 325,000 tons of vegetable oils disappeared into the gaping maw of the Nazi monster. Everything was welcome—from tobacco and woollens to any variety of foodstuffs and fruit. As to the latter, practically the entire apple harvest of 1940 was requisitioned by Germany. And in the meantime tens of thousands of head of cattle, and horses, and poultry by the millions made the trip eastwards . . . never to return. But all the while the controlled radio at Hilversum was commanded to repeat, week upon week, that "all this talk about enormous stocks which are supposed to have been built up in this country" was downright nonsense.

But the Dutch people, in their majority, knew how gigantic a lie this statement was.

An orderly nation with a strongly developed sense for law and justice, now entered upon the most chaotic relationships. Caught in a net of measures and decrees, forced to adopt a "catch-as-catch-can" mentality, they could not fail to see that the systematic ravaging of their country was not merely economic plunder but ultimately intended to break their physical and mental resistance. And apart from the obvious robbery, there were many subtler ways in which the Netherlands Commonwealth could be and was impoverished without the masses becoming aware of it.

Only a few days after the surrender of the Dutch defense forces, for instance, the military authorities decreed that henceforth the Dutch guilder would equal R.M.* 1.50. The mark was thus "stabilized" at the rate of 66 Dutch cents, much too high a quotation in comparison with pre-invasion rates. But less than two months later the guilder was further devaluated and now the mark equalled 75 Dutch cents! How much this difference of approximately 15% has cost the Netherlands Commonwealth is hard to estimate; it is certain that this "gift" to the soldiers of Adolf Hitler took hundreds of millions out of the Dutch treasury.**

Despite this ingenious method, the Germans were none too generous in their payment for requisitioned goods, or for the care of their soldiers. A common soldier had to be "boarded" by any civilian at the rate of ten Dutch cents per night—the equivalent of 6c. For this price he could, however, not claim a bed; should he wish such a luxury, the payment was to be doubled! The best-paying German guests were high-ranking officers who would sacrifice as much as 1½ guilders (or about 80c) for a night's rest between clean Dutch linen sheets.

Towards the end of February, 1941 Netherlands claims on the German army totalled 35 million guilders, or about 20 million dollars. For this huge sum commodities of every kind had been delivered in fabulous quantities; yet, only a fraction of the claim was settled. But let it be clearly understood that this total merely represented purchases from private persons and had nothing whatever to do with Holland's responsibility for the upkeep of the entire army of occupation. Even now, after two and a half years of German domination, it has not been possible to ascertain with any measure of certainty the exact total reserved each year for this purpose. Suffice it to say that Dr. Hans von Brucken Fock, a Dutch Nazi financial expert, estimated this item at no less than one billion two hundred million guilders, or about 648 million dollars, yearly —and this friend of Germany can certainly not be accused of exaggeration.

The Nazis did a thorough job, taking everything they could lay their hands on. It stands to reason that the gold reserves of the Netherlands Bank were included . . . as far as they were there. Fortunately, the Dutch Government was able to carry to safety

---

*Reichsmark.

**The American journalist Howard K. Smith in his "Last Train From Berlin" describes a similar method employed in occupied France to allow the Occupation Army to buy "things for the folks at home." ("The economics of decline"; page 116.)

the greater part of those reserves; but in obedience to the law sufficient gold had been left behind to cover paper money in circulation. This gold was very welcome Nazi booty and to it was added every gold piece and every bar of unminted gold in the possession of Dutch citizens. To part with those treasures would, according to the Nazis, be nothing much of a wrench. After all—the "age of the gold standard" had practically run its course . . . The New Order would bring new standards and it was, so to say, a blessing for the Netherlanders to find the Nazis willing and ready to take over their "useless yellow metal." Requisitioning of this privately-owned gold started in October, 1940 and lasted for several months. It was strictly forbidden to withhold a single gold coin—not even for sentimental reasons. In this way gold to a minimum value of 72 million dollars was carted away to Germany and replaced by paper currency.

After this, new economic and financial measures followed one another swiftly. All foreign shares in the hands of Dutch investors had to be registered. Dollars, Swiss francs and Swedish crowns were to be relinquished immediately. Any interests or dividends due to Netherlands holders of shares in German enterprises were payable only to the clearing house of all German-Dutch business transactions. German firms which had floated loans in the Netherlands, were authorized in the beginning of February, 1941 to lower the rate of their interest to 4 percent. If anyone did not like this idea he could get his money back . . . , that is to say: the equivalent of his original investment in a special kind of German Reichsmarks which possessed only 50 percent of the value of the *real* Reichsmark! Or, if the unfortunate investor preferred, he could get the entire amount of his loan refunded in a payment to the so-called "Verrechnungskasse" (Clearance Center). But should he try to get that money out of Germany, he would find that no less than seventy percent of the total was due to the Reich as a "special tax." Were he to invest the money in Germany himself, no one would give him more than the four percent interest he was already getting.

In this way the Dutch investor in German loans was given very little choice. He had to resign himself to the reception of small mercies; but this lowering of the interest rate is obviously costing the Netherlands Commonwealth many millions of dollars each year.

An immediate result of these and other German manipulations was that the exports from the Netherlands to Germany rapidly overlapped the total of Dutch purchases in the Reich. While during 1939 Holland imported approximately 124 million dollars more than it exported to Germany, the situation had been so drastically changed in the first six occupation months that by the beginning of December, 1940 the country possessed an export surplus of over 30 million dollars!

The reasons were obvious. While the Dutch were mainly exporting foodstuffs, the Germans sent to Holland almost exclusively raw materials for their own war industry. On Netherlands soil these materials were changed into weapons—only to be re-exported to Germany immediately afterwards.

In numerous ways the impoverishment of the Netherlands nation made rapid progress. Dutch industries would get orders for German enterprises, ofttimes for fabulous sums—but allowing only the smallest profit margin. For—as the Dutch Nazi Dr. H. J. von Brucken Fock once explained in his crypto-fascist monthly "De Waag": "The German Commissary for prices examines the cost calculation of every firm with the utmost care." This frank admittance of Nazi exploitation methods did not altogether tally with the honeyed words spoken by the General Director of the "Reich's Industrial Group" during a meeting at The Hague in March, 1941. Had not that gentleman, in an address to his Dutch colleagues, solemnly declared, "We offer you our hand and you only have to grasp it—to the benefit of the entire Dutch industry!"

At every turn of the road the Germans found new and ingenious ways to swindle and rob the Netherlands Commonwealth. During the first occupation year they forced tens of thousands of Dutch laborers to accept work in Germany, and those men had to yield part of their weekly wages for the support of their families at home. But do not believe that the huge amounts thus held back from the payrolls of these workers were actually transferred to the occupied country. No—the money remained in Germany and the Netherlands State was politely invited to advance the necessary funds in exchange for a claim on the Reich. Roughly speaking, this yielded the German Treasury a total of forty-three million dollars for the first twelve months of Holland's subjugation.

There was a general rush of Nazi hyenas to get out of Holland whatever they could. The Amsterdam Stock Exchange probably never sold as many shares to German buyers as it did in those autumn days of 1940. Nazi soldiers were allowed to send 1,000 marks each month to their people in the Reich and whenever these men passed the Dutch-German frontier they were at liberty to carry on their person a further amount of one thousand marks.

Every German in the Netherlands could buy Dutch commodities to a total of 5,000 Reichsmarks per month. It is obvious that where so many rivulets came together, they formed a turbulent stream of insatiable buyers. Steadily the Netherlands was emptied of all it possessed in movable commodities; many Germans who had no opportunity to visit this Land of Cockaigne themselves sent money to their soldier friends or relatives with the sole desire to get as much as possible—no matter what—out of fabulously-rich Holland.

Before the close of 1941 German financial penetration of Holland's industrial and commercial life had grown to monstrous proportions. Motor cars, machinery, commodities, horses, cattle, poultry and a thousand different other things had been requisitioned or "bought" with Holland's own money. In various industries the Nazis had, by hook or by crook, obtained a majority of the share capital. The Dutch people had been robbed of all their investments, national and international, and of all their gold. What they had been given in return were gigantic paper claims on the Reich and huge piles of German shares which, in case of a German defeat, would naturally prove to have very little value.

Should Germany, on the other hand, emerge victoriously, the people of Holland would never get back a single penny of their financial reserves. Worse than that: they would be exposed to Nazi robbery and exploitation, in an ever-changing variety of forms and without a let-up. The appearance of normal commercial and financial transactions would no doubt be preserved for relations which, in reality, were considerably worse than the methods of the stick-up man. Theft of foodstuffs; theft of labor. Plunder of money and shares; robbery of a thousand and one different staple goods which, as Seyss-Inquart so suavely declared, had been "voluntarily yielded to our common economy by the people of the Netherlands."

*

But it would be very naive to believe that the Nazis were satisfied with the loot obtained in so simple and straightforward a series of highway robberies. They wanted much more.

Why should little Holland have its own well-developed industries if after the war the enormously-developed German war industries could well take care of all peace time needs of the entire New Order? Why allow these Netherlanders to possess beautiful ports along the North Sea coast? The little Dutchmen were to be reduced to gardeners, peasants and freight-carriers in the service of the mighty German Herrenvolk. This was the adopted Nazi policy for the second occupation year—and it sums up practically all that happened to the economy of Holland till this very day.

No longer does Holland possess an independent foreign trade. Since August, 1941 the German-instituted "Central Service for Imports and Exports" has taken over the task of licensing every single exportation, no matter how small the article or the quantity involved. Besides, all payments must take place via Berlin and in many instances such payment has been asked for not in money, but in other goods. The world-renowned radio and electric-light bulb factory of Philips, Eindhoven, sent a shipment of its articles to Spain in exchange for a cargo of oranges. In a similar manner Turkey promised to export fruit, Sweden a small quantity of wood, cellulose and paper in exchange for machinery, chemical products and more Philips' radio sets and bulbs.

To tell the cruel truth: there was no Dutch export left to speak of. World-wide, a most important part of the national income only a couple of years ago, it had now shrunken to dwarfish proportions.

The heavy industry, the blast furnaces, shipyards, machine factories and electrical and technical plants had all been crammed with Nazi orders until the summer of 1941. But gradually the Germans reorganized their war industries and concentrated much of their manufacturing in their own plants. The Dutch enterprises were slowly but unmistakably cut off from all Nazi war activities. Soon enough it became clear why. New machinery was taken from Dutch plants and carted to the Reich; and the men needed to work them were forced to leave their homesteads to migrate.

By now the safes of the Netherlands Bank were filled with worthless German paper received in exchange for Dutch currency. Netherlands industrialists who had been paid in German marks and who had readily obtained the equivalent in their own Dutch guilders, discovered that the possession of so much ready cash was of little use. The purchase of fresh supplies of raw materials was as impossible as the acquisition of new machinery. Some of these men switched over to black market activities; but those not attracted by the lures of "illegal" trading, found nothing left to do but to deposit their superfluous cash with their banks. These institutions, in their turn, exchanged the deposits for Treasury Bills, with the result that the Netherlands Commonwealth obtained tremendous "credits" from millions of banking accounts—unusable credits covered by nothing but Treasury Bills. Meantime, to fulfill its obligations toward the occupying power, the State of the Netherlands was obliged to print more and more of those Treasury Bills.

For the average Hollander it was hard to discover how rapidly his country was being brought to the verge of bankruptcy, and with how much perfidy this was done. But the Dutch financial and economic experts were well aware of the truth. All they had to do was to look at the Weekly Statement of the Netherlands Bank. When in June, 1941 the Dutch-Nazi Meinoud M. Rost van Tonningen brought out his first yearly report as Director of the Netherlands Bank, the Amsterdam daily "Telegraaf" dared to ask him for "greater frankness concerning the way in which the Treasury is being financed." The paper asked more information regarding the manner in which the items "Various accounts" and "Paper claims abroad" were mentioned on the weekly balance sheet. But, of course, the "Telegraaf's" inquisitiveness was not rewarded with any revelations by Rost van Tonningen.

Instead, the influence of this ambitious and in his way capable Nazi traitor greatly increased when in December, 1941 the entire Dutch banking business was placed under the supervision of a Secretary-General for Special Economic Affairs. It was ordained that the new official would have to consult the President of the Netherlands Bank only on matters of principle; but since both positions were held by the same man, these consultations must have taken the form of rather curious monologues. The truth was that with this extension of Rost van Tonningen's power, it became impossible for any bank to guarantee its clients the slightest degree of secrecy.

The financial debacle towards which the Netherlands was heading with breakneck speed became so obvious that even Rost van Tonningen himself could no longer ignore it. And so—in December, 1941—he wrote an article in Mussert's weekly "Volk en Vaderland" in which, after admitting that the national debt was rising rapidly, this Dutch accomplice of the Nazi robbers remarked reassuringly, "But does this mean that at the end of the war our country will be in a state of hopeless financial chaos? In full confidence I can answer, No. For the difference between the last war and this one is that even while I speak the entire economic structure of the Netherlands is being reorganized."

But it must have chagrined him considerably to see that some of his close friends did not seem to share his opinions and were, on the contrary, well aware of their exceedingly hollow sound. The N.S.B.'er Dr. Von Brucken Fock, personal advisor of Anton Mussert and since March, 1942, director of Seyss-Inquart's "Institute of Economic Research," contributed an essay to the Nazi press in which he painted a clear picture of the road to financial ruin along which the country was being dragged.

"Against our probably greatly increased national income there is no proportionate increase of goods in circulation," Von Brucken Fock wrote. "It is true that our claims on Germany show a temporary increase, but the question is: what will remain of those claims at the end of the war? Besides, the protection of our territory (meaning: the upkeep of the Army of Occupation) is a costly business . . . The orders of the German Army do not bring new commodities into circulation . . . We must not forget, moreover, that a huge amount of private claims on the Netherlands Bank, mainly in the form of bank notes or current accounts, is no longer offset by adequate activa. At best we can speak of a doubtful claim on the German Reich with regard to the gold it took away from us."

*

A never-ending stream of new taxes began to flood the country. Increased income tax, dividend tax, a special "victory tax" of 4½ % on all wages . . .; a tax on limited companies; a new capital levy on all legally recognized businesses . . . The nazified Nieuwe Rotterdamsche Courant calculated that any enterprise making a profit of no more than 5% on its capital investment would have to pay taxes representing 87% of everything it had earned.

But all this was far from enough for the German usurers.

During 1941 loans were placed on the market to a total of over one billion guilders (approximately 540 million dollars). Only 30 million guilders were represented by private emissions; the rest had been placed by the Government. In October, 1941 for example, a State loan of about 270 million dollars was issued at the rate of 3½ %, with voluntary subscription. However, this announcement was accompanied with the threat that, should the required amount not have been fully subscribed, a compulsory loan would be issued at an interest rate of 2½ %. The loan, though it would have to be paid up in full, would not be quoted higher than 75—so that every person forced to invest his money in that manner would be certain to lose at least 25 % of his capital. However, the "voluntary" loan was subscribed and for once a piece of German bullying went haywire.

The cost of living was meanwhile mounting by the hour. While salaries had not risen to any appreciable extent—the Germans had, in fact, put a ceiling on all wages long ago and only tolerated insignificant raises—the few commodities still on the market became more and more expensive. Besides, as taxes increased, the amounts available for the purchase of foodstuffs dropped proportionately.

But the scarcity was not confined to foodstuffs. The Netherlands, with its limited natural resources for raw materials and dependent as it was on supplies from abroad, was left with very little to keep its industries going. It was too late now to collect the metals of utility objects inside the country; the marauders had been too quick for the Dutch and had beaten them by several lengths. In June, 1941—only a couple of days before the invasion of Soviet Russia—all articles made partly or entirely of brass, copper, tin, lead, nickel and their alloys, had been requisitioned. The Nazi order specified no less than thirty-seven such metals which could no longer be used. The list, beginning with ashtrays, birdcages and flower pots ended with stands, service trays, vases and a host of other articles in general use. The only exceptions made were for public monuments and grave memorials, church clocks, liturgical objects, organs and pieces of historical value in the care of museums. Also excepted were decorations, coins in circulation and such objects as could be considered of high scientific or artistic value. As usual, the Netherlands Bank paid for all objects. In other words, the people of the Netherlands took money from one pocket to put it in the other. Within fourteen days each community had to install the necessary number of receiving centers; within a month the entire requisition was to be completed.

The N.S.B. insisted upon having at least one of its members in each branch office, to make sure that every citizen would be treated "fair and square" . . . Much to their disappointment, their wish does not seem to have been acted upon everywhere. In fact, the artistic norm which most of these bureaus set themselves was very low indeed. Millions of objects never reached the Nazis because the bureaus readily decided that they were "of undoubted artistic value" . . .

All in all, the number of objects brought to these centers was not particularly large. One of the reasons for this poor result may have been a passage in Mussert's radio speech of June 28, 1941 in which he shouted, with his characteristic lack of tact, "Bring all your copper—*we* need it to win the war!"

To be sure, this appeal could not have been made with greater clumsiness. Max Blokzijl, the former Dutch journalist from Berlin who was serving the Nazis as press and radio man, tried a couple of weeks later to save the situation by broadcasting that "According to my information the sacrifice asked of you is not to benefit the German war machine but will be used to manufacture material for our electro-technical industries . . . It may be hard," Blokzijl continued suavely, "to give up one or more of your souvenirs to the State. But great heavens—what does this mean if compared with the perils of our days?"

Rarely has a Nazi decree been more thoroughly sabotaged. There were humorists who brought a few thumb-tacks and asked to be paid for the value of the metal. The most insignificant objects were offered for sale at the receiving centers. According to a conservative, neutral estimate no more than one per cent of all goods falling under the decree was handed over to the authorities. The rest was hidden away in safe places. In the spring of 1942 the occupying power started a check on the metal claimed and as a result—obviously with the intention of frightening the masses—sent four Netherlanders to concentration camps.

But the requisitioning of these articles was by no means the only trick the Nazis used to rob the Dutch of their valuable metals. Bronze and silver coins, huge quantities of which were in circulation, were held back by the Netherlands Bank at the order of its Nazi Director and replaced by a quaintly-stamped coinage made of zinc. In a way this measure came too late because many Dutchmen had seen their chance to build up large stocks of small change—bronze as well as silver. Now and again the German police traced such "criminals," as in the case of an Amsterdam shopkeeper who was found to possess several herring vats filled to the brim with silver "kwartjes" and "dubbeltjes,"* to a total of ten thousand guilders.

*A kwartje is about the same, in buying value, as an American quarter; as to the dubbeltje, it equals approximately an American dime.

The new zinc coins (see illustrations opposite this page) were not very warmly welcomed. It was not only the insignificance of their weight but also the extraordinary pagan symbols with which they were covered, which evoked the aversion of the Dutch people. When, moreover, the Dutch Government in London declared in January, 1941, in a broadcast to the occupied country, that "everybody who keeps in his possession bronze, silver and nickel change may be sure that these coins will be restored as legal tender immediately after the liberation of the Netherlands," the majority of the Netherlanders were less than ever inclined to take to the Nazi light-weight coinage.

One industrial group after the other was affected by the ever-growing shortage of raw materials. The importation of wood, for instance, had dwindled to almost negligible proportions. Not a single plank arrived from Russia or the Baltic States, and for a while the building industry came to a complete standstill.*

The demand for reclaimed raw materials increased by the day. There was a veritable rage to discover ways in which old and rejected materials could be made usable once more. Nothing was to be thrown away; not even the flimsiest packing. Regular services were instituted to receive this, and every other kind, of scrap. Even human hair was included and no less than 6600 lbs. per week of this novel raw material were gathered and used as filling for pillows and furniture. A particularly optimistic "inventor" tried to gladden the hearts of his fellow countrymen by announcing that he was getting along nicely with the perfection of a new discovery: that of spinning human hair, and of weaving it into strong material which, one day soon, might yield suits and costumes for a multitude of Netherlanders.

It stands to reason that one of the first enterprises to suffer from the absence of building and other materials was the huge scheme for the reconstruction of Holland's war-scarred areas. Throughout the second occupation year very little was done to provide new homes for the tens of thousands who had been robbed of their shelters during the five days' battle of May, 1940. The Germans withheld practically everything needed for this purpose. In Rotterdam, with 26,000 homes reduced to rubble, only 1,300

*Wood is of great importance in the Netherlands as a building material—not so much for actual construction but mainly to ensure the laying of staunch foundations. As most of Holland's soil is soft and soggy, it is necessary in at least seven-eighths of the country to drive huge piles into the subsoil on which to rest the actual building foundations. One outstanding example of this age-old method is known to every schoolchild; it is that of the famous seventeenth century Royal Palace in the center of Amsterdam which, as a time-hallowed rhyme says, "is built on 13,659 piles."

families had been given new living quarters by June, 1941. In November of the same year there still were nine hundred Rotterdam families living in temporary structures, and in The Hague more than 1,200 Rotterdam refugees were entirely dependent on charity.

The situation was even worse in the smaller towns which had suffered the effects of the war. The Germans announced, for instance, that whatever had been destroyed in the North Brabant city of Breda would not be rebuilt. In a considerable number of Zeeland villages where great damage had been done during the last days of the battle, reconstruction work advanced at snail's pace. In the beautiful capital of Middelburg where so many examples of the best Renaissance style—edifices which had withstood the centuries—were turned into rubble by German artillery, only one house had been rebuilt by August, 1941. In fact, the clearing of the debris had at that time not even been completed. By way of doubtful consolation the people of Middelburg were told in January, 1942 that it was "the intention to rebuild the center of your city before the end of this year . . ."

Much more attention was given to the rebuilding or repairing of farmhouses, wherever they had been destroyed or damaged. The Nazis defended this by declaring that "everything possible must be done to further the production of foodstuffs"; and to prove their point they went to the length of reconstructing the stables long before the farmer's living quarters got their turn.

But during that second year of the occupation traffic conditions suffered more than anything else. There was no gas. Whatever the Germans could lay their hands on, was very badly needed for themselves. One of the great Dutch oil companies which had imported fabulous quantities from the Netherlands East Indies, now tried to locate new sources by drilling wells somewhere in Overijssel province—a terrain which had never before been considered of the slightest importance.

Road traffic, through the absence of gas as well as motor cars, fell back to one percent of the normal. Whatever cars were still in use had rebuilt their motors and had installed generators which, as a rule, were burning peat, wood or anthracite. But to build such a clumsy, heavy generator into your car was no simple matter! It required an endless amount of red-tape and patience; all in all only a few licenses were granted. No ordinary taxi, for instance, could obtain permission to use a generator, so that by the end of June, 1941 Amsterdam, once teeming with taxis of every size and shape, had four cabs left for public use. The municipal buses were still running, but their services had been drastically cut; and in February, 1942 a decree was published stipulating that no motor bus would be allowed to operate anywhere in the Netherlands on Sundays. Private cars had completely disappeared. Gas was only given to ambulances—and that in the most minute quantities.

The results of these tragic cuts and restrictions were, nonetheless, rather amusing at times. Throughout the country ancient wagons, derelict stage-coaches, old hansom cabs and horse-drawn tram cars were brought out of museums and other hiding places, though lack of fodder had made the average horse unfit for long trips. Ingenious youngsters invented novel means of conveyance, such as the so-called "cycle-taxi"—a light wooden structure built over one or more cycles in which the driver or drivers worked diligently with their feet, to transport their clients at the breakneck speed of . . . 10 miles per hour. These crazy vehicles became very popular, but they were not allowed to stay. In May, 1941 the Nazi authorities, with a histrionic display of hurt dignity, forbade the use of cycle-taxis as "these carriages set in motion by man power, were not in accordance with a sound, European feeling of self-respect." Rapidly the cycle-taxi was replaced by the pony-taxi in which a horse took the place of the briskly-pedaling drivers. The tandem, too, became a very much wanted "vehicle," and hundreds of owners of those useful "bicycles built for two" did a brisk business.

Naturally, such stop-gaps were not able to improve the situation to any appreciable extent. And things became even worse when the scarcity of rubber began to affect the sale of cycle tires. In few European countries was the cycle so widely used as in the Netherlands where one in every three citizens possessed a bicycle and covered many miles on it each day. Statistics published shortly before the outbreak of the war showed that more than three million bicycles were in constant use. And little wonder; the average Dutch child rode a bike almost from the moment he could toddle around by himself. There is no exaggeration in saying that a large majority of Holland's schoolchildren went to and from their schools on bikes. The adolescence of the Hollander was, with few exceptions, very closely interlinked with his bike. After school hours the Dutch boy and girl would meet their friends on the cycle; their holidays would be used for long cycle trips.

And many a love affair found its start, as well as its development, on the bike. Visitors from abroad would often be greatly amused to see loving couples—arm in arm, their heads close together—cycle swiftly along the special cyclists' paths, laid out at the side of all of Holland's highroads.

Throughout the course of his life the Netherlander had good use for a bicycle. In the industrial centers no less than in the big towns one could see endless processions of cyclists morning and evening—going and coming from their work.

Considered in this light it will be easy to understand the hardship of being prevented from using one's cycle with the easy freedom of prewar days. To get a new tire was a most intricate business and generally, after an avalanche of red tape, one's application was rejected, without the possibility of protest. The cycle, until then an article within the reach of even the smallest purse, began to rise in value like the shares of a suddenly productive gold mine; and simultaneously the number of cycle thefts reached fabulous heights throughout the country. During 1941 an average of 400 bicycles were stolen each week in Amsterdam alone. In March, 1942 this average had risen to 715; often the thieves had no other purpose than to obtain a set of new tires, or inner tubes. The renting of bicycles which at one time had been a lucrative enterprise, became of questionable interest as many unscrupulous clients replaced the good tires of their hired bicycles with threadbare seconds.

In the autumn of 1941 an industrial group published the details of a contest which asked inventors to devote a good deal of their time to finding a practicable substitute for bicycle tires. There were more than two thousand answers—some amusing, some curious, some starkly naive—but only three considered good enough to be rewarded with a prize of one hundred guilders each. Certain inventors suggested the replacing of the inner and outer tires with a length of discarded vacuum cleaner tubing; and there was quite a large harvest of complicated ideas for tires made of wooden hoops, or wooden blocks mounted on spring coils.

Meanwhile, the genuine article could only be bought in the black market where applicants gladly paid twenty-five guilders per tire or inner tube, which in normal times would cost no more than one, or one and one-half guilders. Prices for cycles—no matter how much they had been used—soared sky-high; reports from the occupied country have since repeatedly confirmed that buyers were eager to pay as much as one hundred guilders for cycles which formerly would not have yielded more than one-fifth of this sum.

Finally, in July 1942, most civilian-owned bicycles were suddenly requisitioned. The reason given by the official German-language paper in the Netherlands, the "Deutsche Zeitung in den Niederlanden," was "the urgent needs of the occupation army." In reality, the move may have had to do with defense maneuvers against a possible Allied invasion. To soften the blow a little, certain groups—such as factory hands, miners and farm laborers—were told that they would get their cycles back before August 15 . . . ,* but this never happened.

*

However inconvenient such restrictions, however hard to bear this theft of one of Holland's most necessary means of transportation, there were other and greater hardships to be borne. There was the tragic every-day struggle for food and clothing, for warmth and some degree of personal safety. The overwhelming majority of the Dutch were not in the least impressed by the stream of new titles, new functionaries, new decisions. One feeling surged uppermost in every loyal Netherlander: deep resentment against the foreign marauders who were plundering and ravaging, stealing the very nourishment of Holland's children and adolescents. With every new decree or restriction the general chaos intensified.

Now and again, in a particularly expansive mood, the occupying power would allot "special rations" of some commodity or other; but it did not take long to discover that such extras were only granted to camouflage further severe cuts of essential means of sustenance—butter and fats, bread and potatoes foremost among them. Hunger was no longer a mere word. Millions made the discouraging discovery that the possession of rationing coupons was by no means a guarantee for obtaining the promised articles. To live the "legal way" was a certain road to undernourishment and subsequent self-destruction. To get a minimum share of

---

*Speaking at Waubach, in the province of Limburg, deputy Reich's Commissioner Schmidt revealed a few days after this requisitioning that it "had met with failure." He continued: "It was not our intention to take bicycles from workers and peasants, but it was necessary to act quickly. Had the prosperous classes been more willing to make sacrifices, the bicycles could have been returned to the laborers. But even when thirty policemen searched one house after another, the total haul was only forty-two bicycles." Schmidt added that those "hidden" cycles would be taken anyhow—the owners should not "imagine the authorities did not know where they were hidden!"

whatever had escaped the voracity of the German hyenas, other methods had to be applied.

It was, therefore, little wonder that the so-called "black market," from a half-hearted attempt to disobey the German rulers, swiftly developed into a nation-wide institution. No one who bought or sold in the black market could plead innocence of the great risks he ran; but even the most ruthless penalties handed down by Nazi-appointed judges were incapable of stemming the tide. To acquire or dispose of commodities "illegally" began to be looked upon as a patriotic act and Anton Mussert's weekly, "Volk en Vaderland" was constrained to admit in one of its issues of April, 1942 that among the peasantry black traders were "revered as saviors of the direly-imperilled Dutch people." It was not difficult to follow the line of reasoning leading to this approving attitude. As the invaders were taking away Holland's food supplies by using the markets and public auction halls—both of them normal means of exchange—it was the obvious duty of all patriots to keep out of German hands everything it was possible to withhold from those auctions and markets.

There was a strange but rather amusing side to the black market problem. Everyone took part in it: rich and poor, young and old, and among them—unbelievable as it may seem—was a large percentage of Dutch Nazis. Although their leaders never tired of fulminating against "the irresponsibles who by buying in the black market disobey the occupying power," the illegal trade blossomed as much among Mussert's followers as amidst the most zealous loyalists.

As a rule, purchase and sale in the black market rarely concerned very large quantities. Obviously, this was a very necessary precaution against discovery. But even if the authorities caught a black market "criminal" red-handed, there were a few loopholes, however small, left for him to try out for escape. For example, there was no law or decree forbidding the Dutch to make each other a present of rationed goods. If, therefore, a parcel was delivered at anyone's door while an inspector of the "Central Crisis Control Service" happened to be busy asking some pertinent questions, there was no need to get panicky. The parcel was, of course, sent by a solicitous relative, or friend . . . At the worst the benevolent sender might be sentenced to pay a small fine which the recipient was only too willing to share with him. Another possibility was that of being stopped in the street by one of the ubiquitous inspectors of the Distribution Service while transporting a conglomeration of the most coveted delicacies—a fat chicken, maybe; or a dozen eggs, or even a pound of butter. In that case the only necessary precaution would be to make a timely arrangement with some friendly grocer who, if asked, would gladly confirm that the foodstuffs were bought in his store.

Only too often people who in normal times never dreamt of breaking the law, were forced to take recourse to black market practices. Again and again men accused of illegal buying would defend themselves before the Economic Judge by saying: "We didn't have enough to eat." "My wife is ill and in need of restoratives." If the Judge remarked, as he steadfastly did, "But others are in the same position, and whatever there is left must be shared equally," the answer would be: "Do you mean to say that my family (or my sick wife, or child) must suffer because of that?"—a poser to which even the glib Economic Judge failed to know the answer.

The black market has no ceiling prices. If in September, 1941 it was still possible to buy a pound of butter for three and a half guilders (or two dollars), double that sum was required a year later to obtain the same quantity. Loaves of bread which normally cost fifteen to eighteen Dutch cents (about $0.06 to $0.10) were hard to get at the rate of one and a half guilders (or about 85c) each in the middle of June, 1942. Second-hand goods were sold at colossal prices. In April, 1942 a well-worn suit of clothes plus a second-hand pair of shoes were offered for sale for four hundred guilders, or approximately $225.

Soon this buying rage spread to everything saleable. There was too much ready cash about with which nothing could be done in the way of commercial or industrial investment. And so this huge latent buying power turned towards every other possibility. Gold coins normally worth ten guilders, found buyers at prices ranging from thirty-seven to fifty guilders apiece. Bad quality material for men's or women's clothes brought an easy four to six dollars per yard. Books fetched prices three or four times the rate at which they had been offered in every Dutch bookshop at the time of their publication. There was money available for everything—even trees were bought in large numbers. Not with the purpose of felling them, but with the idea in mind that at least some of them might still exist after the war and then be worth something. The people of Holland fully realized that the German manipulation of their finances had brought about the unavoidable devaluation of the guilder and that the only thing left to do was to convert ready cash into solid objects, no matter their nature, with the faint hope that the war would at least leave untouched the intrinsic value of those tangibles.

There also was a strange, disquieting flight into art-collecting. Painters whose work had thus far been little known and even less demanded, found themselves able to sell their pictures at comparatively high prices. Less scrupulous artists signed their canvases with good sounding names of well-known colleagues; but even this brazen deceit did not withhold the buyers who, on the contrary, were willing to pay preposterous prices for such products. Many shopkeepers and tradespeople, including barbers, tobacconists and café-owners took up "art-dealing" on the side, as a welcome addition to the sadly-depleted income from their regular trades. Amidst barber chairs, on tables and in show-cases, normally given over to the display of less artistic objects, the art works of known and unknown painters were on constant exhibition, attracting an uncommonly large number of dabblers who acquired the canvases "because you never can tell."

Genuine art benefited by this same buying fever. At an auction in The Hague held during the summer of 1941 a number of Old Masters were sold at prices not seen at similar auctions for many a day. A small Jan Steen, "Samson and Delilah," fetched no less than twelve thousand guilders (about $7,000), while a "Girl's Hat" *after* Vermeer was sold for 5,600 guilders, or approximately $3,000.

The anxiety to acquire something "worthwhile" before it was too late made people pay ridiculously high prices for antique Dutch furniture and for a variety of very doubtful Dutch Masters.

Finally, this unsound trading urge degenerated into barter, pure and simple. The newspapers published column upon column of advertisements in which the most unusual offers appeared, such as that of an overcoat for three pounds of coffee, a sun-lamp for one hundred cigars, a hall rug for a pound of tea, or "some butter and tea for a cycle tube." Another original advertisement offered a quarter ton of coal for one solitary cycle tire.

There was little the Germans could do against these excesses. It did not help them much to send hundreds of inspectors out on the roads, or to issue sharply-worded decrees forbidding price increases. Two hundred of the most active and most intelligent officers of the Municipal Police Corps, the Marechaussées and the

Customs were picked to form a special anti-black market force. Half of them were destined to institute razzias all over the country, while the entire new police division was to be supplemented with 25 State bureaus, each having its own department to trace offenders against the price ceiling laws. And indeed, the joint inspectors managed to get hold of no less than twenty thousand "criminals" of this kind between February, 1941 and February, 1942, extracting from them a little more than five million guilders* by way of fines.

It must be admitted that some of these fines were well-deserved. A number of less scrupulous wholesale traders had been abusing the situation freely, forcing their clients to pay exceedingly high prices. There was, for instance, the wholesale greengrocer who induced his clients to leave, quite accidentally of course, a couple of banknotes on the bottom of their empty returns. If they failed to do so, there were no more supplies for them in the future. Or again, there was the case of thirty-two cheese manufacturers who had felt like selling only when they were sure to receive substantial "tips" in addition to the totals of already sky-rocketing bills.

The retail trade produced its own offenders. An ordinary glass ash-tray filled with a small quantity of low grade candy was sold for fifty cents; and a tiny metal toy with a few bits of similarly worthless stuff was offered at the bargain price of a dollar. There were shopkeepers who refused to sell any marmalade or jams unless worthless sweets were bought with them; there were greengrocers who withheld their potatoes unless an expensive vegetable could be delivered at the same time.

The number of sentenced people grew with alarming swiftness; in the end every jail was filled to capacity and condemned men were allowed to go free until others had been released. Awaiting the day of their incarceration, the majority of these black marketeers quietly returned to their old handiwork.

The chaos grew worse by the day. A lively trade ensued in rationing cards, with a particularly strong demand for butter and fat coupons. The occupation authorities were well aware of this new evil, but its eradication appeared impossible. All they could do was to threaten—even with the death sentence.

In the summer of 1941 a rationing office in the town of Amsterdam was broken into and robbed. Coupons were stolen

*Approximately $2,800,000.

representing a total of more than four and a half million pounds of bread, 650,000 pounds of butter, 570,000 pounds of margarine, 16,500 tons of coal—and a long, impressive list of other commodities. Only a small fraction of this haul was retrieved; the bulk of the stolen coupons disappeared into the black market and found a legion of eager buyers. From October to March the Dutch police investigated this gigantic theft, arresting 150 accused persons. But suddenly the occupying power took the authority out of the hands of the Dutch Economic Judge, declaring him "unauthorized to express an opinion because the matter of an ever-growing unity of interests between Germany and the Netherlands is more than a Dutch affair." On May 7, 1942 the German Obergericht sentenced six of the first batch of twenty-three accused to be shot by a Nazi firing squad. In August, three more underwent the same fate.

These death sentences were a last desperate effort made by the German authorities to stem the economic chaos. They evidently hoped that this ruthless punishment would intimidate the huge army of black marketeers and reduce their activities considerably. There is no evidence, however, that the shooting of a few Dutchmen curbed the black market to any appreciable extent. Plainly enough, such an improvement could never be expected as long as the basic reason for the existence of black market dealings had not been eliminated.

For this chaos, this bewildering increase of criminality resulted from one solitary factor only: the unrestricted Nazi pillaging and looting which in a little over two years had managed to bring a once rich and prosperous land and a thrifty people to the very edge of starvation. In condemning to death nine Netherlanders gone astray under their bad Nazi management, the German invaders pronounced sentence upon themselves.

4

THE SPECTER OF MALNUTRITION

"Deliveries on military rationing cards and coupons take preference over all other deliveries."

Decree of the Reich's Commissioner of January 15, 1941.

"Everyone of us will agree that we truly lived in a Land of Cockaigne!"

The "Haagsche Post," The Hague, of August 30, 1941.

The standard of living now prevailing in the Netherlands is not adequately expressed in its lowered financial status—however disquieting this may be. There is no lack of cash in the occupied country; on the contrary, the total amount of ready money has risen by leaps and bounds. A reliable impression of the gravity of the situation can, therefore, only be attained if one considers the stocks of still available commodities. What good is the possession of money, if there is nothing for which to exchange it?

While national economy had suffered greatly through the invasion, with shipping and fisheries reduced to shadows of their former selves, two sources of national income were producing more than before May, 1940—agriculture and the civil service. Though the greater part of Dutch agricultural produce was claimed by Germany, there was at first an unmistakable upswing in the earnings of farmers and their help. But this increase was of little consequence if compared with the tremendous sums paid to an army of new government officials. The distribution of foodstuffs and a host of other new offices required the expansion of many civil service institutions.

Yet, even though the total income of these two groups showed a sharp rise, this did not put extra stocks of bread, meat or fats in the market. The truth was that a completely fresh category of willing customers had been created who, unfortunately, found nothing much to buy.

Another class of newly-recruited buyers were the German soldiers who by order of Seyss-Inquart were to be served first and best in all circumstances, at the obvious expense of the Netherlands people. It is no exaggeration to state that the presence of those occupation troops raised the total number of people to be fed each day by something between one-half and three-quarter million. Even in normal circumstances this would have meant cutting a slice of more than ten percent from all available foodstuffs. But the conditions were abnormal. Some supplies were cut off, and what in the early occupation days was not eaten by the German military or "bought" for relatives and friends in the Reich, had disappeared along legal commercial channels . . . to the same destination.

During the second half of May and up to June 15, 1940 no mention was made of rationing. The occupation troops were buying and consuming freely and although in immediate reaction prices began to rise sharply, there was still enough left to buy, for the average Dutch purse.

But on June 17, hardly more than a month after the surrender of the Dutch armies, rationing started of a most important staple food—bread. This first distribution measure was a very lenient one; no less than 4½ lbs. of white bread became available per capita per week, and for those preferring rye bread, (which, for example, has since time immemorial been a stock food in the northern provinces of Groningen and Friesland), no less than 5¼ lbs. per head could be bought every seven days. It seemed little more than a precautionary measure; and even the fact that throughout the summer of 1940 the bread dough contained 5 percent potato flour failed to produce any anxiety or grumbling.

In the late autumn all pastries and other fine quality bake goods were placed on the rationing list. They could still be had for the asking, but bread coupons to an equivalent weight had to be sacrificed. About the same time the quality of the bread began to get worse and by the first of January, 1941 when the rye bread rations were reduced to a little more than 4 lbs. per head per week, the color of the bread had changed completely. As an apology, one of the largest Dutch bakeries published the fact that "our home-grown wheat and rye are not particularly fit for baking purposes; and as we are no longer receiving these products from abroad, the quality of our bread cannot be the same as before." The total consumption of bread at that moment showed a decrease of 15 per cent.

But meantime, and in ever-increasing tempo, a great many

other commodities had been rationed. As early as July, 1940 all kinds of groceries were placed on the distribution list—at first in fairly generous quantities which were soon drastically cut. Butter, margarine and fats were also rationed and cream disappeared from the dairy shops in the early summer of 1940, to become exclusively obtainable on doctor's prescription. In the beginning the less privileged classes were enabled to buy butter on their fat coupons but in September, 1940 this arrangement was discontinued. The price of butter underwent a sharp rise and the enormous consumption of this article by the German occupation troops led to a decree by which the purchase of margarine became obligatory.

Next followed many products of which there had always been plenty. Cheese, milk, eggs—each one of these received the special attention of the distribution authorities and promptly became very hard to get. By the first of April, 1941 fifteen percent of well-established Dutch dairies had ceased to exist and the daily milk ration—which the German authorities described as a "very welcome addition to the menu"—consisted of a ½ pint of milk per head. Only children from 4 to 14 could get as much as a pint a day and for babies there was a theoretical portion available of no less than a quart! In reality, however, it was almost impossible to buy so much, especially for townspeople. In the country things were a little less difficult, though even there it was hard enough to get the weekly egg to which the rationing coupons entitled every citizen.

Until now the authorities had found the introduction of the rationing methods smooth sailing. But when in the latter half of September, 1940, the distribution of meat commenced, there was an immediate shortage of supplies. The farmers appeared none too willing to offer their cattle which represented the bulk of their business capital, for slaughter in return for some practically worthless money. It soon became clear that the meat ration had to be drastically reduced and by December it was legally impossible to get more than ten ounces of meat per person each week. The Municipal Council of Amsterdam declared courageously that "this will greatly increase the number of malnutrition cases in our city and is going to end in a catastrophe." And even though soon afterwards the Nazis forced the Dutch farmers to give up their cattle so that by the first of March, 1941 they had placed on the market no less than 200,000 head, there was at best no more than a quarter of this total available for consumption inside the country. The remainder had disappeared mysteriously, or was used for the German occupation troops. To heap insult upon injury the Nazis declared suavely that the shortage of meat was solely due to the fact that "the rationing boards in Holland do not function as smoothly yet as they do in the Reich."

By the spring of 1941 even the sale of horses' and sheeps' flesh was "regulated." But meantime the rations of every variety of meat had been reduced over and over again, with the bankruptcy of numerous butchers for an immediate result. These middlemen, though their expenditures remained virtually unchanged, received so little meat for distribution that they were doomed to failure; meat rationing had reduced the total consumption to less than a third of normal.

Still unrationed were poultry, game and fish. Their prices were high, of course, and this despite the fact that a strange prejudice had sprung into existence against the consumption of ocean-caught fish. For many people believed that these fish, caught in the North sea off the Dutch coast, had fed upon the corpses of war victims . . . Game could sometimes be had at reasonable rates—but in those cases it was unquestionably poached. That such delicacies were beyond reach of the lower classes stands to reason; but as yet those people could eat their fill of potatoes. It was a great reassurance for them when the engineer S. L. Louwes, head of the Netherlands Rationing Board, announced emphatically that no potato rationing was contemplated, as "potatoes are the last refuge for our laboring masses."

That statement was made on April 18, 1941 . . . ; and nine days later the official distribution of potatoes was a fact. All of a sudden the authorities had, it seemed, reached the conclusion that the Dutch working men and their families would be just as well off without a generous helping of potatoes for their daily dinner. Only a few days previously the rationing Chief had voiced the opinion that "even an average of ten pounds of potatoes per head per week is insufficient;" but now it appeared that four pounds per person must be considered plentiful for seven consecutive days.

For the first time there was a public outcry against a rationing measure. Large groups of the populace found their staple food drastically curtailed. It helped them little to hear that owing to the inundation of May, 1940 the potato crop was very poor. Or that there had been a devastating potato disease. Such excuses could not fill empty stomachs. Besides, the quality of the available potatoes was, to say the least, very doubtful. They were of a variety thus far almost exclusively used for cattle fodder. And soon the Dutch, who by the grace of Heaven never lose their well-developed sense of humor, began to describe the rationed potatoes as "N.S.B.'ers." Why? Because like the hated members of the Nationaal-Socialistische Beweging (the N.S.B., or Dutch Nazi Movement) they were "black on the outside and rotten to the core!"

It is obvious that if so dire a necessity was stringently rationed, luxuries such as coffee and tea would hardly be allowed to remain in the open market. They were not; and in their case the usual method was followed. At first the rations were reasonably large, but by the summer of 1941 there was practically no more tea or coffee to be had. In their stead had come an avalanche of substitutes: tea made of bramble leaves and potato peelings; coffee brewed of even more fantastic ingredients, such as flowerbulbs and barley. "You do not quite know what to think of them at first," radio Hilversum admitted apologetically, "but with a little sugar, some milk and a lot of imagination you may even get to like them." The announcer forgot to add where the milk and sugar were to come from. Yet, the demand for these substitutes was so great that in the spring of 1942 the Germans forbade the unauthorized picking of beech leaves, the leaves of huckleberries, brambles, raspberries and rose bushes.

The black market had little tea and coffee to offer; the importation of both articles had ceased long ago, while the bulk of the available stocks was transported to the Reich soon after the invasion. That is why in February, 1942 some well-to-do citizens of the Netherlands were ready to pay forty guilders, or about $23, for one pound of tea and fifty guilders, approximately $28, for a pound of coffee.

But far more serious than the rationing of these commodities—however much the people of Holland had come to consider them a part of their daily diet—was the lack of soap. No extensive medical knowledge was required to realize that this shortage would inevitably lead to a lowering of the hygienic standards. Whatever soap became available was, moreover, of such bad quality that instead of cleansing it damaged the skin and generally succeeded in ruining the laundry.

During the second occupation year rationing became truly catastrophic at times. Bread-flour, after undergoing many changes, finally consisted of 43 percent wheat, 40 percent rye, 7 percent barley and 10 percent beans. To this mixture was added a goodly portion of potato flour. Often the bakers were forced to add too much water, so that the total quantity of dry ingredients became even smaller. This "bread" was black and sticky, and looked far from inviting. But worst of all, there was not enough of it; and in August, 1941 this led to a full-fledged rebellion at The Hague. The people requested delivery of bread without rationing coupons but the bakers refused as they could only get new "flour" in proportion to the number of coupons they received. Thus bread became a much demanded article in the black market, and in places throughout the country a pound loaf of bread soon cost as much as two guilders, or approximately $1.08.

Sometimes the bakers tried to buy bread coupons from their clients. A typical case of this kind occurred in the town of Bussum, near Amsterdam. In November, 1941 a baker who at first had been rather generous in his deliveries to a clientele of about eighty laborers' households, suddenly discovered that he was seriously short of coupons. In desperation he asked his clients to give him their coupons a week in advance; but even this failed to help him much. Finally he asked and got the entire bread rationing cards of several families. As meantime he had continued to sell some of his bread on the black market without coupons, the day unavoidably arrived on which he had neither bread nor coupons to obtain fresh supplies of flour. The indignant people first stormed the baker's shop and then the police station. It was then revealed that the baker, afraid of police investigation, had burned the bread rationing cards of his clients. He was arrested—but this did not change the fact that eighty families were left without bread. The local rationing Board asked the Central Office at The Hague to send new cards to the poor victims. However, that Office answered it would do anything rather than that. The poor dupes had to wait for the next bread card to become valid—several months later. Apart from this, a strict investigation was threatened, to ascertain in how far they were liable to judicial prosecution.

After August 1, 1941, only skimmed milk was available and that with no more than one-tenth of one percent of cream. "This should not be taken too tragically," the official announcement declared, "for skimmed milk has excellent nutritive values." The "excellent" milk was a bluish liquid, known by the ironic name of "Victoria soda water"—after a popular brand of that fluid.

In the course of that second year of German suppression eggs disappeared entirely from the legal market. Holland's poultry stock had been cut once again by a third and so, in the autumn of 1941, only hospitals remained entitled to receive a small number of eggs. Yet, the production of eggs was still such that the demands of all consumers' groups could have been satisfied. But the occupying power, carefully "watching the health of the Dutch," saw to it that no Hollander should be tempted to upset his digestion by eating too many eggs!

Clandestinely eggs were still to be bought in almost any quantity, at the minimum rate of 25 Dutch cents apiece. Butter was sold at five guilders, or almost $2.80, per pound—and this in a country which until recently had been one of the world's foremost dairy-producing centers.

During the course of 1941 the meat rations were cut and cut again. In July the sale of meat was entirely prohibited on Mondays and Tuesdays. In January, 1942 the rations were reduced once more; although the consumer was still entitled to approximately 11 ounces of meat per week, there generally was nothing approaching this ration available. Those without means to buy on the black market, got no meat at all.

Illegal slaughter increased correspondingly. At first the Nazi authorities tried to "horrify" the populace out of this practice by showing them films which represented clandestine slaughter as a most dangerous thing for the people's health. Pictures would appear on the screen of large chunks of meat, covered with crawling, hopping and sliding insects and worms.

But the effect of these super-graphic performances was surprisingly small. An official German instance revealed in the middle of July, 1942 that a minimum of 600,000 pigs had been killed and sold on the black market. Heavy punishment was dealt out to people caught in the act of slaughtering illegally, or holding clandestinely bought meat. A minimum imprisonment of six months awaited every trespasser, and the Nazis threatened with "less lenient" methods for the near future.

And still the illegal butchers' trade flourished. There were always buyers galore for clandestine meat; people were willing to pay prices as high as seven guilders (or about $4) per pound. As a next step the Germans decided to punish not only the sellers but also the buyers of the forbidden meat. In the town of Groningen they once caught a few ladies who had bought a quantity of illegally slaughtered meat. They were sentenced to pay a fine of no less than ten thousand guilders, equal to about $5,400.

Naturally, the illegal poultry trade was doing just as well. During the Christmas holidays of 1941, chickens fetched an average of $3.25 per pound. At The Hague a lover of turkey paid $14 over the fixed retail price for one bird; and when the police intervened, forcing the poultry shops to sell their wares at regular rates, there was a general run on those establishments. To buy poultry at pre-invasion rates was an undreamt of boon!

Each week fish became scarcer and more expensive. Prices were bound to be high because of the tremendous risks the Dutch fishing smacks were running. In May, 1942 smoked salmon sold at twenty-six guilders, or about $14.50, per pound, the superstition and prejudices of a year ago having disappeared into oblivion. The fishermen of the drained portion of the Zuider Zee, now known by the name of IJssel Lake, "forgot" to bring large portions of their catch to the public morning auctions, and dumped them on the insatiable black market. Many of them went to sea in little boats, making their catch as far out from the Dutch coast as they dared to go. In case they were caught, there was nothing easier than to throw their catch overboard, well weighted down with cork so that with some luck it could be retrieved. At times they made arrangements with "the trade" to meet somewhere in a lonely spot along the Zuider Zee dike. There one of the men would jump overboard, swim calmly to the nearby shore . . . and deposit the salty bags with freshly-caught fish. Soon a cart would appear upon the dike, stop "accidentally" in the right place and swiftly collect the booty.

Even potatoes became a black market commodity, and little wonder. For in the course of the second occupation year the potato ration underwent repeated changes for the worse. The largest ration was 5½ lbs., the smallest less than 3 lbs. per week. During the winter months the rations were on the "generous" side, but at other times there were no potatoes at all, no matter the number of coupons due. Often the laboring masses were compelled to obtain potatoes at any price. They mounted their bicycles and rode into the low-lying polder land, persuading farmers to sell them small quantities at only slightly increased prices. But the better-situated classes who stayed in the towns and expected to get their potatoes delivered, were fortunate if they could buy a few pounds at rates 300 or 400 percent above the normal.

Similar conditions soon prevailed in the vegetable and fruit markets. The bulk of Holland's production was claimed by the Reich; as much as 80 percent of all lettuce, cucumbers, tomatoes and other food disappeared in the bottomless well of Germany's needs. And when the truck gardeners began to throw ever more of their produce on the black market, the occupation authorities simply bought up everything that was offered for legal sale at the long-established morning auctions. Great was the embitterment of the Dutch people about this shameless theft of their indispensable vegetables and fruit. True, it was called "export"—but everybody realized only too well that the country's Treasury was paying for this exportation. The general dissatisfaction did not fail to reach the ears of the German authorities who swiftly assigned a Nazi expert to give a plausible explanation. "Well," said this amicable German for the benefit of the disgruntled Dutch, "don't forget that the bulk of those vegetables of yours is very perishable. To store them would have been useless as everything would have decayed . . ." Of vegetable canning this gentleman had evidently never heard.

During June and July, 1941 the prices of vegetables and fruit soared sky-high. An apple would fetch as much as fifty-three cents (about 30c). A head of lettuce normally worth no more than a couple of Dutch cents, was cheap if offered at the rate of 15 Dutch cents. In August the authorities intervened and fixed ceiling prices; but thereafter the chaos became worse than ever.

The ceiling prices were so low that truck gardeners refused to deliver, wholesalers declined to buy and the shop-keepers took no notice whatever of the officially fixed rates. There was a frantic run on nearby farms and gardens. In their hundreds townspeople "invaded" the countryside and bought whatever the farmers were willing to sell. Soon the morning auctions shrunk to sixty percent of their normal proportions. The police stood powerless to stem the run on the farms. There was no law prohibiting the transportation of foodstuffs and if at times they arrested a few people transporting vegetables or fruit on their cycles, the invariable excuse would be, "Oh, but we picked this from our own little garden outside the town!"

In the end truck gardeners who found hardly any buyers for their legally-shipped produce beside the Nazi authorities, were forced to become black marketeers. A typical example was that of a fruiterer to whom in the course of a full month fruit had been apportioned to a total purchase value of less than 300 guilders. The price stipulations entitled him to a 30 percent profit, or approximately 90 guilders. Obviously, no shop-keeper could hope to earn a living if his weekly gross income was thus officially limited to about 22½ guilders.

It was, therefore, not particularly astounding that the introduction of ceiling prices gave rise to serious disturbances in Amsterdam. On August 14, 1941 it came to a wholesalers' strike, followed by the sequestration of their stocks. Throughout the town fruiterers closed their shops rather than sell at prices which in many instances lay considerably below cost. To quote one instance: onions were to be sold retail at a nickel per pound. Unfortunately, the purchase price for this commodity was . . . a cent and a half above the fixed rate of sale.

In less than a month after the initiation of the maximum rates more than two hundred retailers had been arrested and were waiting for their cases to come up in Court. All over the Netherlands fruit and vegetable traders were compelled to trespass upon the law. Some of them simply ignored the ceiling prices; others carefully displayed those official rates per kilo (2.2 pounds) but provided their clients with only half that quantity. Finally, the Germans were constrained to admit that "it was very hard indeed" to cut out this "utter confusion."

*

Obviously, the Rationing Board did not fail to bestow its attention on other commodities than foodstuffs, and textiles were at the head of the list. A little less than three months after the invasion special "points" coupons had been printed by the carload and distributed among nine million Dutch citizens. Each card contained a hundred points, and for every article bought a certain number of points had to be yielded. From time to time that "certain number" was changed, purportedly in proportion to the available stocks, but in reality in accordance with the whims of the men in charge. Nevertheless, it is possible to give an idea of the approximate value of a complete textile rationing card. Clothing, underwear and household linen—they all had to be bought on the same card. The Dutch housewives found themselves burdened with the extra worry of calculating whether to buy a frock, some highly necessary underwear for the children or a couple of bedsheets—as long as those were still to be had. A man's suit consumed no less than 80 points; a shirt from 15 to 24, all according to size and quality; a pair of pajamas 45; a raincoat 65 and a pair of socks 8 points. A lady's frock required 42 textile points, a nightgown 20, a chemise 20.

But many pieces of clothing could not be obtained on the textile cards at all, and required special permits. A new winter coat for men or women could only be bought if an old one, in a reasonable state of repair, was produced in exchange. Woolen blankets, of which only shortly before the invasion the country manufactured and exported immense stocks, had disappeared as if by magic; and shoes were rarely obtainable without a special "pass." If from time to time a shop was able to offer shoes, no matter their quality or style, without requiring special permits, the news spread like wildfire. Long files would form outside so remarkable a place—with the result that at the end of the day most of the applicants returned to their homes as shoeless as they had come. In May, 1941 shoes with wooden heels were equally rationed, and by that time a pair of shoes never fetched less than 35 guilders,* or about five times the normal price, in the black market.

With clothing and shoes so hard to get, tailors and cobblers were kept extremely busy, the former with the repair of old suits and the turning of whatever promised to be wearable again after that drastic operation, the latter with the patching of threadbare footgear. Turning an overcoat soon cost more than the normal price of a new one. And so, slowly but surely, the Dutch people began to look shabby and neglected. The scarcity of clothing was such that some old rags used to outfit a couple of scarecrows in a field near the town of Alphen, were stolen under cover of night.

Worse than any other shortage was the acute suffering of the people owing to the lack of fuel. In October, 1940 all fuel supplies were carefully checked and rationing coupons equal to the individually available stocks were torn off cards, and destroyed. But only in rare cases had people been able to cover their needs for the entire coming winter, and the rationed quantities were not only small but often failed to arrive in time. Transportation difficulties made it hard, if not impossible, for many provincial coal dealers to replenish their stocks; the result was that throughout the winter thousands of families suffered bitterly from the cold, even though in each home only *one* room was allowed to be heated.

The winter of 1940-41 was exceptionally severe; yet, for

*The guilder is approximately 54 American cents.

invalids and old people there was not a single lump of extra coal available. Towards the end of January, 1941 this inhuman measure had caused such privations that the authorities were compelled to rescind it. Placatingly the people were informed that "from now on there will, indeed, be extra fuel rations for invalids" . . . provided they remained ill for no less than a week. Anyone forced to spend fewer than seven consecutive days in bed—behold the strange reasonings of the German mind!—could well do without the necessary heat.

Immediately there was a marked increase in the consumption of gas and electricity. But this did not last very long; for without delay the Nazis clamped down upon the "sinners" and ruled that no one was to use more gas and electricity than in the corresponding month of the preceding year. Goodbye to gas stoves and electric heaters . . .

During the second occupation winter the fuel situation became much worse, despite the fact that Seyss-Inquart, in a speech at Amsterdam on October 3, 1941 had assured his listeners that "all coal mined by the colliers of Limburg since last September, will be put at the disposal of the Dutch. We may safely say," he added, without mentioning to whom the production of the remaining months had gone, "that we here in Holland will get through the winter all right."

And indeed—the country came through the winter; but it is better not to ask how.

Up to February, 1942 fuel was available in modest rations; there even were small extras for the invalids and aged. But in that month the fuel supply went completely haywire and swiftly the situation became untenable. Large quantities of coal had been requisitioned by the Germans to keep the railroads running, to produce gas and electricity and, in a few cases, to assure heating for some of the more important hospitals. For private citizens no more coal became available—no matter the number of coupons they might be holding. Finally, at the urgent request of the Health Service, minute rations were distributed to families with a baby not older than six months. The schools closed down and remained closed for many months so that most Dutch children were confined to poorly-heated homes. Public reading rooms, the Royal Library at The Hague among them, locked their doors and even the Department of Education, Science and Culture was forced to inactivity on two days each week—Saturdays *and* Sundays.

The lack of fuel was by no means restricted to the towns; the country districts suffered as much, if not more. A veritable rush ensued for anything burnable and in the late autumn of 1941 the authorities had to publish a warning to "beware of cutting down indispensable forests all over the country." Nevertheless, by sheer force of circumstance entire woods disappeared in the succeeding months. Large piles of mine supports, ready for shipment to southern Limburg, were stolen; and in the heart of a twenty year old forest practically every tree was clandestinely felled. The inhabitants of Vught, a small place in the surroundings of 's-Hertogenbosch, North Brabant's capital, turned out one moon-lit February night and hewed down several acres of excellent trees before the police could interfere. On the island of Walcheren, in Zeeland, hundreds of trees were uprooted from along the roadside, and in the town of Hilversum the general rage for wood attained such dangerous proportions that the municipal authorities strictly prohibited the carrying of axes, saws and wood-cutters' knives.

On rare occasions there was in certain localities some "extra" fuel to be had. In Utrecht, for example, small quantities of practically useless cinders were sold at high prices to people ready to cart them away from the huge Central Railroads' cinderdumps. In March, 1942, with the extremely severe winter still refusing to relent, fishermen of the "drained" island of Urk accidentally fished some coal from a hole in the thick ice covering the tiny harbor. It was part of a deposit formed in the course of many years during which unloading barges unavoidably spilled some coal overboard . . . and no one ever gave it another thought. But now the authorities swiftly organized the winning of this "buried treasure." It became a real business, with each privileged person's coal-fishing time limited to two hours weekly, and to a maximum "catch" of four bags full.

In the same month of March the occupying powers announced that the scarcity of fuel was really and truly due to the Dutch themselves. Their colliers did not work on Sundays—so what could the people expect? If only the mines would stop idling on the Sabbath! The colliers would be welcome to one hundred percent extra Sunday pay and a few cigarettes in the bargain!

But the workers in Holland's mines revolted. They knew quite well who would benefit from this extra labor. The results of their Sunday work would swell the "export" . . . to the Reich. For more than two months those colliers refused to go down the mines on the day of the Lord. Once again they proved to belong to the most irreconcilable elements of the Nazi-resisting working classes.

*

Compared with the intense suffering caused by the lack of fuel, the absence of such luxuries as cigars, cigarettes and liquor would seem no more than trivial. Yet, to be robbed of a smoke between working hours or a drink in the evening, was an added vexation for the Dutch masses. The legal tobacco trade was practically non-existent; the situation was, in fact, very similar to the stagnancy in the butchers' trade. To do legal business gave ridiculously low returns, with bankruptcy for a certain finale. Quite naturally the trade in cigars and cigarettes soon changed into an almost exclusive branch of the "black market." The guileless would-be client expecting to buy his packet of cigarettes at the fixed ceiling rate, met invariably with the same answer: "Sorry, Sir—I'm entirely out of stock." But anyone willing to pay fancy prices could still get his few cigarettes or a couple of cigars per day.

In May, 1942 the Germans made a desperate effort to reopen the legal tobacco trade by introducing a smokers' coupon card, good for 40 cigarettes per month for men over 18 or women over 25 years of age, or—alternatively—for 10 cigars or nearly 2 ounces of pipe tobacco per week, but this for men alone. All non-smokers would be entitled to 10 ounces of candy per month instead.

Suddenly the shop windows were filled again with the most delectable cigars and cigarettes, and with delicious-looking candy. Why? Simply because every shop-keeper had been officially informed that new supplies would only become available in proportion to the number of coupons he was to deliver at distribution headquarters at the end of a set period. For a few days the black market in smoking articles and candy received a serious setback. Retailers vied with one another to attract clients. It was like olden times—it all seemed too good to be true.

Unfortunately, this transition measure worked out rather differently from what had been expected of it. For those dealers who had thus far honestly offered for sale whatever they possessed and kept clear of the narrow path of black marketeering, now found themselves unable to compete. Much to their chagrin they saw their less conscientious colleagues gather an avalanche of the coveted coupons. However, as soon as the coupon-gathering came to a close, the shop windows were empty once more. And the rationing was not to start for another month.

Towards the end of the second occupation year, in May, 1942, black market quotations for tobacco products had reached ten times the level of normal prices. Even then the supply of cigars and cigarettes was very small. Substitutes of a mixture of oak and beech leaves, rationed since June 1, 1941, rose in price and cost as much as $1.20 per pound, despite the frank admission of an Amsterdam daily that the "ersatz" was "dank, unhealthy and impossible to light."

With most of the tobacco factories closed down and with no domestic harvest to speak of, many inveterate smokers tried to grow their own crop, in little front gardens or in boxes filled with earth and placed before their apartment windows. The majority of them, however, soon discovered that cultivating tobacco under such conditions was not very satisfactory. And the few who succeeded in raising a small crop met with fresh difficulties—foremost among them the problem of how to cure the leaves. Some buried their tobacco in hay; others put the leaves between newspapers in wooden boxes. Misguided souls tried to cure their valuable crop by soaking it in a solution of saltpeter, drying the leaves in a neat pile and pressing them under a heavy board. But almost always the results were disheartening, as the leaves rotted and were utterly spoiled. A tragi-comic instance is that of a man who sent a mess of sticky, shriveled leaves to a professional tobacco processor with the following note: "Here is my crop. I have counted the leaves; there are 673. You will notice that I attempted to cure them but the results have not been very pleasing as I was told to boil the leaves. Will you now please cure them the right way so that I at last can begin to roll my own cigarettes?"

As to beer and liquor, they too were drastically rationed. By November, 1941 the consumption of beer had shrunk to 50 percent of normal. And many liquor stores were forced to close down when in the spring of 1942 the deliveries of beer were stopped entirely because there was no coal to keep the freight trains running. The use of gas for delivery trucks was, of course, entirely out of the question. A glass of cognac, "vilely smelling like ether, and burning your throat," as a Dutch newspaper wrote, found thankful consumers at the price of 1½ to 2 guilders, or about one dollar.

Looking at the aspects of the food situation after two and a half years of German suppression, only one conclusion can be reached: that the level of absolute insufficiency has been passed long ago. The constant loss of calories is enormous for children as well as adolescents and adults. Of the 3150 calories per day which, according to a publication of the League of Nations on the subject of popular diet, are needed by every adult each 24 hours, only 1480 could be obtained in August, 1942 if every valid rationing coupon could actually be exchanged for the foodstuffs it promised. For adolescents the situation was hardly better, and children between the ages of 3 and 13 as well as pregnant women and young mothers, were getting only 60 percent of the calories they required.

These figures look bad enough; but they become considerably more disquieting if the available foodstuffs are examined at their intrinsic value. The lack of fats, for example, means the absence of proteins indispensable to the human body—more especially albumen and calcium. Children suffer most from these shortages but young mothers also fail to receive anywhere near the adequate doses.

It is, therefore, not surprising to learn that a higher death rate closely follows the curse of malnutrition. During 1941 deaths increased 17 percent over 1939, a total not including the deaths resulting from direct war action. For children the situation was even more alarming; here the total soared from 30 to 40 percent over the figures for 1939. The greatest increase of fatal cases was found to be due to contagious diseases, or ailments of the respiratory system. During 1941 grippe or influenza cases with fatal results increased to 224 against every hundred in 1939, while the figure for other contagious maladies, outside of grippe and "flu", was 198 in 1941 against every 100—two years previously.

This preposterous setback in a country which had proved to be well able to cope with such scourges as tuberculosis, diphtheria and other highly communicable disorders, was mainly due to the fatal shortage of vitamins A and C. They are to be found plentifully in butter, cheese, fresh vegetables and cod-liver oil—exactly the products which are no longer obtainable in anywhere near sufficient quantities.

Such were conditions in the summer of 1942 and things have grown worse ever since. The natural resistance of adults and children alike is now thoroughly undermined. Frequent reports show beyond doubt that dysentery, diphtheria and other ofttimes fatal diseases, are on the upgrade in every part of the Netherlands. They confirm that the Nazis are, at last, succeeding in the physical ruination of a once proverbially healthy people.

The average daily rations of the Germans, whether they live within the Reich or are the "guests" of occupied Holland, never reached so low a level. Yet, in the beginning of his infamous rule Seyss-Inquart had solemnly promised the Dutch that their standard of living would never be allowed to fall below that of their "German brothers" . . . But that "vow" was made long ago; and so it was possible that in the autumn of 1942 the same Reich's Commissioner could make a speech at Arnhem in which he stated that a general raising of Dutch food rations to the German level could not be envisaged "because the people of the Netherlands are not as ready as the Germans to make supreme sacrifices for the war against Bolshevism."

If the fact is faced that many commodities are now sold for twice or more of what they cost in 1940 while the average income of the working classes has not increased, it becomes evident that many of the most indispensable commodities remain outside the reach of the Dutch masses. Those able to pay any price may still succeed in finding the necessary foodstuffs on the black market; the others see the specter of hunger coming nearer each day. Voluntarily established communal kitchens which since their foundation in November, 1940 had done splendid work in providing the poor and needy with sufficient nourishment, were pressed into Nazi service less than a year afterwards. They now prepare exclusively special rations for certain types of laborers who cannot be expected to turn out satisfactory work on the official food allotments. With the disappearance of those kitchens untold thousands saw themselves robbed of their last hope of keeping body and soul together.

In two and a half years of continuous marauding the Nazis have turned a land of plenty into a desperately barren waste.

5

LABOR'S DOWNFALL AND ENSLAVEMENT

"The Dutch laborers in Germany distinguish themselves particularly through their inexhaustible capacity for grumbling and their 'love of liberty'—which is nothing but an egotistic shirking of the duties the Commonwealth quite naturally lays upon the shoulders of its members."

"Nationale Dagblad," March 12, 1941.

"A large number of Dutch 'unemployed' have been sent to Germany to help win the war. But through opposition, and all kinds of sabotage the right people did not always get into the right places—which caused difficulties. Besides, workmen were sent of whom one felt ashamed. They did not know how to behave; they were a rowdy, undisciplined lot . . ."

A representative of the nazified National Center of Trade Unions, as quoted by "Volk en Vaderland" of March 20, 1942.

Long before the outbreak of the second World War the Nazis never failed to pride themselves on their remarkable achievements in coping with the Reich's unemployment problem. And indeed, hundreds of thousands of men who were out of work before Hitler came to power, had found a job. But this was by no means a miracle. It is never a difficult matter to place even millions of laborers on uneconomic projects as long as the cost is borne by the entire populace. During those long years of preparation in which the Germans were building equipment for the gigantic wars of the future, the Nazis wisely abstained from drawing the world's attention to the peculiar character of this employment. But in their propaganda they knew how to make good use of the fact that as time went by fewer and fewer men were left without steady work and a regular wage.

It was a prime necessity—both for propaganda and utilitarian reasons—that in Holland, too, unemployment should visibly diminish. The manner in which this was to be done mattered little. To begin with: no laborers were to be dismissed from the work they were doing at the moment of subjugation. Whether or not the enterprise in which they were engaged had sufficient work for them was immaterial; the main thing was to avoid at all cost an increase of the unemployment figure. The Director-General of Labor decreed that no dismissal would be valid unless sanctioned by the Labor Inspection Board. If scarcity of raw materials was the reason for the employer's desire to dismiss part of his labor, the Board was to investigate whether, perhaps, a different type of raw materials could be used. If an enterprise had lost its main outlets through war conditions, the Board was to ascertain whether this factory could produce some other article fit for the home market. Was coal shortage at the bottom of lack of work, the "cure" was to replace coal with electricity. And if all this appeared insufficient to stimulate a given trade, then the employees picked for dismissal had to be the unmarried. Next came women, or married men of more than 65 years of age.

As could be expected, only a handful of requests for the dismissal of workmen was accepted by the Labor Inspection Board, though up to the end of November it had received no less than seven hundred fifty such appeals daily.

A factual increase of the unemployment figure was thus prevented; more than that, the Nazis really decreased the number of those out of work which, according to a statement made in June, 1940 by the German Commissary-General Fischboeck, totalled around 300,000. To this purpose they applied a variety of tricks. To begin with, the number of laborers employed in the execution of public works was maintained despite the shortage of raw materials. It had not been an easy matter to find work for some 50,000 men but somehow or other the Nazis succeeded in locating those "opportunities"—never caring whether there was the remotest justification for their existence.

However, this inventiveness could hardly solve the unemployment problem, particularly in regard to the hundreds of thousands of demobilized soldiers whom the Fuehrer, in his boundless generosity, had released from Dutch and German prison camps and returned to civil life. For them the Nazis created a new kind of organization upon which they bestowed the resounding name of Reconstruction Service. Apart from making long and strenuous marches and going in for a good deal of outdoor sports, the former soldiers who entered this Service were supposed to assist in every way possible in the reorganization of civil life. For example, about a thousand men were sent to northern France to help reap the belated harvest. A further few thousand were employed in demolishing the fortifications of Holland and those along the IJssel river. But by far the largest group was put to work in devastated Rotterdam where for many months they were helping civilian workers in clearing the rubble and leveling the burned and scarred surface of the town's bomb-blasted center.

All the same, in the late autumn of 1940 it began to be hard to find fresh work for these large masses of former soldiers. And so the Nazis ordered all men over 25 and all petty officers of more than 35 years of age to leave the Service. They were given the choice of joining the Air Raid Precaution (A.R.P.) or emigrating to northern France or Germany. Those who after this severe curtailment remained in the Reconstruction Service, were to be trained for a new Nazi institution, the Netherlands Labor Service. They were given a series of Germanic titles, all of them more or less military in sound. And on November 1, 1940 they were even provided with a grayish-green uniform, very much akin to that of the German Labor Service. During December more details of the new institution were published; it was to be based on purely National-Socialist principles and would eventually absorb all men between the ages of 18 and 23. To begin with, however, the glorious opportunity to join voluntarily was offered to 10,000 "eager young Hollanders."

Unfortunately for the German organizers, Dutch youths displayed alarmingly little enthusiasm. Several times the Labor Service leader, a former Major of the Dutch Army, delivered rousing speeches via the Hilversum radio. He did his best to paint an alluring picture of what the Labor Service would be like, describing it as a sort of Scout movement for adults, calling it an "unique opportunity for Netherlanders of every class and rank to meet, with the same rights and the same duties, and to form within the nation a small, select group of men who, forgetting their usual conditions, will share the same kind of life."

He also tried to impress possible candidates with the fact that "the Labor Service will have no political background." "I myself," he said in one of his most desperately urgent talks, "remain entirely outside the political arena . . . I regret the existing political divisions and would love nothing better than to bring about a unity embracing our entire people. I have no particular preference for the manner in which this unification can be materialized. And so, as long as the divergency of political opinion remains a fact, I shall take the utmost care that under my guidance the Labor Service will not be linked to any political party. In our camps there will be no mention of politics at all." But far from encouraging patriotic Dutch youths to sign up, this quaint defense of a severely "neutral" standpoint made them even more suspicious. They did not wish to sit back and be opinionless. They wanted to fight, combat the German suppressors and their Dutch Nazi helpers. What was the good of a Labor Service which would not tolerate the discussion of burning political issues?

The Dutch Nazis showed hardly more enthusiasm than these patriotic youngsters. From their standpoint the creation of a labor organization which emphatically proclaimed to be neutral and which would, therefore, be of no use in disseminating Nazi ideologies, was not worth a second thought.

Thus the Netherlands Labor Service never grew to more than sickly, anemic childhood. At the zenith of its doleful existence it possessed . . . two labor camps with a couple of thousand followers. Throughout the early part of 1941 there had been public announcements of great plans, according to which the Service, in the course of the next year, would become the proud sponsor of at least fifty camps with a total membership of more than one hundred thousand. But on April 15, 1941 the unfortunate Major's Labor Service was officially pronounced dead; and the poor corpse was not even considered worthy of a decent burial.

It is very doubtful whether the Germans ever wished this movement to meet with success. Far more likely the occupying powers, still going through the period of suavity and good-will, were out to impress the Dutch with their "genuine efforts to help solve the unemployment problem." At the back of their minds, however, they surely enjoyed the abject failure of the Labor Service. For now, with a gesture of profound regret, they could safely point out to Holland's hundreds of thousands of unemployed that it had proved impossible to find work for them inside the Netherlands. In their own interest it would be much better for them to travel a little and find pleasant and profitable work in Germany, or northern France.

And indeed—the German-directed employment bureaus got exceedingly busy. Before the summer of 1941 had passed, 120,000 Netherlanders had found work in the German metal and building industries and in the textile plants of northwest Germany. The majority of them had no desire whatever to leave their families and go to the enemy's country for employment. But there was no alternative. They were forced to emigrate by the simple practice of suppressing their rationing cards. On November 22, 1940 the nazified Dutch press had published the following short but meaningful statement: "The Dutch Social Welfare Board has sent a circular letter to all its members, in which they are informed that the authorities do not object to transferring the care for starving laborers' families, be it in the form of money or foodstuffs, to private and religious institutions. This only refers to cases in which such laborers refuse suitable employment in Germany, or decide to discontinue such work once they have accepted it."

The German authorities had acted with typical Nazi perfidy. The non-conforming were pushed into the hands of private or church institutions upon whom the burden was placed of protecting them as well as they could against complete starvation. It would be hard to work out a crueler system of forcing free human beings to sell their working power to their nation's foes. Nonetheless, in a speech of March 12 the Reich's Commissioner dared to say: "Naturally, our opponents' atrocity stories tell you that foreign labor is engaged under duress. But I declare that not a single Netherlander in Germany has been brought to his work by our police force."

The "apology" was as transparent as it was crude. Indeed, the Nazis took good care not to apply any outward force as long as they could obtain the desired results by the application of underhand means. Their strength lay in nothing more nor less than blackmail.

*

Towards the end of November, twenty-eight Hollanders lost their lives when during a British raid a Nazi plane fell down upon a Dutch labor barracks in Germany. The official communiqué concerning this accident revealed that "despite the air alarm the men had stayed in their beds from sheer fatigue." In fact, these foreign slaves were very haphazardly cared for and finally, in unanimous protest, they nominated a Committee of representatives to negotiate with the Germans for better living conditions. Reluctantly, the Nazis provided the abused Dutchmen . . . with some books and illustrated papers and even let them have their own daily paper. But this propaganda did not work out very well; and so—obviously with the intention to build up their morale—the nazified Dutch press of mid-February, 1941 published a leader in which the Dutch workmen in Germany were called "soldiers of the Fuehrer"—a distinction which they utterly failed to appreciate. They behaved accordingly. Complaints about them grew in frequency and in many cases their own foremen were hastily summoned from the Netherlands to re-establish some sort of order. The men objected particularly to the harsh Teutonic commands ringing out all day; and their implacable attitude infected masses of other forced laborers who had been recruited from different occupied territories. They found fault with their food, their lodging, their work, their foremen—in short, with everything they could think of. In the end the Germans had to admit that no group of foreign workers had proved to be as unruly as "those damned Hollanders."

Quite naturally, the members of Mussert's National-Socialist Movement were the first to shake their heads and exclaim their indignation at this "impossible conduct." It was, they asserted, "nothing but an egotistic shirking of the duties which the Commonwealth quite naturally lays upon the shoulders of its members . . ."

*

During the second year of the occupation the labor problem became, if possible, more urgent even for the Reich. Up to the invasion of Russia, Germany had disposed of a huge army of laborers totalling no less than 25 million, of which one million were prisoners of war while 1½ million had been recruited from abroad. The remaining 22½ million were made up of German men and women. However, the war in Russia claimed no less than 3 million male laborers who, in their turn, had to be provided with the necessary equipment, clothing and nourishment. Following the accepted rule that for the upkeep of every one soldier the full labor capacity of two civilians is needed, there was a sudden shortage of no less than nine million workmen.

But this problem did not seem to frighten the Nazis. Had not the mighty Fuehrer promised them that Russia would be on its knees before the winter? . . . And did not this mean that before long the majority of the three million new soldiers would be demobilized and given back to their various industries?

But alas—things did not quite work out that way and when the Russian winter had fallen upon Hitler's armies in its full atrocious severity, there was still the same—and even a greater—shortage of labor in the Reich as in June, 1941. By the spring of 1942 Germany was in dire want of four million men, skilled and hard-working laborers. And it was clear that in the near future even more would be required to offset in some measure the rapidly increasing war production capacity of the Western Hemisphere.

As a result the last remnants of Germany's labor reserve were called to action; men of over 70 who had long ago been sent home to their well-earned rest, were once more placed at the lathe. No longer were workers dismissed because they suffered from diseases—even contagious ones, such as open tuberculosis. Thousands of women were recruited but all this meant no more than a drop or two in an ocean of necessity. The most important source was and remained that of foreign labor shanghaied in the overrun countries.

Besides, there were reasons of a more technical character for swelling the importation of foreign workers. When during the first half of 1940 the German Army occupied a great part of western Europe, it found huge quantities of raw materials. Nothing was more practical than to exhaust these stocks on the spot. As far as Holland was concerned, the Netherlands' enterprises best equipped to use those raw materials, were summoned to turn them into war material. But in the end the reserves were exhausted while the requirements of the Russian campaign grew by the day. To those difficulties must be added the scarcity of means of conveyance and of fuel for the manufacture of electric current.

In the beginning of 1942 the Nazis were therefore obliged to change their policy fundamentally. Production was concentrated in special, centralized plants, most of them situated in Germany. The remaining factories were going to be closed down.

And so a variety of decrees were published most of which sounded quite innocent. In their entirety, however, those rules and regulations clearly betrayed that they meant to expand German power over an ever-growing number of Netherlanders. For example, in the middle of January, 1942 factories and other industrial enterprises were granted permission to discharge personnel which on May 10, 1940 had not been in their service for a minimum of three consecutive months. The result was, of course, a wholesale dismissal of superfluous staff, placing thousands of Dutch workmen within the grasp of Germany's insatiable war machine. During the next month a further decree appeared, stipulating that no industrial or commercial enterprise was to maintain or introduce a shorter work week than forty-eight hours. With one stroke of the Nazi pen a splendid plan of many patriotic employers had been killed. It had been that of giving their men a shorter work week rather than rendering them workless, exposed to the danger of being sent to Germany. Simultaneously, all unemployed were ordered to register with their district Labor Exchanges. The German Dr. Boening, who had been sent to the Netherlands as Adolf Hitler's special "crimp" of Dutch labor and who called himself the "leader of the Social Department of the Reich's Commissioner," stated publicly that it was an "imperative claim of Germany that Netherlands workmen who were not fully employed in their own country, should be put to work elsewhere to satisfy the demands of Greater Germany." In the future every Hollander could thus be forced to leave his country and work elsewhere—no matter where, or for how long. Boening added that the "employment of Dutch labor in the great German living space would continue on a voluntary basis." But this reassurance was immediately followed by the threat that force would be used "as a last resort, and only on people who are obviously in need of some education." No one can deny that Herr Boening expressed himself admirably.

Soon afterwards, to make things a little more impossible for Dutch labor, Boening wrote another piece of literature in which he declared that the hiring of any Dutch workman under forty would require official sanction if he was not required for agriculture, shipping or fisheries. "The decision," Boening added, "would be favorable only if the worker concerned were found unfit to be employed abroad."

Although these stipulations were sufficient in themselves to force many a Dutch laborer to leave his homeland, the Nazis still tried to keep alive the legend of voluntarily offered assistance. A large-scale propaganda campaign was launched during the spring days of 1942. Practically every newspaper contained huge ads addressed to Dutch "laborers and office help" and most pleasantly and suavely worded.

"Netherlands' workmen," one of them said, "there is no need for you to be unemployed. You will find plenty to do in Germany. Good pay is awaiting you and you will have the same rights as your German colleagues. Just think—you will be enabled to keep your family well." Another advertisement philosophized, "Are you helping the enemy through working in Germany? No. Because if that were true, then every kind of labor in Holland will also help the enemy. Do not allow yourselves to be frightened by foreign propaganda, but accept work wherever it is to be had. It *is* offered to you right now—in Germany."

And by way of final persuasion: "Netherlanders! To take care of your wives and children is, of course, one of your prime interests. But you are best able to look after your family if you are regularly employed. You can now make good money in Germany! Do not lose time but apply *at once* at your local Labor Exchange."

Conscientious objections did not count. After all, the Nazi propaganda reasoned, it was impossible to be consistent. "The result would ultimately be that no Dutch cow would be milked because that would benefit the German Lebensraum. Besides, whatever pangs of conscience a laborer might feel, they would disappear completely if compared with the great economic and social advantages resulting from his active participation in the task of building a new Europe."

But still the majority of Dutch workmen, whether for conscientious reasons or otherwise, steadfastly refused to consider employment outside the boundaries of their own country. They preferred to live on the edge of famine. It was a terrible decision to arrive at, especially for married men who knew that by taking this stand they were exposing their families to incredible suffering. And so, in the early autumn of 1942, the number of Hollanders at work in Germany had only reached a total of 180,000. Most of them were engaged in the reconstruction of destroyed areas. When towards the end of June some 25,000 of this total had left their jobs and returned to the Netherlands without Nazi permission, they were given the choice of going back to the Reich immediately or being put to heavy galley slave work in the "Wadden," muddy shallows north of the provinces of Groningen and Friesland.

On the whole these modern slaves were well paid—which by no means meant that they were able to send generous contributions to their deserted families at home. On the contrary, the deductions made by the Nazi authorities for taxes and other war purposes were so high, that on an average no more than twenty guilders, or about $11, per week was left for the support of wife and children. Besides, food was bad and the housing poor. The men found themselves in a strange and unsympathetic land, with every semblance of family relationship missing. Towards the end of January, 1942 the Dutch Nazi Commissar of Labor, H. J. Woudenberg visited several Dutch labor camps and on his return made hesitant mention of difficulties "of a psychological nature" he had met with. "In most cases, there is not much evidence left of a comradely spirit," he admitted. And he concluded that Dutch workmen in Germany "should show more understanding of what is happening in the world these days." Indeed, that was the difficulty. These Netherlanders could be compelled to work for their enemies but they could not be forced to show sympathy for the National-Socialist cause. On the contrary, they never failed to demonstrate their distaste for the harangues on Hitlerism which both German and Dutch propagandists showered upon them. The official propaganda leader of Mussert's National-Socialist movement, Ernst Voorhoeve, got a taste of this when in February, 1942 he tried to address a large group of Dutch workmen in their ramshackle barracks near Munich. In a subsequent radio-broadcast Voorhoeve described the scene as follows: . . . "Men sat at tables in indifferent attitudes, their hands cupped around their heads. Some of them turned their backs upon me . . . and the only reaction to my speech was, that one of the laborers got up and in a very sensible and polite manner voiced many complaints about their living conditions."

A couple of months later the Nationale Dagblad, official daily organ of the Dutch Nazi movement, came with an equally depressing picture of conditions in another German labor camp for Hollanders. There was a great deal of unrest in that camp where seven hundred men were very poorly lodged. They crowded around the Nazi correspondent to air their grievances, and many of them had particularly bitter things to say about the bland way in which the Germans disregarded the terms of the contract they had entered into before leaving the Netherlands. The general plaint was that they "were worked much too hard," with the result that at the end of the day they were too exhausted to leave the camp, and find some sort of distraction.

Most disputes, however, arose at the close of each week when the disgruntled workmen had to give up a substantial part of their hard-earned Marks for a variety of purposes. Evidently, the "Nationale Dagblad" writer had little sympathy to express; he placed the blame fullheartedly upon the Dutch laborers themselves. "Their fatigue," he asserted, "is merely due to the fact that when they were engaged they pretended to possess skills which in reality they lacked, but which entitled them to better pay . . ." As to the wage deductions, "these men," the correspondent said, "have little understanding of the new times. They are adventurers of the sort that will make trouble anywhere."

*

So as to obtain full power over the fate of all able Dutch workmen, the occupying authorities found it imperative to take over complete control of all Dutch trade unions. To achieve this the Germans applied the same old effective recipe—mixing equal parts of servile cajolery and brute menaces, and flavoring the concoction with high-sounding speeches and broadcasts in which the "rights of the proletariat" were mentioned with emotion, and capitalism attacked as the vilest form of tyranny.

Black indeed was the picture which those Nazi propagandists painted of the past. The laboring classes of Holland were reminded of the "rightlessness which had been their heritage." And a particularly perfidious emphasis was laid upon the alleged contempt with which in the pre-Nazi era workmen were looked down upon by their employers. At the same time the praise was sung of pre-capitalist periods in which "masters and servants spent their leisure hours in the same games, enjoyed confidential chats and shared the same vicissitudes." In fact—mediaeval conditions underwent a most remarkable metamorphosis in the mouths of these speakers. They conjured up a time both idyllic and prosperous. And outside that period and the future glory of the National-Socialist State there was nothing but the black, ill-smelling pool of capitalist misery and exploitation . . . "The revolution through which we are going," said the Hilversum radio in April, 1941, "will bring happiness to millions of people, millions who will at last be free from the fetters of a dark past."

A particularly moving appeal was made to the paupers, the least privileged of all. For this purpose an announcer was hired who, assuming the accent of a "Jordaner"—the popular name given to people hailing from the poorest section of Amsterdam, the Jordaan—"descended" to the level of these underdogs and tried to work upon their feelings by the daily reading of so-called "letters" in which their neighbors or friends were supposed to have unburdened themselves about the sufferings of the past. But the sum total of these efforts was not very encouraging for the Nazis. On the whole their pleadings and persuasions fell upon deaf ears. The modern trade union movement was too well organized and developed not to understand the cheap methods of the German Propaganda Bureau to "divide and rule" Holland's working classes.

Besides, the standard of living had undergone a drastic change for the worse since the coming of the Nazis, and this could hardly be called an inducement to listen to German promises and flourishes with any display of confidence. A constantly undernourished mass of laborers is not a particularly fit and patient public to applaud propaganda speeches.

Other efforts to overcome the objections of Holland's workers were, if possible, even less successful. As early as June, 1940—barely two months after the start of the occupation—Meinoud M. Rost van Tonningen, that "intellectual genius" of the Dutch Nazi movement who was destined to become the czar of Dutch financial life, had been appointed Commissary for the entire Dutch labor movement. He began with a series of "friendly conferences" with the leaders of the S.D.A.P., the Social Democratic Labor Party. Those leaders who had witnessed the awful fate of their comrades within the Reich, had no illusions of the future of their movement. In fact, on the day of capitulation they burned all their membership lists and their archives. They did not refuse to accept Rost van Tonningen's invitation. But neither did they restrain their laughter when this traitor tried to make them see that "at last the materialization of true Socialism has come." When finally he realized that his warblings made no impression, Rost van Tonningen closed the conference, stressing that the negotiations had been of a strictly "confidential nature." In answer to this the Dutch Socialist leaders told him plainly that the word "confidential" had no place in the National-Socialist vocabulary and that they would hasten to inform all laborers organized in the modern trade unions of the gist of their talk.

Almost immediately afterwards Rost van Tonningen, exercising his power as General Commissary for Labor, disbanded the Communist Party for the Netherlands as well as the Revolutionary Socialist Labor Party. Throughout the summer he tried to find a weak link in the armor of the S.D.A.P. and in the end, after many more rebuffs, declared the Social Democratic Labor Party illegal and prohibited. But in making this declaration before the microphone, Rost van Tonningen assured his listeners that the work of the S.D.A.P. was to be taken over immediately by a new organization he himself had founded. It was to be known as the "Socialist Workers' Commonwealth." Only in February, 1941 the head of the new party, a former propagandist of the National Center of Trade Unions, (known as the N. V. V.) was allowed to address the people of Holland over the radio. And on that occasion this man who had been ousted from his former job for reasons of incompetence, declared in a whining voice that: "We often feel doubtful of our ultimate success, more particularly when we see how sadly misunderstood are our intentions . . ."

The fall of the S.D.A.P. also meant the discontinuance of the multitude of institutions and organs which belonged to the modern labor movement of the Netherlands. The most vital link between the two million voters of the S.D.A.P. representing nearly a quarter of the entire Dutch population, had been forged by the development of an important daily paper, "Het Volk." In the years preceding the German invasion this daily, appearing simultaneously in seven of the most populous Dutch cities, reached the vast majority of organized labor and formed a splendid means for their unification. Now "Het Volk" was "taken over" by none other than the director of the Dutch Nazi weekly "Volk en Vaderland."

Y. G. van der Veen, the man who had spent his life in the service of the S.D.A.P. and especially in the development of the Socialist press, did not await the final humiliation of transferring his work to the enemy. On the morning after publication of the change-over, he committed suicide in the office from which he had so long directed the fate of his beloved paper.

Tens of thousands of readers refused to be treated to a daily dose of "Nationale Dagblad"-type of literature and subscription cancellations came in with such dazzling speed that in August, 1940 the new head of the Labor Press addressed a desperate "plea" to the remnants of his readers' circle, begging them to remain faithful to their paper. How well this prayer was answered is evident from the fact that shortly afterwards the morning edition of "Het Volk" was discontinued because of a universal lack of interest in what it had to say.

*

Far more effective than the killing of the Labor Press was the throttling of the Socialist trade unions. They, assembled in the N.V.V. (National Center of Trade Unions), were placed under the supervision of the Dutch Nazi H. J. Woudenberg. Without delay this gentleman who long before the arrival of the Germans had been known for his pronounced Nazi leanings, started with the "reorganization" of the N.V.V. and after a few months of arduous work he had got rid of twenty-eight of the chief executives who, he declared, "are not capable of doing the positive work which will be required of them in the direction of a new Europe." The remaining 272 officials, by the grace of the new Nazi head, were allowed to go on with their task. On twelve of them was bestowed the particular honor of forming a personal Advisory Board for dictator Woudenberg.

If one should question why the N.V.V. did not, as the S.D.A.P. had done, virtually disband itself, the answer very simply is that it could not do so without delivering into the hands of the oppressor the care for thousands of unemployed, ill and infirm workers who thus far had been looked after by their trade union Center. And so the N.V.V. pretended to jog along with the enemy but already outlined its future attitude which was one of firm resistance and unwillingness to conform with the demands of their unwanted new leaders.

It cannot be denied that a handful of these 300 Dutch labor officials yielded to the temptation and became more or less willing tools in the service of Nazism. For this treachery they have paid dearly; it has cost them the confidence of the Dutch laboring masses. It will cost them more on the day of Holland's liberation.

It was to be expected that as a possible bait the Germans would introduce in the Netherlands their famous "Kraft durch Freude"* movement. Towards the end of October Woudenberg notified the laboring classes in a solemn broadcast that they "who never had a share in the cultural life of their country," would now witness the realization of a great change. The new movement, to be known by the name of "Vreugde en Arbeid" ("Joy and Labor") would be initiated officially with a monster concert of the world-renowned Concertgebouw Orchestra, conducted by its "great and genial leader, Professor Willem Mengelberg."

But when the third of November arrived the baptismal party of the new institution became . . . a dismal one. Woudenberg was present in the concert hall and with him countless Nazi functionaries as well as the "great and genial Mengelberg." But Amsterdam's laborers had remained at home. The immense auditorium set aside for this "grand" occasion, was less than half-filled. And in the course of the next few months this lack of interest increased, if anything. "Vreugde en Arbeid" turned out to be a still-born Nazi child.

"Strength through Joy," which has its counterpart in Italy under the name of "Dopo lavore."

Meanwhile dictator Woudenberg left little doubt that it was his intention to transform the N.V.V. into a labor organization equal in all respects to the German "Arbeitsfront" (Labor Front). As early as April, 1941 he declared in a public speech that the N.V.V. could never be more than the "foundations upon which the trade union movement of the future will be built." It took some time to strengthen those foundations; and it was, therefore, not before the first of May, 1942 that Reich's Commissioner Seyss-Inquart issued a decree ordering the establishment of a Labor Front to replace the N.V.V. It stands to reason that Woudenberg became its leader; but from now on he would be closely watched and supervised by Meinoud M. Rost van Tonningen, who was given a high-ranking position in the new organization.

On that very day the installation of Woudenberg took place "in the large and quiet workroom of the Reich's Commissioner" —as a Nazi radio announcer described the solemnity. In his inaugural speech Seyss-Inquart complained of a "certain lack of understanding here and there." And he concluded with the statement that he had decreed the institution of the Labor Front with the purpose of "bundling together" all Netherlanders employed in the country's industrial life. The new front would have to assure peace among labor by educating its membership "in the National-Socialist sense." Every workman would be welcome—with the exception, of course, of the Jews.

In the afternoon the new Labor Front held a mass meeting in the Amsterdam Concertgebouw in which Woudenberg admitted that immediately after the publication of Seyss-Inquart's decree many of the officials of the National Center of Trade Unions had tendered their resignation. This, he contended, would not prevent him from reaching his aims. The words "Netherlands Labor Front" were by no means translated from the German, as rumor had it. They were Dutch out and out . . . But in the same breath Woudenberg agreed that in choosing this name he had been inspired by the mighty German "Arbeitsfront." "And thus," he concluded rather incoherently, "it should be clear to everybody that the new Labor Front will not be linked to any political party . . ."

In the intervening year Woudenberg had had plenty of opportunity to convince himself how thoroughly hated he was among Holland's workers. On one occasion he had made a propaganda tour through several factories, more particularly in the southern section of the Netherlands. In a report on this trip printed in "Het Volk," the writer naively admitted that "nowhere was the carpet put out" for Mister Woudenberg. On the contrary, "he had to convince each man separately. He must put up a tough fight before he gets people to listen to him . . . When Woudenberg speaks, there is heckling without end . . . Sometimes they (the laborers) do not come anywhere near the speaker and look at him from a distance with obvious distaste. In one town not a sound came from the loudspeakers which had been placed in various parts of the factory. Woudenberg spoke but nobody could hear him; was that an accident, or was it sabotage? In Maastricht the leader tried in vain to enter a large ceramic factory; the workmen had locked and bolted the front gate." And finally, describing still another of Woudenberg's unfortunate visits, the reporter said: "There is a tremendous uproar when the Commissar enters but at last he begins to speak, above the noise and the clamor . . ."

*

Whilst the National Center of Trade Unions had thus gradually been converted into a duplicate of the German Labor Front, the Nazis abstained from interfering with the so-called Confessional trade unions, in which the Roman Catholic and the National-Christian laborers were organized. Nonetheless, there was little doubt that they, too, would get their turn. And indeed—on July 25, 1941 the nazified Dutch press announced that Woudenberg had now also been appointed to head the "confessional trade unions." Upon this news item followed the "reassuring" message that this nomination would by no means "interfere with the religious convictions of the members of these organizations."

In a special appeal to his new victims Woudenberg beseeched them to 'remain members of their respective organizations."

Adopting the true German blackmail style, he stressed that they should do so first of all to be able to help build the New Order "in which the working man will find his justified place." Secondly, so as not to forfeit their rights to relief money in case of unemployment and illness and to remain entitled to receive legal assistance and help in closing their collective labor contracts. Thirdly, to avoid that in the future they should suffer a setback which "may be in store for those who were never organized or who have left their organizations. Workers," the appeal concluded, "beware—do not listen to *malicious advisers!*"

This friendly epithet no doubt meant to describe the Catholic bishops who only a week after the coordination of the religious trade unions drew up a letter of protest which was read in all churches and chapels and which is an irrefutable proof of the spiritual strength of the Netherlands in the second year of its occupation.

"We have long been silent about the multiple injustices done to us, Catholics, during the last few months," the message read. "We have been ordered to abstain from public collections for our charitable and cultural institutions, even among our own co-religionists . . . Our Catholic Radio, for which during a number of years we sacrificed so readily, has been taken away from us. Our Catholic daily papers have either been banned or limited in their activities to such an extent they can hardly be called Catholic organs any longer. Our religious teachers have been robbed of 40 percent of their income . . . Countless priests and nuns have been forbidden to head their schools—not because they lack the necessary legal authority, but just because they are priests and nuns. The new law on non-commercial enterprises and institutions deals a heavy blow to smaller foundations, such as the St. Radboud Institution of our University which has to pay 143,000 guilders* of the money which it gathered everywhere in cents and dimes. Our youth leagues, such as the Catholic Boy Scouts, the Young Guard and the Crusaders have been disbanded without a word.

"But now something has happened which forbids us to be silent any longer without betraying our spiritual duties . . . The Reich's Commissioner has decreed that the Board of our Roman Catholic Trade Unions is to abstain from all further action and that in its place a Commissary will be appointed with complete authority. This official is a member of the National Socialist movement.

"Virtually the Roman Catholic trade unions are therewith destroyed, as they are prevented from continuing their religious and morale-building task . . . It is clear that a Catholic league cannot be placed under the tutorship of people whose mental attitude is completely contrary to Catholic principles and whose intention it is to propagandize that attitude in the organizations which have been placed in their care.

". . . Our trade unions, being pressed into the service of the National-Socialist movement, therefore become its sub-organiza-

*Approximately $80,000.

tions. Consequently, Catholics may no longer be part of their membership . . . Whoever fails to leave the organizations will be considered a member of the N.S.B. and the Holy Sacraments will be refused to them . . . Publicly and loudly we raise our voice against the injustice done to thousands of people by robbing them of one of their social institutions. We protest against the unheard-of practice of trying to force upon them an attitude towards life which is contrary to their religious convictions . . ."

The reading of this remarkable document made a deep impression. Within a few hours the whole of Holland knew of the courageous message and found in its noble wording new strength to fight the oppressors. During the next few days, the Dutch-Nazi press as well as the newspapers under German control published columns upon columns of venomous comment upon the attitude of the bishops. The letter of protest was described as a "disquieting symptom of mental aberration." That "civilized men who know what is happening in the world today, are able to compose a letter in which the high spiritual values and the meaning of National-Socialism are thus denied," was something leaving these writers speechless with indignation.

Some newspapers tried to "explain" Woudenberg's appointment by saying that it was an attempt to end party politics in labor organizations and heal the split between "ordinary" and "religious" labor movements. As to Woudenberg himself, he declared with trembling voice that the pastoral letter "had nothing to do with religion but was merely another way of waging war against us. Its only purpose," said Woudenberg, "is to create an attitude of martyrdom."

Despite these frantic efforts to win over the denominational trade unions, their members were leaving by the thousands. Of the original total of about 200,000 members, comparatively few remained by the beginning of August, 1941.

It was obviously time to try other means of persuading the Catholic and National-Christian workers to place themselves behind their new boss. Maybe material advantages would make them see reason. And so Woudenberg announced that all members of the nazified N.V.V. would be entitled to considerable increases in the various reliefs they had thus far been receiving. For example, old age pension would undergo an increase of 40 percent; sickness relief would be increased 65 percent and the pension of widows and orphans was to be raised by more than 50 percent.

Moreover, a new arrangement was made entitling organized workmen to greatly expanded medical help from their panel doctors. It cannot be denied that this form of bribery had a certain measure of success. But the great majority of the workmen could not be caught. Rather than listening to Woudenberg's siren song, they helped each other as well as they could with food and money.

By November 10, 1941 the membership of the denominational trade unions had decreased so far that Woudenberg felt obliged to publish a general pardon in which he begged the confessional workers to rejoin their unions on particularly advantageous conditions. They would not be forced to pay their back dues; immediately and automatically they would be reinstated in all their rights. This "special offer" was to remain valid for three weeks only; but its draw was so small that it had to be extended time after time. In fact, it remained in force throughout the next winter, spring and summer. Finally, on September 30, 1942, when the whole of Holland was laughing at the eternally extended "pardon," Woudenberg announced over the Hilversum radio that it would now quite definitely "expire at midnight." It is not known exactly how many laborers had by this time returned to the fold—but their total was no more than a small percentage of the erstwhile membership. Certain is that Woudenberg was far from pleased with the result of his alternate cajolings and menaces; for as late as the beginning of September, 1942 he stated in an article published in the official organ of the Labor Front, "De Arbeid," that "labor leaders are trying hard to reduce the membership of our Labor Front and, to achieve this purpose, do not hesitate to cooperate with employers." And he added, by way of a final growl: "But we would have these men know that we are keeping an eye on them and will get hold of them when they go too far."

With this disgruntled remark the Nazi labor leader provided conclusive proof that the spirit of rebellion among Holland's laboring classes could not be bridled by a Woudenberg—even if he were supported by Seyss-Inquart himself and a thousand German crooks or Dutch Nazi traitors besides.

During the following months the working classes of the Netherlands intensified their slow-down campaign to hamper production for the German war machine to such an extent that "De Arbeid" (Work) published a wrathful article in which the writer complained that "laborers were making a suspicious habit of mislaying precious raw materials which are difficult to obtain. Factory managers," he said, "were cooperating in all kinds of ways." As a "typical" case he mentioned the factory manager who paid full wages to his men during illness, "to encourage absenteeism, never caring whether this attitude caused dislocation of production."

Soon after this outburst the leader of the Nazi-instituted Literary Guild, Professor Jan De Vries, broadcast a New Year's speech via the Hilversum radio. It was a fervent plea to Holland's laborers to "stop their slacking and grumbling" and to work more diligently for the German authorities. "Your country's future," De Vries said, "depends on your work. If you make a bad impression on your employers, your attitude will be considered symptomatic of what can be expected of all Dutchmen."

Although he evidently meant to direct this appeal to Netherlanders employed within the Reich and to those who in the near future would be drafted for such slave labor, it also applied to all workers in occupied Holland. For by that time the laborers of the Netherlands, irrespective of their former political adherences, had unitedly taken their places in the front ranks of resistance. They were the patiently burrowing moles of the underground movement. Once organized in strictly separated unions, they had now found one another outside all labor organizations. They were held together by the same intense desire to regain their lost freedoms and do their share in the construction of a stronger and a better Netherlands.

6

PLIGHT OF THE PEASANTS

"Give us two years—and we will form the best Germanic Commonwealth of peasants there ever was!"

E. J. Roskam, Nazi farmers' "leader," on June 21, 1941.

"As leader of the Nederlandsche Landstand I am authorized to declare that no deliveries from Holland will be made to the Reich as long as the Netherlands' food supply is not superior to that of Germany. A healthy exchange of goods will be promoted . . ."

E. J. Roskam in his inaugural speech as head of the "Nederlandsche Landstand," (Netherlands Agrarian Cooperative), October 25, 1941.

A furious fight is being waged between the Nazi authorities and their accomplices on the one side and the masses of Dutch peasantry on the other. In the first few occupation months the battle was almost entirely one of strong Dutch common sense against a veritable avalanche of confusing Nazi propaganda. Through the gagged press and the controlled radio the farmers of the Netherlands were constantly reminded of the "improvements" which Nazi intervention had brought and would continue to bring in their existence.

Now that all their available produce could be exported to the "natural outlet," the insatiable markets of the Reich, prices would soar higher and higher. In short, they would only have to realize that the end of the "liberal-capitalistic" period had come and that the "revolution" would bring them all and more than they had ever dared to hope for. But these effusions, despite their synthetic enthusiasm, were, to say the least, very coolly received, particularly because such jubilations and pleasant promises found little justification in the obvious decline of the living standard and the general circumstances in which these peasants had to work.

Moreover—conservative as they might be, the farmers of Holland were by no means blind to the fact that the ultimate aim of the enemy was to "coordinate" them as much as any other group of their compatriots. The majority of them understood that farming would shortly be organized on the German standard pattern, in the same way as Dutch industries were already being remodelled. That their surmise was right became clear when during the summer of 1940 the Germans ordered the Dutch Nazi movement, the N.S.B., to establish an organization which was baptized the "Agrarian Front." To its leadership was appointed a certain E. J. Roskam, a former store-keeper who was twice declared bankrupt during his business career. The intention was to bring under this man's jurisdiction an ever-widening circle of National-Socialist peasants. Finally when that was achieved, the Front was—as will be seen later in this chapter—discarded, making place for the one and only "Landstand," or Agrarian Cooperative.

It began with strenuous efforts to induce other peasants' organizations to amalgamate; but almost everywhere the new Front met with utter disdain. The only exception was the case of a small organization of farmers, "Landbouw en Maatschappij," which counted most of its membership in the barren, poverty-stricken province of Drente. That first "conversion" happened in November, 1940—and not until former Minister of Agriculture Folkert E. Posthuma* had set a "glorious" example by joining the Nazi party and pleading for collaboration.

Thus the Dutch Agrarian Front was formed; with the immediate result that the most important agricultural associations, gathered in the so-called Central Agricultural Organizations,** broke all contact with "Landbouw en Maatschappij," the Drente apostate.

As might have been expected, the Dutch Nazis reserved all leading positions in the new Agrarian Front for their own men. Posthuma saw his treachery rewarded by becoming the head of the Advisory Council as well as of the Council of Assistance. An Agrarian Council was also installed; in this body representatives from all sections of the country were seated. They called themselves "Gouwleiders" (district leaders), evidently proud of their Germanic titles. There were many more Boards and Councils in this complicated Teutonic structure; it became a standing joke of

*This man was Minister of Agriculture, Commerce and Industry during the first World War when his most important task was that of regulating the supply and distribution of foodstuffs. After the war he became one of Holland's leaders in the field of agriculture, more especially for dairy produce. Through this work he came in close contact with the Germans and long before the Nazi movement reached its ruling stage, Posthuma gave frequent utterance to his profound admiration of totalitarian methods in general and Nazi ideologies in particular.

**There existed three such Central organizations: the Roman Catholic, the Protestant and the Royal Netherlands Agricultural Committee.

those days to enquire who was the solitary member of the Agrarian Front that did not occupy a place on one of its manifold Councils.

For example, the Front had a special Culture Section and a Scientific Council. It also comprised a separate economic organization composed of main groups, each in their turn sub-divided in specialized groups. Here the old Woltersom plan* came into play; the same program was followed as worked out for the "coordination" of industrial and commercial groups in the Netherlands. A special effort was made to organize into guilds separate and still smaller groups of men engaged in allied occupations. In Amsterdam, for instance, such a guild was formed exclusively for dealers in hides; and soon afterwards another guild made its appearance, this time of "agricultural scientists."

Such was the new set up; and the only remaining difficulty was to attract a reasonably large membership. To overcome the natural resistance of the farmers, the Nazi propagandists exhausted themselves in words of praise for Holland's peasantry. As in the case of Dutch labor, the country-folk were now told how they who had "always been outcasts," would at last be enabled to enjoy their natural rights. Besides, following the old Nazi method which had proved so useful inside the Reich, the Dutch farmers were solemnly assured that they, in contrast to the pools of immorality into which most of Holland's towns had been turned, had retained the pure "Germanic racial values" of past centuries.

"Leader" Roskam, in one of his most desperately poetic and mystic efforts to attract the crowd, said in a Hilversum broadcast around the middle of January, 1941, "We shall furnish fresh blood to our towns—but our peasants' blood is too costly to bestow upon a medley of races. We shall establish special schools to which the grandchildren of those peasants who moved into the towns, can eventually return. Thus their progeny will, in its turn, be the generation to give its blood to the development of our old, indestructible national power. Emigration from country to town . . ., all right. But next to this a return from the town to the country. 'Farming land in farmers' hand' will finally do away with a thousand year old injustice done to our people.

Then and then only our nation will regain its old style and face the new times with self-reliance and strong straightforwardness. Then we, the farmers of this land, will once more be the beating heart and the panting breath of our nation."

---

*See page 48.

A few weeks previously this same inspired speaker had had slightly different ideas on the future of Holland's peasantry. In similarly exquisite verbiage he had then told his listeners that the "racially pure generations of our peasants and land workers must possess and work 40,000 farms of their own, within the living-room which will be yielded to us in the framework of a New Europe." Roskam had obviously made up his mind that in the Netherlands itself there would not be sufficient living-space for 40,000 such "racially pure" farmers. The solution was simple enough. The overflow was to be provided with miniature farms in east Germany, northern France and probably in parts of Poland. He said as much—but so as to prevent his public from appreciating to the full the immense distinction of being thus exiled on a tiny plot of land in a foreign country, he hastily added that such favors would be reserved exclusively for "energetic and racially immaculate young Dutch peasants."

But these glad tidings were not only for the deserving sons of Holland's peasantry, the girls too, would take part in the miraculous future. Specially appointed female propagandists addressed those young women, extolling their future role and exhorting them to "remain themselves." "Do not," said one of these N.S.B. ladies in March, 1941, "try to be 'modern.' Do not powder your faces and—above all, do not resort to the unwomanly practice of smoking. Return to what you were: girls of untainted quality, women of the greatest simplicity."

But all this seemed insufficient to entice the farmers, and their sons and daughters. Even the ardent plea of another Dutch Nazi who pointed out that collaboration with the Germans would not mean a loss of independence but on the contrary, "a great measure of safety inside a large German federation," found little response. "The occupying forces have not come to us as an army of conquerors," he said. "They have not murdered us, ravaged or plundered us—as used to happen in former wars. All they did was to offer us their hand of friendship and full equality of rights."

It all proved to be of no avail; nothing much could be expected of the voluntary collaboration of the peasants. Well then—they would, once and for all, be told what was expected of them. Towards the end of 1940 a decree was published, to the effect that no land was to be sold at rates exceeding those of 1939; and that such sales could only take place to "users of the soil." In other words, peasants alone would in the future be allowed to purchase arable lots. "Farming land in farmers' hand"—that was to be the new slogan . . . If the German authorities and their Dutch Nazi fellow travelers had expected this measure to find an enthusiastic welcome, they were sadly mistaken. The Dutch farmers showed little elation; they disliked the new decree, rooted as it was in the basic principles of National-Socialism. In fact, many of them complained bitterly of the German ruling in the meetings of their agricultural associations. Their farms carried the burden of heavy mortgages; henceforth they would be obliged to keep those mortgages alive indefinitely. Until the Nazi interference there had at least been the chance to turn themselves into tenant-farmers by selling their property, thus transferring the mortgage debts to others. The only people to sell to now would have to be brother-farmers; and it was easy to see that few of those would be prepared to acquire heavily-mortgaged farmsteads and lands.

The next Nazi measure was the introduction of the so-called "Productieslag" (production control).* The cultivation of many commodities would have to be greatly restricted and, far worse, the cattle herd was to be drastically reduced. The Germans blamed this on the Allied blockade which had, of course, considerably reduced the importation of artificial manure and fodder; but the real fault lay with the invaders who from the moment they became masters of the Netherlands, dug deep down into its supplies, and exported without restraint. For example, in May, 1940 there were stocks of superphosphate sufficient for one year. It is not hard to guess where the greater part of those stores went to during the ensuing months. Whatever doubt there might have been concerning their destination was completely dispersed by a statement the Director of the "State Bureau for the Distribution of Fertilizers" made on March 5, 1941. "Part of the superphosphate stocks of this country," he said, "had to be designated to a different purpose" . . .

Agricultural lime was supposed to be imported from Belgium, but little or nothing arrived as the necessary means of transportation were practically impossible to find. Lime saltpeter and nitrogen were still available, but at very high prices. The most serious shortage of all was that of phosphoric acid. Had there been sufficient quantities of other fertilizers this would not have mattered very much; however, there was an almost immediate lack of everything.

---

*See page 119.

It is unnecessary to emphasize that in these circumstances Dutch farmers found themselves in the gravest straits long before the close of the first occupation year. But greater perils were threatening. Germany was taking whatever percentage she could get of Dutch farm labor; inexperienced boys and girls hailing from the bigger cities were told to replace those shanghaied for work in the Reich. As could have been foreseen, the total number of townbred youngsters volunteering for farm work was very small; those who did register knew nothing of agricultural and horticultural problems and turned out to be of small use in their new surroundings.

The next blow was as serious—and even more harmful. The Germans requisitioned large numbers of the best farm horses. In the beginning of December, 1940 all farmers were ordered to relinquish their horses of three years or over, with the exception of the stallions. As the Nazis realized that many of the farmers would kill their horses rather than give them up in exchange for money of doubtful value, they forbade the slaughter of horses.

The initial requisitioning order had mentioned that no more than 25,000 horses would be asked for but as soon as this total had been reached a further requisition was made. The province of Zeeland, internationally known for its beautiful breed of extraordinarily strong farm horses, had to sacrifice more than 5,000 out of a total of 18,000 animals. Many peasants saw themselves bereft of their only work horse. In most cases this meant more than the loss of an indispensable tool; it meant the sad parting from an animal to which these workers of the soil were truly attached. Richer farmers who were left with more than one horse came to the rescue. Committees were formed and meetings held to settle the question how the available number of horses could be best divided among the thousands of smaller farming enterprises.

Quite naturally this shortage of animal help, led to a considerable "black market" trade in horses, so that in April, 1941 the occupation authorities intervened by fixing maximum prices. They stipulated, besides, that no purchase or sale of farm horses could take place without special permits.

The scarcity of farm horses was hardly worse than that of machine help. Owing to the lack of fuel thousands of tractors and other agricultural machinery stood uselessly in barns and sheds. And to top it all, there had been an enormous demand for Dutch cattle; huge quantities of cows and calves were slaughtered even during those first months of the occupation.

Rapidly the situation had grown alarming for all of Dutch peasantry. No fertilizers; an ever-increasing loss of cattle and horse-power; the use of makeshifts instead of experienced hands—and still the Nazis wondered why the farmers of the Netherlands showed no interest in their fanatic propaganda for a New and Blissful Order!

Breeders of live-stock found themselves in a sorry plight. It was virtually impossible to get the necessary corn for their chickens and ducks, so that a gigantic reduction of the poultry stocks became unavoidable. During the summer of 1940 fourteen million chickens, out of a total of twenty-two million, were slaughtered. The killing of so many birds was a veritable shambles; thereafter astronomic quantities of chicken meat were canned to go "the way of all flesh"—that is, to Germany.

Thus live-stock breeders were brought to the verge of bankruptcy. Whoever had possessed five hundred hens now had only ninety left; and of every additional lot of five hundred hens only twenty were allowed to remain alive. Poultry breeding for a living had become the most precarious enterprise imaginable.

But heaviest of all was the sacrifice made by cattle raisers. Those farmers who, between them, possessed one million six hundred thousand cows and a million two hundred thousand calves when the Germans invaded Holland, were told to drive their animals to the abattoirs in droves. In yielding their cattle, these hardworking peasants did not surrender a mere product of their farms, but their sole means of production.

It is true that the shortage of fodder, resulting from the difficulty to import worth while quantities from abroad, was an undeniable fact. But the farmers realized full well that the Germans had done nothing to combat this serious obstacle to the keeping of a large cattle herd. On the contrary, they had again and again requisitioned colossal quantities of hay and straw.

The British blockade *did* make it hard to obtain fodder—but it can be said without fear of exaggeration that the overwhelming majority of Dutch cattle raisers recognized its necessity. They did not feel bitter towards the English; their resentment was focussed upon the occupying powers who never ceased stealing and robbing, while whispering sweet words of advice to hide their crimes. It was only natural that those thousands of small farmers were loath to dispatch their cattle to the slaughterhouse.

But, as usual, this reluctance was pounced upon by the Germans to replace the "voluntary" sacrifice of cattle with obligatory requisitioning. Every farmer was allowed to keep five "free" cows; of each following five animals at least one had to be killed—and this before December 1, 1941. In vain did the peasants plead for the postponement of that fatal time limit to April 1, 1942. All they obtained was a promise that after this butchery no further demands would be made upon the Dutch cattle herd. But subsequent decrees made it clear that the entire cattle herd would be reduced to only a million and a quarter head.*

It was not the people of the Netherlands who benefited by this wholesale slaughter; most of the meat was used for the German occupation troops and for exportation to the Reich.** The same fate was in store for Dutch pigs; nor was it allowed to kill goats without official leave, a ukase which merely resulted in an extension of clandestine slaughter.

As had happened in all branches of industry which the Nazis had "reorganized, regulated and restricted," their orders to the cattle breeders ended in a real catastrophe. The victims of their new decrees received large sums of money with which they could do nothing practicable. Their cattle was gone and replacement was out of the question. Moreover, the poor remnants of their herds suffered considerably from the lack of good fodder and gave much less milk than normally. In the province of Friesland, known the world over for its splendid type of cows, that loss—after ten months of occupation—equalled two-fifths of the usual milk yield. As a natural consequence it had been necessary to raise the price of milk. This opened the door to new hardships for masses of consumers throughout the country, people who could ill afford to pay more for the little milk which was still being put at their disposal.

The healthy appearance of Holland's cattle which used to arouse the unstinted admiration of all foreign visitors, disappeared completely. These cows had been changed into scraggy animals—

---

*It is in this respect worth while remembering that the Nazis never reduced their own herd to an appreciable extent before the late autumn of 1942. Only then, with all stolen fodder supplies exhausted, the Germans ordered their peasants to "slaughter enough of their cattle so that the remainder may be fed by fodder produced on the farms."

**The innate sense of humor of the Dutch allows them—fortunately—to see a comic side to most of the tragedies which have come in the wake of German occupation. Thus the export of thousands of head of cattle gave rise to the following joke which circulated throughout the country:

"Did you hear the story of the cow who chewed up a German communication cable?"
"No; what happened?"
"Well, she was at once arrested and shot as a saboteur."
"You don't say . . ."
"Yes. But listen to what happened further. The Nazis immediately rounded up another fifty cows and carried them off to Germany as hostages . . . !"

as unlike the proverbially sleek Dutch cattle as the Nazi methods differed from the conceptions of generations of liberal-minded Netherlanders.

In the midst of all their troubles the peasants thought they had found a means of obstructing the enemy. If he requisitioned so large a percentage of full-grown cattle, there might be some sense in keeping much larger quantities of calves than was the habit in pre-invasion days. Obviously, this had a detrimental effect on the milk yield, but it seemed that such a disadvantage was acceptable as against the advantage of possessing considerable numbers of young cattle if—by a stroke of exceedingly good luck—the war were to end favorably during the course of 1942. The hope that this policy would remain unobserved by the Nazis soon turned out to have been idle. In April, 1942 Dutch cattle breeders were ordered to give up all their "excessive" calves.

As a prelude to this further bleeding the Dutch Nazi G. J. Ruiter, who had meantime been appointed Director-General of Agriculture, declared in a radio speech towards the end of March that the situation in most cattle raising enterprises was "dramatic" and that it could only be understood by those who know "how attached these people are to their cattle." With a synthetic catch in his voice this Nazi described the "empty stables and the meager, bony cows which are living reproaches to the farmer of his unwise exploitation methods. Thin, forlorn-looking, young animals may be seen trying to graze in wintry meadows, devoid of grass, or lowing pitifully alongside snow- and ice-covered ditches."

In this way, painting a gloomier picture than was warranted by the truth and working upon the sentiments of the farmers, Ruiter endeavored to prepare his victims for the additional requisitioning.

For still the Germans were not satisfied. Early in July, 1942 they ordered the plowing up of 187,000 more acres of pasture land on which rape-seed was to be grown, this being an important source of vegetable oil. At the same time the slaughter of about one hundred thousand cows, which had hitherto grazed upon this land, was ordered. This new sacrifice reduced whatever remained of the original dairy herd by at least 30 percent.

The killing of so much cattle produced 48 million pounds of meat and fats, all of it destined for Germany. In addition, the Nazis expected to derive a minimum of 70 million pounds of vegetable oils per year from the new rape-seed fields—as against an average yield of 30 million pounds of fats which might have been obtained from the milk of the slaughtered cows.

To redress the damage done to Dutch dairy farming in less than three years of German destruction will require a minimum of five years after the war; and still the end is not in sight. In a broadcast over the Hilversum radio made during the early autumn of 1942, Ruiter declared that "there was still far too large a cattle herd in the Netherlands." He asserted that the total number of cattle under one year old had "surpassed the normal"; and this led to the announcement that more calves would have to be slaughtered before the year was over, so that the ratio between cows and calves would become 5 to 1.

Not long afterwards the German authorities notified the Dutch farmers that silages would no longer be available for sheep and cattle and that in the winter of 1942-'43 *all* fodder, of every description, would be scarce. Farmers were ordered to surrender all of their grain, with the exception of a small quantity of oats for their horses. Hay and straw stocks would also be requisitioned before the winter set in; stockmen were ordered to render detailed reports on their cattle and fodder stocks by October 15 at the latest.

*

Horticulture, too, had been going through the worst time it had known for many a year. Yet, at first sight, it had looked as if after the subjugation of the Netherlands truck gardeners would be doing exceedingly well, as a new and almost insatiable market had been opened up to them.

Indeed, the quantities sold at the daily vegetable auctions exceeded considerably those of pre-invasion days. German propagandists did all they could to play this fact up in their regular broadcasts over the Nazi-controlled Hilversum radio. But those mouthpieces of Joseph Goebbels conveniently forgot to mention that the larger turnover of Holland's vegetable auctions had not brought an equivalent increase in earnings for its market gardeners. They were obliged to pay higher prices for all their requirements. Above all, the subsidies which they had received from the Government until the invasion, had been withdrawn immediately by the German authorities. It was, therefore, very doubtful whether the average proceeds of their production under Nazi supervision came anywhere near the minimum rates they made in pre-invasion days, in addition to the state subsidy. And so the "Nieuwe Rotterdamsche Courant," early in 1941, had the courage to publish an article in which it criticized the endless rejoicings of Hilversum's broadcasters and pointed out that thousands of horticultural workers lived "on the edge of their minimum requirements."

But this protestation failed to carry the slightest weight. Instead the truck gardeners were politely invited to do everything in their power to make the state-controlled production of certain specified vegetables and fruits "a roaring success."

At the head of this campaign, which was advertised as the "Productieslag," (a literal translation of the Teutonic "Erzeugungsschlacht") was placed the former Minister of Agriculture Folkert E. Posthuma, who was thus rewarded for having turned Nazi and throwing his full weight into the German effort to coordinate Dutch agricultural associations. He had started his inglorious task in favor of the enemy a fortnight earlier, on March 6, 1941, by delivering a broadcast in which he took it for granted that the occupying powers would grab more than half the total yield of Holland's horticulture. Should the harvest exceed expectations, he *hoped* that his compatriots would be allowed to retain that surplus . . . Trying to explain this strange standpoint, Posthuma lost himself in complicated calculations of which, to be sure, his farmer-listeners understood one thing only: that they would be mercilessly robbed.

The various agrarian organizations, such as the Protestant, Roman-Catholic and non-sectarian Central Agricultural Associations, convened with representatives of the Federation of Dairy Farmers and Poultry Breeders. After long discussions these men decided to collaborate as well as they could with Posthuma's Committee "as long as constructive work can be done for the benefit of our people." But they made it very clear that this collaboration would under no circumstances be more than a technical one. In the minutes of this historic meeting it was carefully explained that "as the task of the Posthuma Committee is confined to technical production problems, it stands to reason that all other duties of our organizations (in the fields of cultural, social and economic welfare) will be continued as heretofore."

Immediately the new authority of Posthuma began to be felt. He forbade the planting of all crops having no immediate bearing upon the production of the most necessary foodstuffs. Rye, beans and potatoes were promoted to first-rank positions; the planting of oats and green vegetables was, on the other hand, severely restricted.

Even if the prices of certain products underwent a not inconsiderable rise, there was little reason for Holland's truck gardeners to rejoice. Their difficulties increased by the day; manure was hard to get, even at rates far above the normal. Transportation became almost impossible and the wages of whatever help there was, soared high above the carrying power of the average producer. Thus Posthuma's campaign did not turn out to be a great success. The market gardeners declined to be held responsible for the new restricted way of raising their crops. In an official declaration made by the Board of the Groningen Agricultural Association—one of the oldest in the country—it was fearlessly stated that "if the farmer is told it is within his power to avoid famine, we feel obliged to say that the necessary factors which might justify such a statement, are not present. One only has to consider the scarcity of manure and fodder to understand our objections. If the shortage of these essential production factors leads to disappointing results, we, the farmers, cannot be held responsible." Moreover, the various associations did not hesitate to make it clear that they were unwilling to join the new-fangled Agrarian Front.

In retaliation, the attitude of the Dutch Nazi Party became ever sharper. Furious attacks were launched upon the "recalcitrant" organizations and their leaders; but the simple fact that the membership of these associations showed a marked increase, was sufficient proof of their vitality and of their resolute decision to fight all Nazi efforts at meddling. The farmers demonstrated no more than lukewarm interest in the German encouragement to plow up soil which had thus far been used as pasture land. Among them there were thousands who remembered that toward the end of the first World War a similar policy of breaking up meadows had resulted in tremendous losses.

Besides, in many cases the cost of converting grazing land into tillable soil was prohibitive, apart from the fact that no fertilizers could be had to help prepare the new fields. A further objection was that even if a cattle breeder tore up all his pasture land, this would not automatically turn him into a capable tiller of the soil. He would have to acquire assistance, often from faraway sections of the country where horticulture predominated. Moreover, he would have to buy new and expensive implements. But above all, he would be obliged to attune himself very rapidly to entirely new work with completely new problems and risks. Even though a certain "premium" was paid for every acre of converted grass land, a simple calculation made it clear that the farmer would, as a rule, suffer large financial losses—mainly because he had no source of income during the transition period.

As usual, the "voluntary" plowing up of grazing land soon made place for enforcement—which only led to further impoverishment of Dutch peasantry. The exceptionally severe winter of 1941-1942 had catastrophic results. The larger portion of all winter corn and of the huge quantities of newly-planted rape-seed were frozen. Considerable damage was also done to the vegetable crops.

When on May 14, 1942 the third occupation year began, the future looked dark indeed for all of Holland's farmers. The cattle herds had been drastically restricted without any benefit to the people themselves; the best work horses were requisitioned. Poultry stocks were practically exterminated; tens of thousands of farm hands had been forced to work in Germany when they were so urgently needed in Holland. Indeed, the farmers had every reason to dislike the New Order from the bottom of their hearts.

Is it a wonder that the peasants began to obstruct and sabotage unanimously every measure taken by the enemy? What was more natural than that they preferred to sell their vegetables direct to the consumer, or that they took up clandestine slaughter with true enthusiasm?

It was quite an easy matter to hide a couple of suckling pigs from each litter, which in a few weeks' time could be sold on the black market. Whatever the Nazis did to halt these practices turned out to be in vain; and it was even rumored that in the villages of North Brabant it became a rule to have a full-fledged bean feast whenever the hundredth pig was clandestinely killed!

The horticulturists did not stay behind. For them, too, the only means of salvation was to take part in the black market trade. Potatoes, vegetables, beans and grain were sold to go-betweens or direct to those consumers who were eager enough to fetch the eatables from the farms. It is estimated that in the province of Brabant no less than 50 percent of the grain harvest disappeared without trace. Milk, too, was sold clandestinely or worked into cheese with the same purpose. The fact that these delicacies cost three or four times as much as normally, did not withhold a single townsman from acquiring at least a small helping.

There were distinct reasons why the black market trade came

to such swift development in Brabant, and also in the southernmost province of Limburg. High prices were paid by buyers from Belgium, because in that downtrodden country famine had already got a strong grip on the majority of the people. No official figures were ever published on the scope of these activities; but it is significant that more than once nearly fifty smugglers were arrested in one night. Rye, grain and beans were favorite commodities. They were smuggled out of the country in huge quantities; in March, 1942, for example, no less than 325,000 pounds of rye were "illegally" exported from one particular section of North Brabant to Belgium.

An additional basis for this interest in the black market was that most of Brabant and Limburg's inhabitants are Catholics. These people were anxious to take revenge for the humiliation and persecution of their co-religionists. They did not intend to collaborate with the German invaders. Against their iron-will to obstruct, all Nazi measures were doomed to miscarry. If the farmers did not throw the bulk of their products onto the black market, they hid their stocks or destroyed them, rather than yield them to the enemy.

*

On October 25, 1941 the Hilversum radio broadcast the report that Reich's Commissioner Seyss-Inquart had instituted an equivalent of the German Agrarian Cooperative. It was to be called the "Nederlandsche Landstand"—a word combination completely foreign to the Dutch language—and at its head was placed the ubiquitous Roskam.

The founding of this new body was another Nazi effort to plant a net of Dutch-Nazi spies throughout the country, spies who were not to work individually but as a well-organized institution. The various "district leaders" would take the place of the infamous "block spies" first introduced by the Nazis in all their large cities for the organized betrayal of any "suspicious persons or irregularities." These local spies were to report to "leader" Roskam who, in turn, would bring about the necessary contact with the German authorities.

Of course, Roskam had quite a different explanation to offer when he first described the task of the Nederlandsche Landstand. "The Reich's Commissioner," he said, "represents the highest power in the Netherlands and with the formation of the Landstand he has created an opportunity for all farmers to regain the honorable position to which their class is entitled and to make true the old slogan that 'farming land should be in farmers' hand.' "

It was a repetition of the old effort to flatter the victims and promise them the golden eggs that would never be laid. For the Landstand did not only mean to be a fairy godmother to the farmers. Horticulturists and fishermen, and all those engaged in afforestation, would henceforth also be working under the auspices of the new Cooperative. As an example of the Landstand's intentions Roskam mentioned the reclamation work of the Zuider Zee. In the future, he asserted, all reclaimed land would be placed in the care of the Nederlandsche Landstand, for distribution among "the deserving."

However, despite these day-dreams the Landstand flourished none too well. Dutch loyal peasantry refused to cooperate with Mussert's Nazis; if anything, they hated these accomplices more than the invaders. The Articles of Incorporation of Seyss-Inquart's latest creation might state that it had been established to "further the interests of the rural population and protect their honor," but the farmers of the Netherlands preferred to do things their own way and denied that they were in need of anyone to play the role of guardian angel in their behalf.

They had no confidence in their newly appointed "boerenleider"* Roskam and his empty verbiage. They merely shrugged their shoulders when Roskam, in his inaugural address, assured them that he was "authorized to declare that no deliveries from Holland will be made to the Reich as long as the Netherlands' food supply is not superior to that of Germany." They fully understood the ominous meaning of his statement that the goods which would be exchanged against other commodities would be "50% of all Dutch horticultural produce, which we do not require for ourselves. The same applies to cattle, for slaughter."

When the Agrarian Front was formed several associations had disbanded themselves rather than enter upon a semblance of cooperation. Dutch farmers' wives had been no less resolute than their men. The influential League of Farmers' Wives refused every form of collaboration with the Front and when in retaliation a Dutch-Nazi woman was nominated a member on its Board, the entire Board resigned unanimously. With the introduction of the Landstand a stipulation was made to prevent a recurrence of

*"Peasant leader."

this policy: automatically every person active in the fields of farming, horticulture and the fisheries, became a member. The entire Agrarian Front was dissolved into the Landstand and great emphasis was laid upon the fact that the same rule would apply to "all other agricultural associations" that, as yet, had managed to stay outside the Front.

But here the Nazis made a grave miscalculation. There was nothing to prevent those associations from hastily disbanding themselves; and even Roskam found it hard to include non-existent organizations in the Nederlandsche Landstand . . .

The Groninger Maatschappij van Landbouw (Groningen Agricultural Association), one of the oldest in the country, resolved in its last public meeting that in the present circumstances it could not continue to exist without great changes to "its character, traditions and work." The Chairman concluded his announcement with the following touching words: "Many of you will feel as moved as we when you consider that our Association, after 104 years of continuous activity, has come to the end of its road. However, we shall bear our fate with dignity. As farmers we shall continue to devote ourselves to our work and we will adhere to the sanctified parable of the single grain that falls into the earth and perishes but in due course will bear rich fruit."

This and similar opposition did not withhold leader Roskam from starting out upon his organizing rampage with unparalleled fury. By February, 1942 he had arranged for a complete and imposing staff of acolytes. He had appointed a deputy leader, chiefs, departmental heads and quite a variety of other "leaders." He also had installed an Advisory Committee, all of them members of the Dutch Nazi party. Finally, he had formed a "Farmers' Council" composed of prominent provincial farmers.

As an "Orlando furioso" Roskam tore around the country nominating and installing representatives and meantime, despite all paper shortage, editing and publishing a special Farmers' Journal in an edition of no less than 350,000 copies. This new weekly, with a separate edition for each of the eleven provinces, was to replace the hundreds of local agricultural papers which had appeared regularly before the Nazis "reorganized" the Dutch press towards the end of November, 1941 and killed hundreds of trade journals.

By the end of March, Roskam had nominated eleven provincial "leaders" who each in their turn were held responsible for the appointment of district heads. Those men would have to find the necessary local chiefs; and thus all of Netherlands' peasantry would at last become conscious of the New Times or—as Roskam expressed it in his peculiar, vague manner—"The folkish cycle of Holland's peasantry would close itself according to the law of creation" . . .

That N.S.B.'ers were nominated to be their masters, enraged Dutch farmers, horticulturists and fishermen more than anything else. Methodically the followers of Mussert were kept out of the community of farmers which was going through a period of unification as never experienced before. Those Dutch Nazi farmers lived on their homesteads in solitary shame. They were abhorred and avoided as lepers. They and their relatives were exposed to continuous digs and insults—very much in the same way as their brothers-in-arms in the cities were shunned by every loyal townsman, throughout the land.

During October and November, 1942 thirty Netherlanders were executed at the order of the German authorities on charges of sabotage against Dutch farmers. They were accused of having set fire to many farms and storehouses and of having damaged railway and transport facilities. These men formed part of a sabotage ring of more than a hundred factory hands, students, and business men, ranging in age from 16 to 56. Their work was mainly directed against Dutch-Nazi farmers and included the destruction of a flour mill by fire; the building was estimated at a value of a quarter of a million guilders.

Most of the damage was done in harvest time; the saboteurs —travelling afoot or on bicycles—visited the fields at night and started fires in several places. These were watched over by special incendiarists who poured chemicals onto the flames to encourage their spreading, where necessary. In many instances farmers lost not only their harvest but also their homes and barns, with irreplaceable tools. It was announced during the trial that about one hundred more saboteurs were to be prosecuted shortly on similar arson charges.

These incendiary attacks were the final form in which the loyal Dutch demonstrated the depth of their feelings against farmers who had constantly shown their sympathy for and readiness to collaborate with the Germans. It was the dramatic climax to a protracted series of warnings given to the treacherous elements among Holland's peasantry.

But that the Nazi farmers, long before the saboteurs took

their material vengeance, had been well aware of the disdain in which they were generally held, was proved by the Nationale Dagblad—official daily of the Mussert movement—when in the spring of 1942 it published an obviously apocryphal diary of one such farmer-N.S.B.'er. It was clear, however, that the manuscript was based upon facts—even though the writing was that of some nazified journalist. The diary was written in a typical Pepys style; a few passages are amusing enough to be quoted in full:

> *Sunday, May 4.* This morning to church with my wife but found the sermon little interesting as the clergyman mixed politics with his speech. Saw the face of H.—better known in the village as our "local Rothschild"—shone with pleasure and now know he familiar with sermon before it was pronounced. Will have to be careful as he may make things difficult for me, my son having joined the Storm Troopers. This laid at my door and must our whole family suffer for the boy's courage.
>
> *Sunday, May 11.* Home from the fields and found my wife in bad mood, as the woman T., who was our servant for many years, ignored her question how her youngest child is faring. My wife convinced this due to campaign against us, I never having expected such petty hatred possible in this village.
>
> *Thursday, May 15.* Heard tonight our Mayor visited local schoolhead as children singing nasty songs in streets against Germany. Today the Storm Troopers marched through village, this drawing many people. My son also among the marchers. Our policeman escorted the marchers with long face—but nonetheless no disturbances.
>
> *Friday, May 23.* Our son, with two Storm Trooper comrades, in terrific fight during the night, they being treacherously attacked by a gang of "patriots." However, they gave good account of selves.
>
> *Tuesday, June 17.* Tonight our Agrarian Front meeting badly disturbed by urchins making tremendous row outside gathering hall, so we could not understand each other. Upon our asking café-owner to chase the boys away, no result. This explainable as the man secretary of the local Patriots' League, or Netherlands Union—and we certain they sabotaging our meetings.
>
> *Saturday, November 23.* My son having left for Storm Troopers' training, he sends us long letters about service

which not easy. He writes of having met some old acquaintances—which is always pleasant among strangers.

With this philosophic effusion the diary of the "simple Nazi peasant" came to a sudden end. But during the few months of its appearance it had furnished invaluable information on the bitter struggle between usurper Roskam and his unwilling "material." The obstructionist policy of the rural population was such that even one of the most energetic and successful Dutch Nazi propagandists, a certain Dirk van den Hul, admitted in one of his regular Saturday broadcasts towards the end of February, 1942:

"To tell you the truth, listeners, there are moments in which I think: I'm through with it all! I would rather stay home quietly Saturday nights near the fireside, with my wife and my cup of coffee. What is the good of all this talk? . . ."

Indeed, what *was* the good?

7

MUSSERT'S SCHOOL FOR TRAITORS

"It may sound somewhat arrogant but we National-Socialists are entitled to say that we are the only true patriots."

Anton Adriaan Mussert, leader of the Dutch-Nazi Movement, in a press conference on November 9, 1940.

". . . The chasm between the Dutch people and ourselves has never yet been so profound. Our nation has lost its bearings, but the N. S. B. will point the way to unity."

Idem, in a speech at Roosendaal, September, 1941.

"I must say that the bombing of this town (Rotterdam) was quite a good thing, because something infinitely more beautiful than was ever conceived will be built in its place."

Idem, addressing the Technical N. S. B. Guild of Utrecht, November, 1941.

"We stand and fall with Germany."

Ernst Voorhoeve, Propaganda Leader of Mussert's National-Socialist Movement, April 11, 1942.

In the democratic Netherlands of pre-invasion days the National-Socialist movement, founded by the engineer Anton Adriaan Mussert, never succeeded in attracting more than a minuscule section of the people. There were many political and common sense reasons for this lack of public appeal; but in addition the very personality of the self-appointed Dutch Nazi leader acted as a formidable brake on the development of his party.

Mussert, born in 1894 as son of a village schoolmaster, grew up a difficult, self-centered youth whose life ran none too smoothly. He wanted to study at the Technical University of Delft but his father's means did not allow such expense. And when, after many heartaches, young Anton finally went to Delft, it was only because of the magnanimity of his mother's sister who put up the necessary funds. In June, 1918 Mussert got his Civil Engineer's degree; it marked the end of an uneventful study period. Immediately afterwards he entered the service of the province of Utrecht; and in the following years he went through the conventional stages of an average, slowly-progressing and obedient Civil Servant. It cost him almost a decade of competent though uninspired effort to reach the rank of Chief Engineer.

Throughout this up-hill struggle Mussert was consumed by an overweening ambition. He wanted to be heard and seen in public; he was greatly inspired by the appearance on the political horizon of Benito Mussolini who by martial speech and acts of dictatorship was beginning to show the world how the people of Italy were to be "regenerated."

In 1922 Mussert married his aunt, by way of recompense for her financial sacrifices. The truth is that the ambitious lady had asked her eighteen years younger nephew to take her in holy matrimony. She did not want her monetary investment back; all she desired was a share in the slowly-rising social standing of her protégé. Owing to their blood relationship the marriage required the Crown's special consent which was readily obtained. It is hard to say whether this easy approval delighted or disappointed the young bridegroom; but it is an unassailable truth that there was much for which he had to thank his wife. From the first day of this union "auntie" Mussert proved to be a powerful driving force behind little Anton's social and political aspirations.

She wanted to see him publicly "recognized"; above all, she wished him to emerge as a political leader of his fellow countrymen. She persuaded him to offer his services to the Liberals; but when they turned down Mussert's proposal to adopt him as their candidate for the coming parliamentary elections, she goaded him to the formation of his own party. A new political movement, all his own . . . ; something of which, at last, he would be the unchallenged boss!

That is how the Nationaal-Socialistische Beweging—known from the very start by the initials N. S. B.—came about. A small group of hotheads soon joined the Utrecht engineer. He also attracted one or two disgruntled intellectuals, among them a university professor who undertook to work out the party program. Irony of fate had it that, though Mussert's sympathies still went out to Mussolini, his party program became more or less a copy, in parts even a literal translation, of Hitler's Nazi platform as fully explained in "Mein Kampf." Almost before Mussert realized it, this German-inspired program had been officially submitted to the membership, and adopted. From that moment the N.S.B. was bound to develop into a secondhand version of Hitlerism.

Right from the start things did not run too smoothly for the new movement, or its leader. Of the curious hundreds who had joined the N. S. B. to find out "what it was all about," many dropped out again after a few months—completely disillusioned. And when in 1934 the Netherlands government forbade adherence to Mussert's party to all Civil Servants, the military and the police forces, it suffered further—and almost fatal—setbacks. In the next year Mussert was dismissed from his responsible position as engineer of the State's Waterways, as the Government held the opinion that his political views were incompatible with the dignity and patriotism required of any Civil Servant.

It did not last long, however, before—parallel with the increasing significance of the Nazis in Germany—Mussert's party began to find financial backing and meet with widening interest. The "leader" staged large-scale gatherings and outdoor meetings, the necessary funds being provided by a few sympathizers among Dutch capitalists who meant to find a bulwark against the dangers of Communism in Mussert's efforts. New applicants turned up throughout the country; and not long before the outbreak of the second World War, the N. S. B. was officially announced to possess a membership of just below forty thousand persons.

It is worth while scrutinizing somewhat more closely the elements of which this membership was made up.

During the end of the 19th and the beginning of the 20th centuries, Socialism had reached the large majority of the Dutch working classes. Among the early leaders of this evolutionary movement there were many of the best and noblest whose influence upon the masses was great indeed. Steadily the Social Democratic party had grown in size and influence; and several of the more significant social reforms were introduced and adopted because of its indefatigable efforts. Along legal lines and within the Constitutional framework of the country the position of Holland's labor had been improving slowly but considerably.

It was not among those Socialists that Mussert could hope to find his supporters. On the contrary, his followers were mainly the "odd remnants," impetuous, disappointed, embittered, lazy or dissatisfied people usually encountered at the lower levels of any community. These residues of society did not join the Mussert movement for reasons of idealism. They were not fighting for something to be achieved in a far-away future. All they desired, and expected to get sooner or later, was a good time; they wished to get ahead of all those envied others—the gifted and energetic, the more successful. Their new-fangled leader was to make them rule supreme, so that they might take revenge upon the democratic elements for all imaginary humiliations and deprivations they had experienced in years gone by.

There were, of course, some capable men amongst them; but they had been spread thinly over the various National, National-Socialist and Fascist parties that endeavored to make themselves heard in the Netherlands of those days. Consequently, they were of no particular value to any one of the revolutionary movements. The unbalanced elements which formed the "enthusiastic audience" of Mussert's meetings, could not possibly envisage social changes by means of legal—and at times protracted—procedure. They clamored for the "revolution"; and soon, in touching imitation of Germany, their attacks obtained that unmistakably Teutonic, personal flavor which distinguished Nazism from any other political movement in the world. For them it was not a matter of changing laws or replacing threadbare ideas but an uncontrollable urge to attack certain people who in the most irresponsible, ludicrous manner were declared guilty of having brought about economic situations which in reality had taken many decades to develop.

Yet, though they reserved their right to criticize freely and call anyone the most dastardly names, these great reformers turned out to be hypersensitive; they themselves could not bear the slightest unfriendly remark. Rather amusing evidence of this may be found in the fact that in less than three years the N. S. B. Documentation Bureau employed, in rotation, the labor of no less than 120 party members for the task of cataloguing the numerous clippings which during that period appeared in the Dutch press about the N. S. B. Evidently none of these officials could bear the avalanche of distinctly unflattering remarks which the Netherlands press of all political nuances used to employ when it was forced to mention the unspeakable Mussert and his fellow-travelers.

Inside Mussert's "house" conditions were not very satisfactory either. Almost from the start distrust ruled supreme in the heart of the party. In December, 1941 when the N. S. B. celebrated its ten years' existence, the financial director—a certain Van Bilderbeek—naively confessed in the Special Jubilee issue of "Volk en Vaderland" that "from the beginning I was accused of accepting bribes from traders who were allowed to make deliveries to our party." This gentleman also revealed that in the early days, when the necessary funds were obtained by open collection, several party members voiced the opinion that "collecting in a Storm Trooper's cap always yielded more money." "But I," Van Bilderbeek added, "soon discovered that those collections ultimately brought *the party* considerably less cash than a collection in safely-locked boxes . . ." It is hard to decide what to admire most: the discretion with which "comrade" Van Bilderbeek expressed himself or the generosity with which he allowed his readers to take a peep in the National-Socialist party-kitchen.

As their most typical characteristic, the bulk of Mussert's followers displayed an unparalleled measure of stupidity and tactlessness. None other than propaganda leader Ernst Voorhoeve* provided an excellent instance of it in February, 1942 in an article published by the Nazi weekly "Volk en Vaderland." He related how after much discussion he had persuaded one of his wavering friends to attend a public gathering of the Nazi movement. However, a couple of days before the rally the candidate for Nazism had to visit an office where several uniformed Dutch Nazis were at work. One of these, taking it for granted that the visitor was a party member, started a confidential talk. He said, "You see, I'm wearing my uniform now, but after office hours I put on civilian clothes, go to the cafés and listen-in carefully to people's conversations. The notes *I* make . . ., and the things that happen to those people! You'd be surprised."

The result of that quaint incident was that Voorhoeve had to start all over again with his victim's conversion; and he concluded his story with the following moral: "It is a most subtle and responsible task to be a propagandist for the National-Socialist movement. Therefore, district leaders must be very careful indeed picking their men and giving them the necessary training."

This story is a fair sample of the "integrity" inside a movement which had the audacity to call itself "the symbol of the honor and conscience of the Netherlands' nation," and "the political party without which Holland would have no future." It should, moreover, be remembered that this incident took place more than ten years after the founding of Mussert's party. A full decade had been insufficient to produce more than a very limited number of intelligent propagandists.

---

*Before joining Mussert's movement Voorhoeve was the leader of the Flemish-inspired "Verdinaso" party.

In the summer of 1940, after the German invasion, a few hundred persons of dubious quality—most of them living on the fringe of Dutch intelligentsia—had thrown in their lot with Mussert but none of these men planned to give leadership. Everyone of them had his own axe to grind. Things had not been different before the war; only on rare occasions had intellectuals been attracted by the N. S. B. During those first years of Anton Mussert's political career it was quite an event if an intellectual decided to join him. And thus it was that the entry—early in 1935—of a youthful-looking, boyish-mannered fellow who had made some sort of name for himself in public life, was considered a veritable milestone in the party's development.

The man was Meinoud M. Rost van Tonningen. He was born in the Netherlands East Indies, of partly native parentage. At the start of his career there had been nothing to betray the strange turn it was destined to take. In 1922, at the age of 28, Rost van Tonningen obtained his Doctor of Law-degree and was made secretary to the President of the American-Norwegian Arbitration Court. In the next year he was appointed secretary to the Commissar-General of the League of Nations in Vienna, and for three consecutive years did excellent work, resulting in a complete reorganization of Austria's disrupted finances.

In 1931 he became financial adviser to the Austrian Government. For five years he devoted himself to this task; a Netherlander who used to meet him frequently and knew him intimately during that period, described him as "an intelligent, entertaining and outspoken man." Yet, even then certain internationally-known financial experts who in some capacity or other had to collaborate with Rost van Tonningen, said of him that his character was "complicated and turbid—that of a man who might ultimately do the most surprising things."

In 1936 Rost van Tonningen, through the assistance of certain well-placed connections, became departmental head of Hope and Company, Amsterdam, one of the oldest banking establishments in the Netherlands. From the moment of his return to Holland he made it a habit to announce on every possible occasion his conversion to the extreme right. He would admit at the slightest provocation that he had turned completely against democracy and liberalism. This man who at one time prided himself on being a bosom friend of Dr. Dollfuss, Austria's unfortunate Chancellor, never lost an opportunity to confess his profound admiration for Adolf Hitler. As yet he carefully refrained from claiming the Nazi ideology for his own; but he gave sufficient evidence that mentally he was living the life of a fanatical Nazi.

When after four years of hesitation Rost van Tonningen at length decided to join Mussert's party, this podgy leader was so overjoyed with his first worthwhile catch that he immediately made him "Chief Essayist"—Nazi slang for Chief Editor—of his scurrilous daily "Nationale Dagblad" which was then painfully worming its way into Dutch lower middle and working classes.

Until that time Rost van Tonningen had on the whole been able to control the ugly instincts that seethed within him. Now he let himself go without restraint. He could at last venge himself on all those people who in past years had "disliked or hated him." In his distorted imagination there existed many such individuals; and against them he started a systematic slander-campaign. The "Nationale Dagblad" became a deadly weapon which he wielded with great cunning—particularly against those who at some time or other had confided to him their abhorrence of Hitlerism.

There was Sir Eric Phipps, for example, who for years had shown Rost van Tonningen the warmest friendship. He had received him with exemplary hospitality in his home at Paris where, at that time, he occupied the post of British Ambassador. The names of former Dutch colleagues and superiors, among the latter Eelco N. van Kleffens, (now Foreign Minister of the Netherlands), were equally besmirched and their persons menaced because of their avowedly anti-Nazi principles. Throughout 1938 and 1939 Rost van Tonningen constantly attacked these and other representatives of democracy, and he never missed a chance to describe his "blood"-friend Dollfuss in slighting and disdainful terms.

Benefiting by the very election system which he never stopped condemning, he got a seat in Parliament and here he fought a rabid obstructionist's fight, stubbornly attacking not institutions but personalities. He abused his parliamentary immunity to call his enemies unspeakable names and to utter the direst threats against them, especially against those among them who happened to be of Jewish birth.

At last this psychopath had reached his long-set goal. Whoever had ignored him or refused him assistance in his struggle for social recognition, now found themselves reminded of the most insignificant, long-forgotten incidents. His newly-acquired power, no matter how feeble it still might be, turned Rost van Tonningen's head completely. He became more dangerous than the average uneducated Mussert man; his dark and tortuous mind made him into an implacable, blood-thirsty enemy whose vengeance for imaginary insults soon proved to be terrible.

It was evident that after the rape of the Netherlands by Hitler's hordes the progress of this exemplary Dutch Nazi would be swift. He had given ample proof of possessing the right mentality. There was, besides, no denying that as a financial adviser to the Austrian Government he had been a hard, conscientious and efficient worker. All this explains why only a few months after Seyss-Inquart's arrival on Dutch soil Meinoud M. Rost van Tonningen was picked to head the Netherlands Bank.

In previous chapters* it has been made clear how he showed himself a willing tool in the hands of an enemy out to destroy Holland's economic independence. Time and again he was instrumental in robbing the nation's treasury to support the Nazi war machine. He pressed upon his fellow countrymen huge loans to the Reich, loans which *must* be fully subscribed to, the only alternative being a compulsory loan at a ludicrous rate of interest and with the certainty of immense losses to all subscribers.**

To this unbalanced, maniacal mind are now entrusted the interests of all banks within the occupied Netherlands. The blackest of magic has provided him with a position of such far-reaching power as even he cannot have hoped for in his wildest dreams.

*

It must have filled the hierarchy of Mussert's Nazi party with impotent rage to find that the occupation of the Netherlands by their German "brothers" did not bring their immediate elevation to that rank of all-powerful leadership they had so confidently looked forward to. On several occasions one of Seyss-Inquart's righthand men, the German Commissar-General Schmidt, publicly declared that "the N. S. B. would obtain full power." But nothing much happened. Even Mussert's interview with the godhead Adolf himself, towards the end of September, 1940, bore no visible fruits. Worse than that—if before the invasion the Dutch Nazis were generally disliked and attacked not only with the pens of honest democratic writers but also with the fists of strong and indignant working men, these feelings now culminated in a fierce and general hatred. More than 98% of the Netherlands' people

*See pages 58 and 100.
**See page 59.

were unwilling to let "bygones be bygones." They would never forget the shabby role played by Mussert's followers before and, more particularly, during the unwarranted German attack.

In his boundless imbecility Anton Mussert, far from trying to convert his recalcitrant fellow countrymen by some show of diplomacy, managed to make himself more despised than ever through an endless chain of gratuitous insults and blunders. The sayings of this pitiful "leader" mentioned at the head of this chapter, have been chosen from a wide range of similar effusions—all of them betraying the obtuseness of his mind, his lack of common decency and his failure to understand that these genuflexions to the enemy not only made his very name anathema with every loyal Hollander but also earned him the unconcealed ridicule and scorn of many a German "colleague."

Why did not the invaders take more kindly to Mussert and his crowd? What made Hitler procrastinate until the close of 1942 before he endowed Mussert with something akin to the power this henchman had so eagerly solicited for himself and his friends throughout two-and-a-half years of occupation?

There were several reasons. First, and most important, the Germans fully realized that Anton Mussert could not claim power of any sort on the ground that he represented an important section of the Netherlands' people. It was no secret to them that altogether the N. S. B. comprised only a fraction more than one percent of the population. It was, therefore, imperative that Mussert and his fellow collaborationists should first show themselves worthy of distinction through an arduous propaganda campaign. In the second place, the Nazi authorities had ample opportunity to ascertain that it would be a dangerous move to place Mussert immediately upon the throne of political power. This might conceivably lead to a state of chaos, and ultimately to revolt. Chaos, because when the Germans took over—and for a long time afterwards—the N. S. B. counted only a handful of truly capable organizers. To them no more than a small number of more or less responsible posts could be entrusted. But once these men were employed, there would remain no executive manpower reserves whatever. To place even a major part of the intricate government machine in the hands of the Dutch Nazis, was therefore excluded.

And thus, whilst keeping Anton Mussert constantly asway between hope and fear, the Germans encouraged him and his associates to set about an intensive campaign among the masses of patriotic Hollanders. The results were not very heartening, thanks to the peculiar make-up of Mussert and of the majority of his helpers, who never missed a single chance to make themselves more obnoxious to every patriotic Netherlander.

Only a few weeks after his assertion that "the N. S. B.'ers were the only true fatherlanders," Mussert wrote in his weekly, "Volk en Vaderland": "Many years ago I argued, and I was duly jeered at for having said it, 'without the N. S. B. our people have no future.' This has now come true. Those who were laughed at and made fun of as degenerates and traitors, have become the carriers of our nation's fate."

But this was only the beginning of a long row of equally outstanding dictums. In a Utrecht meeting he praised Adolf Hitler as the "man who to the entire Germanic world is a gift of God such as is made only once every thousand years." To celebrate the coming of 1941 he sent a telegram to his revered Fuehrer, wishing "a continuance of the wisdom and power which have distinguished you." He even grovelled in the dirt at Seyss-Inquart's feet, thanking him for all he and his collaborators "had done in the past year to improve relationships between the German and Netherlands' peoples. May your aspirations be crowned with success during 1941."

To achieve this success Mussert would give his wholehearted cooperation. To be sure, he was quite willing to supersede Seyss-Inquart at any time his German bosses would let him. Meanwhile he had to be satisfied with small mercies—now and again a trip to Berlin, where he was even admitted into the inner sanctums of Goebbels and Goering. From early January till the end of March, 1941 Mussert constantly travelled around, alone or in the choice company of Seyss-Inquart. He also talked with Heinrich Himmler, fiendish head of the monstrous Gestapo, and with Rudolph Hess who at that time must have been rather preoccupied putting the finishing touches to the plans for his spectacular flight to Scotland.

On his return to The Hague Mussert told a meeting of his acolytes that "Hitler means well with the people of Holland." And he added triumphantly, "I know it from the best sources! Therefore, do not hesitate any longer to join the N. S. B. Later you will deeply regret the days you are now losing." But still the people of the Netherlands refused to flock to his group houses and rowdy gatherings, so as to be "in at the kill"; and Mussert was forced to carry on his quixotic campaign with undiminished vigor.

As the next step towards winning the love and trust of all his compatriots he sent the Fuehrer a congratulatory telegram on his birthday, April 20. In this document Mussert made one or two revelations too good to be lost to posterity.

"If my National-Socialist party had been in power in 1940," he assured Hitler, "the Netherlands would have stood shoulder to shoulder with Germany in this war. We rejoice to see that already large numbers of our membership have joined the battle of their own volition."

This sample of super-treachery which widened the chasm between Dutch loyalists and Mussert still further, proved to be too much for some of his own followers, and for quite some time frequent references were made to an opinion expressed by the fascist weekly "De Waag" (The Scales) a few months previously. In an article on the N. S. B. leader this paper had made the following statement: "He is not the right man to act as the only, all-inspiring Fuehrer. Somewhere in his make-up there is a psychological flaw which time and again makes him say or do things which turn the people at large more and more away from him."

However, despite this regrettable lack of success with the masses, the N. S. B. was busily "coordinating" itself. The German example was closely followed; during 1941 every Nazi institution existing within the Reich got its counterpart in the Netherlands. To mention only a few of those Teutonic organizations: Mussert founded a Law Front* in which judges, lawyers, notaries public, tax collectors and councillors, inspectors and policemen were jumbled together. He also established a Medical Front, a Students' Front, an Economic Front, a Front of the Netherlands Middle Classes, a Netherlands National-Socialist Teachers' Organization, a Technical Guild and several National-Socialist women's organizations. Naturally, the already existing "Weer-afdeeling" (the equivalent of the German Storm Troopers), the Netherlands SS and the National Youth Storm—a replica of the Hitler Jugend—were formations which greatly expanded their membership as well as the fields of their activity. The obvious purpose of all these Fronts and organizations was to help the Germans obtain control over all strata of Dutch life.

*Rechtsfront.

As to the magistracies, here too a Nazi association was formed which under the name of National League of Civil Servants meant to "mature all Civil Servants for the acceptance of National-Socialist principles." To dispel any doubts in the minds of the men concerned, a Dutch Nazi playing an important part in this new League, declared in January, 1942 via the Hilversum radio: "The government official who does not adhere fanatically to the principles of the new world order cannot in the long run expect to be maintained as a Civil Servant." This brutal threat caused great unrest among Netherlands officials, even so that the Germans were obliged to announce it was not their intention to make membership of the N. S. B. a matter of obligation. That is . . . : for the time being!

It has since become perfectly clear that right along the Germans intended to give all official positions to such N. S. B.'ers as they thought trustworthy. In the autumn of 1942 the list of Mussert men occupying leading positions in every government department already was a long one, and it grew by the day. Besides, the number of Nazi burgomasters, whether or not capable of occupying such posts, was overwhelming. In fact, many of them soon proved to possess so few commendable qualities as mayors that the party hastily organized a "correspondence course for burgomasters," for which no less than three hundred comrades registered at once. The course consisted of three months' schooling climaxed by a week's "practical experience" at The Hague. In some cases the successful pupils were sent to Germany for final instructions; but even without this finishing touch they were supposed to be quite ready for the burgomaster's office. Indeed, if being the leader of a community means no more than the passive execution of orders given by the occupying power, without the assistance of aldermen-advisers or a municipal council—both of which the Germans have completely eliminated—then even three months' schooling is much too long.* The investiture of such makeshift burgomasters was not always a pleasant experience for the gentlemen concerned. In the town of Axel, for example, a member of the Council present at the inauguration snatched the

*A typical example of the men turned out by the Burgomaster Correspondence Course is the present mayor of Amersfoort, a town of more than 40,000 people in the center of the country. This new official was a clerk in the office of a notary public. As he failed to distinguish himself in any way, his firm transferred him to an even less attractive job in an insignificant village. There the man became a subscriber to the correspondence course and simultaneously joined Mussert's party. After completion of his "studies" in the spring of 1942, this new "magistrate" was solemnly initiated as the head of the city of Amersfoort.

chain of office from the hands of the temporary mayor who was preparing to hang the token of his dignity around the neck of the newly-appointed Nazi burgomaster. In Utrecht all aldermen resigned from office before they could be dismissed, as a protest against the removal of the loyal mayor, Dr. Gerhard A. W. ter Pelkwijk. In Baarn the new burgomaster was welcomed with a speech which stated that the news of his appointment "had been received with mixed feelings." The new functionary, obviously confused by this hearty welcome, observed in a peevish tone, "I do not know you and you do not know me; so what can you have against me?" He begged the community to "give him a chance" and assured his listeners that he would only rule in a purely National-Socialist fashion. "I hope," he concluded, "that Baarn will soon give more recognition to and show better understanding of all the Dutch Nazi movement stands for."

The installation of another Dutch Nazi as burgomaster of Schiedam had to be postponed because the necessary quorum failed to appear. In the small town of Wouw the officiating alderman welcomed the burgomaster by assuring him that "there would doubtlessly be plenty of clashes."

Nevertheless, at the end of the second occupation year the burgomasters of all important towns were N. S. B.'ers or sympathizers with the Nazi movement. The burgomaster of Rotterdam, after having borne courageously the brunt of endless Nazi attacks which often took the form of brawls and fisticuffs during Council meetings, finally resigned from office in July, 1941. Ten weeks later his place was taken by a certain Frederik Ernst Mueller who had been Nazi Commissar for the province of Utrecht since the preceding February. Promotion was swift indeed for this offspring of a German industrialist family.* But even in those places where no Dutch Nazis had been put at the head of municipal or provincial Councils, the invaders found a way to nazify municipal authority through "coordination" and the introduction of the "leadership principle."

By a decree published in the official "Verordeningenblad" of

*A synopsis of this man's career gives an excellent idea of the type of people the Germans were eager to entrust with responsible jobs. Frederik Mueller was of German origin; and though his relatives had been settled in the Netherlands for almost two generations, he was sent to the Reich to finish his studies as an engineer. After obtaining his degree, he returned to Holland and worked in his father's factory. At the death of the latter, in 1935, he became technical leader of the Utrecht chemical plant which the Muellers exploited under the name of P. Smits & Zoon. Almost at the start of Mussert's movement, in 1931, Mueller joined up and occupied various functions in the movement's "inner circle." Finally he became leader for the town of Utrecht and Commissar for the Utrecht district.

August 12, 1941 all city and provincial Councils and all colleges of aldermen and deputies were suspended. The authority of the municipal councils was transferred to the burgomasters. The Councils were bereft of every vestige of influence and their poor remnants, henceforth called advisers, were burdened with the task of choosing a mayor from among the inhabitants of their communities. A further duty of these advisers would be to "make the people understand and accept all measures of the burgomasters."

In a similar manner the Provincial Assemblies were "reorganized"; as to the provincial commissars, they were placed under the immediate supervision of the Secretary-General for Home Affairs.

The new measure caused the virtual dissolution of municipal councils and provincial assemblies as independently governing bodies. Thus far town councils had possessed far-reaching autonomy and even though the National Parliament was disbanded after the invasion, the municipal councils had continued to wield great powers.

All this was over; from now on the new "leadership principle" enabled the German authorities to keep a close check on the activities of any mayor. No longer could the inhabitants of a town follow their own free will for the good of their community. They became utterly dependent upon the decisions of the Nazi Provincial Commissar under whom their mayors were graciously allowed to operate.

Before this decree was published Seyss-Inquart is sure to have realized that it would cause an exodus of aldermen and deputies refusing to be turned into impotent puppets. He therefore added a special clause stipulating that if any one of those officials resigned his post, he would automatically lose his rights to claim either retention money or a pension. This clause also prescribed that no one chosen to be active as an "adviser" of a town or province, had the right to refuse acceptance of this distinction—unless "the appointee had already fulfilled a public office for more than six consecutive years, without pay." The decree listed a few more legal excuses such as "being in the necessity of leaving town on frequent occasions and for long periods, being an invalid, having reached the age of 60 or over, or fulfilling an ecclesiastical position."

As a further measure to avoid an epidemic of protests, Seyss-Inquart instructed one of his men to deliver a "reasonable" speech upon the subject. "The Netherlands' people," this mouthpiece said, "will at a later date be given the opportunity to decide whethei this decree—which is carried out by the German authorities merely as an administrative necessity, in complete accordance with international law for the Maintenance of Public Order and Safety—is suitable to serve as a base for a new Netherlands Constitution. We must remember," the speaker concluded on a persuasive tone, "that this great authority for the governing bodies of cities and provinces was demanded years ago by the ablest Dutch specialists in the theory and practice of the country's administration." This speech was repeated parrot fashion in countless places throughout the Netherlands—simply to prove that the Germans had merely complied with long-standing requests of numerous Dutch burgomasters, professors and other people, ranking high in public and economic life . . .

In this sweeping decree the Dutch Nazis eagerly tried to recognize a wide-open gate leading them to almost unassailed power in the government of communities and provinces. It would now, they thought, be an easy matter to place N. S. B.'ers in and around all key positions. For they did not have the slightest doubt that the "advisers," drawing a tight ring around any burgomaster of the old school, would be exclusively members of Mussert's party. Unhappily, this whole affair turned out to be another disappointment. So near to much-coveted authority, the Dutch Nazis were turned back again by the German announcement that for the time being and until further order there would be no nomination of advisers. This "further order" never came.

The immediate repercussion to the new decrees was a wholesale tendering of resignations by aldermen, deputies of provincial assemblies and burgomasters. But none of these officials was allowed to leave their posts before substitutes had been found; and it was not until April, 1942 that all vacancies were finally filled. In the province of Limburg no less than 52 mayors out of a total of 170 refused to stay on. In some communities the administrative apparatus become so depleted that special calls had to be made upon the citizens to fill the posts of self-dismissed municipal workers.

Yet, throughout 1942 the Nazi newspapers, Nationale Dagblad and Volk en Vaderland, continued to publish complaints of N. S. B.'ers who had been passed by for municipal jobs which were "rather given to boys of 15-18 years of age than to experienced members of the Nazi party." Hardly an issue appeared without letters from disgruntled members expressing their disappointment that the German authorities still refused to allow the nomination of new "advisers."

Meanwhile the loyal citizenry never failed to show its disgust when a Dutch-Nazi traitor was foisted upon them for their ruler. The measures and decrees of these new officials were systematically sabotaged and those who had been forced to resign—mayors, aldermen and deputies alike—were certain of the practical sympathy of all who in former days had worked with them. The peculiar thing was that these ousted officials rarely left the communities in which they had worked. As late as April, 1942, Max Blokzijl, in one of his revealing radio talks, told of cases known to him in which dismissed burgomasters had rented apartments in the towns which they had headed so that, Blokzijl added sneeringly, "they would be immediately available when the Tommies—who always win the last battle—march into the Netherlands to the edifying tune of 'It's A Long Way To Tipperary.' "

*

If Mussert's disciples had not, therefore, penetrated into the magistracy without much trouble and many heartaches, it took them considerably longer to take root in other government departments, more especially the Department of Justice which included the Netherlands police force. Only on July 1, 1941 a member of the N. S. B. was chosen to a high judicial position. On that date professor J. J. Schrieke, once a well-known teacher at Leyden University, became Secretary-General of Justice. After that other appointments followed in fairly quick tempo. The age limit for judges had been reduced from 70 to 65, which enabled the Germans to place quite a number of N. S. B. lawyers on the judge's bench. A sympathizer of the New Order, Professor Dr. Johannes van Loon who had thus far taught law at Utrecht University, was promoted to the rank of President of the Supreme Court; a few months afterwards he was joined by two fellow-travelers who took the places of Vice-President and Councillor. It was, nonetheless, an exasperatingly slow process and in the beginning of January, 1942 Max Blokzijl impatiently demanded "a radical house-cleaning among all those hypocritical saboteurs in the service of the state, the provinces, and the municipalities who make it a sport to stymie all good measures of the New Order, in the vain hope that the people at large will reproach *our* men for the absence of visible results."

As to the police, N. S. B. penetration has become disquietingly thorough after thirty-five months of steady burrowing. In practically all important towns Mussert's men were nominated to the posts of Chief of Police, or Police Commissioner and throughout the ranks loyal police were as far as possible replaced by believers in Nazism. Moreover, the fact that the *entire* police force was placed at the disposal of the infamous Rauter, German head of the imported Green or Security Police, has drastically reduced the influence of loyal policemen upon the activities of their less reliable colleagues. In many instances the Dutch police have been forced to cooperate with Rauter's hooligans in rounding up innocent victims and dragging them to concentration camps, or packing them into freight cars for transportation to some unknown "destination."

How bravely the reliable elements among the police took a stand against the bestial excesses in which they were often compelled to play a part, becomes clear from the list of nearly one hundred patriots who in May, 1942 were shot "because of subversive action." Among them were quite a number of policemen. In most cases those men had refused point-blank to obey such Nazi orders as would oblige them to arrest innocent people. But apart from these martyrs, there are many more who even now, at the definite risk of losing their liberty if not their lives, will not obey the standing Nazi order to keep "hands off" any brawl or fight in which N. S. B.'ers are mixed up.

Towards the end of 1942 the Nazis made the final move to strengthen their hold upon the Dutch police. By announcing a merger of the various police divisions—such as the Marechausseés or military police, the gendarmes and all municipally directed police units throughout the country—they brought the entire police force of the Netherlands under their immediate control. This decree followed exactly a fortnight after the significant announcement that Gestapo Chief Heinrich Himmler had appointed two high German police officials to posts in Seyss-Inquart's offices at The Hague. One of them was Inspector-General Lankenau, of the Munich police force.

Unhampered, with no more than negligible opposition from whatever loyal elements succeed in holding their own under the new arrangement, this nazified police force can devote itself completely to suppress the "spiritual organizers of hostile action, whether or not there is evidence of their participation in such acts," as Seyss-Inquart explained soon after the fusion of the police forces.

No doubt the "Weer-afdeeling," or Dutch Storm Troopers, and the Germanized SS or Elite Troops, will be relieved to see the wings of the Dutch police thus drastically clipped. More than ever before their well-organized marches may now provoke Dutch loyalists at any time of day or night. From the very start of the German occupation the "heroes" of Mussert's Storm Troops, yelling their martial songs at the top of their voices, used to make every town and village unsafe. The rhythmic tramping of their heavily-shod feet was an ominous sound; and their challenging glances at anyone crossing their path were as many invitations to utter the first word of protest. Any obstruction sufficed to justify the generous use of bludgeons and knives which burned in their vengeful fingers.

These hooligans, from the simplest *weerman,* or soldier, to the *Opperheerbanleider,* or "Super Army Division Leader," were out to show themselves not a hair less pugnacious and ready to terrorize than their German colleagues of the notorious S. A. Their processional marches were the zenith of their ruffian's lives, and in their weekly, "De Zwarte Soldaat,"* many a flamboyant description appeared of those edifying activities. An issue for April, 1941 for instance, brought the following report of a Storm Troopers' march through the center of Amsterdam:

"When the Leidscheplein, in the heart of our town, has been 'purified' (of Jews and other undesirables) our detachment marches through the surrounding streets and along the canals. The atmosphere among our men is tense. They all hope something else will happen. They wish to fight for their ideals; they want to see results. At the end of the evening our Storm Troopers line up near the Town Theatre and their 'headman' addresses them as follows: Men—you were splendid tonight. Authority and again authority, that's how they will get to know our uniform; that's how they will learn to obey us, and submit to our will."

On the whole the Storm Troopers were not disappointed in their desire for a fight. Quite regularly the infuriated loyal Dutch gave battle and on more than one occasion a Storm Trooper was beaten within an inch of his life—or even killed. But soon the people began to realize that to go in for street brawls with the Storm Troopers was actually playing the game of the N. S. B. For

*The Black Soldier.

wherever the Storm Troopers had been "attacked," the National-Socialist party, backed by the German authorities, would declare with obvious glee that the Dutch police was "no longer in a position to keep the situation in hand," and that it was imperative to dismiss more old-timers and replace them exclusively with members of Mussert's movement.

The underground workers, therefore, rapidly distributed a leaflet in which all patriots were besought not to interfere with the Storm Troopers, allowing them to strut along the streets rather than to give them the slightest reason for "complaint" against loyal police officials.

In several communities where the black-shirted Storm Troopers had no detachment, they would organize a march through and parade to encourage the swift formation of local W. A. troops. Generally they found all shops locked, their blinds down and the vast majority of the inhabitants encloistered in their homes. In some places the citizens, ignoring the unwanted visitors, would stroll along their streets in a leisurely fashion, unanimously displaying the national red-white-and-blue, or an orange emblem.

In Hoogeveen, a small town in the province of Drente, a group of men who signed their pamphlet "Some citizens of this community, also good patriots," circulated a warning in March, 1941 after it had been announced that a Storm Troopers' visit could be expected on the next Saturday afternoon between 5 and 7. "Fellow citizens," the circular said, "this is not the time to take our fight against the Storm Troopers—that hateful phenomenon of moral decay—into the open. Let us preserve complete neutrality. Every good Netherlander is to stay at home next Saturday afternoon. Our streets must be completely desolate. In this way we will prevent the Storm Troopers from disturbing our peace. In this way only can we be of real help to our local authorities.

"Should you fail to follow our advice and brawls ensue, there is no doubt that the N. S. B. will insist upon the dismissal of our authorities whom, we need hardly say, we prefer to Mussert's rowdies."

*

If the black Nazi rabble thus ruled the streets of the entire country without fear of real opposition, another and even more authoritative organization began to make itself felt. That was the

Dutch section of the German SS, or "Schützstaffel," which originated in the so-called Mussert Guard: the pre-invasion body guards of the none too courageous Dutch Nazi leader.

The members of the Dutch SS, also known as Standarte Westland, were a type far "superior" to the ordinary Storm Troopers. They had to fulfil many high requirements—not only with regard to the undiluted purity of their Aryan blood, but also concerning their physical characteristics, including height, build and the color of their hair. They received a special training, first in Holland and later in Germany, to become worthy of their distinguished positions. Towards the end of February, 1941 a special contingent of six hundred SS men left The Hague to join the German Army. In his official send-off Mussert jubilated that "this Dutch battalion is our guarantee that later, when the construction of a New Europe is taken in hand, we shall be looked upon as equals."

During the first year of occupation some 1500 Dutch SS men and eligible Storm Troopers had joined the Standarte Westland or were serving the German war machine in the "National-Socialist Motorized Corps.*

For them National-Socialism was a religion, and Adolf Hitler their God. "Storm," the SS monthly appearing in the Netherlands, declared in its issue for March, 1942, "We follow our Fuehrer blindly. We do not know where he leads us, but we believe in him—and that is enough for us." They called themselves a "league of fighting men who at all times will defend their holy Germanic character." Juggling with the words "Germanic" and "folkish" was one of their strong points; at the same time they never hesitated to show their disdain for Christianity and insisted on speaking of the apostles as "that Jew Paul" or "that Jew Peter." Their influence upon a group of youthful Netherlanders was tragic. Here follow, as a sole example, some quotations from a letter which an eighteen year old provincial girl, true reader of "Storm," wrote to that worthy paper. The letter was recited in a weekly SS broadcast over radio Hilversum. "Did you see the poster which early this year was distributed to invite contributions for charity to children?" the girl wrote. "It represented a raceless child, a hash between Malayan, Jewish and the Lord knows what. Above that portrait was the legend, 'For to them is the Kingdom of Heaven.'

*National-Sozialistische Kraftfahrer Korps.

"I asked myself whether Heaven is to be reserved for this sort of creature and I began to question the entire theory of tolerance and love of neighbor.

"I am convinced that one must hate everything bad. For instance, I could never love a Jew or a bestialized Russian because they would pull me down with them into the abyss of perdition. I must hate the bad in order to live; yet, I dare not confess this openly so as not to be derided by my friends . . ."

The SS announcer had particular praise for this epistle which he called a "clear, honest and straightforward statement of a young Dutch woman who well understands the true nature of things."

A sadder example is hard to imagine of how during the last few years the National Youth Storm had been poisoning the minds of thousands of adolescents, in every corner of the land.

The Youth Storm, already in active existence before the invasion of 1940, was swiftly coordinated after the subjugation and transformed into a duplicate of the infamous Hitler Jugend. The deputy leader of the N.S.B., Van Geelkerken, became its Head Stormer and under him a long line of officers, provided with weighty Teutonic titles, was installed to help in the education of a "truly National-Socialist Dutch youth."

Boys between the ages of 10-14 were called "gulls" (meeuw) ; for girls of the same age the strange Germanized word of "meeuwkes" had been adopted, denoting the female gender. From 14-18 the members were known as Stormers, or Stormsters. All Youth Stormers must wear blue shirts symbolizing faithfulness —because "blue is true." One of the leaders of the National Youth Storm explained why that particular name was chosen. "National," he said, "because bound to nation and soil, with love for people and fatherland. These are the principles in which our youth will be formed; those national values will be revered in all circumstances . . ."

But meanwhile, in anticipation of the great day on which National-Socialism would be the only and therefore the leading thought in the Netherlands, very little of this prophesied reverence was shown to the misguided children and adolescents of the National Youth Storm, or to their Nazi leaders. One follower of Mussert drew a succinct picture of the situation when in a radio broadcast he described the Dutch Nazis and their offspring as "the lonely ones—a people within a people. A group of pariahs."

Max Blokzijl had a busy time sorting the piles of letters

which reached him from despondent N. S. B.'ers. Youth Stormers had been ordered to leave public buildings, including churches; members of the party were described as "ridiculed, spat upon, slandered, pestered and sneered at when they marched through town." Children of patriotic Dutchmen made it a sport to smash the windows of Dutch Nazis. The home of the new-fangled Nazi Student Front at Utrecht was set afire; speeches by Nazi leaders were effectively "jammed" by the ringing of cycle bells in unison or by a quasi-enthusiastic applause lasting so long that the speaker never got a decent chance to air his viewpoints. In several towns, but particularly in Utrecht, daylight attacks were made on members of the Nazi party, sometimes with fatal results.

*

All this was not just a passing phase, a violent reaction against the presence of the enemy inside the country. Loathing for Mussert's men, especially in the light of their cowardly behavior during the tragic May days of 1940 when they eagerly helped to spread confusion and prepare the ground for their German confederates, was so deep-seated that time could only strengthen it. Nearly one and a half years after the subjugation, Mussert was constrained to admit in public that "the past eighteen months have been a harder strife than we experienced throughout the eight years of party life prior to the invasion."

Both the Storm Troopers and the SS were known and shunned as the lowest scum. Under a mask of haughty aloofness the people of Holland tried to hide their bitterness about the licentious behavior of the German plunderers and their Dutch helpmates. Quite naturally their desire for revenge went out, first of all, toward the traitors who in years gone by had belonged to their business associates, or even—maybe—to their circle of acquaintances, or trusted friends. The great masses remained demonstratively unwilling to grasp the meaning of "the Nazi revolution which must inexorably lead to a new World Order." Apart from Blokzijl's meanderings, the Nazi papers themselves provided the best evidence of the situation. One day the "Deutsche Zeitung in den Niederlanden" contained the following boldly-printed advertisement: "Which Dutch or German comrade will correspond with N. S. B.'er, 21 years of age, son of an industrialist? He has lost all former friends on account of his political convictions, and he now wholly depends upon congenial spirits from some other town. Would gladly establish connections anywhere."

In Mussert's weekly, "Volk en Vaderland" another believer in Adolf Hitler and Anton Mussert, his prophet, confessed that he had lost all the friends he had before the war. "Since May, 1940 I walk around as a lonely man. In fact, even our neighbors make me feel that I am suffering from some contagious disease. They pretend not to see me in the street and at best give me a stiff little nod of recognition. Wherever I go, in cafés, cigar shops, at the barber's, I am always aware that I am not exactly a welcome guest. I am not complaining; but I only want to state some hard and undeniable facts."

During the second year of occupation the general boycott of Mussert's followers became complete and the hatred of patriotic women was, if anything, fiercer than that of their husbands and sons. There were a few isolated cases in which loyal Hollanders endeavored to "save" former acquaintances who had gone the Nazi way. They tried to talk to them and persuade them to cease playing the part of traitors to their own nation. Those talks were in reality final warnings to mend their ways. If the hint was not taken, the N. S. B.'er in question could be certain that shortly his mail would begin to contain a regular stream of menacing letters. In his radio talks Ernst Voorhoeve, the official propagandist of the N. S. B. who in August, 1942 was forced to join the "voluntary" army fighting in Russia, repeatedly quoted examples of this kind. In the small Limburg town of Groesbeek, for example, a Dutch Nazi café owner received a letter from which the following quotations are lifted, as typical of the notes sent to many who openly admitted their love for Anton Mussert.

"You are a member of the N. S. B., yet you pretend to be a good Catholic. But you cannot belong to the Church, as you are confessedly a follower of Mussert—and the N. S. B. is openly fighting the Roman Catholic Church. Perhaps you think, 'Well, then the Church must be wrong.' But that is not so. Now think of your café. Look what has become of it. Your son Piet has been sent to some place far away; he will probably never return. When you hear of his death the N. S. B. will console you by saying, 'He has died for the New Order'—but that will not do *him* any good . . . People hate you because you are an N. S. B.'er. What are you going to do when the tide turns—as it doubtlessly will? Consider this well. Come to church as you used to; join your old comrades. Speak again with decent people and there is sure to be a place for you after the war. Otherwise . . ."

It was, indeed, most unpleasant to be a Nazi and defy the scowling glances, the unspoken threats of one's fellow countrymen. The N. S. B. insignia which its members had so proudly fastened in their buttonhole the moment the German troops entered the Netherlands, became a dangerous mark of distinction. Gradually thousands of Dutch Nazis left off wearing it—so that, in the end, their "leaders" were obliged to make its display obligatory. Even Reich's Commissioner Seyss-Inquart had to admit that to be a Nazi in the Netherlands was "a very uncomfortable business."

Finally the German authorities installed a number of so-called Peace Courts all over the country. It was their main task to prosecute all "misdemeanors" against members of the Dutch Nazi party. The new judges, generally N. S. B.'ers themselves, set about their work with a vengeance. An endless procession of "criminals" passed through these farcical Courts and were duly sentenced to heavy fines or imprisonment, or both, for offenses ranging from some explosive but heartfelt remark at the address of a Dutch Nazi to beating up a disciple of the great Mussert. To choose a few stray examples from a wide variety of material: a baker at The Hague was sent to jail for fifteen days for buying some caricatures of N. S. B. leaders, which offense the judge described as "an act of incitement." Similar punishment was meted out to a shoemaker who had confided to a local N. S. B.'er that in his opinion "all N. S. B.'ers are traitors and should be hanged." A twenty-one year old girl was imprisoned for 25 days because she stared with obvious disgust at a Nazi professor when he passed her in a park. The learned man had overheard the girl express her opinion of him in one short but picturesque word, "louse."

Gradually the sentences handed down by Peace Court judges became more severe. The hard-headed Dutch "obstructionists" would have to learn obedience somehow. In Amsterdam two women and a man were sent to prison for a year because of "having shouted malignant and unrepeatable words at members of Mussert's party leaving for the Russian front." In defense of that conviction the Amsterdam daily "De Tijd" published an editorial which concluded: "Germanic volunteers fighting Bolshevism shoulder to shoulder with German soldiers, are under the special protection of the Dutch Nazi SS formations. Hence those who dare insult them must be ruthlessly punished."

A technical official of the municipality of Eindhoven, in North Brabant province, was arrested in October, 1942, peremptorily dismissed and sentenced to a fortnight's jail term because he had refused to obey the Dutch Nazi burgomaster's order to raise flags on all the city's public buildings in honor of N. S. B. leader Anton Mussert who came to visit the town. The accused had asked his subordinates whether they would object to carrying out the burgomaster's order, and when their reply was in the affirmative he simply abstained from giving them instructions.

But the distribution of anti-Nazi literature was considered an even worse offense; and in the city of Maastricht twenty Dutchmen were given prison terms ranging from five to fifteen years on this particular charge.*

Never before have the people of the Netherlands fostered so intense and fierce a hatred as in the years of Nazi occupation. It is crushing the lives of the traitors among them. It has withheld many a wavering soul from joining up with Mussert. It is a hatred which cleanses the country's atmosphere, drawing a sharply dividing line between the black night of Dutch Nazism and the clarity of true patriotism.

Peace Courts, occupation authorities, the entire apparatus constructed for the protection of the Dutch Nazis, is no more than a flimsy fence behind which Dutch patriots are waiting for the day on which the "German protectors" will be driven out forever and the hateful black pest of Nazism can at last be eradicated.

As Anton Mussert himself expressed it in one of his speeches: "if the English invade the Netherlands the Dutch mob will exterminate all N. S. B.'ers." And among the many perishable sayings of this deplorable creature that tremulous utterance, so full of dire forebodings, must be preserved for posterity as the only one of unassailable truth.

*Further sentences of the Peace Courts are listed in Appendix II. There they are compared with cases in which members of the N. S. B. stood accused of acts of violence against patriots.

8

UNHOLY CRUSADES

"We and we alone are candidates for power in the Netherlands."
Speech by Ernst Voorhoeve, propaganda leader of the N.S.B. (Berlin, May 27, 1941).

"Our leader will be Head of State."
"The Black Soldier," Dutch Storm Troopers' journal, March 6, 1942.

"Is it something to be ashamed of that after ten years of lack of appreciation we sometimes lose heart?"
"Volk en Vaderland," Mussert's weekly, May 29, 1942.

On December 14, 1942, the eleventh anniversary of the National-Socialist movement in the Netherlands, Reich's Commissioner Seyss-Inquart made a momentous announcement. Just returned from a special conference in Berlin with Adolf Hitler, Heinrich Himmler, Anton Mussert and the Dutch Nazi burgomaster of Rotterdam, Frederik Ernst Mueller, he solemnly revealed that the Fuehrer had recognized the Nationaal-Socialistische Beweging (or N.S.B.) as the only bearer of political life in the Netherlands and had appointed Anton Mussert, the N.S.B. chief, as Leader of the Netherlands' people. "He and his party," Seyss-Inquart declared, "will henceforth be consulted on all important matters concerning the administration of Holland."

During the Berlin meeting Hitler had laid down three principles for the German attitude towards the Netherlands. They were:

1. The Germans will not treat the Dutch as a vanquished nation. They are to share as equals in all consequences, rights and duties of the New Order. There must be an authority to assume responsibility for such a partnership.

2. The Netherlands must be National-Socialist. That is, the Dutch people must prove to be "safe" for the New Europe and must make a total effort to assist in the materialization of the New Order.

3. The N.S.B. and Mussert will be considered leaders of the Netherlands' people.

There was great rejoicing inside the ranks of the N.S.B. At last, after thirty months of strife and wrangling, the "God-given Fuehrer" had plainly told the world that Anton Adriaan Mussert was to be his one and only prophet—for the eternal benefit of Holland. However, those who were not carried away by the frenzied outbursts of enthusiasm and had listened more critically to the cautious wording of Seyss-Inquart's announcement, had not failed to observe that the "additional" power with which Leader Mussert found himself endowed, was not of much significance.

True enough, all attempts at recognition of competing Nazi parties and groups had been suppressed once and for all; and it was equally evident that the last obstacles to a swift increase of N.S.B. influence in the administrative machinery had now been taken successfully. Nonetheless, there was no mention of forming a Dutch Nazi government authorized to take its own measures—subject, of course, to ultimate approval from Berlin.

Instead Seyss-Inquart removed all doubt that the new glory would *not* include responsibility for any really important measures. He emphasized that the "Germans would continue to control the country as long as the war lasts." Adolf Hitler was leaving his own officials actually ruling the Netherlands because he did not as yet wish to decide the country's future place in the New Europe. Such a decision could only be taken when the frontiers of that New Europe had been determined. To forestall every chance of misunderstanding as to Mussert's executive power, Seyss-Inquart concluded, "Of course, military matters will take precedence, and I will therefore be solely responsible for all final decisions."

So as to soften the blow a little he had a suave compliment for the N.S.B. "If we had not had Mussert and the N.S.B.," he declared dramatically, "things would have shaped up badly for the Netherlands. The German attitude remains unaltered. The future freedom of the Dutch people depends upon themselves. They can now share the task of reconstructing Europe as our equals and our partners."

It was, indeed, a very small crumb of ruling power which the Germans threw to Anton Mussert. But something had to be given to him, some kind of payment was long overdue. The Dutch Nazi leader had pleaded so long with Hitler for a little authority, he had so consistently demonstrated his readiness to collaborate, to sell his country to the New Order with everything and every person in it. From among his followers Mussert had provided a few thousand "warriors" who had hastily been shipped to the abattoirs of the eastern front; something had to be done to encourage him in the not inconsiderable task of providing more Hollanders to fight for the Fuehrer in Russia.

Throughout the years of occupation Mussert had been beset by the untiring activity of competitors, each and every one of them considering himself the best man to play the role of chief Quisling. This intrigue and squabbling had cramped the "leader's" style. It had been instrumental in withholding from him the support of thousands of Nazi sympathizers who followed their own little Fuehrers, in the hope of seeing them come out on top. Here was something the Germans could eliminate without sacrificing a single iota of their own authority.

As a matter of fact, the N.S.B. had already been the only officially acknowledged political party in the occupied Netherlands since late in September, 1941 when its last important rival—the N.S.N.A.P. (Nationaal-Socialistische Nederlandsche Arbeiders Partij) *, headed by the annexationist Dr. Van Rappard—was disbanded. Until that time Van Rappard seemed to stand as good a chance as Mussert to win the ultimate and complete "confidence" of the Germans. He had openly taken up the cudgel for a Greater Germany of which the Netherlands would be an integral part. Besides, the N.S.N.A.P. had recognized Adolf Hitler without reserve as "the highest Fuehrer."

As often as he got the opportunity, Van Rappard publicly emphasized the importance of the Greater German idea, as contrasted with Dutch nationalism and "narrow-mindedness." "There is no such thing as Dutch culture," he once exclaimed, "there is no Netherlands' history and the existence of a Netherlands' language is hardly more than an illusion."

This strange Hollander, more of a Teuton than the most fanatical Heinrich or Fritz, would have liked nothing better than to see the independence of the Netherlands—so dearly bought by his ancestors in an eighty years' struggle—exchanged for a German declaration that henceforth it would again be part and parcel of the Reich. In him the Nazis had found a super-traitor whose very enthusiasm made him too hot to handle. Whatever their ulterior wish might be, to have elevated Van Rappard to the rank of leader

---

*See page 34.

of the Netherlands would no doubt have met with a wave of revolt and ridicule. It would have aggravated the chaos which already had got a firm hold upon the administrative machine. By his very eagerness to "go all out" for inclusion of his country in a Greater Germany, Van Rappard signed his own Certificate of Political Incompetence.

Yet for many months the occupation authorities wavered between taking a public stand in favor of either Van Rappard or Mussert. They left these two to their endless disputes, thereby reducing the influence of either party and allowing themselves ample time to spy the land. Only a few days before the dissolution of the N.S.N.A.P., Van Rappard addressed a meeting at Rotterdam in which he stressed once more that his party fostered one ideal only: to help bring about the Greater German union. Several "distinguished German guests" were present at this gathering; but none of them gave the slightest intimation that Van Rappard's fate was all but sealed. However, less than a week afterwards Mussert's Volk en Vaderland, obviously acting with the consent of the Germans, invited its membership to tear from fences and walls throughout the country the N.S.N.A.P. posters with legends prophesying the coming "return" of the Netherlands to the Greater German family.

Behind the scenes Van Rappard was having one of the most unpleasant experiences of his life. He was ordered to recant, to don the penitential garb and declare before everyone willing to listen that the N.S.N.A.P. would discontinue functioning "until further order." To sweeten the bitter pill somewhat, Van Rappard was allowed to add that "all district leaders and other officers of the N.S.N.A.P., in full agreement with their membership, had decided to give the Nationaal-Socialistische Beweging of Anton Mussert a chance to work unobstructedly in bringing about the reconciliation of the Netherlands and Reich's German peoples."

It was a triumph of which Anton Mussert bragged times out of number, emphasizing the close friendship existing between himself and Hitler, "reassuring" his audiences over and again that the Fuehrer—"who with Mussolini carries the fate of Europe upon his shoulders"—did not intend to incorporate the Dutch into a Greater Germany. The policy of the N.S.N.A.P. had been one of "inciting the Netherlands nation against their German brothers." Now, as head of the only recognized political movement, Mussert made a bid for the complete confidence of the recalcitrant Dutch.

Why withhold their trust from him who had so constantly fought (and with such outstanding success!) for a lasting independence of the Netherlands within the framework of Hitler's New Order?

To help him in his terrific and thankless battle for public recognition, the Germans—on October 10, 1941—allowed him to publish a letter from the Fuehrer which was supposed to eliminate the last vestiges of suspicion regarding the integrity of Mussert's true Netherlandership.

"Be it said," the Fuehrer's announcement read, "that those speaking of, or striving for, the annexation of the Netherlands by Germany, or the inclusion of Holland in the Reich, act against the clearly pronounced wish of the Fuehrer.

"We emphasize that this declaration is a result of the truly fanatical activities of N.S.B. leader Anton Adriaan Mussert against those who had adopted annexationism for their device. Thanks to Mussert, thanks to this 'conscious' member of the German tribe, thanks to this Netherlands National-Socialist, Holland will not become German. Holland will remain itself."

But soon afterwards Mussert began to use a phraseology which in many respects sounded suspiciously like Van Rappard's oratory. He spoke of the Fuehrer as "the leader of all Germanic peoples"; he discussed a long and involved plan concerning a "Reich's Netherlands," which would be part of a Germanic nation numbering no less than 140 million souls. Slowly but surely, pleasing his masters and adopting an attitude which would ultimately yield the same results as the too impulsive outspokenness of Van Rappard, Mussert was endeavoring to qualify for the coveted post of head of a Dutch Nazi puppet government.

In the interval the only responsibility resting upon the N.S.B. was, in the words of Seyss-Inquart, that of "educating the people of Holland to political comradeship with the Reich." In other words: nothing had changed except for the dissolution of the N.S.N.A.P. and the subsequent infiltration of Van Rappard's followers into the N.S.B.—a not altogether welcome expansion, as every Van Rappard-man carried with him the suspicion of joining with the sole purpose of forming opposition cells within the Mussert ranks.

The next few months turned out to be most difficult, and little encouraging for the N.S.B. The only bright spots came in October and November, 1941 with the arrival of American troops in the Netherlands West Indies. Those Allied safety measures, taken with the full cognizance, approval and collaboration of the Netherlands Government in London and with the sole purpose of strengthening the protection of these strategically vital points in the western hemisphere, with their oil refineries (Curaçao, Aruba) and bauxite mines (Surinam), were decried as "traitorous sell-outs arranged for by the London emigrants. Those sales will never be recognized by the people of Holland as they were made without their consent."

The Nazi version of these defense reinforcements, which in the course of time have worked out exactly as they were planned, told of an outright sale of the West Indies to America. For many days in succession the controlled radio filled the air with vituperations against the "hucksters who for a few silverlings had given away the colonies for which generations of Netherlanders worked and died.'" Prime Minister Pieter S. Gerbrandy was pictured as a creature filled with uncontrollable hatred, performing duties "which remind the observer of the unbalanced meanderings of a madman." "We shall never accept this barter, this looting of our colonies," one broadcaster declaimed with feeling. And a colleague hastened to explain that the "barter" of Surinam had been arranged for by Princess Juliana in person during her visit to President Roosevelt, earlier in the year.

The Dutch Nazis made whatever they could of these two incidents; but the sum total of their fulminations was nothing as compared with the chances offered them by the Netherlands' declaration of war against Japan which followed immediately upon the treacherous Pearl Harbor attack. They never tired of condemning Queen Wilhelmina, her government and the responsible officials in the Netherlands East Indies for thus "jeopardizing the colonial possessions of the Netherlands' people." No opportunity was missed to emphasize how different would have been the relationship with Nippon had N.S.B.'ers held sway in the Indian Archipelago.

"I might be willing to forgive the fugitive Queen that she placed our people in the wrong camp, that she left this country in days of battle," the magnanimous Mussert declared in one of his speeches, "if only she had kept the Indies out of the war. But what happens? War is declared by Japan on England and the United States. The Japanese emphasize that they have no other enemies than China, England and America. I sighed with relief when I read that; I felt thankful because of this chance of survival offered to the Indies. But instead Queen Wilhelmina declares war on Japan . . . To combat such madness is impossible."

Exactly a week after the outbreak of the war in the southern Pacific, the N.S.B. commemorated its tenth birthday. Only a few days previously Mussert had enjoyed another heart-to-heart talk with Hitler and had also gone through the rather discouraging experience of hearing the great man admit in a farcical sitting of the so-called Reichstag that his mighty plans to break up the Russian armies before the winter had dismally failed. Nonetheless, the Fuehrer's bad luck did not mean that Mussert was forced to return to Holland empty-handed. On the contrary, he brought with him quite a number of copies of a beautiful photograph showing Adolf Hitler busily engaged in shaking him warmly by the hand. Soon afterwards these historic documents were offered for sale throughout the Netherlands at the reasonable price of one dime apiece.

Apart from this invaluable present Mussert was carrying back something else. For some time past there had been dark hints that on December 14, 1941 Mussert and the N.S.B. would be officially invested with full powers. The rumors had in no way been discouraged by official Nazi instances; but a stray few courageous journalists took their lives into their hands by publishing editorials in which Mussert was warned that he would take a great responsibility upon himself, "as his task cannot be fulfilled without severe clashes with large sections of the Dutch people who are not ideologically prepared for a change which they fail to see in the light of the actual situation."

The Dutch Reformed Church of Amsterdam invited the believers to Sunday morning services by means of large advertisements—a procedure thus far unheard of in the annals of Netherlands' church life. The advertisements served to announce that in all churches the sermon would be based upon Matthew, Chapter 11, Verse 3, "Art thou he that should come, or do we look for another?"

The N.S.B. birthday ceremonies were held at Utrecht; as usual the meeting attracted a crowd of "comrades." The leader went through the conventional inspections of his Storm Troopers, the SS and the Youth Storm. There was the mass assembly attended by 6,000 enthusiasts who were requested to divest themselves of their overcoats so as to provide more "living room" for their neighbors . . . A feeling of great tension governed this crowd.

It reached its summit during the last-minute ceremonial entrance of Seyss-Inquart, Anton Mussert, deputy N.S.B. leader Van Geelkerken and other high-ranking officials of the German and Dutch Nazi parties.

One address followed the other; numerous pugnacious songs were sung; but none of the Dutch or German speakers brought the message which the gathering had been impatiently awaiting. Finally Seyss-Inquart arose and after many introductory platitudes, came to the vital issue.

"It was difficult for your leader," he said, "to take the right decision in this important hour. But the unfailing instinct of the man and the National-Socialist—whose only care is the well-being of his people—has moved Mussert to decide that his party and he must be placed in the very center of a community which has sworn to build up a new and better order, a happier Europe—even at the risk of their very lives.

"The conclusion I have arrived at on the basis of Mussert's decision, is my decree that henceforth only one political party can be tolerated in the Netherlands, and that is the National-Socialist movement under its leader Anton Mussert. I have accordingly ordered as of today that all societies of a political nature still existing in this country will be considered dissolved.

"This outcome of Mussert's ten years' old struggle lays upon all Netherlands National-Socialists, as well as on the Dutch people, special obligations towards the greater Commonwealth of Germanic nations in Europe. Remain true to the N.S.B.," Seyss-Inquart concluded, "and be hard. For membership of the N.S.B. or of one of its affiliated organizations is, the Lord knows it, no pleasure."

There was the usual hysterical upheaval, the wild, uncontrolled shouts of approval, the mass singing of battle songs. But when all the noise and fury had died down and the true-believers had returned to their hearths, quite a number of them must have realized how cruelly they had been deceived.

What was the meaning of this "dissolution of all other political parties"? Less than nothing. On July 5, 1941 all existing political parties had been disbanded, including the Netherlands Union which as a rallying point for all those bereft of their usual political outlets, had grown too swiftly to the liking of the German authorities and was then comprising more than 800,000 members. One by one competing National-Socialist parties and Fronts had disappeared from the scene. Van Rappard's creation had been dead and buried for nearly three months. Practically speaking the N.S.B. was, therefore, the only tolerated political formation in the country. On this memorable December 14 that fact had been officially recognized—and this was all.

It turned out to be a tempest in a teapot, and the Reich's Commissioner's special appeal for unity carried with it the additional burden of having to adopt the hated followers of Van Rappard in the N.S.B. at a much quicker rate than heretofore. On January 24, 1942 the N.S.N.A.P. was officially fused with Mussert's party. A little later when in the opinion of the Dutch Nazi leader, Van Rappard was priding himself too much on his share in the fusion, he launched an attack upon the newcomers and denied there had been anything like an official fusion. Unfortunately this very expression had not only been used in a number of Dutch broadcasts, but it had also appeared in the official Nazi newspapers. The fact remained that the members of the former N.S.N.A.P. did not exactly flock to Mussert's movement; by the middle of March, 1942 only about a thousand had joined him. On April 24, 1942 Van Rappard, without a word of farewell for conqueror Mussert, left political life and rejoined the German SS to which he had originally belonged. The last that was heard of him was his departure for the eastern front in September of the same year.

Dissatisfaction among the Dutch Nazis was general, but to voice it was a different matter. The Germans themselves cut short any effort in this direction by "encouraging" the publication of an editorial in the controlled press in which the writer said that Mussert would doubtlessly have been better satisfied if he had been made leader of the Netherlands people. "The fact that this nomination has not yet been made, might give some spiteful people undiluted pleasure. But the main thing now is to prove what Mussert meant exactly when he talked of the future connections between the Netherlands people and the New Europe, in the light of a Germanic peace conception."

*

The rest of that winter and of the second occupation year brought no change in the position of the N.S.B. Mussert's status remained as vague as it had ever been; Seyss-Inquart held the reins firmly in his own hands. Despite all efforts to win over large sections of the Netherlands people, the N.S.B. showed no growth whatever. On the contrary, loyal Dutch never slackened in their obstruction and denigration of the Nazis.

Towards the height of the summer of 1942 Mussert made one of his strangest contortions to win the sorely-coveted trust of his unwilling fellow countrymen. For a selected group of Nazi enthusiasts he assailed German imperialism and shouted defiantly that the "German Reich is Germany's affair and Holland is a Dutch affair. Versailles was unable to destroy Germany but neither has there been an enemy, ever since the Spanish wars, who succeeded in subjugating the Netherlands."

Far from unleashing upon himself the wrath of the German authorities, Mussert was invited to print his speech in full in his own weekly, Volk en Vaderland. Besides, the greater part of it was broadcast on August 22, via the controlled Hilversum radio. At one point of this talk Mussert said, "German imperialism desires to undermine the existence of the Netherlands people in favor of German capitalism. It wishes to make the Dutch so poor and cause so many to become unemployed that it will be an easy matter to recruit coolies for work in East Europe among them." He pleaded for a "Federation of European States," composed of European countries with the German Reich for nucleus, and under the general leadership of Adolf Hitler. However, each member of this Federation was to be an independent state, with one common defense machine for all, under German command.

He dwelt upon the part his movement would play in the "independent" Holland of a German-led Confederation. It would leave all churches, with the exception of the Jewish, free to follow their religious practices. "Something" would have to replace the controlling function of the erstwhile Parliament because "otherwise a state of absolutism would exist, leading to a terror system which would reduce the whole nation to slavery for the benefit of a small group of exploiters who lust for power and thirst for gold." The Netherlands State would, therefore, require a national-political core which was to be composed of "clean and corruption-free N.S.B.'ers." "The head of state who, as leader of the N.S.B., would be anchored in the nation, must enjoy the full confidence of the Fuehrer. He must be carried by the trust of the members of the N.S.B. and must win the ever-increasing devotion of the entire people by the righteousness of his actions."

The whole thing was obviously another effort—made with the connivance of the German authorities—to convince the determined Dutch that "Mussert was, after all, *the* man for them." A leader independent enough to call the German imperialists names and to chide them "because they dared speak deprecatingly of the Dutch language, which as a bearer of Art and Sciences is in no way inferior to German," could surely be trusted to have the interests of his own people and country at heart!

However, the huge majority of Netherlanders did not take the bait. There may, at first, have been some astonishment among them about this change of face but it was quickly realized that Mussert would not have dared to say the things he did before they were censored and approved by his German bosses. They definitely refused to accept N.S.B. leadership, or to welcome Anton Mussert as the man who in the new Confederation of European States was going to guide them to the gate of a millenium of prosperity and happiness.

And so the German gift to Mussert's party, on December 14, 1942, its eleventh birthday, was not yet to be what he had so fervently hoped for. He still remained the peon at the beck and call of his masters. Now that all efforts had failed to "popularize" him with the masses, he was given another chance to *earn* the ruling power he had been yearning for. On promise of getting together an army of 100,000 young Hollanders, he was decorated with the as yet empty title of "Fuehrer of the Netherlands."

But after a lapse of seven weeks during which little or nothing changed in existing conditions, the new "Fuehrer" officially announced on February 3, 1943 that he had surrounded himself with an executive body, bearing the name of "The Secretariat of State of the National-Socialist Movement of the Netherlands." Up to that time the N.S.B. had its headquarters in Utrecht; but now it was removed to The Hague—the seat of the Netherlands government until the invasion. To form his Secretariat, Mussert used practically every "topnotcher" in his party, with the exception of Prof. T. Goedewaagen. A few weeks previously this man had, for some unknown reason, been relieved of his duties as Secretary-General of the Department of Culture and Public Enlightenment and as President of the Culture Chamber, and was "kicked upstairs" to a professorship at Utrecht University.

Among the chosen members was C. van Geelkerken, cofounder and second in command in the N.S.B., to whom was entrusted the Secretariat of Home Affairs and National Security. Professor Robert van Genechten, who betrayed Belgium, his motherland, during the first World War and had escaped heavy punishment only by seeking refuge in Holland, was given his second promotion in a fortnight. He was made Secretary of Education, Arts and Sciences in the new Mussert Secretariat. Only a week before he had been appointed to the post of Commissar for South Holland province. Meinoud M. Rost van Tonningen, head of the Netherlands Bank and Director of the Netherlands East Company for the settlement of Netherlanders in the German-occupied Ukraine and Latvia, became Secretary of Finance and Economy.

The remaining Secretariats were distributed as follows: Construction and Roads—W. L. Z. van der Vegte, head of the Dutch Nazi Economic Front and Director-General of Post and Telegraph who had thus far solely "distinguished" himself through ruining the Dutch broadcasting system and by providing the people with new postage stamps, in consolation for a slowly deteriorating postal delivery system. The Secretariat of Agriculture and Fisheries was given to Folkert E. Posthuma,* one time Minister of Agriculture, Nazi sympathizer and finally Chief of the Special Commission on Agricultural Planning for the Netherlands. Public Enlightenment went to Dr. H. Reydon of Haarlem who at Goedewaagen's "resignation" had already been appointed Secretary-General for that department. Before this former editor of Volk en Vaderland could devote himself to his new task, however, he was shot and seriously wounded by an unknown assailant in his apartment at The Hague. His wife, an ardent Nazi devotee herself, was killed.

C. van Ravenswaay, burgomaster of the town of Utrecht, became the new Secretary for Social Affairs.** During the occupation years this official managed to build up for himself a particularly unsavory record. Before being appointed to the mayoralty of Utrecht, he headed the municipality of Zaandam where he became involved in a very unpleasant triangle affair. This disgusted many of his aldermen to such an extent that they expressed a wish to resign en bloc, and remained at their posts only at Mussert's special command. When Van Ravenswaay left Zaandam, he had managed to accumulate a financial deficit for that town of six to seven thousand guilders (about $4,000). As soon as he was installed at Utrecht he appointed a former convict to Director of the Municipal Social Services; a grocer's clerk who had been dismissed

*See page 110.

**An attack was made on Van Ravenswaay on February 12; according to a subsequent Hilversum broadcast, he was killed on the spot.

for fraud, was elevated to the rank of Senior Clerk of the Utrecht municipality. Soon afterwards, however, Van Ravenswaay was forced to announce that Utrecht's financial administration had "run into serious difficulties." Simultaneously he dismissed the non-conformist aldermen of Finance, Social Affairs and Security and usurped their duties himself.

Dr. K. Keyer, until now head of the Nazi Medical Front, was made Secretary for Health. The entire cabinet was placed under the leadership of Dr. J. H. Carp, once known as a splendid jurist and a profound admirer of Spinoza's philosophy. Carp, whose political ideas had been mainly reactionary with outspoken disdain for the masses, had gradually turned towards Nazism. His hatred for anything French was almost proverbial, while his knowledge of and interest in Anglo-Saxon affairs had been very limited. From 1937 on Carp made no secret of his totalitarian sympathies, sentiments which were probably strengthened by the circumstance that he was never offered a chair at Leyden University, to which distinction he had believed himself fully entitled.

Apart from this Secretariat of State the "Fuehrer of the Netherlands," to demonstrate his newly-acquired importance, appointed a personal cabinet headed by Jonkheer D. Blocq van Scheltinga. But even now there were some Nazi leaders left who had not been given a specific place in the new constellation. They, one and all, were made into "authorized representatives" (gemachtigden) with instructions to work under the Secretariat. Among them were the infamous Woudenberg and Roskam, respectively heading the Nazi Labor Front and Nazi Agrarian Front, and Lt.-Gen. Hendrik A. Seyffardt who had managed to make himself thoroughly ridiculous through his vain efforts to form a Volunteer Legion.* He fell by the hand of an unknown attacker (February 5, 1943)—even before the Secretariat could hold its first official meeting. Also included among the "gemachtigden" was Dr. W. A. Herweyer who for some time past had been functioning as Nazi head of the Germanized Hilversum radio.

The formation of these two bodies was a grave menace and so, almost immediately after the latest Mussert move became known in London, Prime Minister Pieter S. Gerbrandy broadcast a clearly-phrased warning to the people of the occupied homeland. "Germany is badly short of administrative officials and talent," he said. "The sooner it can leave the administration of the Netherlands to

---

*See page 176.

others, the better for its war effort—provided, of course, that administration is left to persons who have sold themselves body and soul to the enemy and thus look after German interests first . . . The Dutch Nazi party's task is still primarily advisory and only partly administrative. It will depend upon the future course of events whether the N.S.B.'ers will actually obtain the power they desire so passionately . . .

"It is your legal government's duty to inform you which attitude all Netherlands' Civil Servants must take under the new circumstances . . . They must oppose and undo all measures (taken by or at the advice of the new Secretariat). This especially applies to all those measures aimed at strengthening the German war potential. Not only executive matters in this respect must be opposed and thwarted, but also all preparatory measures intending to feed the German war machine with Dutch goods and people . . . But you should also resist all measures which can support the enemy and injure our own people . . . No Netherlander can now have doubts concerning his duties. The Queen, the government and the country demand your participation in the struggle for the liberation of our territory."

The Nazis were obviously starting a new drive to obtain German acquiescence in their attempts to take over the reins of administration. Soon after Mussert's announcement, the Nationale Dagblad wrote that "the second phase, the battle for the soul of the Dutch people" had begun. "It is a fight to get the Netherlands' nation behind Mussert and the Dutch-Nazi movement," the paper said. And it added: "We know that the number of Dutchmen now behind Mussert is very small. Yet, that does not worry us. The people's greatest deeds have always been performed by a determined minority."

Mussert's weekly Volk en Vaderland, even went a step further, admitting that "the political schooling of the greater part of our party members is not too advanced. Probably only a few of the comrades expected the party to be allowed to take over complete power," the writer confessed. "But evidently the time was ripe to give more authority to our movement. People inside and outside the party may be sure that Mussert would not have accepted these powers unless he were convinced he is able to handle them properly."

The new departure made it clear how dangerously the heads and hearts of Anton Mussert and his satellites had swollen since that memorable anniversary party of December, 1942. But one thing is certain: whatever real or imaginary power the German invaders will decide to yield to these deplorable, cringing creatures, it will never be able to change their position in the eyes of all patriotic Netherlanders. To more than 99% of the population they remain unspeakable outcasts whose names will for all time be synonymous with the blackest treason and the most revolting cowardice.

*

The "threat of Bolshevism to civilization" is an old and well-beloved theme in the Nazi song book and during the first year of the occupation it was assiduously repeated. Goebbels' propaganda plant turned out atrocity tales by the dozen, most of them concerning the Russian attack on Finland which, in truth, had left a bad taste in the mouths of many Hollanders. However, even the man in the street had had plenty of opportunity during the last few years to find out that of all nations Germany was surely the least entitled to the right of championing Christian ideals and tolerance. This sugary-sweet sympathy with "poor little Finland" sounded too much like the fox's pity for a dove which the hunter's shotgun has fatally wounded. To recognize in Hitler the "protector of the rights of the small nations" was asking rather too much of anyone in his sound mind, in view of what had happened only a year or so before, in that fateful dawn of May 10.

After the outbreak of hostilities between Germany and Soviet Russia on June 22, 1941 it became more and more difficult for the Nazis to use their anti-Bolshevist propaganda for the benefit of occupied Holland. Whatever their political hues, the Dutch could not help feeling true admiration for the courage and military prowess shown by the Russian armies. Indeed, this had nothing to do with pro- or anti-Communist beliefs. As the battles grew fiercer and the Russians defended every town, village and street with indomitable steadfastness, the people of the Netherlands realized that—whatever objections one might have against the political Soviet system—the bolsheviks had shown more sense of reality, more preparedness and patriotism than quite a few of the democratic western European governments. It was hard to understand the tales distributed for years, in which Russia was pictured as a full-fledged slave state. When witnessing so unified a defense, so deep a belief in the cause for which a nation of more than 180 million souls was fighting, it was impossible to deny the stimulating effect of such epic behavior upon the democratic peoples under enemy domination.

Goebbels might shout himself hoarse and declaim the horrors of the Tcheka and the secret Soviet police, but the Dutch knew too much of Himmler's Gestapo and of Rauter's Green "Security" Police. The little clubfooted doctor of Berlin might yell his warning against the "bloodhounds of Moscow" who would not halt at the Netherlands' frontiers in their murderous march, but the Dutch had seen the deadly advance of German panzer divisions and witnessed the ruthless attacks of paratroopers and shrieking, heavily-armed Stuka divers.

At times the radio announcers to whom the distribution of Goebbels' latest fantasies were entrusted, surpassed themselves and served up such utter nonsense that instead of raising gooseflesh, as they undoubtedly meant to, they made the proverbially calm and stolid Dutchmen laugh and listen as they would to an amusing comedian. To quote one example, this was what the Hilversum radio made "a voice from the eastern front" say in a broadcast on April 7, 1942:

"I would like to tell you something of the punishment dealt out by the Bolsheviks. Buttons were cut from coats, vests and trousers of prisoners so that they were obliged to hold on to their clothes wherever they went. Apart from the blows they had to endure from their Bolshevist judges during interrogation, they were beaten into unconsciousness with rubber bludgeons. After such tortures the victims were unable to eat as their internal organs, such as kidneys and liver, had been damaged. Their fingers were turned back and pierced with iron pins. Needles were inserted below their fingernails; the skin of fingers and hands was torn off. Cheeks and nostrils were burned with red-hot irons. They were alternately placed in ice-cold and boiling-hot water. They were hung by the neck with their toes just above the ground. Arms and legs were broken, the skin cut open and lumps of flesh torn out. The ears of some prisoners were clipped in the shape of flowers. Sometimes the victims were buried nude, their hands inserted below the skin of their own bodies. They were bound naked to a pole and then slowly choked with red-hot wire. In other cases the prisoners were locked up in rooms of which the floor had been electrified so that they could not stand still for a second."

It was indeed a revealing picture of the innermost workings

FOREIGN TYRANTS, AND THEIR ACCOMPLICES

(*top*:) German officers saluting Nazi troops from the steps of a Ministry at The Hague; (*bottom, left*:) Reich's Commissioner Dr. Arthur Seyss-Inquart, Austrian traitor, now omnipotent ruler of occupied Holland; (*right*:) Air Gen. Friedrich Christiansen, military Governor, head of the Nazi occupation troops.

THE STORM TROOPS MARCH . . .

through the streets of a northern city. (*bottom, left*:) Anton Mussert, "leader" of the Dutch Nazi Movement, addresses a meeting under the 'protection' of the Swastika; (*right*:) efforts to nazify the Dutch: appeals to 'fight with Mussert,' to support the Nazi Winter Help and to join the nazified Trade Unions.

"FIGHT AGAINST BOLSHEVISM—UNDER YOUR OWN FLAG!"

(*top*:) Typical German posters appealing to the Dutch 'brothers' to join the fight in Russia. (*bottom; left*:) Anton Adriaan Mussert, Dutch Nazi "leader," and (*right*:) his intellectual competitor, Meinoud M. Rost van Tonningen, head of the Netherlands Bank.

"FRIENDLY" INVITATIONS

(*Poster on left*:) "Register for work in Germany; youths—make room for older men!"; (*right*:) another 'scare' poster against Russia, presenting Stalin as an oriental-looking monster.

of the sadist Nazi mind. It was a true report on the activities of the Gestapo as they have become known through the tales of victims who managed to escape from torture and from an almost certain death. Every kind of torment the Germans had tried or were to try on their defenseless victims, was described in an indifferent tone of voice, impersonally, as a man would read the latest stock-exchange rates or the tendencies of the commodity market. These tales and many of a similar kind which followed during the next few months,* were an insult to the intelligence of so highly developed a nation as the Dutch.

*

Hardly had the invasion of Russia begun than the Germans started an intensive recruiting drive throughout Holland. They urged Netherlanders between the ages of 17 and 40 to enlist with the Standarte Westland, the Dutch section of the German Waffen SS** and promised these volunteers "adequate reward." At the end of the war, or at any rate at the end of three years' service, the survivors would be endowed with a small farm or some other kind of settlement . . . But very little interest was shown for that splendid offer; not even the Dutch Nazis seemed much impressed by the prospect of becoming "landed gentry."

As usual, Max Blokzijl was picked to voice the disappointment of the German authorities. Three weeks after the outbreak of the German-Russo war, he angrily shouted into the long-suffering Hilversum microphone that "proportionally speaking, only a small minority of our population troubles to give the struggle the support it so fully deserves." He also chided the public for having failed to demonstrate its indignation about the stories and terrifying photographs of Russian "atrocities" in the Ukraine. Even the motion picture "Horrors of Lemberg," which was shown in all cinemas (and at the close of which there was flashed upon the screen the slogan: "Netherlanders—now you know what we are fighting against!") aroused little comment. A reporter of Mussert's Nationale Dagblad went to a performance and described the attitude of his neighbors as follows:

"Lady—why do you turn your head away? Don't you

*The summit was unmistakably reached when in the spring of 1942 the Commander of Mussert's Storm Troopers, a certain W. A. Zondervan, told a meeting at Groningen that with his mortal eyes he had witnessed how two Russian colonels were devouring their own orderly . . . Another "reporter" told of Russian children who "knew no joy, no fairy tales, no dreams. That is how the Bolshevist system has placed its stamp of bestiality on the poor, oppressed people of Russia."

**See page 147.

wish to see it? Do you think this sort of thing ought not to be shown? You refuse to look at such scenes of barbarism? Oh—you prefer to go home? And you, gentleman with your Netherlands Union emblem . . ., why are you laughing? Ballyhoo, you say? . . . Propaganda?"

A speaker for the nazified broadcast sighed wearily that everywhere in the country the rumor was afloat that Stalin had ordered a solemn church service which he would attend "in the front pew. People have now forgotten everything they had against the bolsheviks and hope these godless creatures will come out victoriously. This shows a complete lack of political experience and understanding," he complained.

It was evident that little or no credence was given to anything the German propaganda service tried to plant in Holland; and when "news" was provided under the label of N.S.B. authoritativeness, it found less belief than ever. Three weeks after the start of the German "march on Moscow," the Nationale Dagblad proclaimed that the "Russian armies were in a state of collapse"; and loyal Hollanders exchanged knowing smiles. In fact, the continuous assertions of the Dutch Nazis that Russia "was practically beaten to frizzles" became a source of profound amusement. In July the Dutch Nazi press saw "Stalin and his henchmen taking to flight through the empty wastelands of the Russian steppes." Towards the end of August Rost van Tonningen told an Amsterdam audience that the German armies would be standing at the Volga river "in a couple of weeks." On August 30, 1941 Mussert, with a sigh of relief, informed his followers that "the worst is now over in Russia."

Now and again the Nazi press gave thought to what the Russian leaders would do after their final defeat. The Nationale Dagblad predicted in one of its September issues that "in all likelihood the Soviet rulers are now exclusively thinking of their forthcoming ocean trip, to find refuge on North American soil."

It all sounded suspiciously like whistling in the dark . . .

Throughout the summer and the autumn of 1941 there was a fierce barrage of German propaganda articles in the Dutch press. Wading through this muddy conglomeration of fanfares and lies, leavened with some unassailably true reports of Nazi victories on Russian soil, one is constrained to feel genuine admiration for the people of Holland who, despite it all, never lost their confidence in the ultimate strength of the Allied armies. Wishful thinking took a predominant place in the reportage of those hectic months. As early as July 2, with even the vanguard of the German panzer troops at an enormous distance from Moscow, the Nieuwe Rotterdamsche Courant, once world famous for its reliable foreign news service, printed a five-column headline, "Is Moscow Being Evacuated?" A few days later it repeated the question, "Has Soviet Government Left Moscow?"

By August the same newspaper had had to change its views somewhat. It began to realize that though the Russian armies had been "annihilated" half a dozen times, the war might last throughout the winter. And thus, cautiously and tactfully, it came with the following headline: "Will Operations in Russia Last Through Winter? Berlin Says *Probably* Not."

In the meantime action on the Russian front had come to a virtual standstill. It was not before the first days of October that the Germans launched another terrific offensive against Moscow. On October 4 Adolf Hitler jubilated that the Russian defense had now been definitely broken . . . During the next week Mussert's daily brought the news that "Marshal Timoshenko had sacrificed his last usable army units" and that the Soviet Union no longer existed in a military sense. At the end of this braggadocio the Nazi-controlled Netherlands press was instructed to print the reassurance that "before the winter the war in Russia will be over." An intellectual N.S.B.'er, Professor Westra, prophesied in a learned article how the German armies would then turn towards the west, how the British "seeing the approaching catastrophe of a German landing," would try to throw over their present leaders and by means of a compromise with Germany would endeavor to save whatever there was left to save. Max Blokzijl, adding his share to the general supply of fantastic forecasts, told the world in a thundering tone of finality that "Stalin is lost. It has been a bloody and sub-human interlude—but now the curtain may come down."

However, something had gone wrong with the curtain's mechanism. Three weeks after Blokzijl's assurances there was no noticeable change in the Russian situation. The curtain was still very much up. In a somewhat less certain key Blokzijl informed his skeptical listeners that "the battle is practically decided. Moscow's armies no longer play a part of any importance."

Alas for this bewildered optimist! Leningrad and Moscow, however sorely beleaguered, fought off the enemy. No German ever set foot within their walls. Towards the end of November Timoshenko had chased the Nazis out of Rostov. On December 7, 1941 Russian cavalry penetrated the German lines before the Soviet capital; the German plans had hopelessly floundered. For six long winter months the depleted armies of Adolf Hitler went through indescribable sufferings whilst being pushed back, slowly but surely, towards the confines of Poland and Latvia.

This miraculous comeback of Stalin's armies placed Holland's Nazis in a difficult position. For even they began to realize that the Russian campaign was not, after all, a mere repetition of former German campaigns. Something had gone wrong with German invincibility . . . But there was little choice. They had ranked themselves on the side of the Hitler wolves' pack and with them they must howl in the forest.

The unwillingness of the large majority of Netherlanders to believe the inflated propaganda talk of Joseph Goebbels and his helpmates, was demonstrated again and again, most clearly whenever they were expected to make a real contribution towards winning the German-Russo war. First evidence of this had been given in the beginning of July, 1941 when the "Organization of N.S.B. Women" arranged for a collection in behalf of the German Red Cross. During four consecutive days every street of every town and village was honeycombed. Three weeks later the proceeds were published and the N.S.B. called the results "exceedingly satisfactory." The truth, however, was that this tremendous effort yielded only 80,000 Dutch guilders (approximately $43,200) or about 1/5 of the total amount gathered on a rainy December day in 1938 when quite spontaneously a nation-wide collection was held to assist those Jewish victims of Nazi persecution who had taken refuge in the Netherlands after the November pogroms.

The second failure was the effort to gather money for a Nazi ambulance to be sent to the troops in Russia. The idea was General Seyffardt's, but he did not derive much pleasure from it. More than a month after launching his appeal, only 75,000 guilders had been contributed—in sharp contrast with the generosity shown on pre-invasion occasions, such as the Russian famine of 1922 which elicited an immediate response of more than half a million guilders, or the collections for Finland which yielded one million six hundred thousand guilders.

Throughout the second occupation year the newspapers

were forced to carry a daily appeal asking for ambulance funds. No propaganda means were left unused to soften the hearts of the recalcitrant Dutch and make them part with some money. At their wit's end the Nazis often published spurious lists of contributions in which all of the donors used exquisite slogans exactly fitting the nature of their gifts . . . For example, there were the "wounded Dutch soldier who knows what an ambulance means on the battleground," "someone who has made much money in prewar Germany," "an 'old hand' who has fought in the Boer War," "a father whose son is at the east front," "for the courageous boys who hold our Dutch honor high"—and a host of other descriptions smacking suspiciously of a well-trained propagandist mind.

Now and again news items about "the" ambulance would appear to keep the enterprise from dying an inglorious death, but in February, 1942 the German wounded on the Russian front still had to make shift without their Dutch ambulance. It was announced at that time that the "military and specialist training of the ambulance staff is still to be perfected." At last, late in April, 1942, the car was given a ceremonious send-off . . . , with thirty men short of the necessary crew.

Another failure was the German effort to collect warm winter clothing for the soldiers at the eastern front. Officially, only German citizens resident in the Netherlands were to contribute. But soon the Dutch were graciously "allowed" to give their share in exchange for a "special receipt which at some later date will be replaced with an official document signed in behalf of the German people." A rumor that winter coats and furs would be requisitioned from passers-by in the streets did not appear to be founded. But the German army authorities did not hesitate to rob Dutch clothing factories and wholesalers of all they had in stock in the way of warm cover. Blankets, too, were requisitioned and exported in enormous quantities. This pillage went on throughout 1942, until there was nothing left worth stealing. Yet the shortage of adequate winter clothing for the troops on the east front remained great. It was, for example, not before January 10, 1943 that the Hilversum radio quoted a reporter with the Dutch Nazi troops in Russia who gave a detailed description of the men's sufferings from the cold. And he continued: "Today at last great news circulated through the trenches—*our winter clothing has arrived!* This afternoon overcoats, fur caps and mittens were distributed to some of us . . . We are fostering new hope now," he sighed in conclusion. "Maybe we are to get fur-lined boots, too!"

*

When the Dutch persisted in showing so little eagerness to share the glories of Hitler's armies, a variety of means was used to stimulate their martial sentiments. Day after day all journals appearing in the occupied territory were obliged to carry a "persuasive" one or two column "call to arms." Besides, special favors were promised to the relatives of those who would join the Nazi colors. Time and again the unwilling were invited to follow the "heroic example" of those who even before the Russian invasion had entered the German Waffen SS,* that élite corps whose special duty it was to spy among the members of the regular army—or its Dutch equivalent, the Standarte Westland.**

On the first of July, 1941 these Dutch SS enthusiasts had their baptism of fire. On the next day their Commander was reported killed "by a treacherous bolshevist shot from a cornfield." Thereupon the division marched in a southwesterly direction, penetrating deeper into Russia and assisting in the capture of Rostov. Some time afterwards Seyss-Inquart revealed that the division comprised about two thousand "Netherlanders"—but according to Dutch law these men had automatically lost their citizenship when taking service in the army of a foreign power. In Anton Mussert's imagination this number of Nazi "heroes" grew by no less than fifty percent. For on November 28, 1941 the N.S.B. leader declared in a radio speech: "Three thousand of our Dutch boys have helped to conquer the town of Rostov." He never announced, however, how many of "the boys" were massacred when only two days later the beleaguered town was retaken by the Russians.

As a special favor to the Netherlands sister-nation, Adolf Hitler had graciously consented to accept volunteers of related Nordic peoples for the German armies as from the autumn of 1941. However, the ardor shown to acquire this distinction was so small that the Fuehrer's "special offer" was never repeated. Whether, and if so how many, Hollanders ever did sign up with the regular German armies, was covered with the cloak of secrecy.

It is not difficult to comprehend why the few thousand Dutchmen who took up arms in behalf of the Great Protector, preferred to serve with the Standarte Westland or the SS. In

*See page 147.

**Shortly after the outbreak of the German-Russo war, the Standarte Westland was incorporated in the German SS division "Viking."

either corps they knew themselves among "friends"—safer, at any rate, than in the regular army ranks which harbored so many elements of doubtful reliability. It is a strange phenomenon that none of these men was used for the German Air Force. Evidently they did not inspire their Teutonic masters with sufficient confidence to put armed fighter planes at their disposal.

The poor results of such strenuous efforts to coax the Dutch into supporting the defense of Nazi Germany could not fail to make a painful impression upon the occupation authorities. There was no semblance of coherence between the various so-called National-Socialist groups. Each for itself claimed exclusive ownership of *the* recipe to mold the Dutch into a truly united nation. When one of them, Arnold Meyer, founder and chief of the totalitarian National Front, suggested that all political parties—including the Netherlands Union—should hastily form an independent Dutch Legion, he was fiercely attacked by a bevy of other "leaders." Mussert who, had he acted upon the suggestion of Arnold Meyer, might have opened up the possibility of attracting thousands of new members, declared highhandedly that anyone willing to serve the German cause could do so in the Waffen SS or in the N.S.K.K., the German Motorized Transportation Division in which around 1,500 N.S.B.'ers were already incorporated.*

Van Rappard whose N.S.N.A.P.** was still tolerated at that time, confirmed soon afterwards that Arnold Meyer's plans to form a Netherlands Legion were "nonsensical." "Our boys already fight in the Waffen SS, or are serving in the Standarte Westland!" he exclaimed at a party meeting in The Hague. "Therefore, Meyer's plans are not worth a further thought. Your last chance to save the honor of our nation and ensure the eternal freedom of our people has now arrived," he solemnly declared. "The first page of our new Socialist history is being written. You may now join the victorious German armies." And toward the end of his speech, in his usual effort to outdo the Germans in Teutonic sentiment, he came with the following exhortation: "The same socialist fire burns in your hearts, the same German blood beats in your veins. Unite with your German comrades, save the honor of your socialism, your German blood, your sense of immortal freedom!"

The Germans knew well that whatever help they could ex-

---

*See page 147.

**National Socialist Netherlands Labor Party.

pect, would necessarily have to come from the ranks of the N.S.B. and of other, smaller Nazi parties. At the same time, they realized that no appeal made by Mussert in person or by his party could hope to meet with great success. In fact, the call to arms would have to be based on purely anti-Communist slogans and detached from all connections with the hated N.S.B., or its conceited little "boss."

It must have been a rather unpleasant surprise for Mussert when the nazified news agency ANP, on the morning of July 6, 1941, distributed a report that the formation of a Volunteer Legion of the Netherlands To Fight Bolshevism had almost reached maturity. 'This Corps," the reporter explained, "is to be organized with the assistance of the various political parties and with the help of Dutch officers. Enlistment will be made possible through a special Netherlands Registration Bureau."

The legion was the brain child of 68 year old Lt.-General Hendrik A. Seyffardt, one time Head of the Netherlands General Staff, retired since 1934, and long suspected of strong totalitarian sympathies. It is hard to find an explanation for the attitude of that officer who, though ambitious and conceited, had been known in his day as an efficient and intelligent Chief of Staff. To say the least of it, German propaganda seemed to have got the better of him, so that he was capable of seeing the Nazi attack on Russia exclusively as a struggle against bolshevism, for the benefit of all Europe—a battle in which the people of the Netherlands must take part, to justify their claim to a share in the future advantages.

The first appeal of Hendrik Seyffardt was published on the front page of all Dutch evening papers and signed by the Reich's Commissioner himself. "The Fuehrer," it read, "has given us an opportunity to remain a separate nation. Thus our Volunteer Legion will have its own flag and its own Dutch officers." For the time being registration bureaus were established in Amsterdam, The Hague, Utrecht, Groningen, Deventer, Arnhem and Breda.

As in the case of Arnold Meyer's effort, Mussert showed himself thoroughly averse to this new plan. Immediately he wrote a sharply-worded article for his weekly Volk en Vaderland in which he advised the members of his Storm Troops to refrain from signing up with the new Volunteer Legion. Shortly afterwards he went even further and decreed that any N.S.B.'er intending to join Seyffardt's "Legion," would have to obtain the approval of his Party Headquarters.

At the start the German Propaganda Bureau did all it could to give the people of Holland the impression that the Volunteer Legion was being flooded with applications. For example, no less than six hundred of the Marechaussées (military police) had enlisted. They were, it was said, shortly to leave for the Russian front, led by their own officers. However, not a single word was published about the fate of this particular battalion. If ever it departed, it left Dutch soil in a deadly silence—rather an extraordinary procedure if one considers the publicity given to any subsequent departures for Russia, even of the smallest group.

On the first registration day huge crowds came together outside the various bureaus, not with the intention of enlisting but only to see who would be mad enough to offer themselves for slaughter upon Adolf Hitler's sacrificial altar. At the end of the day the ANP news agency blared forth triumphantly that *two hundred* men had been accepted in Amsterdam alone! It retained a suspicious silence, however, on the results in the other six towns. Nevertheless, it soon became known that in Meppel, for instance, only one applicant had turned up, and he a jailbird with two years' imprisonment awaiting him.

The more depressing the results, the louder the voice in which the Propaganda Bureau shouted of overwhelming successes. On July 23, hardly more than a fortnight after the foundation of the Legion, the Hilversum radio announced with hysterical joy that the total number of applications "exceeded all expectations." Simultaneously, it was made known that further registrations could take place during the following week while the present applicants were to be medically examined immediately. The pay would be the same as that accorded to German soldiers and everyone between the ages of 17 and 40 whose height was not less than 5 ft. 7 inches, would be welcome. Unfortunately, not one soul turned up anywhere, the completely empty registration offices becoming a source of unconcealed amusement to the entire populace.

When nothing else seemed to help, a few N.S.B.'ers were paid to come and "offer themselves spontaneously" once or twice each day in various registration bureaus. Even this crude subterfuge failed to yield results. And finally, on July 28, all registration offices were closed with the exception of those at Amsterdam and The Hague. The former was to remain open until August 1; thereafter only the main office at The Hague would continue to function. The official reason? "The run of volunteers on these recruiting offices has been so great thus far that it is a physical impossibility to handle all applications."

It was a tragi-comedy which gave rise to many a hearty laugh in those difficult days. Throughout the second year of occupation the Legion's registration bureaus remained tightly shut, though at the demand of Professor Goedewaagen's Department for Culture and Public Enlightenment, the "call to arms" continued to appear in all papers—every morning and evening.

Even before the close-down of the registration bureaus, the N.S.B. had found itself forced to print a notice on the front page of its Nationale Dagblad in which the public was informed: "In connection with rumors spread with great cunning and obstinacy by irresponsible elements, we are constrained to announce emphatically that the fight in the east has up till now caused no losses among the men serving in the Standarte Westland." In flagrant contradiction, however, the same week's issue of Volk en Vaderland carried obituary notices on "Obersoldat" L. van Trierum, 27 years of age, "who fell in action before Lemberg on July 2."

With neither the Waffen SS and Standarte Westland, nor the Volunteer Legion attracting sufficient men, Seyss-Inquart decreed in final desperation that "military or civil service in the struggle against bolshevism is not to be considered as service in a foreign army, or for a foreign State." In other words, Dutch citizens could henceforth join the German legions without losing their Netherlands nationality. Generous provisions were, moreover, made for the families of the volunteers. If they were bachelors, no less than 80 percent of their former salaries was regularly booked to their credit. Were they married and without children, their wives became entitled to the payment of 90 percent of their normal income. But most "reassuring" of all: they simply could not be dismissed from the posts they held before joining up. As to the personnel of the Netherlands Bank, for them even more favorable conditions were concocted. Not only were they to receive their full salaries during the period of their service but special allowances were fixed for their relatives, including generous pensions in case of death and high invalid pay should they return from the theater of war incapable of further work.

It was all of no avail. Not before July 26, 1941 was the first contingent of 650 men ready to leave; nearly 300 of them were N.S.B.'ers. Before their departure they listened to an address by Seyffardt who warned them that they were about to face an enemy "whom I cannot even compare with animals because wild beasts are too good for such a comparison. They are devils incarnate!" Thus encouraged, and enriched with an orange, white and blue flag, the new warriors marched to the railroad station which was decked out with green and flowers. Even the engine was hung with garlands of oak leaves. Dutifully the men chalked *"TO MOSCOW"* on each and every one of the carriages, the engines whistled—and off went the first contingent of the Netherlands Volunteer Legion. Two days later it arrived in Cracow for further training. In the beginning of August it left again to march "deep into Russia." All the while the troops were accompanied by Dutch Nazi press men who exhausted themselves broadcasting flamboyant reports to the people at home.

Around that time a second contingent left Holland. There were only 430 men in it, and of these no less than 340 were members of Mussert's movement. Though newspapers and radio gave endless descriptions of this splendid new outfit, eager to throw itself into the battle against Communism, they were in reality transported to Alsace Lorraine only. In late October these men had not yet proceeded any further. By then their initial zeal had waned considerably; one of them even found the courage to write a letter to the Nationale Dagblad in which he complained of the inferior food which was given him and his comrades day after day. He expressed a particular loathing for the German potato soup which he described as "something you try in vain to get used to."

*

In August, 1941 Anton Mussert, with surprising suddenness, changed his mind about the Volunteer Legion. Obviously, he had been made to realize that the N.S.B. was cutting a very poor figure indeed. Out of an alleged membership of 35,000 fighting men, less than 1,000 had thus far shown any inclination to take part in the "battle against Bolshevism." Volk en Vaderland therefore published a statement signed by Mussert in which he heartily welcomed the foundation of the Volunteer Legion and expressed the desire that his party members should no longer join the Standarte Westland or the semi-military motorized troops of the N.S.K.K.,* but enlist exclusively in the Legion. The head of the Dutch Nazi Storm Troopers, W. A. Zondervan, even excelled his chief in fervor by making the public suggestion that all Storm Troops should leave in a body for Russia!

*National-Sozialistische Kraftfahrer Korps.

This idea did not seem to please the majority of the Storm Troopers, however. Nor did Mussert like it very much; he needed these blackshirted ruffians too much for his own protection and that of his colleagues. Consequently, he hastened to announce that "new contingents of Storm Troopers will be allowed to leave only when I have made sure that a minimum of 10,000 men will remain available for the struggle on the home front." At the same time he ordered all male party members between the ages of 18 and 40 to join the Storm Troops without further delay, and warned all eligible members shirking to enroll that they would—without exception—lose their party number and be transferred to the non-active list.

These decisions caused little less than a panic among the heroic street brawlers. In the town of Enschedé they were summoned by their local chief and told that a new Storm Troopers' regiment of 3,000 men was being formed to help the Germans fight Bolshevism. A certain number of "volunteers" must be yielded by their section, and the moment had arrived to make a choice. Deep silence greeted this announcement. Finally the chief said, "I'll leave you alone for an hour; that will give you plenty of time to make up your mind who among you will go." When he returned to the meeting no choice had been made. He then suggested a draft but this idea, too, was rejected. Finally, he was forced to make the choice himself . . . That is how Enschedé delivered its quota.

In other townships the collaboration was equally "spontaneous" and all in all it took quite some time before a total of 1,400 men had been recruited. The remaining 1,600 had to be found among Hollanders domiciled within the Reich.

Faced with this sadly dwindling eagerness to serve the great cause, the Dutch SS issued a summons ordering all men liable for service in the Storm Troops to attend a meeting in which the matter of enlistment would be discussed. No apology would be accepted; attendance was compulsory.

But even this did not influence recruitment very much and it was October 11, 1941 before the first Volunteer battalion of a thousand N.S.B.'ers stood ready to depart. Mussert came out in person and made them take the oath to Adolf Hitler as "your Germanic Fuehrer." Defending himself against an unspoken accusation he later announced by radio that for this oath he took full responsibility upon himself, "as I am firmly convinced it was made in the interest of our country." By way of further sacrilege the ceremony took place in the courtyard of the Binnenhof, between the ancient buildings which for so many generations had been the seat of the Netherlands government.

For some months after their departure the W.A.* crusaders were lost from sight. They were, it appeared, going through their final training somewhere in East Prussia. On New Year's Eve of 1942, however, Anton Mussert, in the company of a few prominent N.S.B.'ers among whom were the Dutch "Lord Haw-Haw," Max Blokzijl, visited his braves. It transpired that "the boys" had experienced considerable difficulty in adjusting themselves to German discipline. In subsequent broadcasts Blokzijl, however hesitantly, had to admit that the habitual shouting ("*anschnauzen*") of the Prussian officers "had now and again been misconstrued." There was much in their treatment, he revealed, the boys had failed to appreciate. "But," he concluded, "grouching and grumbling is part and parcel of the make-up of any Hollander."

Around the middle of January, 1942 Anton Mussert launched another call to arms "for the defense of Europe, from the Grebbe River to the Ural Mountains." The appeal was heard but generally ignored. And so the inimitable Blokzijl was given another chance to say "a word of encouragement." Towards the end of April, after a protracted and rather painful silence of several months on the subject of triumphs in Russia, he jubilated via the Hilversum radio that "within a few days—or even a few hours—the signal will be given for the final attack upon the bolsheviks." Two more months elapsed, however, before the Germans started their colossal summer offensive against the greatly reinforced Russian armies.

Meanwhile, during the month of February, the Volunteer Legion had at last been thrown into action, and was suffering heavy losses. Though no clear picture was ever obtained of the hardships to which these misguided men were constantly exposed, details of their untenable living conditions would filter through from time to time. In the spring of 1942 one of them managed to make it known in Holland how the most fortunate among them were obliged to exist. "If the food-supply trucks or the field-kitchen fail to come our way for some days," he wrote, "we can choose between hanging around and starving, or trying to 'collect' ingredients of a kind, with which to prepare a meal. If you do

*W. A. = Weer-afdeeling, the name of the Dutch Storm Troops.

not wish to be in on those hunts, you may pretend to have rheumatism . . . and perhaps they will take you to the field hospital. We all complain of the bad food, the lack of news from home, the freezing cold, the stormy corners where we have to stand guard and where your ears and feet get numb in no time. There are lice and vermin too and, above all, there is the Russian malignancy we have to cope with . . ."

As if to underscore this doleful effusion, there came official confirmation that thousands of Dutch Nazis had been annihilated fighting on the eastern front. The few who did return to the Netherlands, either disabled or on furlough, found themselves exiled in their own country. To quote one example which was published in a nazified local paper: "Nobody showed the slightest interest in a certain volunteer who had just come back from the front and was eager to unburden his heart. He found himself surrounded by the wall of silence against which," the writer said, "every member of the National-Socialist movement is bound to hurt himself some time or other. Finally he could stand it no longer," the story proceeded. "This 'iron man' who throughout a long winter had gone through unimaginable privations, broke down and burst into tears of despair."

In one of its September issues the Nationale Dagblad disclosed that Dutch Nazi headquarters were receiving a steadily increasing number of anonymous letters containing newspaper clippings of death announcements made by relatives of N. S. B.'ers fallen on the eastern front. Most of these clippings had "congratulatory" slips attached to them. One of these read: "Splendid! Our warmest felicitations. Another 15,000 would be mighty fine!"

The Catholic clergy adhered rigorously to its policy of refusing to say mass for Nazis killed in action. One such case in particular was related of a Storm Trooper whose son had volunteered and was shot in Russia. One morning, soon after the death report had become known, the man found four words painted upon the wall of his house, "I killed my child."

By this time fear of being forced into fighting on the Russian front was all but paralyzing the Nazi Storm Troops; and Mussert's daily found it necessary to "pipe down" somewhat. Rumors that all Storm Troopers are to be drafted for service in Russia, it said, are absolutely unfounded. Mussert has only asked his Storm Troops if they would "care to join the Dutch regiments serving in Russia." In fact, enlisting for eastern Europe remained voluntary and would not be extended beyond a part of the W.A. formations. The need was still great to maintain quite a number of them on the home front, "where people are unable to behave well, even under the most decent occupation conditions."

Furthermore, as a special attraction for Dutch recruits, the press was made to announce that the Nazi authorities had greatly simplified marriage formalities for all men belonging to either the Dutch SS or to Seyffardt's "Volunteer Legion." Firstly, a member of these forces serving outside the Netherlands might be exempted from the need of requiring parental consent if his bride were less than 30 years old. Henceforth the German authorities would give such exemption. Secondly, a permit for marriage-by-proxy would no longer be required, the German military authorities being empowered to sign the necessary documents. Lastly, a widow or divorced woman need no longer wait the customary 300 days before remarrying, if her bridegroom belonged to the Dutch SS or the "Volunteer Legion."

But none of these efforts to coax Dutch Nazis into signing away their lives, yielded more than poor results. Besides, when in the early autumn the first "warriors" returned from the eastern front disabled in one way or another, they soon spread the news that all was not "beer, skittles and glory" in the Russian war zone. The presence of those disillusioned men proved a psychological boomerang to the recruiting efforts, because of their harrowing stories of hardships and horror.

As time went by, the number of death announcements in the Dutch newspapers grew alarmingly until in the end their publication was forbidden. The general attitude towards the few who managed to come back alive was by no means improving and in May, 1942 the German Commandant of the small town of Heiloo was forced to issue a warning in which he wrote, "It is outrageous that Dutchmen returning from the eastern front should be spat upon, as happens in this community. If the people do not immediately refrain from this provocation, I shall take the strongest measures against it."

In the summer of 1942 General Seyffardt—who had meantime obtained his first reward "for services rendered" by being nominated President of the Military Division of the Nazi Peace Courts*—began to pay sympathy calls on the relatives of Dutch Nazi volunteers whom he had sent to their death in Russia. He

*October 18, 1941.

offered these people his condolences, not only for the loss of their relatives but also because "you are living under such extremely difficult circumstances. Your neighbors only show you enmity; you are indeed having a very tough time." More than that, he presented the bereaved mothers with flowers, gave tobacco to the fathers and candy to the younger brothers and sisters. Thus the commemoration of the lost heroes became something in the nature of a beanfeast.

But abusive letters continued to be sent to such families, so that the Nationale Dagblad finally demanded the death penalty "for the criminals who write this filth."

The fact remained, however, that in hundreds of Netherlands households the departure of one of its members for the east front had brought about complete estrangement between him and his relatives. They refused to have any further contact with the "fighter against bolshevism." The number of those outcasts was so great that finally the N.S.B. was forced to create a special organization to look after their material and spiritual needs. In October, 1942 that institution placed large announcements in the newspapers. "Many of our comrades," it said, "have lost all connection with their relatives by volunteering. They cannot spend their leaves in Holland because they have been deprived of their homes. It is our obvious duty to help them. All volunteers on furlough from the east front should be welcomed in Dutch health resorts; and special homes and receiving centers must be arranged for them." As a further consolation for the Nazi heroes on leave, Peace judges went so far as to extend their protection to them under all circumstances. One such soldier, for instance, had removed a portrait of Prince Bernhard from a tavern wall and was subsequently ordered to pay a fifty guilders' fine (about $30) by a local police authority. Immediately the Peace Court reversed this sentence, the officiating judge declaring solemnly: "Any man who because of his love for his country, offers his life in the fight against bolshevism, cannot be expected to have regard for other people's views on the subject of royalty."

Shortly afterwards there was a Nazi meeting in Utrecht where Mussert, carefully repeating what his bosses had instructed him to say, told mothers, wives and fiancées of his volunteers that "the Allies would have invaded the Netherlands to open a second front if the Germans had not occupied our country." He also asserted that Germany had been forced into the war with Holland only

THE "CALL TO ARMS" . . .

Nazi posters in occupied Holland. (*left*:) 'Fight against bolshevism in the Elite Guard.' Its companion (*right*) has a similar appeal. In the background: silhouettes of historically-great Dutchmen: South African President Paul Krueger, and 17th century Admiral Michiel Adriaenszoon de Ruyter.

Voor Führer Volk en Vaderland sneuvelde op 18 November 1941 aan het Oostfront bij Schönfeld (Dnjepper), oud 25 jaar, onze beste Kameraad

BERNHARD YPEY

Vaandrig W.A.
Stamb.nr. 2734
Schütze Waffen-ϟϟ

Hij bracht het hoogste offer voor een Vrij Nederland in de komende Nieuwe Europa.

Namens de kameraden
Kring 34 der N.S.B., en Nederl. ϟϟ.
De Kringleider.
Maart '42.

Heden ontving ik het droevig bericht, dat op 24 Februari 1942 aan het Oostfront is gevallen in den strijd tegen het bolsjewisme, mijn innig geliefde man,

CORNELIS FREDERIK VAN RIJSSEL

in den leeftijd van 29 jaar

Hij stierf den heldendood voor Leider, Volk en Vaderland.

K. VAN RIJSSEL—THOMAS.

Zij offerden zichzelf Leider, Volk en Vaderla…

Heden ontving ik bericht, wederom twee Kameraden …ven hebben geofferd in …rijd tegen het Bolsjewism …meraad

DIRK LAMMERT ZINNEMERS

uit Zutphen (Kring 75)
Stamboeknummer 125426.
…eboren 14 Januari 1922 …
…neuveld op 14 April 1942 …
…lilipy.

…meraad

GEERARD PEDDEMORS

Doesburg (Kring 75 …nchem). Stamb.nr. 136230. …en 30 Januari 1912 en ge…eld op 16 Febr. 1942 bij

…e Kameraden werden op …leldenkerkhof te Selo …eraardebesteld. …roote inzet van deze kameraden strekke het …nt tot voorbeeld. Wij … deze kameraden door …k voor de Beweging ge…

De Districtsleider van D. 7
Geldersche Achterhoek:
A. W. J. BORGGREVEN.

Op 23 November 1941 viel bij Bolschekreperf-kaja in den strijd tegen het Bolsjewisme

---

… Lentemaand 1942 is …atilipy gevallen voor … Volk en Vaderland …rouwe kameraad

HUBERTUS SCHOLL

Sturmmann Legion Niederlande

…ger Verwundetenabzeichen in zilver.

Voor Leider, Volk en Vaderland gaf zijn leven aan het Oostfront

Legion Schütze

CORNELIS PIETER MASTRIGT

Rijswijk Z.-H.,
12 Juni 1942.

Bezoeken kunnen …gens uitstedigheid … worden afgewacht.

Heden bereikte ons de droeve tijding dat in den strijd tegen het Bolsjewisme onze lieve dappere zoon en broer

ARIAN KNIP

ϟϟ Schütze

op 20 Juni 1942, in den leeftijd van 22 jaar, den heldendood vond bij Stalino.

Hij werd ter aarde besteld op het Heldenkerkhof in Us…enskaja.

…emster, 12 Juli 1942.
…iddenweg 114

…ed forstoar rêstich ûs ljeave …n, Heit en Pake

KLAAS BARTELE VRIES

… binei 63 jier.

…tergeast, 23 Febr. 1942.

M. VRIES—Fokkema.

Apeldoorn:
Ir. J. B. VRIES i.i.
G. J. VRIES—Muller.

Hiermede heb ik den treurigen plicht het overlijden te melden van onzen Kameraad

C. van der Horst

in den ouderdom van 67 jaar.

De teraardebestelling heeft plaats gevonden op Dinsdag 9 Zomermaand op de Nieuwe Oosterbegraafplaats te Amsterdam.

Castricum,
9 Zomermaand 1942.

Namens Groep 188
Herbschleb

. . . AND ITS FINAL RESULTS

Death announcements culled from nazified Dutch newspapers. They all concern Dutch Nazi soldiers at the Russian front. The mark at the top of the announcements is the Runic "R" — one of the many symbols adopted by the Nazi "heroes."

because the Dutch people had stubbornly refused the formation of a National-Socialist government.

As an afterthought the "leader" had a few flattering words for his volunteers. "If our Storm Troopers had not gone to the Russian front," he shouted, "the people of this land would have no future. They had the choice of being soldiers, shoulder to shoulder with the Germans, or of becoming slaves. Already my Storm Troopers have made their choice—but the day and hour will come when our entire population must choose."

But neither such cajoleries nor the thinly-veiled menaces directed against all loyal citizens, swelled the ranks of Dutch volunteers. Though the Nazi party, according to Mussert's own statement, counted approximately 100,000 members with 30,000 men between the ages of 18 and 40, the total number serving the German war effort in any military capacity did not exceed 10,000 men. It was a far from impressive figure and the German authorities had no doubt made this very clear when in December, 1942 they decided to nominate Anton Mussert as leader of the Netherlands' people. The day after Anton's "promotion" Max Blokzijl said over the Hilversum radio that he had been "reliably informed" the Volunteer Army would be increased to 100,000. How this was to be done the renegade journalist did not bother to explain, but he added, "It's high time the Netherlands people open their eyes to realities and try to get a more complete picture of the political landscape. The time of totally independent peoples and communities," he concluded significantly, "is long past."*

It was and remained a shoddy affair, this "Volunteer" stunt —and the people of Holland knew it. Even the most lyrical effusions of the special Nazi propaganda unit which was giving the Dutch the full benefit of its on-the-spot reportage, failed to make any other impression than that of unendurable rhetoric and shameless lies.

The volunteer crusade had conclusively proved to be an unholy crusade; and the final word about it was said on February 5, 1943 when through the hand of an unknown assailant the turncoat General Seyffardt, founder of the entire "Volunteer" movement, was killed in front of his home at The Hague.

*Pretending to form a Territorial Guard, Mussert—in February, 1943—called upon his followers to join a new formation, the Nederlandsche Landwacht. He also invited "sympathizing elements" between 17 and 50 who before the invasion served in the Dutch defense forces. The Landwacht was to be part of the German Waffen SS, under the command of Rauter, head of the German Security Police. Obviously, this was a further, desperate effort to create the large Dutch "Volunteer" Army Mussert's German bosses demanded.

9

"A MIGHTY FORTRESS . . ."

"Many clergymen abuse German leniency through open incitement in their churches, by praying for the Queen and the House of Orange, and by skilfully chosen texts and still more skilful explanations."

Volk en Vaderland, April, 1942.

"These bishops are the fiercest enemies of the Nazi New Order in Europe; those people simply ask for religious persecution."

Volk en Vaderland, September, 1942.

The Protestant and Roman Catholic churches of the Netherlands have been in the front ranks of those who from the very start of the occupation forcefully opposed the invaders and their Dutch Nazi accomplices. It is difficult to exaggerate the importance of this fact.

During the first confusing weeks following upon the subjugation of the country, the people had often been at a loss which attitude to take. Belonging to a nation of individualists, there is no doubt that on their own accord many thousands of Dutch men and women reached the conclusion that the struggle for liberty and independence must be continued at all cost. But the masses were in dire need of an outside stimulant; they looked to their spiritual leaders for the decisive word of deliverance. Consequently, the churches of towns, villages and hamlets were more crowded than in a score of years. It still seemed possible to find solace within their hallowed walls; here was a haven in which to contemplate and regain one's balance, so badly disturbed by the incredible cruelty of every day's events.*

If in those days the clergy of the Netherlands had not silently, and practically without exception, decided that there could be no question of a compromise with the enemy, how much more

*Typical of the entire situation is the fact that the Calvinist churches increased their membership by 11,000 during 1942, bringing the total to 684,505. The services have, as a rule, been so well attended that the Council was forced to inaugurate additional ones.

painful and slower, how hopelessly retarded would have been the renaissance of Holland's spirit of defiance.

But the attitude of the churches could hardly have been different. Ministers and priests alike had seen what happened to the churches and religious organizations of the countries thus far subjugated by the Nazis. It was evident that the intruders, despite their suave assurances of friendship and untrammeled liberty, would at some time or other attack the Christian character of Dutch civilization. The lesson of a Niemoeller and of the Catholic leaders of Germany perishing in the squalor of concentration camps, had not been lost upon these Netherlands churchmen.

Had not Hitler himself confessed in "Mein Kampf" that even if the older generations must be considered "spoiled," there were plenty of young people available—blank pages to be filled with a detailed story of the Nazi creed? Quite naturally this dogma would not allow the church to influence its youthful members; history had proved this abundantly. Despite the Nazi assurances of 1933 to the Vatican, that the Church would continue to enjoy spiritual liberty, thousands of Catholics had been incarcerated and tortured to death. Nuns and priests were molested, hordes of Hitler Youth-ruffians destroyed crucifixes; and the non-Catholic part of the German population were told glaring tales of immoral conditions existing in Catholic institutions. Religious schools had been closed; all church organizations were disbanded. No longer was the Sabbath used to rest and go to Church; it was turned into a marching day for every member of the Hitler Youth.

Very much the same prescription had been followed in the suppression of the Protestant section of the German nation. Here, too, the church was degraded into becoming an instrument of the State, while preaching and Christian devotion were made almost impossible. That State, on the other hand, promoted the "New Paganism"; the return to Wodan and the Valhalla, to constant glorification of the "greatness of the Aryan tribes."

Of all this the Netherlands church authorities were well aware; and rather than submit or wait in silence for the things to happen, they spoke their minds fearlessly. Less than four months after the beginning of the occupation, the General Assembly of the Reformed Churches in Holland made a number of courageous decisions and, translating these into German, hastened to submit them to Seyss-Inquart. They read:

1. The General Assembly declares that in its opinion legal

authority still rests with Her Majesty, the Queen. Through the occupation of our country the factual power fell into the hands of the occupation authorities, but the sovereignty of the Netherlands Government, and more especially that of the Queen, have not suffered thereby. Our form of Government and our relationship with the House of Orange—matters which, according to the Reich's Commissioner's declaration, the Netherlands people must decide independently—are no subjects for deliberation. The churches have their firm opinion on these points; they do not mean to forsake a historical link which dates back more than three and a half centuries.

2. The General Assembly decides to instruct its representatives in the Convent to obtain as close as possible a contact between the Convent and the oecumenical movement. The General Assembly believes it to be of the highest importance in these days that the oecumenical character of the Church in its relation to the authorities is emphasized.

3. The General Assembly declares that the meetings of each community must be preceded by the prayer for Her Majesty the Queen and for our Government.

The Reformed Churches did not halt at this terse declaration of principle. Even though their first approach had not elicited the slightest answer from the Reich's Commissioner, they did not hesitate to send him a second letter of protest, couched in equally proud and dignified terms. On October 24, 1940, soon after the Germans had announced the peremptory ousting of all Jewish civil servants, they signed a joint declaration in which Seyss-Inquart was reminded of his initial solemn promise not to force Nazi ideologies upon the people of Holland. "We are profoundly moved by the meaning of these measures," they wrote, "touching, as they do, upon important spiritual interests and being against Christian mercy . . . Besides, these restrictions will also apply to members of our church who, having embraced the Christian faith during these last generations, were accepted by us in complete equality of rights, as the Holy Script emphatically desires."

Although the sole reply to this protest was the cold information that "the authorities take such decisions only after careful preparation," the voice of righteousness was not to be silenced so easily. When the press had been gagged and turned into a vehicle for Goebbels' propaganda, numerous stenciled pamphlets were circulated discussing the attitude Dutch Christians should take towards the German enemy and the Jewish "problem." In one such leaflet the writer endeavored to show the right path as lying between "the abyss of unbridled hatred and unprincipled fraternization with the invaders." Describing the feelings which live in the hearts of millions of Hollanders who base their existence upon the Gospel, the author said: "In our daily tasks, our thoughts, yea —even in our dreams, we never leave off fighting the enemy. Our hopes and prayers are directed against him; our greatest desire is the speediest, most conclusive and merciless defeat for him. Such sentiments may seem incompatible with the Christian doctrine that we must not only pray *against* the enemy, but they do mean that in these difficult days we must continue to follow Christ and listen to his commandments." These pamphlets were widely distributed and greedily read. In the eyes of the Germans they became "dangerous political sentiments"; and they were as swiftly as possible confiscated.

Time and again the Protestant Churches came back to the same vital issues. As the Germans extended their measures and regulations against Holland's Jews, they found the church authorities constantly and violently opposing them. In March, 1941 when almost every day brought new rules still further circumscribing the public and private life of Netherlands Jewry, clearly betraying the enemy's firm decision to eradicate the Jews completely from Holland's economic structure, the Protestant Churches addressed the Secretaries-General of all governmental departments. They "felt obliged to say how deeply the development of things was disquieting" them. "The Church considers it a holy duty to defend right and justice, truth and love," the protest continued. "Whenever in public life those high principles are threatened or attacked, the Church is compelled to make herself heard. That these principles are now seriously menaced can hardly be denied by anyone observing the state of affairs among our people . . . Clear symptoms can be seen in the treatment reserved in ever-growing measure for the Jewish minority of our Netherlands nation. There is increasing uncertainty of justice, continuous limitation of the liberties which form the indispensable basis for the fulfilment of our Christian duties. Those symptoms not only arouse the conscience of our fellow countrymen; they also go against the meaning of God's word.

"That is why our churches feel constrained to turn to you with the urgent prayer that you, as far as you are able, will see that truth and mercy remain the leading motives for the behavior of the authorities."

In September, 1941 the Reformed Church once more defied the German authorities by publishing a pastoral letter in which it counselled disobedience to all Nazi decrees which are contrary to the laws of God. Then the Apostolic words "We ought to obey God rather than man" become valid, the letter declared. "The authority which fails to respect this limit, degenerates into tyranny. In that case, one serves the authorities by acting in accordance with God's will. The Christian Church then accepts suffering, for the sake of the Gospel." The letter ended with another clear reminder that the people of the Netherlands would have nothing to do with the baiting of a defenseless minority. "According to God's providence, the Jews have lived among us for centuries and are bound up with us in a common history and a common responsibility. Our Saviour's commandment to love our neighbors as we love ourselves, applies to them as it applies to any other neighbor."

The next protest was staged in close collaboration with the Catholic bishops and took the form of a personal interview with Seyss-Inquart. A delegation saw the Austrian traitor on February 17, 1942 and its spokesman, pointing out that he addressed the Reich's Commissioner for "every Christian Church in Holland," asked him to "recognize, in the name of God, the spiritual distress of the Netherlands people, and to avoid doing further harm."

In a memorandum which the delegation then handed to Seyss-Inquart, the writers stated that "the churches are once more compelled to utter their emphatic and most serious objections to the present development of events. Without entering politics, they yet must raise their voice when the principles of justice and charity are being denied. The churches would be forsaking their duty towards the authorities if they, representing the majority of the population, did not express their anxiety over the feeling of tension increasingly existing among all classes of the Dutch people."

Describing the present state of affairs in the subjugated country, the memorandum decried the "almost complete lawlessness" exposing Hollanders to imprisonment without stated charges or a hearing, and the deprivation of the personal liberty of many people, for an unlimited time, by transferring them to "camps or elsewhere," without trial or condemnation.

This obviously referred to the rounding up of thousands of

Jews. But so as to leave no possibility of doubt on that point, the memorandum continued: "Numerous Jews arrested during last year have been sent elsewhere; subsequently official reports were received dealing with the high death rate among them. The churches would fail greatly if they did not ask the authorities, in the name of Christian charity, to keep their measures within bounds." Finally, the document emphasized that the churches continued to reject the National-Socialist viewpoint and to resist "the attempt of the authorities to force Nazism upon the Dutch people of whom only a small minority accept this creed. The resistance of the churches is based on the fact that Nazism assails justice, charity and freedom of conscience—all of which are inseparable from the Christian faith."

There was no beating about the bush in this memorandum, and Seyss-Inquart could hardly do more than stammer a grossly inadequate reply. The Nazis, he asserted, administered "justice" *as much as possible.* Imprisonment was "often in the nature of protection of the prisoner who, if allowed to continue along his chosen path, would become guiltier still" . . . He added, rather incoherently, that "the people of Holland do not know how well off they are, compared with the soldiers on the eastern front." As to the Jews, there could be no question of charity. The "Jewish problem" would be conclusively "solved" by the Germans. Forcing Nazi ideologies upon the Dutch might, he admitted, indeed conflict with the Christian creed. But such conflicts would be avoided "if the Christian Church keeps strictly to her vocation" . . .

With great courage the spokesman of the delegation expressed his dissatisfaction with Seyss-Inquart's answers. He said that on taking office, in May, 1940, the Reich's Commissioner had solemnly declared he would not touch the foundations of Dutch life. Now he was nonetheless attacking those foundations, in the form of Holland's Christianity.

In all likelihood, no better result had been expected from this historic interview. At any rate, the churches were not discouraged by the attitude of Hitler's Austrian stooge. On April 19, 1942 a further letter, signed by all Reformed Churches, was read from the pulpits of every town and village. "Great concern is felt within the Church," the message said, "over the way in which the three basic principles of our life—justice, charity and freedom of conscience and conviction—are being violated . . . Lately the Nazis have encroached upon the domain of Christian education and deprived it of its organ, the Joint Council of Religious Schools, and the Society for Christian Education . . . There are, besides, many other examples demonstrating that work founded on the Gospel is becoming increasingly involved in the heavy struggle wherein many have sacrificed their personal freedom."

The only answer made by the occupation power was the rounding up of foreign Jews who had found a place of refuge in the Netherlands after Hitler's rise to power, and their wholesale deportation. In July, the Germans extended this horrible persecution to thousands of Netherlands' Jews who were shipped to eastern Europe, never to be heard of again.* Once more the churches, Protestant and Catholic alike, sent a petition to the German assassins. This time, they approached Air General Friedrich Christiansen, German military commander in Holland, and urged better treatment of the Jews. Simultaneously a flaming protest was read in all churches against the horrible annihilation decrees.

A few days afterwards the Germans actually answered the latest joint petition of the churches. They ordered Commissar Schmidt—who also functions as Deputy Reich's Commissioner—to announce that "the Jews cannot stay in Holland; within a short time one of their strongest bastions will have been cleared away. They will return to the place they came from, just as poor as when they left it, covered with lice. Those sympathizing with them will be treated in the same way."

The menace was clear indeed, and subsequent executions of hostages and imprisonment of church dignitaries were tragic evidence that the Germans refused to tolerate further utterances of pity for the Jews. But in doing so, they only gave the churches new and stronger reasons for protest. In a broadcast over the Hilversum radio on January 30, 1943, Seyss-Inquart shouted indignantly that the Protestant church authorities had recently sent him and General Christiansen another letter in which protests were made against the "mounting tide of executions."

"It is intolerable," he howled, "that there are organizations** which try to endanger the safety of this territory, in the rear of the men who fight in the east. We must be hard, and we are becoming still harder. The churches should understand the significance of our struggle. All denominations can fully practise their faith

---

*See Chapter 10 "Slaughter of the Innocents," page 225.

**Seyss-Inquart was apparently also hinting at the activities of the excellently functioning Underground movement.

under Nazi occupation. They are even allowed to express their viewpoint regarding the measures we take. I, therefore, believe they are under the moral obligation at least not to *hinder* the German prosecution of the war" . . .

*

As already seen from her close cooperation with the Protestant institutions, the Roman Catholic Church did not differ in her firm attitude against the tyrants. Before the invasion both the Pope and the Netherlands bishops had repeatedly denounced National-Socialism; there was little need to reiterate those denunciations. But despite this fact, the bishops thought it desirable from time to time to underscore their firm decision not to close a pact with the Nazi enemy. Exactly half a year after the German aggression, on November 10, 1940, a pastoral letter was read from all Catholic pulpits, which pointed out that "the world is threatened by a nationalistic and materialistic outlook in which there is no place for Christ." The same message urged the believers to fight for the maintenance of their spiritual treasures, more especially their religious schools.

Some months later a further episcopal letter was read in which the Catholic standpoint against National-Socialism was clearly defined. Obviously, the various N.S.B. mouthpieces did not fail to answer. They were furious that the bishops had dared to reiterate their ruling that no Holy Sacraments were to be given to any Catholic "about whom it is known that he supports the national-socialist idea to any degree of importance." Cautiously, no specific Nazi movement had been mentioned—but those whom the glove fitted were quick enough to put it on.

Only a few weeks previously, the bishops had sent a special instruction to the secular and regular clergy. In it specific attention had been given to the N. S. B. and the various organizations which served it as a false front. The instruction forbade every connection with Mussert's national-socialist movement, either in the form of membership or by supporting it with money. No exceptions were made. Even force, or fear of monetary losses were not recognized as legal reasons to disobey the instruction. No meetings, assemblies or processions of the N. S. B. were to be witnessed by church members. It was forbidden to read Mussert's newspapers, or other material distributed by the N. S. B., to make propaganda for the movement, or to represent it in any way in any other public body.*

The punishment for those trespassing upon the regulations, would be a refusal of absolution and of the other sacraments. Those who had thus far been allowed the sacraments must first receive a personal warning except when they publicly admitted to be members of the N. S. B., either by wearing its uniform or displaying its emblem. To them access to the sacraments was to be refused without warning.

As to marriages, they could be performed only with the ritual the Catholic Church reserves for mixed marriages. Such ceremonies were not allowed to take place at the altar, but had to be relegated to the vestry. Interment in sanctified soil had to be refused if the deceased had not shown signs of penitence, or died unconverted. In no circumstances, however, would funeral processions be allowed to carry Nazi banners or flags, or to comprise men or women in N. S. B. uniforms. Equally prohibited was membership in the N. S. B. "false front" organizations, such as the Agrarian Front or the Culture Circle and, later, of the Nazified Center of Trade Unions, the erstwhile N. V. V.

It was to be expected that the contents of this very lucidly worded document would soon—and often—have to be applied to practical life. In April, 1941, for instance, a Limburg Storm Trooper had been killed in a street brawl and the church refused to permit his burial in sanctified ground. Representatives of Mussert's party hurried to the Reich's Commissioner who gave out a formal order for the funeral. In accordance with the regulations, the clergy on that occasion restricted the service to the reading of the funeral mass and the absolution, but could not prevent uniformed Nazis from drawing a cordon around the cemetery.

Numerous were the cases in which the Catholic clergy refused to solemnize the marriage of N. S. B.'ers. It soon became a habit to mention this in bold lettering at the foot of the marriage announcements appearing in the Nationale Dagblad and Volk en Vaderland.

Slowly but surely the relationships between Mussert's party

---

*The only exception made was for people who might be given the choice of joining the N. S. B. immediately or losing their means of livelihood. However, they were not at liberty to accept membership until they had obtained the permission of their father-confessor who was instructed to examine each case most carefully. But even if the priest's advice was in the affirmative, such membership had to remain rigorously passive, while it was to be made clear beyond doubt that the person concerned became a member only *under duress.* In other words, this circumscription reduced the "exceptions" of this kind to virtually nought.

and the Catholic Church grew more pointed; in the end the occupying powers seemed to consider it necessary to have their say. Commissar-General Schmidt was promptly ordered to "tell the clergy off" and in a subsequent speech in Limburg province this German lackey shouted: "We know quite well how to distinguish between a good shepherd whose task lies with his community and the clergyman with political ambitions who abuses the pulpit to agitate against us!"

As might have been expected, Herr Schmidt's statement failed to make much impression upon the church dignitaries. Nor were they moved by the childish way in which the N. S. B. endeavored to advertise Germany as the "protector of European culture against bolshevism." Volk en Vaderland might try to frighten the clergy into shivers by predicting that Europe would fall a prey to Communism, in case of a German defeat. It might prophesy that "those priests who now pray for England, may yet finish their days on earth as woodcutters in the forests of Siberia, or as slaves in the mercury mines of the Caucasus" . . ., the clergy concerned did not seem unduly stirred by those uncomfortable prospects. Also, perhaps, because Siberia happens to be as devoid of forests as is the Caucasus of mercury mines.

In August, 1941 the Nazi decision to discontinue separate denominational Labor Unions, was openly condemned from the pulpits of all Catholic churches. A pastoral letter, signed by Archbishop J. de Jongh of Utrecht and four other bishops, was read, in which he bluntly stated that "virtually the Roman Catholic trade unions are therewith destroyed, as they are prevented from continuing their religious and morale-building task . . . Publicly and loudly we raise our voices against the injustice done to thousands of people by robbing them of one of their social institutions. We protest against the unheard-of practice of trying to force upon them an attitude towards life which is contrary to their religious convictions . . ."*

There was every reason for the Catholic clergy to be satisfied with the results of their protest. A vast majority of workers refused to be either cajoled or threatened into joining the new Union. In a joint Lenten Letter of the Dutch archbishop and bishops, read on February 22, 1942, gratification was expressed with this attitude of the faithful "who have so far withstood tendencies and aspirations which offer a serious threat to Christian

*See Chapter 5, Labor's Downfall and Enslavement, page 105.

faith and morals." At the same time the bishops complained that "many means of spreading, deepening and defending our faith are taken from us." They urged the Catholic Netherlanders to be "ready, armed with truth, justice and responsiveness to the Gospel of Peace against a menace which becomes stronger as the pressure on us increases." The message which sent the Germans into the usual paroxysm of fury, concluded by quoting from the epistles of St. Paul: "May the gift of words be given me. May I continue to be outspoken, which is my duty."

To this firm decision the Church adhered throughout the ensuing year. Best proof of it was furnished by the same German puppet, Commissar-General Schmidt, when in February, 1943 he addressed a combined Netherlands-German Nazi meeting at Utrecht. In the sharpest terms he outlined the German attitude towards still another pastoral letter which on the preceding Sunday, February 21, had been read from the pulpit of all Catholic churches.* It was high time, he said, to "send the clergy back within the limits of their churches and the law."

"Why do they not accuse Bolshevism which is out to destroy *us* who allow everyone to have their own religion?" Schmidt fulminated. "We do not retreat a single step from our program; we will not name Dutchmen and Jews in one breath. In their pastoral letter the Catholic bishops wish to intercede on behalf of those who are affected by the occupying powers; in a letter to Seyss-Inquart, the Catholic Church complained about "injustice' done to the Netherlands people . . . I ask, what has the Church said about the injustice done to the German nation for twenty-five years?

"When the Churches protest against the shooting of hostages, we say that we must protect ourselves against crimes which can only be stopped by the severest measures. Hostages are only shot to atone for assaults on the German military; no hostages have died yet for crimes against members of the N. S. B.** because Mussert said that Dutch blood 'should not be atoned for by more Dutch blood.' But the strongest measures must be taken to bring the incited 'Volksgenossen' (racial comrades) to reason.

"In the pastoral letter harsh treatment in concentration camps is condemned. But the writers forget that the people concerned

---

*For full text of the Catholic letter and for a synopsis of the Protestant protest, see Appendix III.

**Schmidt obviously referred to the shooting of various members of Mussert's newly-instituted Secretariat. See chapter 8, pages 164 and 165.

are men who conspired against Germany at a moment when the German people were fighting for the whole of Europe. The pastoral letter complains that Dutch youths are sent to Germany and from its wording you would think that the Reich is a fortnight's journey from Holland! The bishops also talk of contradictions between our measures and the meaning of the Gospel. All we can ask is whether it is not contrary to the Gospel and its commandments that they refuse burial services to members of the N. S. B.

" 'God's commandment is above worldly power,' the pastoral letter states. But we Nazis comment that our faith and our creed guarantee a victory over Bolshevism."

Commissar-General Schmidt, working himself up to a fine frenzy, sharply denounced the bishops' advice at the end of their pastoral message: to refuse all cooperation in the execution of important war measures. "If these clergymen care to incite civil servants to a non-cooperative attitude toward the occupation authorities," Schmidt shouted, "we can only say that we will face with tranquillity, but also with hardness, everything they may try to do.

"It is the Reich's Commissioner's duty," Schmidt continued, "to send all laborers to Germany who can be spared here in Holland. By the same token we shall dismiss all recalcitrant mayors and, if necessary, replace them with intelligent laborers.

"As to young people, I can only underscore what Mussert said in Amsterdam: that decent youngsters may continue their studies; but the others will be sent to concentration camps where we shall guide them back upon the right path."

*

Meanwhile the Nazis had, of course, thought of other ways than speechifying to "break the spell" of ministers and priests upon their congregations. They put the microphone of the Hilversum radio at the unlimited disposal of those among their membership who still called themselves adherents to the Protestant or Catholic Churches. To quote one single but typical utterance of such a spokesman, the secretary of the N. S. B. "Catholic Council" delivered an address which culminated in the following edifying metaphor: "It is the duty of the State to see that every party member gets his bread and butter; as to the Church, she is obliged to see that every party member goes to Heaven" . . .

The "Protestant Council" of the N. S. B. did not stay behind, but in its turn tried to convince its radio listeners, if any, that the New Order would shower great benefits upon the Church. "Cede all desire for secular power—and you smooth the path to a purer conveyance of truly religious thought . . . Under the New Order the Church will be allowed to remain itself just because it will be a church alone—in the right sense of the word."

This was poor propaganda indeed; it might have been to the advantage of the N. S. B. if it had not taken recourse to the assistance of such mealy-mouthed apostates. Far from being lured into the National-Socialist camp, both Protestants and Catholics now came closer together than in many preceding decades. Old-time squabbles which only too frequently had sown discord among the numerous factions into which both religious movements had gradually split, were easily brushed aside. Bygones were left bygones. No long and weighty parleys were needed to make the Dutch people understand that unity in the Christian Church was a first necessity.

To live in Holland under German tyranny is to wander through a bewildering, upside-down world. Today's existence is the reverse of the complete independence and personal liberty which were taken for granted until the invasion of May, 1940. Of course, it is sad to suffer the pangs of hunger; and to see one's children deprived of the most necessary nourishment is wellnigh unbearable. But the tortures of the soul are still harder to bear. To witness how depravity and injustice are elevated to the rank of highest virtues, to stand aside impotently when tens of thousands of fellow countrymen are systematically annihilated just because they are Jews—such things cannot be borne long by decent people unless they have found support in a higher power.

Through the churches that support had been forthcoming. In the darkest days the people searching for comfort, found it within the walls of their temples and in the hallowed words of the Bible. Throughout the country "Bible Study Groups" were formed, not as debating clubs or for the pleasure of organizing social receptions, but mainly to come together, to feel of one mind and one desire. To escape, if only for a few hours, from the rapacious elements that had fallen upon the Netherlands' nation as buzzards settling down upon their prey. To live within the trusted world of the Bible and find courage in the joys and tribulations of those who founded the Christian Church was—and still is—so great an encouragement to millions of tyrannized Hollanders that it enabled them to remain themselves, impervious to all Nazi propaganda.*

In the churches courageous men addressed their flocks giving form to their unspoken thoughts of disgust, disdain and rebellion. Time and again, after all other means of free utterance had been paralyzed, brave words of protest have been heard from hundreds of pulpits. Many a significant Bible verse was fearlessly quoted, and little perspicacity was needed to find out to whom the words applied. When in a Protestant church the minister dared to conclude his sermon with Chapter 6, verse 23 of Job: . . . "Deliver me from the enemy's hand. Or, redeem me from the hand of the mighty . . .," the leaders of the N. S. B. protested furiously that such quotations had nothing to do with religion but were exclusively meant as political demonstrations.

What these Nazis failed to see, however, was that the Bible was not merely used as a rich arsenal of appropriate sayings against the German oppressors, but that the contemplation of those ancient Bible words brought deeper understanding to the masses than they had known in times of peace and prosperity. As one theologian expressed it in a public lecture: "Whoever among us thinks simply and in a Christian way, feels inclined to distinguish—next to God's judgment—a subconscious judgment of self." The majority of the Dutch who, as most other peoples, have long been inclined to live a surface existence and render hardly more than lip service to their churches, began to think and search for the inner sense of the terror by which they were surrounded. They tried to gauge the guilt of humanity and find courage for the future in the wisdom of the past. Once again Bible and reality dissolved in one another.

Indeed, Holland's clergy knew no fear. These men of God did not fail to appreciate the worldly power of the German invaders. They knew that words spoken from the pulpit might bring swift retribution, imprisonment or even death. They did not search for martyrdom, but neither did they try to avoid it.

Despite all prohibitions these ministers and priests insisted upon pronouncing prayers for the royal house and for their legal Government at the beginning of every service. They expressed

*The establishment of these Bible Study Groups had still another purpose. Judging by the attitude of the Nazis in Germany, it was to be expected that the invaders would try to eliminate at least some of the leaders of the obstreperous Protestant Churches. Conceivably this might disorganize the churches, and throw the dependent masses into utter confusion. To avoid that possibility, the formation of "laymen apostolates" was greatly encouraged and the heads of the Bible Study Groups were, as a rule, men capable and willing to give spiritual guidance if a community should be robbed of its religious leader.

their thoughts in many ways, but the following is a fair sample of those heartfelt prayers: "We pray for all those whom Thou art deigning to place over us. Above all wilt Thou give them understanding of and respect for Thy Kingdom and Thy creed. We pray Thee especially for our respected Queen and her House and her Government, that Thou wouldst be near her and console her and guide her by Thy spirit. We pray that Thou givest her and her Government wisdom in their sore need, to do what must be done, to tolerate what must be tolerated for the true salvation of our people. We pray that Thou wilt grant the alien rulers whom in Thy dark ordinance Thou still allowest to rule over us, to bow down before Thy commandments."

In their sermons these churchmen often fell back upon the thrilling history of the Netherlands; and frequently the eighty years' struggle against Spanish domination* was spoken of as a time of great hardship and oppression, personally experienced. And indeed, the analogy was obvious enough: once again liberty of body and mind, that invaluable treasure for which the ancestors had so bravely fought, was at stake.

On dates of historical significance many a sermon attained such actuality that it deeply stirred the congregation. In a Leyden church, on October 3, 1941, for instance, the minister chose for his subject a story which every schoolchild in Holland knows, that of Leyden's resistance to the Spanish tyrants, three and a half centuries ago. It is a tale of steadfastness under duress, of men ready to die rather than to surrender their liberties and their beliefs. Despite hasty Nazi measures to prevent its distribution, the gist of this vivid recital reached every corner of the Netherlands in a surprisingly short time.

The unnamed Leyden preacher besought his hearers to take courage from the epic struggle carried on within their very city walls 367 years before. He emphasized that the present situation was but little different from that in which their ancestors had found themselves. They, too, were confronted with the same hardships and temptations, the same dangers, the same godless oppression. "Again we live in the midst of overwhelming and terrible perils. Once more our nation finds itself in a decisive crisis of its history," he exclaimed. Ostensibly describing the struggle for freedom of so many centuries ago, he warned his congregation

*From 1568 till the Peace of Munster in 1648, interrupted only by a twelve years' truce (1609-1621).

against the insidious traitors from within. "Certain burghers of our city asked themselves," he said, "if it would not be better to surrender at last, rather than wait still longer for a raising of the terrible siege. Would it not be far better to give in, or at least to negotiate with the enemy? That was the temptation which some well-spoken citizens dangled before the eyes of their exhausted fellow townsmen.

"For that matter, there were 'sneaks.' They represented a very small group of the citizenry, but they were responsible for an immense, uproarious tumult. Here was a handful of mean-spirited traitors who—asway on the boundary line between two worlds—did not know their place and willingly made themselves into the enemy's ready tools. Frequently those sneaks addressed their fellow citizens with grandiloquent words, or in cunningly devised letters and writings just to blind them with their very lies . . . At first they flattered, then they threatened. But the stolid people of Leyden, though giving them a patient hearing, refused to walk into the trap."

The comparison was too clear to be missed by anyone. Yet, as if to exclude any doubt, the minister thereupon dropped every pretense of speaking only of past tyrannies. "God will have none of despotism," he exclaimed. "He will have none of the arrogant tyrants who seek to mould all to their will. It is His wish that both people and government bow down humbly before His word, and that they shall not prevent anyone from serving Him according to his conscience."

*

For some time religious dailies and weeklies, too, became platforms for fearless speakers. But as a rule the Nazis suspended such "trespassers" and sent their responsible editors to concentration camps. Foremost amongst them was Dr. Hendrikus Colijn who, after having served his country thrice as Premier, had taken upon himself the editorship of the prominent Calvinist daily "De Standaard," at Amsterdam. For years he had filled this post with great distinction. Despite the strict German control upon the press, Colijn had continued to publish outspoken editorials. In meetings, too, he never hesitated to speak his mind. During the first occupation winter, for example, he addressed a mass gathering in which he said, "Whoever knows anything about our people knows that we will have nothing to do with imported extremism. We have shown the occupying power that we cannot put aside our national characteristics when choosing the political path we wish to follow . . ." In Colijn's place the Germans appointed the renegade Dutch journalist Max Blokzijl who a short while previously had come "home" from Berlin to help the Germans rule the Dutch press and radio.

To replace the disbanded religious journals the Nazis started a weekly of their own under the name of "Volk en Evangelie" (People and Gospel) which made it a point to enumerate, from issue to issue, all the "crimes" committed by religious organizations. In this manner it revealed that believers were busily carving capital V's in church pews when the famous "V" campaign was at its height. Other carvers took more time and trouble and engraved such slogans as 'Long live Queen Wilhelmina' and 'Bravo, Churchill.' "And the ministers are taking no action to halt this abominable practice," the paper wailed. It told of Mussert-men who were refused admittance to their churches, not only to attend services but also for the solemnization of marriage. "In some cases," Volk en Evangelie revealed, "those unfortunates are obliged to go to a German church because Dutch Protestant clergymen refuse to perform the ceremony."

No issue of the Nationale Dagblad appeared without some complaint against the Protestant or Catholic church authorities. Propaganda leader Ernst Voorhoeve once wrote that he as well as Mussert had repeatedly tried to get a hearing from the Catholic bishops and the Protestant authorities, only to ask them, "Why are you so much against our National-Socialist principles? What do you not like in our practices? But," Voorhoeve concluded dejectedly, "it has all been in vain. These men have never wanted to speak with us."

On another occasion Mussert's paper announced the following ingenious discovery: "Let us agree for argument's sake that there are certain things in the National-Socialist movement dangerous to religion and morals. If that is so, would it not have been the duty of the bishops to send as many Catholics as possible to enroll with the N.S.B. and ward off that danger by their influence? The Catholics call themselves the salt of the earth. But of what use is salt if it refuses to be mixed with other matter, thus preserving it from deterioration?" . . .

That the German Roman Catholic clergy does not refuse the sacraments to Hitler's followers, was often repeated but without causing the slightest change in the attitude of the Catholic authorities in Holland. Gradually the persuasive, argumentative tone changed to high-pitched yelling and a calling of names. One propagandist, completely losing his temper, shouted through the Hilversum microphone that he would "love to send five political bishops in a sealed railroad wagon to the Pope with a request to exchange them for five *real* priests." In March, 1942 Mussert's weekly, Volk en Vaderland printed a letter purportedly coming from an N. S. B. spy who had taken part in a Catholic retreat. He declared that the priest had warned those present against seeing German films and had "eulogized the Dutch Merchant Marine now serving the Allied cause."

Once De Misthoorn (Fog Horn), a rabidly anti-Semitic extremist paper, advised the bishops of the Netherlands to "thank God for the rescue of the Church by Adolf Hitler. The bishops pray to God Whom they beg to keep the gate of Heaven closed against us," wrote De Misthoorn. "These bishops, whose robes smell of camphor, do not realize that they lose by praying for the Government (in London) which now carries on intrigues with the Bolsheviks."

A few months afterwards the same paper asserted that "Christianity is a veneer which for some time has given brilliancy to European life. But it also is a strait-jacket hindering seriously the true development of Germanic culture. It is absolutely unimportant whether or not Christianity takes part in building up the New Europe." In a following issue the editor, returning to the attack, railed against Netherlands clergy for "stirring up discontent among the people. Priests and ministers are competing in their efforts at veiled incitement against those now ruling the country," he wrote. "One day when the authorities cease to be lenient, hard blows will fall—and then the Germans will, of course, be accused of religious persecution . . ."

In fact, shortly after the publication of this threat something very akin to religious persecution happened. About this time it became a habit among Catholics, male and female, to display a little cross. The idea had originally been propagated by "De Residentiebode," a daily of The Hague, "as a visible token of faith, so that good Roman Catholics may be able to recognize each other as such." For weeks in succession Volk en Vaderland had fulminated against this "annoying habit" which came to be looked upon as a challenge to the Nazis. In truth—many non-Catholics, but all of them patriots, had also started to wear a small cross.

"Every reactionary wears it," Volk en Vaderland raged. "All family members decorate themselves with it and even schoolchildren have it pinned to their clothes. They are birds of greatly-varying plumage . . .; you may find free-thinkers amongst them, anti-Papists, Jews and even members of the disbanded Marxist and Communist parties." Over and over again the paper decried the practice as "a great provocation, to goad Germans and members of the N. S. B. into tearing the crosses from people's clothing." It soon became clear who was the author of such articles; for in a subsequent meeting at Utrecht propagandist Voorhoeve openly demanded that cross-bearers be molested. "We must make an end to this business," he exclaimed.

But his zeal had carried him too far, and he was promptly subdued by the party leader. Eager to maintain at least a semblance of Christian sentiment for his membership, Anton Mussert immediately countermanded Voorhoeve's implied order to attack. A sort of armed truce ensued—until, a few months later, the occupation authorities ended the conflict by completely prohibiting the wearing of the emblem of faith.

*

That interdiction was not the first hostile act against the churches. In their usual truculent way the Germans—after having given the religious leaders of the Netherlands a few months in which to conform to Nazi policy—had taken off their mask of "friendly persuasion." Without further delay they had started upon their habitual series of warnings and menaces, alternated with occasional castigations.

It began during the first occupation winter when the invaders tried to make the charitable church institutions subservient to their own Winter Help. To this purpose instructions were issued that before a certain date complete declarations would have to reach them of all funds received through church collections. Immediately the General Synod of Protestant Churches convened to consider this decree and rejected it, as well as a special command that for every collection permission must henceforth be obtained from the authorities. The Synod concluded that no further interference could be tolerated in the matter of voluntary collections and advised its congregations rather to discontinue the gathering of funds outside the church. As to collections held during the services, they continued to take place without interruption since the Nazis still hesitated to show public disrespect for the inviolability of the churches.

No financial statements were ever sent to the Germans, even when—as a final gesture—the Nazis granted a few weeks' respite to obey the order. If anything, this "grace" resulted in a stream of extraordinarily generous contributions to the church collection—which did not fail to irk the enemy greatly. For his own Winter Help he had hardly been able to gather a few thousand guilders, and that under duress . . . Finally, the Nazis forbade all collections throughout the country except those they organized themselves. But even this order was sublimely ignored inside the churches.

Next followed a sustained German effort to curtail the influence of the denominational schools. As early as March, 1941 priests who headed Catholic schools, were peremptorily dismissed and two months later an entire Jesuit college at The Hague, the *Huize Katwijk,* was sequestrated. Salaries of priest-teachers were severely cut and many institutions of learning forced to close down.

Next the attack shifted to primary Protestant and Catholic schools. Numbers of them were discontinued without further explanation and closely upon them followed the denominational teaching colleges. The latter were forbidden to accept freshmen, and the state subsidies they had hitherto enjoyed were withdrawn. It will, therefore, be impossible for them to survive the graduation of their present enrollment.

More and more Catholic dailies and weeklies were suppressed. The Rotterdam "Maasbode," for example, for generations the leading daily of Dutch Catholics, was completely disbanded. Others, like the Amsterdam "Tijd," were allowed to appear—but only as mouthpieces of the German Propaganda Bureau.

Toward mid-summer of 1941 something happened which had long been foreseen by Protestant church leaders. Dr. K. H. E. Gravemeyer, Secretary of the General Synod of the Netherlands Reformed Church, was sent to prison. The authorities charged him with having drafted one of the many Synodal messages in which cooperation with the invaders was bluntly refused. In several ways Dr. Gravemeyer had been responsible for the revival in the Protestant Church; it was, therefore, obvious that through his arrest the Germans hoped to deal a severe blow to that rejuvenation movement. Subsequent events clearly proved, however, that all measures to prevent such a collapse had been taken. The absence of Dr. Gravemeyer* in no way weakened the unity of the churches; if anything, it made their repeated protests more urgent and vehement. As in the case of their first anti-Jewish decrees, the Germans discovered that by singling out a small group for enforcement of their tyrannical measures, they found themselves immediately opposed by the entire population, irrespective of creed.

During that same summer month the Archbishop of Utrecht, Mgr. J. de Jongh, was sentenced to pay a fine of five hundred guilders (approximately $270) because he had refused to participate in the Nazi-sponsored propaganda campaign against Bolshevik paganism. The verdict was announced by Goering's own paper, the "Essener National Zeitung" which in an editorial comment complained that "it is not understandable, though unfortunately only too true, that all Catholic organizations in the Netherlands refuse to acknowledge the German fight against Bolshevism as a battle for Christianity." As soon as the news of the sentence became generally known, a veritable rain of money orders poured down upon the desk of Mgr. de Jongh. From all over the country Catholics and non-Catholics wished to contribute something to help pay the impudent German levy upon the daring Utrecht prelate.

Another dignitary to suffer much from Nazi vengefulness was Mgr. J. H. G. Lemmens, bishop of Roermond, in the province of Limburg who—because of his opposition to several German rulings—was deprived of most of his residence. The main sections of his palace were turned into storerooms for gasoline.

These and similar incidents, no more than pin pricks at first, swiftly changed into a stream of arrests and imprisonments. Several Protestant clergymen were rounded up mainly on charges far removed from the actual reasons for their incarceration. While, for example, the Germans would accuse these men of buying in the black market or of having listened to prohibited foreign broadcasts, they had in reality been arrested only because the Nazis still hoped to wreck the organized protestations of the Church by taking away her leaders.

Books and pamphlets written by outstanding theologians were destroyed. In fact, with a single stroke of the pen the German authorities could have put a stop to all remaining Church activities. But the invaders were as yet not unwilling to leave the Churches

*After some time Dr. Gravemeyer was freed, only to be rearrested during the summer of 1942. This second imprisonment lasted until February, 1943 when the Germans once more released him from a concentration camp in the Netherlands.

almost alone—if only they showed sufficient preparedness not to interfere with the practical application in the Netherlands of Adolf Hitler's ideologies.

The Churches remained adamant, however. Throughout the difficult years of 1941 and 1942 no hesitation was discernible in their attitude. Their servants never tried to hide their contempt for all tyranny, intolerance and religious persecution. Time and again Protestants and Catholics, either individually or as united leaders of the two great religious movements, expressed their abhorrence of serfdom to Nazi Germany. It might be a single priest who spoke his mind without beating about the bush—like the reverend who said of Mussert's followers, "They live like dogs. That's why they should be buried like dogs." Or it might be one of those fearless protests in the name of all Christianity which once again brought it home to the Germans that the churches of Holland would never yield.

During the latter half of 1942 the accumulated acts of German persecution began to make themselves felt in leading religious circles. The Catholic University of Nijmegen, for instance, not only saw its acting Dean, its regent and one of its professors arrested, but the institution was also blackmailed into paying about a quarter of a million dollars for the "privilege of continuing its activities"—under sharp and constant control of the Germans.

In quick succession the death of several priests and ministers in German concentration camps was announced. Dr. Hein Hoeben of Breda, leader of the largest Catholic Press Bureau, also died in a Berlin jail from wounds inflicted on him during more than ten months of torture. His organization, collaborating with a similar press center in Belgium, had been the chief means of informing the outside world of religious persecution and atrocities against members of the clergy within the Reich. Hoeben was only 42 years old and a journalist of international repute. He had been an editor of the Koelnische Zeitung and for many years headed the Catholic German Press Agency. When the Nazis invaded Holland, Hoeben had fled to Paris; but after the subsequent fall of France he was caught by the Germans, never to see freedom again.

Towards the end of the third occupation year things were going from bad to worse. Several more leading theologians, among them the famous Professor Hendrik Kraemer of Leyden University, were imprisoned. Kraemer had been Chairman of the Youth Commission of the Dutch Reformed Churches; with his incarceration the Synod lost its third prominent leader.* No less than fifty Protestant churchmen were now in German camps or jails; the vituperous attacks of Dutch Nazis increased by the day. More Catholic institutions were "taken over" by the military, and their inhabitants ordered to find lodging "elsewhere." In one instance priests of the Order of the Sacred Heart found refuge in a dilapidated brewery. But because these men attempted to make the brewery fit to live in by taking along some of their own furniture, they were severely lectured by the local German Commander who termed their conduct "selfish and un-Christian."

Confusion became general; without the slightest reason and with as little warning, monks and priests were deprived of their living quarters and sent to other districts. Things became so bad that the bishop of 's-Hertogenbosch saw himself obliged to publish an appeal in which he urgently asked the priests and institutions of his diocese to try and keep him posted of their "latest addresses."

Thus the Germans, with great cunning, and eagerly supported by Mussert's followers, proceeded with their systematic efforts to paralyze the influence of Holland's churches. They rarely resorted to closing down places of worship; nor did they put any restrictions on the religious services themselves. They preferred to break down religious life in stages. At first all political parties including those representing the religious groups in the Netherlands, had been disbanded; afterwards they focussed their attention upon the discontinuance of all religious teaching and finally came their attack upon the denominational trade unions.

It is nonetheless a remarkable truth that thus far all this tireless German burrowing has shown only very small results. Under great provocation and in common hardship, a unity of purpose was born which bound the people of Holland very closely. It turned the Churches into impregnable strongholds. Never could the spiritual inheritance of the Netherlands have found better defenders than those who were watching the ramparts of these castles. Time and again the enemy might attack; he might even succeed in damaging the outer walls. But unattainable for him, because of their intangibility, remained the symbols decorating the highest bastions: the Christian cross and the colors of the Netherlands.

*The other two were Dr. K. H. E. Gravemeyer, aforementioned, and Professor Paul Scholten, Chairman of the Advisory Council of the Church.

10

SLAUGHTER OF THE INNOCENTS

"We Nazis do not consider the Jews a part of the Netherlands people. They are our enemies, with whom we neither wish to conclude a truce nor a peace."

Reich's Commissioner Seyss-Inquart on March 12, 1941.

"The Synod complains erroneously of the treatment of and the lack of pity for the Jews. They form no part of the Netherlands' nation and cannot be made a part by giving them civil rights. Our people are a blood community, not shared by Jews."

Volk en Vaderland, June, 1942.

Throughout the greater part of the nineteenth century the Jews of Holland lived on a footing of complete equality with their compatriots of other creeds. The Napoleonic era had broken down the last obstacles in the path of their emancipation. Schools and universities which had hitherto been closed to Jews, were thrown wide open to students of all denominations. Not only could they practise their religious rites in absolute freedom; they also became full-fledged citizens of the country in which their ancestors had already resided for a century and a half.

Soon the practical wisdom of this levelling process could be observed. Many Jews reached the front ranks of commerce, science and the arts. As time went by, Jewish Netherlanders, now completely absorbed in the life of the nation, were met with in every class and profession. Among them there were large numbers of laborers and artisans, shopkeepers and small traders. Quite a few internationally known jurists were Jewish, such as Asser, Oppenheim and Meyers. Journalism, too, had its share of Jewish contributors, and among the best essayists and playwrights of the country Israel Querido and Herman Heijermans distinguished themselves. On the stage, actors and actresses of the Jewish faith attained stardom. Painters and sculptors, like Josef Israels and Mendes da Costa, gave the world their treasures of lasting value. In short, not only did this tiny Jewish minority help the people of Holland in the extension and consolidation of many trades and industries, they also assisted largely in the cultural development of the nation which had adopted them as its sons and daughters.

During the forty-two years of Queen Wilhelmina's liberal and broadminded reign, the last boundaries between Christians and Jews were entirely effaced. His racial origin disqualified no Jew for the pursuance of whatever profession he wished to follow. The process of assimilation had, so it seemed, reached its final stage. Intermarriages between Jews and gentiles were numerous, even so that apart from the 120,000 "full" Jews no less than 60,000 part-Jews were settled throughout the land, living in perfect harmony with their co-nationals. Thus men and women of the Jewish creed were well represented in almost every layer of the country's structure when, in the early 30's, the German Nazi viper began to rear its ugly head and spit the poison of fanatic anti-Semitism.

This does not mean, of course, that isolated instances of prejudice were unknown before the advent of Nazism. Inborn, unreasonable dislike of the Jew could indeed be met with here and there. A snobbish club or fraternity might frown upon the admittance of Jews to its membership; in certain circles the Jew might still be spoken of with some disdain and asperity. But such cases, apart from being comparatively rare, were in no way more serious or disquieting than the prejudice which, though seldom publicly admitted, existed between the Catholics and Protestants of a number of Dutch provinces.

It came, therefore, as no surprise that the gentile citizens of Holland did not stand idly by when early in 1933 the persecution of German Jews became an official "function" of Adolf Hitler's Third Reich. On the contrary, an overwhelming majority of them showed as much pity for those first innocent victims of Hitlerism as did their Jewish compatriots. Tens of thousands of German Jews received a hearty welcome on Dutch territory. They were fed and clothed; they were given a chance to try and forget their terrifying experiences. They found an opportunity to rehabilitate themselves.

As things grew worse and the economic spoliation of the Jews turned into a shameless man hunt, with the German "Aryans" out to kill, the Netherlanders did not hesitate to express in public their loathing and disgust at Nazi barbarism. Both in the press and in spontaneous mass meetings, the Dutch nation fiercely condemned the anti-Jewish excesses in central Europe. Simultaneously, the bond between all Hollanders, no matter their religious adherences, was drawn closer than ever before. After the revolting pogroms of November, 1938, staged throughout Germany in retaliation for the Paris shooting of a Nazi official, one single day's street collections for the relief of the victimized Jews yielded more than half a million guilders. In every town and village of the country Netherlanders, young and old, withstood the inclement December storms to help make this collection a success. Every faith and class contributed, and even the ghastly "humor" of some Dutch N. S. B.'ers who deposited worthless German mark notes in the collection boxes, proved beneficial to the cause. For those pieces of paper, dating from the inflation period of the early 20's—and on which the Nazi heroes had written such edifying slogans as "To Hell With All The Jews"—were sold by auction and eagerly bought as "keepsakes." They yielded more than many a generous-minded citizen had contributed in hard Dutch cash!

*

Whoever was familiar with these pre-invasion events, knew that the Christian population of Holland was far from ready to accept anti-Semitism as one of the blessings of Hitler's New Order. Even the Germans themselves, despite their inability to understand the workings of a non-Teutonic mind, must have had an inkling of the true situation. There is no other explanation for their initial leniency. After the subjugation of the Dutch defense forces almost three months went by before the Nazis made the slightest mention of anti-Semitic measures.

Perhaps the enemy hoped that if the disinheritance of the Jews were brought about step by step—allowing sufficient time to lapse between one decree and the next—the majority of the Dutch would fail to be disturbed by it. What the Germans forgot was that both the gentile and the Jewish sections of the people never expected them to display greater tolerance in the occupied Netherlands than they had shown in their own country, or in any of the central European states which they had subjugated. As the days went by without the introduction of the Nuremberg Laws or any other restrictions, Jews and non-Jews, far from regaining their confidence and believing that in Holland an exception would be made to Hitler's rule of blind vengeance, grew more and more suspicious. Something sinister was in the offing; a heavy storm was brewing and the only question was, when it would break loose.

In the early days of August, 1940 the Nazis were obliged to realize that their "game was up." Not only had their conciliatory attitude in general yielded scant result, but even their non-interference in the life of Holland's Jews had given them no advantages. And suddenly, without further efforts to conceal their true intentions, they started out upon their long-expected anti-Semitic campaign.

The first attack was made upon the Jews as a mass. On August 7, 1940 ritual slaughter of animals was peremptorily prohibited. No longer were Jews allowed to kill their cattle by throwing, severing of the arteries and bleeding; they had to adopt the generally accepted method of stunning and shooting. The Nationale Dagblad attained the great distinction of being the first to applaud the Nazi decree, and welcome it as a "measure which will at last cleanse our Dutch national honor of this Palestinian smudge of cruelty to animals." Shortly afterwards "Aryan" and Jewish butchers were strictly separated in the Amsterdam slaughterhouses; at the same time the numerus clausus was introduced for the meat trade. As 15% of the town's population were Jews, no more than a similar percentage of the butcher's trade would be allowed in their hands.

There was a month respite after the introduction of those first discriminations. But around the middle of September came the next ruling. Many public markets in Amsterdam were forbidden to Jewish merchants—a cruel measure directed against hundreds of small Jewish traders who eked out a precarious enough living selling odds and ends in the streets. Yet, even this was merely another introductory pin prick. In October, 1940 the first serious blow was dealt to the existence of Holland's Jews. The Civil Service was completely closed to Jews, or to gentiles married to Jews. Those already employed in the service of the State, could make no further progress.

By way of immediate response came a significant protest from the joint Protestant churches. These powerful institutions drew up a fierce denunciation of the new measure and sent it to Reich's Commissioner Seyss-Inquart under date of October 24, 1940.* The only reply the Germans made was in the form of a further decree, on October 7. All Jewish enterprises were obliged to register at once. This order applied to every business directed by a Jew—and according to the Germans people with three Jewish

*See chapter 9—"A Mighty Fortress"—page 188.

grandparents, and even those with two Jewish grandparents but married to Jews, belonged to this category. Also, if a Jew served on a Board of Directors, or if more than a fourth of the share capital was in the hands of Jews, immediate registration was required. Consequently, more than 30,000 businesses had to register; tens of thousands of citizens were to be exposed to slow pauperization.

After this "heroic" performance the enemy allowed himself a further month to digest the spoils. Then, on November 28, came a decree which eliminated *all* Jews from the Civil Service. The only reason given for this discrimination was the "action of world Jewry against the occupying authorities." In Amsterdam alone eight hundred officials were deprived of their living, among them hundreds who were the issue of two "Aryan" and two Jewish grandparents. They had never belonged to a Jewish group, or community.

This crude measure did not fail to shock the entire nation. Some of the newspapers which, though under strict Nazi control, still tried to assert themselves from time to time, mentioned the decree as one which "cannot leave the Dutch people untouched." All Jewish professors, teachers, doctors, clerks and other official personnel were dismissed, without a single exception. The following Saturday morning was to see the end of their employment by the State. None of them would be "expected to return" on the next Monday.

But that Saturday became an unforgettable morning. Clinics, classrooms and workshops were decorated with flowers. In many towns children came to school in the company of their parents, to take official leave of their trusted teachers. Throughout the country Christian workers honored their Jewish colleagues, and particularly impressive demonstrations took place at Holland's ancient universities.

When, for example, the students of the Technical College of Delft heard that their Jewish professors and other "non-Aryan" teachers were to be ousted, they decided to stage a mass protest. That "last Saturday" the Technical College was crowded with students. A procession of indignant young men and women milled through the college halls and corridors. It was of little avail that the authorities had cancelled the last lessons to be given by the dismissed teachers. Neither was much attention paid to the few seniors who tried to placate their fellow-students by reminding them of the Sermon on the Mount, "Blessed are they which are persecuted for righteousness' sake." Spontaneously the decision was taken to stay away from College for two full days. Thus the Germans could hardly pretend to be in doubt as to the opinions held by Holland's intellectual youth. The next Monday and Tuesday the Technical College lay barren and desolate.

Leyden's ancient university did not stay behind. Its students had not forgotten that Prince William of Orange, the "father of the fatherland," had given the town its university as a reward for its valiant share in the fight for liberty against Spanish tyranny. On its faculty there were several Jewish professors—among them men of world repute. Most outstanding of these was Eduard Maurits Meyers, a great scholar, admired not only because of his authoritative position in the world of law, but also beloved as a sympathetic friend and faithful guide to the hundreds of students who had been his pupils during more than thirty years.

Immediately a special meeting was convoked by the rector magnificus* of the college. Leyden University was to pronounce sentence upon the impudent Austrian traitor Seyss-Inquart. The news spread like wildfire; the rector magnificus himself was to address all students in the large auditorium. Once this professor, Rudolph Pabus Cleveringa, had been a pupil of professor Meyers; later, as colleagues, they had become great friends. The younger scholar had a profound admiration and devotion for his former teacher. When next morning he arose in the overcrowded hall and pronounced the first words of his speech, the trembling of his voice betrayed his deep emotion. He had received the letter of dismissal for professor Meyers, he said, and paused a moment. Then he continued quietly:

"I give you this information in all its crudity; I will not try to qualify it. Whichever way I were to choose my words, I am afraid they would fall far short of expressing the feelings of bitterness and pain in me and my colleagues. But I sense that I can abstain from this qualification, because in this moment our thoughts and moods are very much alike.

"Were I to give form to our mutual feelings I could, I believe, do no better than to cease here and now, leaving it to the terrifying silence which would follow, to speak for us all. But I have no desire to guide your thoughts to those who instigated Meyers' dismissal. Their action qualifies itself.

*Dean.

"All I desire at present is to leave them below us and out of our sight, and to look up with you to the height where stands the great figure in whose honor we have gathered. It seems right to me, that in this moment we should try to realize clearly who is the man that, after thirty years of fruitful labor, is now pushed aside by a power which has no other support, in Heaven or on earth, than brute force alone."

In feeling words this stolid Frisian, known to his students as a cool and little emotional scholar, spoke of the unparalleled scientific merits of the great Meyers. He described him as "one of the most important lawyers of many countries and many periods." Then he continued:

"He also was an excellent citizen, who, had not his natural modesty forbidden him to do so, could have pointed to much labor and unselfish effort for the sake of his community. It is this Netherlander, this noble and true son of our nation, this man, this father of his pupils, this great scholar who has been ousted from his post by the strangers now ruling over us as our enemies. I said that I would not speak to you of my feelings. To this decision I shall adhere, though at moments I have the impression that my body is like a seething volcano from which the boiling lava of my indignation will burst forth . . .

"The Netherlands Constitution does not distinguish between creed and race. According to Article 43 of the International Law, the occupying power is bound to respect the country's laws except in such cases where the absolute necessity of safeguarding his own military interests prevents him from doing so.

"There was no reason whatever why the authorities could not have left Dr. Meyers in the place he occupied. We had hoped to be spared this injustice . . . Now, without committing useless stupidities—from doing which I must strongly dissuade you—we can but bow before superior power. Meanwhile we shall wait, and trust and hope. In our thoughts the image and figure of Dr. Meyers will continue to live, because we cannot cease believing that he should be here and that, if Fate will it, return he shall."

Slowly the rector magnificus of Holland's most venerated University sat down. And slowly the seven hundred students who had crowded the hall, arose to sing the ancient anthem of the Netherlands, the "Wilhelmus," which perhaps has never sounded so beautiful and inspired as on that memorable morning.

The same afternoon professor Cleveringa was arrested and transported to the dreaded Buchenwalde concentration camp, in Germany. Promptly both Leyden and Delft Universities were closed by the occupation authorities, "until further order."

That similar protests were not launched in other universities was merely due to the fact that their Boards declared the institutions closed as soon as they received the German instruction to dismiss their Jewish staffs. But the outcry against the ousting was so universal that in the end the Nazis were forced to publish an "elucidation." "The dismissals have taken place," they said, "because of the world action of the Jews against the German nation." And so as to forestall the objection that, even if it were true that such an action was afoot, the Jews of Holland had always proved to be capable and dutiful citizens, the Nazi authorities added, "It does not in the least matter whether these Dutch Jews have or have not played a part in the activities of international Jewry. We consider them capable of doing so, and it is our right and our duty to act preventively."

From then on the introduction of harassing restrictions against the Jews was considerably speeded up. Before the year was out, gentiles were forbidden to accept domestic employment in Jewish families. Infringement of this decree was to be punished with a maximum prison term of one year, and/or a maximum fine of $5,000. Jews had also been barred from all movie theatres, "because," the decree explained, "the disturbances which recently took place, have been mainly the work of Jews."

As yet the Germans refrained from doing any bodily harm to Netherlanders of the Jewish faith. There were many other restrictions to be carried out first. They ordered the special registration of all Jews and half-Jews; they had the names of Jewish blood donors stricken from the lists of clinics and hospitals. They introduced the numerus clausus for all Jewish students, and thought of a number of other discriminatory measures. Not until the second half of February, 1941 was the first physical attack made upon a mass of Jews.*

Dutch Nazis had staged a provocative march through the so-called Jewish quarter of Amsterdam, one of the most ancient and picturesque sections of the city. The procession soon degenerated into attacks on passers-by and on houses inhabited by Jews. However, to the surprise of the Nazis, the Jews, assisted by gen-

*See chapter 7—Mussert's School for Traitors—page 145.

THE ANCIENT JEWISH QUARTER OF AMSTERDAM

(*top:*) The Raamgracht, typical 17th century canal; (*bottom, left:*) the Weigh-House (Waag) in which an interesting Jewish Museum was located; (*right:*) the Montelbaan's Tower, built on the remains of an ancient defense wall.

THE ANCIENT JEWISH QUARTER OF AMSTERDAM

(*top:*) The busy New Market (Nieuwmarkt) with its open air fair; (*bottom, left:*) a dark, narrow street, reminiscent of the old Ghettos; (*right:*) eve of Passover in the Jodenbreestraat.

THE PORTUGUESE SYNAGOGUE, FOUNDED IN 1675

(*top*:) Main entrance, and cobblestone courtyard; (*bottom, left*:) interior of Synagogue, practically unchanged since its foundation; (*right*:) the closed Ark of the Covenant.

Vij hebben afscheid moeten nemen, af-
cheid van gasten, die sinds eeuwen 'or
rood z.g. met ons deelden en de be
tukken voor zich zelf wisten te ve
en. Wij hebben ze uit
iebben hun een laatst w
pen, daar op een terrein
veg in Amsterdam-Oost.
roote insignes, zespuntige
laar achter het hekwer
varen, dat zij behoorden
et reisgezelschap naa
De joden zijn dus officieel uit Ned
erdwenen. Wel wandelen er nog een
ond, maar die zullen de dappere ach
ioede vormen.

chter de „tralies". Wij hadden een beel
n den klaagmuur in onze gedachten
r de werkelijkheid was anders. D
muur was er, maar die was buite
aar werd door de nie
aagd om hun verlore
len echter zag het er ander
ormaliteiten, die door de lede
lschen raad werden vervul
zich afspeelde onder ee
je, zochten de „heeren
plaatsje in de zon op. I
hadden zij niet zooveel zon genote
juist op dezen dag van hun verhu
ng. Enkelen zal het misschien de oud
dagen in Zandvoort in herinnering terug

END OF THE TRAGEDY

Section of a despicable article in *Storm*, organ of the Dutch Nazi Elite Guard. It "describes" the deportation of the last Jews from the Netherlands. "Afscheid" (Farewell) in top photograph, as well as "Jood" (Jew) on the "Jew Star" (which became compulsory as from May 1, 1942, for every Dutch Jew of over six years) are in quasi-Hebrew characters. (*top*:) Jews behind barbed wire awaiting deportation to Poland; (*bottom*:) gentiles helping Hitler's victims with their baggage, and waving goodbye to them.

tiles, met the aggression with a strong counter-attack. As a result several Dutch Nazis were "left on the field." So as to teach those foolish Jews who thought they had a chance to sell their lives dearly, that defense against Nazi brutalities lay outside their human rights, the Germans rounded up four hundred young Jews, picking them at random from the streets. These youngsters were sent to a concentration camp at Schoorl, in the province of North Holland. There they underwent the most humiliating treatment, including regular assaults and starvation. This evidently was only a preliminary "softening up" course, for soon afterwards they were transported to the sulphur mines of Mauthausen, in Austria. Only a few weeks later the news reached Amsterdam that they were dead, one and all. Several parents were offered the ashes of their sons against payment, the "prices" varying from 75 to 125 guilders.

To make it quite clear that any further protests against such bestialities would be of no avail, Seyss-Inquart, in a public speech on March 12, 1941, took particular care to point out that "we Nazis do not consider the Jews a part of the Netherlands people. They are our enemies, with whom we neither wish to conclude a truce nor a peace. The only thing we might be willing to consider, is the introduction of a reasonable transition period."

Now decree followed closely upon decree. Jews were not allowed to establish new businesses or sell those they still possessed. But neither could they discontinue their enterprises, or farm them out to others. Next followed the nomination of "trustees" in all Jewish business houses; the cost of this German supervision was, of course, to be borne by the enterprises concerned. Moreover, the Reich's Commissioner reserved his right to liquidate or stop any Jewish business, or to sell it to others without the consent or even the knowledge of the original owners.

What several generations of Jewish traders and industrialists had constructed, was now alienated from them by the stroke of a pen. Nazis, both German and Dutch, took their places—in the largest industries as well as in the smaller trades. Slowly, but surely the Jews found their own doors closed to them. They were being transformed into pariahs, people of no standing and with no future.

A short while after these specific decrees came a further general rule intended to destroy the few amenities a Dutch Jew might still discover. He was no longer allowed to possess a radio set. The Jews—it was asserted—were distributors of detrimental rumors.

They listened to the broadcasts of Radio Orange, in London, and played the part of living newspapers. This was to end immediately. Volk en Vaderland, Mussert's weekly, jubilated rather foolishly, "Here is a blow of the first magnitude for Radio Orange. Now it has lost all its customers in one go." The truth was, of course, that the forbidden radio was listened to more eagerly than ever before and that thousands of Christians made it a practice to invite their Jewish friends to their homes, to hear the broadcasts.

There were many other ways in which the gentiles showed their abhorrence of the sadistic German persecution game. Generally their feelings were expressed by special kindness and thoughtfulness towards Jewish compatriots. In the streets, in the shops and in whatever public buildings the Jews were still allowed to visit, they experienced great friendliness and sympathy. People made it a point to talk to Jewish acquaintances, or to greet them ostentatiously.

Unfortunately, this splendid attitude sometimes acted as a boomerang, as when, during the month of April, a Jew was elected President of a High School Parents' Association, at The Hague. That same day the poor creature was dragged to a concentration camp, accused of "presumptious behavior" and the "Deutsche Zeitung in den Niederlanden," a German daily issued by the Nazis in Amsterdam, threatened all gentiles with severe reprisals if "such a scandalous election were ever to happen again" . . .

On the first of May, 1941 entrance to the Stock Exchanges of Amsterdam, Rotterdam and The Hague was forbidden to all Jews. A further stipulation ordered Jewish doctors, dentists and pharmacists to treat Jewish patients only. A few days afterwards all Jewish musicians playing in subsidized orchestras were peremptorily dismissed. To crown the list of decrees for that May month, the burgomaster of The Hague issued an ukase excluding Jewish citizens from hotels, boarding houses, furnished rooms and public gardens, as well as from the boulevards of the adjoining seaside resorts of Scheveningen, Wassenaar, Kijkduin and Monster.

This splendid example was soon followed by Nazi mayors throughout the country. Zandvoort, near Haarlem, forbade Jews to appear in public buildings, cafés, or on the sea boulevards. Haarlem, Hilversum and Zaandam refused to allow Jews to settle within their municipal limits.

Around the same time the first attack was made on a Jewish church. The synagogue at The Hague, an unpretentious building set back from a street in the Jewish district of the town, was fired by Dutch Nazis and went up in flames. In various other towns more synagogues and other buildings belonging to Jews were besmeared with paint and otherwise desecrated. But these crimes were deftly turned against the Nazis. Secretly many photographs were taken of the disfigured buildings and thousands of prints were distributed among patriots throughout the Netherlands. Needless to say that this palpable evidence of Nazi barbarism increased the hatred and loathing for Mussert's followers.

A further act of terror took place in Enschedé, center of the textile trade in the eastern province of Overijssel. Three weeks previously, the town had been condemned to pay a fine of fifty thousand guilders* "to atone for an act of sabotage." Now ninety-five people, both Jews and gentiles, were deported. Among them were bank directors, industrialists, educationalists and all the officiants of the synagogue.

A patient was lifted from his bed by the Gestapo while being attended by his doctor. The doctor picked up his bag and left, but by the time he reached his own home, he found Gestapo men awaiting him, too. A fear psychosis followed upon this savage attack. Many people did not dare to return to their homes and took refuge in the surrounding woods.

In June a further round-up of young Jews took place. This time more than seven hundred were imprisoned, accused of having staged a bombing attack on a house in Amsterdam's south district which was used by the Germans as a "jamming-station" for foreign broadcasts. Before being sent to Buchenwalde these men, their hands stretched above their heads, were forced to parade up and down for more than an hour in front of the Amsterdam main synagogue. Some time later the parents of many among them were informed that the ashes of their sons were obtainable against "adequate payment."

June, 1941 . . . only a year after the beginning of the German occupation, no Jew or half-Jew was left with any certainty of life. Leaving his home in the morning, he might never see his family again. He might be caught and bullied into making genuflections before smirking Nazis throughout the hours of the morning or afternoon. He might have to undergo unbearable humiliations and tolerate the most cowardly attacks. He might be knifed and tortured—and not a soul in the whole world could help him.

---

*About $27,000.

No freedom, no feeling of content for any Jewish Netherlander—not even for his children. Every uniform, each newspaper, every poster and each new regulation was a reminder of his condemnation to suffer and to perish. One hundred eighty thousand Netherlanders had been turned into outlaws, their children were nervous, puzzled and frightened; their youth was left without a future; their adults, men and women, were destroyed by anxiety, their aged were left without the quiet and care which are the smallest possible rewards for a lifetime of labor and worry.

The persecution of Holland's Jews not only hurt the immediate victims. It has made a deep, incurable wound in the soul of the entire Dutch people. To be sure—long before 1940 tales of horror had come from Germany and Austria. But it is a different thing to see such injustice, cowardice and acts of cruelty perpetrated on one's own soil, in one's own home, without being able to stop them. When in a certain Dutch town Jewish boys were rounded up in the streets and driven closer and closer together between nets which slowly tightened around them, "Aryan" men and women were seen to cry like desolate children.

This genuine, heartfelt pity of almost the entire Dutch nation has been the only ray of light in the Calvary of Holland's Jews. Time and again the outspoken attitude of the churches buoyed up their power of resistance. Even if their difficulties did not diminish one iota, it was good to know that a vast majority of compatriots suffered with and for them. To see and hear the protests of gentiles, protests which welled forth from true mercy and a strong and purer religious belief, gave them the courage to go on living.

Throughout the Netherlands, in towns and villages, non-Jews found countless opportunities to show their true colors. Clubs disobeyed the order to "throw out" their Jewish members. Many societies resolved to disband rather than to forbid entrance to members of the Jewish faith. Denominational school teachers refused to give up the acceptance of Jewish pupils, and when, at a later stage of the persecution, Jews were sent forth from various townships, gentile friends and neighbors made it a point to accompany them to the stations. They insisted upon carrying their baggage, and in conspicuous places along their tragic route streamers had been fastened with a significant "Till we meet again."

*

The summer of 1941 brought blow upon blow for Holland's

Jewry. No freedom of movement was left to them. Amusement had become unattainable, no matter in which form. From the end of June, moreover, they were forced to keep their shops closed on Sundays and in the northern section of the country, where for generations many middle class Jews had been engaged in the cattle trade, they were forbidden entrance to the cattle markets. Meanwhile, the gentiles were forced to visit motion picture houses where the infamous anti-Jewish film "Der ewige Jude" (The Eternal Jew) was being shown.

But the most criminal decrees of those black summer months were the sequestration of all arable land belonging to Jews and the concentration of all Jewish capital in one bank, that of Lippman, Rosenthal and Company of Amsterdam which had some time previously been placed under German control. No Jew was allowed to possess more cash than one thousand guilders, or about $540. The power to dispose of his own possessions in money and valuable papers was completely taken away from him.

Towards the middle of August a further colossal theft was "legalized" by a decree instructing Jews to register all their real estate, whether vacant lots or houses, before September 15. Automatically they lost the last vestige of authority over their immovables.

In the early autumn and with the reopening of the schools, the Germans focussed their malevolent attention upon Jewish children. Following their habitual underhand methods, they published a decision that the children of Jews could henceforth only receive tuition from Jewish teachers. However, as those teachers had been eliminated from all schools as far back as November, 1940, the real meaning of the decree was that these children could no longer attend the schools in which they had felt themselves in every way similar to their classmates.

A last vestige of human shame must have remained in the Nazis who drew up this ruling; halfheartedly they promised the opening of special schools for Jews. Actually very little came of this. In The Hague and Amsterdam a few primary schools for Jewish pupils were opened, and a report made the round that a Jewish lyceum for classic and modern languages would follow "shortly." But in the provinces little or nothing was done for Jewish children. Excluded from the company to which they had belonged, they were thrown back upon the desolate homes of their parents and steeped in the abject misery of their people.

Apparently informed that some Jews were still "enjoying" the use of certain public institutions, the Germans decreed that "from now on no Jew is to take part in public meetings or use public institutions in so far as these mean to bring relaxation, amusement or enlightenment to the people." No public park, hotel or boarding house; no theatre or cabaret; no gymnasium, concert hall, public library, reading room or museum; no sleeping or dining cars; no swimming pools for "Jewish" use. They were, furthermore, strictly forbidden to visit a railroad station for any other reason than to go on a trip. For this a special permit had, of course, to be obtained. Jews were not allowed to have telephones or even use the public phone booths. They could not enter "Aryan" barber shops, or offices, and whatever shopping they had to do, was to take place between 3 and 5 in the afternoon. A new restrictive decree eliminated them from the professions of auctioneer, auditor, professional advisor, or dealer in steel.

Towards the end of October, 1941 a further ban was published. Jews were forbidden to be members of any society or establishment with an economic purpose, unless the entire membership was Jewish. The same decree stipulated that a Jew might be obliged to obtain a special permit for any kind of profession or enterprise. Also, his work or business might be declared "forbidden" at a moment's notice. Thus the complete pauperization of Holland's Jews was made an easy matter.

Within a month 1400 Jewish textile dealers had closed their shops; their stocks were requisitioned by the State Bureau for Textile Products. The Germans allowed the N. S. B. to establish a special bureau which was to "take over" further groups of Jewish businesses. Here Aryans could be registered for the "purchase" of such stolen goods. The Nationale Dagblad joyfully summed up the available enterprises. There were jewelry shops, and shops for photographic and optical equipment; book stores and shops for musical instruments; electro-technical stores and businesses in art, antiques, stamps, household articles, poultry, meat and fish. To this "first" list was added the promise that "soon many more types of enterprises will become available."

In March, 1942 the N. S. B.'er Van Maasdijk estimated that the total amount looted through the "Aryanization" procedure, exceeded 150 million guilders, or about eighty million dollars. The liquidation of Jewish-owned real estate would yield a further 200 million guilders and the requisitioning of Jewish capital approximately 150 million guilders. Altogether more than half a billion guilders* had been stolen from the Jewish minority of the Netherlands people.

But much worse was to come. After the complete elimination of the Jews from Holland's economic set-up and the theft of everything they possessed, new attacks were launched upon their persons. From every corner of the country Jewish citizens were transported to the large centers, particularly to Amsterdam. Here they were herded together in special ghettos. Soon those narrow, ancient streets were packed to overcrowding. But this did not prevent the Nazis from bringing in more and more Jews. The living conditions of those unfortunates were no concern of theirs.

Simultaneous with this new measure, unmarried young Jews were called upon to register for work in "labor" camps. Knowing full well that this meant a quick death in some concentration camp, hundreds of Jewish couples married hastily. But this road to escape was open for a few days only; then it was rigorously barred by the Nazi fiends. Numerous Jewish men were forced to depart. Volk en Vaderland, Mussert's scurrilous weekly, wrote sneeringly of the "soundless end of those lazybones and parasites." The writer hoped that this would be a lesson "to many intellectual Dutch Judeophiles who are now sweetly offering the use of their safe deposit boxes to hide unregistered Jewish property."

Whoever was ordered to move into the Amsterdam ghetto had to leave behind all he possessed. From their well-kept little homes in coastal towns and villages, hundreds of Jewish families were forced to move into foul-reeking, because hopelessly overcrowded, buildings, often sharing one dank little room with two or three families. Their household goods and everything they had attained and cared for throughout the years of their life, were requisitioned by the Nazis. Much of it was subsequently transported to Germany as "voluntary gifts from the sympathizing Netherlands people to those who have suffered most from the regular R. A. F. bombings."

During April, 1942 the enemy rested. After doing so much evil, even the Nazis had to catch their breath. But the planning of further restrictive measures went on uninterruptedly and on April 29, 1942 a special order of Commissar-General Rauter, head of the German Security Police, made it known that from May 2 every Jewish Netherlander over six years old would be obliged to display

*Equivalent in American money: around 270 million dollars.

a Jewish star, or "Star of David," described as "a sextangular black star on a yellow background. It is to be as large as the palm of a hand and to bear the inscription "Jood" (Jew) in black letters."

From that moment no Jew was allowed to display his military decorations or other honorable distinctions. Instead he got his Jewish Star which had to be clearly visible, even if he showed himself at the door of his home, or in his own garden. Moreover, a similar star was to be attached conspicuously to the entrance of each Jewish home or apartment.

This further step backwards, this return to one of the most barbaric institutions of the Middle Ages, aroused country-wide indignation. With the same spontaneous urge that brought about the strikes of February, 1941, the gentiles of Holland demonstrated. Wherever they encountered Jews wearing their star, they put themselves out to greet them with particular warmth, even if they had never before set eyes upon them. Non-Jewish girls made it a point of honor to walk arm in arm with star-marked Jewish boys; and the reverse was an equally common occurrence. Whenever a marked passenger entered a trolley car, some "Aryan" would get up and offer his place. Better still: large numbers of gentiles wore large yellow flowers in the place where their Jewish compatriots were ordered to wear the Star. Or they even displayed an emblem closely resembling the Jewish Star, with the word "Dutchman" written across it in black letters.

Immediately the Nazis retaliated by threatening these courageous Hollanders that, if they persisted in their "subversive" actions, they would be subjected to all regulations in force against the Jews. On repetition of their "offense" they would be punished with even greater severity, including despatch to a concentration camp.

All this happened in May, 1942—just after the turn of the third year of occupation. By that time little hope was left in the hearts of Jewish Dutchmen. Their fate seemed sealed. Whatever was to happen, it was clear that they were to suffer, to bear the full brunt of Nazi vengefulness and paranoiac hatred. They were completely helpless. Their own authorities, the Jewish Council which had been formed at the behest of the invaders, were equally powerless.

Every fortnight or so there was new panic in the homes of all Jews. Another round-up was in the making; "they are fetching a few hundred more" was the tremblingly whispered message among the terror-stricken. Some thousands would find shelter with friends in the country, or in far-away towns. But their life was like that of an escaped criminal. Their fitful sleep brought no relief; the slightest sound was sufficient to bring them back to the unbearable realities. The things they had loved and lived for—family, friends, books and work—had all dissolved into the abyss of boundless fear. Only one way was left to escape from it all. Many hundreds followed it; from week to week the number of Jewish suicides grew. Men and women took their lives and those of their children, rather than continue to go through the whole gamut of Nazi torture, with death for its only possible end.

*

The summer of 1942 brought the expected climax. For many months, ever since the despatch of Jewish families from provincial districts to the ghettos of Amsterdam, there had been frightful rumors of early mass deportations. No one dared to give definite form to such tales. There still was a glimmer of hope that the Jews would "only" be sent to concentration camps . . . But meantime reports came filtering through that many more "prisoners" of the Jewish race had died in Germany, or Austria. They averaged fifty per week and radio Orange, the free Netherlands broadcast in London, charged repeatedly that the Germans sent these people deliberately into the poisonous vapors of their lead mines, without the slightest protection. The rumor persisted, moreover, that droves of Netherlands Jews were used for experimental purposes; lethal gases and other means of wholesale destruction were said to be tried out on them.

Thus vegetating under a heavy pall of sorrow and suffering, the Jews of the Netherlands awaited their final ordeal. It came at the beginning of July, 1942 when the Nazis published a decree that all Jewish citizens between the ages of 18 and 40 would be deported in quick tempo. They were to be "disposed of" at the rate of 600 per day; to this message the German fiends added a little calculation. "In that way," they said, "the Jewish problem will be 'solved' in a little less than a year."

The edict caused great consternation among the entire Dutch people. From all sides protests were launched against this unheard-of treatment of Netherlands citizens. In a few weeks the composite force of those protests had become so strong that the Nazis, much against their ordinary practice, were obliged to start "explaining." Speaking over the controlled Hilversum radio, a Dutch-

Nazi stooge declared there were very good reasons for the elimination of the Jews. *They* were chiefly responsible for the general resistance in Holland against Hitler's New Order. *They* were the main instigators of armed opposition to the German occupying power.

"And because our Germanic nation has shown itself receptive to this Jewish propaganda," the speaker said, "the Germans are taking away all the Jews. Only when the Hebrews and their blood-brethren are gone, can we be sure that the good qualities of our race will once more become evident to all the world."

On the next day, the infamous Reich's Commissar Dr. Schmidt emphasized the portent of this message. In a public meeting he said, "The Dutch look upon the entire (Jewish) problem through glasses of ridiculous humanitarianism. Because of their passive attitude, we Germans have taken over the solution of the Jewish problem and have started to send Jews to the East . . . Their fate is hard, but no one should forget that they came to Holland poverty-stricken and in rags. We are no barbarians and so we plan to deport entire families together . . . In the East they are to begin with the clearing and repairing of destroyed townships. Whoever obstructs us in this task—no matter their nationality—will have to expect the same fate as that meted out to the Jews. They will be punished with all the severity of the law."

But this was not all. The Jews, despite the many handicaps to which they were subjected, "had been the principal organizers of revenge propaganda." In their homes—so the noble spokesman divulged—a large number of hatchets had been found, all ready for the "day of vengeance."

Very closely following these speeches, the menace of mass deportations became a horrible reality. It began on July 14. That day, at 1:30 p.m., the first group of Jews was rounded up under the supervision of a strong police force. They were to leave the country the same night. The round-up was one of the most gruesome spectacles ever witnessed in Amsterdam's colorful streets. The Germans made an attack on the isolated Jewish quarter and ordered the few gentiles still living within the pale to depart with speed. Then the wholesale arrests began.

Aided by Nazi soldiers, the German police apprehended all men and women wearing the obligatory "Star of David" on their clothes. Every Jew or Jewess between the ages of 15½ and 40 was detained. After the first confusion those in the streets had rushed into their houses, in the vain belief that they might be more or less safe behind their locked and barred front doors. But the Nazis forced an entrance into the ancient buildings, and dragged their residents into the open. The raid lasted more than two hours; finally the hundreds of arrested Jews were marched off in large groups, leaving behind their helplessly wailing relatives.

With typically German sadism this horrible tragedy turned out to be . . . a dress rehearsal. Late that same day the prisoners were allowed to return to their homes. "You will be sent to Germany some time soon, anyhow," the Nazis told them.

In the ensuing days the situation became unbearable. Every hour brought more suicides, and many Jews lost their reason. When was the final blow going to fall? How long would this torture have to last?

Nine days after the loathsome cat-and-mouse game of July 14, the entire thing was repeated in every detail. But this time the play had actually begun; it was the first performance of a long and "successful" run. Every evening, and often also during the night, people were taken from their homes.

"We are on the point of death," wrote a victim whose letter reached Allied territory after many wanderings. "You cannot imagine the suffering that goes on here. Throughout the long nights we listen for the sound of footsteps, and wonder whether they will halt before our door. Age no longer makes a difference. Several of our friends and neighbors, including a woman of 80, have disappeared. Presumably they have been sent to the slaughterhouses of Poland . . . *They* even take pregnant women now, in their sixth month."

An Amsterdam "Aryan" stated, in a letter written early in September, "It is bad enough that we are all living in constant peril of our lives. At any time an Allied bomb may mutilate us, or we may be annihilated by slower-working means, such as hunger. But it is a shameful thought that there are people (the Jews) living amidst us who have so much more to fear than these common dangers. My old teacher has gone—I do not know where. I can only hope he will turn up again after the round-ups . . . This morning I had my daily share of the general misery. My old friend Mrs. S., a Jewess, came in to cry her heart out. She cannot forget her poor boy of 16 years—a half-Jew—who was murdered last year at Mauthausen. She is killing herself with grief."

Among the first deportees were several hundred foreign Jews who long before the invasion of the Netherlands had sought and found shelter on Dutch soil. Those refugees were ordered to appear before a Central Committee for Jewish Emigration which had been established at Amsterdam. Here they were made to fill out numerous forms, all of them pointing to the possibility of a mass emigration. Particularly sharp questions were asked concerning their financial status. Fortunately, the legal Dutch government, during the war days of May, 1940, had ordered the destruction of all archives concerning refugees. There was, therefore, no means of verifying the refugees' statements.

After this gruelling investigation the foreign Jews were allowed to return to their homes. Many among them were filled with new hope; for a moment—and unbelievable as it seemed—it looked as if they would be allowed to depart in peace.

Depart they did soon enough—but not in peace. When shortly afterwards these would-be emigrants received notice to appear at the Amsterdam Central railroad station with their baggage, their hope turned into despair. There was an ominous sign: the luggage of each family member had to be packed separately—a clear indication that families would not be left together. Eight hundred German, Austrian and other foreign Jews were packed into cattle cars and railroaded out of Holland. Not even the Dutch police authorities or members of the Jewish Council were allowed to witness their departure. Their train of death disappeared into the dark night; they were never heard of again.

That same week the Germans started the deportation of Dutch Jews. Parents of babies under three months old were temporarily allowed to stay behind; the same "regard" was shown to people who had recently undergone a dangerous operation. But the tragic fate of their foreign co-religionists had been a lesson to the Jews of Holland, and a good many of those called upon from night to night to gather at the railroad station, disappeared from sight and went into hiding. Thanks to the eagerness of their gentile compatriots to help wherever possible, scores of them saved their lives, or, at least, obtained a stay of execution. Soon, however, the depraved ingenuity of the German rulers discovered a means of revenge. Whenever Jewish citizens whose turn had come, failed to appear, an equal number of Jewish hostages were rounded up at random, and deported instead.

To this purpose the German "Gruene Polizei" (Green Police) which was constantly employed for this dirty work, used to throw a cordon around the heart of the Jewish quarter, the ancient Weesperstraat, and tear the required number of hostages from their families. More than once, in the indescribable panic which ensued, men and women threw themselves into the waters of the Keizersgracht, one of the famous canals that intersect the city of Amsterdam. The Germans forbade their rescue and let them drown. Later their corpses were carried to the Jewish hospital, close by.

Yet, after a while this system did not appear to function satisfactorily. The number of Jewish deportees diminished visibly. Quickly a new method was worked out. Instead of allowing the victims to come to the railroad station on their own accord, they were driven in herds to a small theatre in the Jewish district, a place which—ironically enough—used to subsist mainly on the patronage of Jews. Here they stood pressed together for four full hours; towards midnight began the tragic exodus through the pitch-black streets of Amsterdam, to the waiting cattle trains.

In August, 1942 a further change was made. The Germans, still dissatisfied with the result of their nightly endeavors, staged a gigantic round-up in which no less than 3,200 Jews were apprehended and deported without delay. This time no notice was taken of age, or state of health. Men, women, girls and boys, were driven through the streets before the German barbarians. Without luggage or food, they were transported to the concentration camp at Westerbork, in the north-eastern province of Drente. There the final sifting took place. Families were torn asunder, and morning after morning huge trainloads of Netherlands Jews left the country of their birth, for an unknown destination in the East.

For a while the average trainload of Dutch Jews used to be exactly one thousand. Then the Germans added an extra ten per transport and volunteered the explanation that "at least one per cent of them will 'peg out' on the way, and we'd like the train to arrive at its destination with a minimum of a thousand live ones."

All that is known of their ultimate fate was expressed in the memorandum to President Franklin Delano Roosevelt submitted at the White House on December 8, 1942 by a delegation of representatives of important Jewish-American organizations. Together with thousands of fellow victims from other countries, they were starved in the ghettos of Poland, worked to death in mines and factories or killed outright in droves, either by the German firing squad or by means of electricity.

*

To those Jews still left in the Netherlands, existence became an intolerable nightmare. The curfew ruling was now so rigidly enforced that they were even forbidden to lean from windows or show themselves on balconies overlooking the street, between the hours of 8 p.m. and 8 a.m. At all other hours, when standing before a window, they had to display their David Star. Pending their deportation they were subjected to a physical examination. The reason for this soon became evident. Large numbers of them were put to forced labor in work camps, or transported to Germany to help in the reconstruction of war-destroyed cities.

A Dutch-Nazi broadcaster brought the necessary "elucidation." This hoodlum, who under the pseudonym of Jan Hollander had built himself a reputation as a slick and dangerous mouthpiece of the Nazis, blamed the increasing R. A. F. bombings of Germany and the subsequent destruction of property on "Judah's declaration of war on Mother Germania. Let those Jews be compelled to build up with their own hands what was destroyed by their guilt," the Nazi exclaimed. "That will do them more good than dabbling in European politics!"

After a while the forced labor edict was slightly changed. Only Jews between 40 and 60 years of age would be sent to the devastated areas of German-occupied Russia, or to Germany itself for hard labor. The fate of those between 18 and 40 remained unaltered; they disappeared into the extermination centers of eastern Europe.

Certain gentile doctors, filled with pity for the fate of the middle-aged Jews, furnished certificates of inability to many, generally on the ground of heart ailments. But this did not last very long. Some traitor eagerly "gave away the game" and the rabidly anti-Semitic Misthoorn (Fog Horn) denounced specific doctors, requesting that they be sent to the same places as the Jews whom they had furnished with "false certificates."

Degraded, despoiled, humiliated as they had become, the Jews were still considered good booty by several German and Dutch Nazi racketeers. A few Jews actually possessed the homes in which they "lived." But it was the easiest thing in the world to swindle them out of this last bit of property. Real estate agents offered such houses for sale without the knowledge and consent of the Jewish owners. As soon as a would-be buyer appeared, they went with him to a special office which had been set up by the occupation authorities to obtain the eviction of Jews from their property and force them to sell at any price.

The victimized Jew, after deduction of the agent's fee, actually received the purchase price paid for his property. He was not to hold it for long, however, as another decree obliged him to deposit the amount immediately with the Nazi-controlled former Jewish bank of Lippman, Rosenthal and Company at Amsterdam. Once the money was paid into this depository for all Jewish wealth, it was lost to its rightful proprietor.

Thus the house owner was not only robbed of his property and his money, but he also had to pay a commission for the privilege. Moreover, the new owner became rightfully entitled to claim payment of rent so that the victim, at the conclusion of the transaction, found himself without house and money, but with the obligation to pay a preposterously high rent for the favor of remaining a while longer in his own home.

Everything imaginable was done to make impossible the lives of those who were still "at large." The German Security Police, for example, communicated with the Jewish Council of Amsterdam and informed it that any Jews found seated on public benches not especially assigned to them would be deported at once, *with their families*. The "Joodsche Weekblad," only tolerated Jewish weekly, published by the Jewish Council, printed a warning on September 18, 1942 that those trying to avoid the consequences of the latest decrees which compelled them to work in Germany or elsewhere, "would meet with severe punishment."

For a while certain exemptions were made from the compulsory labor law. Jews married to gentile women and having children could apply for exemption; Jewesses married to Christian men were also eligible for this favor, even if they were childless. But later in the autumn the stipulation was rescinded. Half-Jews sent for deportation, whether to Germany or elsewhere, could only leave their papers behind "with a trusted person." As long as they were housed in the Westerbork concentration camp, they still had a small chance of being released. But once they had left the clearing center and were on their way to some eastern destination, all hope was gone. They were irrevocably lost.

On February 18, 1943 the "Zwarte Soldaat", official organ of the Nazi SS troops, announced jubilantly, "The majority of

Jews have now disappeared completely from Holland's economic life. Soon all traces of erstwhile Jewish rule will be effaced." And the writer clamored for the abolition of Jewish-sounding names belonging to requisitioned business enterprises . . .

Towards the end of the third year of occupation the fate of Holland's Jewry seems tragically certain. Those faithful citizens, who throughout more than three centuries contributed greatly to the economic welfare and cultural development of their country, are doomed to extermination. As the "invincible" Nazi armies lose battle upon battle, dire vengeance will be taken upon defenseless Jews. Their deportation from the Netherlands is now almost complete and it is very questionable whether a successful Allied invasion will come in time to prevent the Nazi barbarians from killing, scientifically or otherwise, the last remnants of Holland's Jewry.

But the handful of Dutch Jews who have managed to escape and the few who succeed in hiding themselves till the day of liberation, will surely agree that the link between them and their Christian compatriots grew stronger as the Nazi crimes became blacker and more horrible to relate. Countless Christians jeopardized their liberty and their lives to assuage the sufferings of the Jews. Scores of hunted men and women were harbored by gentiles of all classes, and no questions asked. Over and again the churches and other official bodies protested fiercely against the murderous practices of the invaders.

No one could reasonably expect that those glowing protests, that heroic indifference for probable Nazi vengeance, would change the Germans into philo-Semites. But neither was it possible to stand aside and let things happen. As an underground pamphlet, which was swiftly distributed throughout the land, so clearly expressed it, "We cannot be deaf, dumb and blind while our Jewish compatriots are quietly wiped out. We who witness their sorrow, cannot pretend that we do not hear their groans and do not see their despair.

"We are not allowed to utter our disgust and our pity. But God and history will condemn us and declare us accomplices in this mass murder, if at this moment we would look on, and keep silent . . . We therefore demand that our co-citizens shall sabotage the preparations for and execution of this fiendish wholesale deportation plan. We expect that all Secretaries-General, burgomasters and high officials will refuse to assist the German occupying power. We rely upon it that everyone in a position to do so, will thwart the sadistic Nazi measures . . ."

As late as February, 1943 civil servants openly expressed their disapproval of the exclusion of Jews from public benefits. It happened in the small town of Losser, in the province of Overijssel—only a mile or so from the German border—when a representative of the Nederlandsche Volksdienst (Netherlands People's Service) was explaining the aims and working methods of that organization. He expounded that the Service would, among others, look after the people's interests in matters of rationing and forced evacuation. Immediately the head of the local rationing service, a patriot by the name of Hartsendorp, got to his feet and asked the Nazi whether the People's Service would also be extended to Jewish citizens. The answer was in the negative and Hartsendorp promptly declared that he resigned his membership in the Service. Forty-five of the sixty people present joined in his protest and walked out of the meeting with him.

In countless ways the people of the Netherlands have demonstrated that they consider the relentless German persecution of their Jewish co-citizens a despicable and intolerable attack upon the unity of their nation. The Nazis made scapegoats of a staunch minority which, long ago, had been fully incorporated into the structure of the State. The annihilation of this minority symbolized the disappearance of that freedom of word and creed for which the people of the Netherlands have so bravely fought ever since the great Prince of Orange, William the Silent, set their course. To tolerate the endless Nazi bestialities without a murmur, would have been equal to accepting the yoke of German slavery.

That, indeed, is far from the minds of all loyal Netherlanders. Against the heaviest of odds they will continue to fight Nazi tyranny—to maintain the high moral principles with which centuries of cultural progress have endowed them.

11

A RALLYING CRY

"Sympathizers with the old order are ingenious. If they do not wear an R.A.F. emblem, as a sign of their anti-German and anti-Nazi attitude, they decorate themselves with a 'Union' pin."

Nationale Dagblad, April 10, 1941.

"The Netherlands Union is to be blamed for the satanically instigated, cynical deviltry carried on by means of poems, pamphlets, constant whisperings, and writings on walls" . . .

Volk en Vaderland, June 13, 1941.

In July, 1940 the German authorities in the occupied Netherlands "coordinated" the Social Democratic Labor Party and all its affiliated institutions and organizations. Singling out the Socialist Party for coordination was a frank Nazi acknowledgement of its importance as a popular movement. To allow the introduction of something resembling the New Order, the Germans reasoned, many obstacles within the labor movement must be overcome first of all.

Until that moment the political parties of Holland had been left alone, although their representative significance was nullified since the dissolution of the Lower and Upper Houses. No longer did any one of those political groups exercise influence upon the government of the State. They could, at best, be called "clubs" in which kindred souls might meet and find some solace in each other's company.

It did not take the political leaders very long to discover how thoroughly their parties had been paralyzed. If in pre-war days they had often and stubbornly opposed one another, they now realized that only through complete unity some sort of effective contact might—perhaps—be restored with the masses which were left without guidance and exposed to constant powerful attacks of the Nazi propaganda machine.

Less than two months after the debacle, representatives of the most important political parties came together and drew up a manifest to approach the Netherlands people jointly, as a political federation. The difficult task of writing this document was left to Dr. Hendrikus Colijn, leader of the Anti-Revolutionary Party.*

A few days afterwards the first concept was ready and once again the representatives of the Roman-Catholic, Anti-Revolutionary, Christian-Historical, Social Democratic, Liberal and Liberal-Democratic parties gathered. Colijn read his manuscript which emphasized that the Netherlands people, in accordance with international law, were obliged to cooperate with the occupying power in the daily routine of things. However, this statement was closely followed by the declaration that no other future could be considered for the nation than one of "independence under the leadership of the House of Orange."

This formula met with unanimous approval. Seen in the light of circumstances it was, to say the least, a courageous expression of loyalty and confidence. Although the situation in France appeared desperate and there seemed little reason to believe that the British would put up effective resistance against German "invincibility" after the fall of France, these Dutch statesmen dared to make it clear that they would not consider a compromise with the enemy. They remained faithful to the House of Orange which had been closely interlinked with the fate of their country throughout more than three centuries.

The historical meeting was attended by two men who had thus far played no part in the political life of the Netherlands. They had come as delegates of another movement which called itself the "Nederlandsche Gemeenschap" (Netherlands Commonwealth). Their names were J. Linthorst Homan, Queen's Commissioner in the province of Groningen and J. E. de Quay, a Catholic professor of economics at the Commercial University of Tilburg, in the province of North Brabant. To Linthorst Homan fell the task of handing the declaration to Reich's Commissioner Seyss-Inquart.

On July 12 Linthorst Homan reported back to his colleagues. What he told them had been expected: the Reich's Commissioner had refused to agree to the formation of a political movement on the basis of "an independent Holland under leadership of the House of Orange." The Anti-Revolutionary delegates as well as their Christian-Historical and Liberal colleagues declared unanimously that they were not interested in a Netherlands Union which would be forced to remain silent on the subjects of liberty and loyalty to the royal family.

---

*See chapter 9—"A Mighty Fortress"—page 201.

There was some discussion about the possibility of going ahead nonetheless. It would be a simple matter to acquaint the Dutch people with the fact that a Netherlands Union had been formed and that this Union had appointed a National Committee whose task it would be to maintain and further Dutch tradition and opinion. Yet, the German interdiction to mention the most poignant subjects, was an insurmountable obstacle, and all further efforts to come to the formation of a Committee of National Unity proved abortive. It was then that the enemy intervened and dissolved the Social-Democratic Labor Party, the largest political movement but one. Thus was frustrated the foundation of one truly united political party in the Netherlands.

But Linthorst Homan, De Quay and a third non-politician, L. Einthoven, former Chief of Police of Rotterdam, decided to continue their efforts for the establishment of the Nederlandsche Unie (Netherlands Union)—if only as a counterweight against the growing power of Mussert's National-Socialist movement. On July 24, 1940 the first manifest, signed by this "Triumvirate" and addressed to the Netherlands people, was published.

"Out of the stress of our days," it said, "a new duty is born, and we urge you to take up that task with us. We call upon you to strive with us for a new Netherlands unity, in accordance with our Netherlands character and through joint, courageous labor. A first necessity to achieve this is the acknowledgement of a change in our relationships. National cooperation on the broadest basis must follow, next to harmonious economic rehabilitation, in which the entire labor section of our people is to cooperate. Social justice, too, would be a prerequisite, so that young and old, strong and weak, will find work to do.

"These aims can be materialized only in our own, Netherlands way—with full respect for our traditional spiritual liberty and tolerance.

"We are willing to do our work in cooperation with the Dutch authorities and the occupying power. Netherlanders, give your utmost strength to our common cause. He who stands aside to 'wait and see,' will only harm the good of our country. Join us now!"

Then followed a detailed program, a few points of which should be mentioned.

"The Netherlands Union," the program explained, "desires to maintain and strengthen the unity of our people in the political, cultural and social-economic fields . . . Culturally it will endeavor to do so by maintaining and strengthening those Dutch characteristics which gave our nation power, and the place it obtained in the world. Also, it will try to uplift the people's ideals above materialism and egoism. It will protect and develop its civilization and customs. It stands for freedom of religion, church, principles and education and will try to further the position of the Netherlands in the framework of Europe's cultural life."

The program then continued to describe the social-economic measures for which the Netherlands Union would fight. Foremost among these was mentioned the organic planning of the commonwealth of labor, with the exclusion of class controversies. An acknowledgement followed of the duty of every Netherlander to work and of the commonwealth to enable every Dutch subject to share in the common labor pool. Politically the Netherlands Union declared to stand for a strong nation, in close relationship with the overseas territories, the Netherlands East and West Indies.

It was a boldly-worded program, drawn up by three able Netherlanders whose loyalty to their fatherland was above every suspicion. Three men who would do anything rather than betray the Dutch cause. This Triumvirate clearly realized the dire peril of a situation in which Mussert's National-Socialist movement would no longer be opposed by a united patriotic front. In all probability the politically colorless middle classes would prove to have insufficient resistance power, if no new and forcefully-worded slogans were put at their disposal, with which to ward off the constant danger of Nazi contagion.

But the founders of the "Unie" movement were not solely urged by this and similar negative considerations. They—and with them hundreds of thousands of others—obviously believed that the system of Parliamentary democracy had truly reached its end. In the upheaval of those days they saw the initiation of a new era; and they were out to discover the new social and political forms which might suit their country best under the changed circumstances.

That is why the Netherlands Union advocated some measure of collaboration with the German authorities, and propagated certain ideas which, at times, came disquietingly close to a well-intentioned but nonetheless doubtful kind of "New Order."

It admitted that the Netherlands machinery of state had been too slow, that too much parliamentary friction had existed. And even though the program did not mention the matter of the people's representation with a single word, nor broached the vital subjects of independence and loyalty to the House of Orange, there were huge groups of Netherlanders who found they could wholeheartedly subscribe to several of its many points. Almost every political party discovered one or more issues coinciding with its own program. In fact, there was "something for everybody."

Soon the general enthusiasm for the "Union" showed how deeply the entire nation was hankering after leadership and willing to give its confidence to any party striving for the old ideals, even though it might be forced to make certain concessions to changed conditions. The people of Holland flocked to the new party; only six weeks after the formal establishment of the Netherlands Union, the first number of its propaganda journal "De Unie" (The Union) appeared. In a leading article the Triumvirate hastened to emphasize that all political reforms would have to wait until after the peace, "because we believe that such reforms are purely Dutch matters on which the Netherlands people will have to pronounce judgment in full liberty."

The Union strongly and repeatedly attacked all those who preferred to stand aside and wait for further developments. But many Netherlanders were anxious to see the last vestiges of their doubt cleared away before joining the new movement. Generally that doubt had a bearing on the political standpoint of the Union. While on the one hand it seemed willing to cooperate with the New Order, it reiterated endlessly that it could only do so if the free character of the Netherlands people be recognized within that New Order. If, for example "De Unie" declared in October, 1940 that "our people will know how to conquer and maintain its place next to Germany in the new Europe," the paper stated only a month afterwards that the Netherlands were "part of a territory in which Germany, in conformity with her geographic position and importance, will indisputably occupy a leading position." Yet, to confuse the issue even further, the Union emphasized on every possible occasion that it would have none of a nazification of Holland.

When the first anti-Semitic decrees were introduced, the Triumvirate hastened to announce, "it is not true that the Jews living in our midst have ever tried to usurp or wrongly influence the life of the Netherlands people." And the conclusion was reached that "we do not believe in the necessity or desirability of a change of attitude towards our Jewish compatriots."

This declaration was the first of many which slowly but surely clarified the position of the Netherlands Union. When the occupying powers and their accomplices began to speak more and more urgently of "the new socialist Commonwealth," the Union stepped back another pace from its originally ambiguous program and declared to be socialist. "We wish to achieve a socialism," the Union leaders explained, "which is reduced to its most fundamental values."

Labor was to be the basis of all social and economic relationships, but "the realization of such a socialist Commonwealth is not to be bought at the expense of imperishable Dutch principles."

*

The reaction of the various political parties to the appearance and activity of the Netherlands Union was, generally speaking, unfavorable. Hendrikus Colijn spoke for many political leaders when he emphasized that his party, that of the Anti-revolutionaries, remained aloof simply because it could not, and would not, forsake its two main principles: independence, and leadership of the House of Orange. Later Colijn added that collaboration with the Union was also impossible because the new party clearly envisaged the foundation of new institutions of a totalitarian nature, and the dissolution of existing bodies.

The Liberals were not a whit less emphatic about the Union than Colijn. Their spokesmen pointed out that already great similarity could be seen between the N.S.B. on the one hand, and the party politics of the Netherlands Union on the other.

Other parties still wavered—now advising collaboration with the Netherlands Union, then again giving out the order that their membership should in no way associate itself with the new political group. Even the Catholic Party, through its leading paper, the "Maasbode" of Rotterdam, uttered words of warning. The only important daily taking up the defense of the Netherlands Union was the liberal "Algemeen Handelsblad," of Amsterdam.

Indeed, the founders of the new party had no easy time. Their intentions were often considered in need of clarification; and a particularly severe attack upon their integrity was made by a young theologian, Dr. Eykman, who had been known in Amsterdam circles as the leader of a Young Christian Movement. Eykman published a pamphlet which he called, "We go on building—but on which basis?"

In this booklet he pointed out that all reconstruction work must be founded upon a pure religious belief and that the "new-builders" should never forget this. And then, to warn against the Nazi elements among these new-builders, he talked of the "traitors who from the outset must be prevented from joining us."

The next passage treated the Netherlands Union which was compared with Peter, the "forsaker."

"What is 'to forsake?' " the author asked. "To forsake is: to ignore a thing, or a person if you are afraid of getting into difficulties by acknowledging them. In doing this you can, of course, make mental reservations. You may continue to think whatever you wish. But on the surface—and for the sake of peace—you forsake. Just as Peter who, though in his heart he still belonged to his Lord, said, 'Verily, I know him not' to the servant. There are many people in the Netherlands who, at the present moment, will not honestly avow their thoughts on quite a number of subjects. Later, when our difficulties have subsided, they will remember them and speak of them. Of course—because then the danger will be past, and everybody may talk freely again.

"But how is it possible to reconstruct whilst thus forsaking? Would it not be better to run out into the dark night and cry, cry . . . because of one's own cowardice?"

In the last part of his pamphlet Eykman analyzed in some detail the program of the Netherlands Union. And he came to this conclusion, "What remains of our typically Dutch characteristics if we have to exclude independence and the House of Orange from this program? . . . I think that many of these new-builders and their sympathizers are afraid. They fear that undesirable Dutch elements will become too powerful. They fear the heavy pressure of these times. They are anxious for their own safety. But this is not a time to find new paths for our people. Later, when our legal government has returned, we shall gladly talk with anyone who would like to suggest new principles for the Netherlands Commonwealth. Then we shall build and reconstruct, build differently from the past—but always on the old foundations, those of Jesus Christ."

Both Dr. Eykman and two other important scholars who had attacked the Union, Professor B. M. Telders, President of the Liberal State Party and Dr. H. B. Wiardi Beckman, chief editor of "Het Volk"—were imprisoned by the Germans and sent to concentration camps.

Meanwhile, however, the Netherlands Union, if only because it was looked upon as a movement against the despised Nazi parties, grew swiftly. There is no doubt that it fulfilled a most important task. Within a few months the Union counted hundreds of thousands of members, all of whom were only too happy to find a chance of joining in organized action against Holland's greatest enemies.

As to the Party's program, the membership never expected much of it. In truth, the Union grew so rapidly that the voices of the Triumvirate were completely drowned out by the clamor of the crowd. The party weekly, "De Unie" (The Union), attained a circulation as in pre-war days had been enjoyed by only a few Dutch periodicals. In March, 1941 this figure exceeded 360,000; by that time the membership was approaching 800,000.

The Triumvirate did all they could to keep up with this mushroom growth. In the large cities local boards were formed, subdivided into districts. Simultaneously the Union established "social advice bureaus," one of the few forms of activity permitted to it.

Apart from this, there were almost no practical results. Some feeble attempts were made to found certain professional centers which were to "study their respective problems, in a nationalist sense." But nothing came of this, mainly because of the lack of cooperation of the German authorities.

The latter became more and more difficult; two months after the party's birth the Nazis prohibited publication of its monthly "Volk en Arbeid" (People and Labor). They also frustrated a plan to rally the youth of Holland. In November of the same year the Union was forbidden to use the Netherlands flag for its banner.

This turnabout by the Germans, who had at first done nothing to discourage the Union's formation, was not entirely unexpected. The Triumvirate had made it very clear that they would not cooperate with the N.S.B., or with any other of the former Dutch-Nazi parties, and that they neither intended to collaborate loyally with the Germans, nor help them expedite the nazification of the occupied country. In fact, the relationship between the Union and the N.S.B. worsened by the week. Time and again the Union spokesmen, without beating about the bush, declared that they considered the N.S.B. a "set of traitors." And having no better means of contradicting this, the Dutch Nazis did their best to retaliate with ofttimes ludicrous accusations and innuendoes.

N.S.B. "leader" Mussert, for example, pronounced sentence upon the movement by saying, "the Netherlands Union stands at the side of capitalism, of plutocracy and international Jewry." And after a few weeks of careful thought, he added, "The Union has been founded as a weapon against National-Socialism, for the gentlemen on top have repeatedly declared that the N.S.B. is the people's enemy No. 1."

As time went by and the Union continued to flourish, the pronouncements of the Dutch Nazis became ever sharper. In April, 1941 Volk en Vaderland described the membership of the Union as "that Dutch clique of Churchill accomplices." And in May the weekly "Union" published the first menacing letter it had received from a member of the Youth Storm. This epistle revealed what N.S.B. circles thought of the Netherlands Union.

"Can you not see that our revenge will be terrible?" the letter asked. "We shall not hesitate to murder you in mass, you Churchill lackeys and mealy-mouthed Papists. Do you not realize that, later, you will be given the choice of National-Socialism, or death by slow torture? The fun we are going to have with you! We are enjoying that little game of ours in advance."

Finally the "differences of opinion" degenerated into street-brawls in which, as the Nationale Dagblad chronicled indignantly, "even tear gas was used . . ." It was a repetition of pre-invasion days' clashes between socialist or communist workers' groups, and the provokingly strutting Storm Troopers of Anton Mussert. In these circumstances the Union could not deploy the action its program had so abundantly promised. It is true that a number of reformatory measures were announced, such as the establishment of a Central Credit Institute, and a complete agricultural program. The latter meant to establish agricultural corporations with "cultural sub-organizations, based upon the spiritual tendencies of our days." Some time during March, 1941 the Union had, furthermore, announced that with the return of normal times, it would be in favor of bestowing greater authority upon the Prime Minister. It would also defend the institution of a so-called Corporative Council, which would rule in conjunction with Parliament.

None of these plans advanced much further than the initial stages, and the half-million people of the Union's membership were as far removed from a renewal of their shaken economic existence as before the Triumvirate's clarion call had sounded.

If until this moment opposition to the Netherlands Union

had mainly come from the side of Dutch Nazis, now the Germans, too, began to show great interest in its activities.

Reich's Commissioner Seyss-Inquart, discussing the characteristics of the Dutch people in an Amsterdam speech on March 12, 1941, said: "I hope that the peculiar make-up of the Dutch will not let them flounder into the same experience we, of the Ostmark,* have had with our so-called Fatherland Front. That Front was a conglomeration of every political opinion devoid of 'folkish' principles, and its only purpose was to keep back a new era by advocating every possible internationalism." It was evident that Seyss-Inquart meant this dictum to apply to the Union; the Triumvirate can hardly have been cheered by the comparison he drew between them and the murdered Dollfuss, or the imprisoned Schussnigg.

Shortly after this reprimand, the Germans began to adopt a severer attitude. Several requests of the Netherlands Union were categorically refused, such as the permission to organize public meetings, and the institution of an Order Service. In April, 1941 canvassing with the weekly organ, "De Unie" was prohibited; within a month nearly 200,000 new subscribers had nonetheless been gained. Two weeks later the new Union flag—a golden lion on a blue field—was banned from public display.

But it was not only the enemy's measures which prevented the Union from spreading its wings. Another, and perhaps just as great, a drawback was the factor of dualism in the party's Program. From the start the Union had declared that it was willing to cooperate in the creation of a "New Europe" if only the occupying power respected the liberty-loving character of the Dutch. The Nazis had conclusively shown, however, that they would not respect Dutch characteristics. Therefore, the more the Germans showed their true tyrannic nature, the clearer became the dilemma before which the Netherlands Union saw itself placed.

It would either have to collaborate with the enemy, or take a public stand against him. The former was excluded; neither the leaders nor the membership wished to go together with the enemy. Opposition, on the other hand, would have meant immediate dissolution of the entire Union organization.

For a long time the Triumvirate wavered; the men at the helm found it hard to make up their minds. Then their members chose for them. When the Triumvirate endeavored to persuade

*"Ostmark," the Nazi name for Austria.

their followers to support the German-organized Winter Help, tens of thousands of disappointed Union men and women resigned.

In January, 1941 an official notice was published, signed by the Triumvirate, to the effect that a number of members had been struck from the lists, "because their loyalty to the occupying power must be considered doubtful." By way of explanation of this move, "De Unie" printed an article in one of its February, 1941 issues in which the writer stated, "It was, of course, unavoidable that among the crowd of hundreds of thousands who became members of our Union, there should be elements not belonging in our organization. There were people who became members solely because of hatred for the N. S. B. There were men who read our weekly faithfully but whose real allegiance belonged to the completely antiquated principles of the "Liberal Weekly,"* or some other paper of party politics. There were men who, though calling themselves members of our Union, took part in the distribution of secret pamphlets, and the spreading of false rumors. They are the people who are in touch with illegal organizations, although our Union has always defended a loyal attitude toward the German authorities."

It was, indeed, a tragically disappointing explanation. While the Triumvirate spoke of a "loyal attitude toward the German authorities," those fiends were planning their first man hunt upon the Dutch Jews. Only a few days after the printing of this unfortunate declaration, tens of thousands of Dutch patriots went spontaneously on strike, to provide the enemy with unmistakable proofs of their loathing.

It stands to reason that in such conditions there was little or no response among the loyal Dutch to the ambiguous intentions of the Triumvirate. To speak of cooperation with the Nazis had always been highly objectionable. Now, however, with the Germans deploying their unspeakable methods of suppression and persecution, that appeasers' talk became utterly unbearable.

The members of the Netherlands Union had waited impatiently for courageous, manly guidance. They had been anxious to assist in constructing, swiftly though solidly, a huge unit which could serve as a satisfactory anti-toxin to the spreading of Nazi dishonesty and meanness. If at some moments they had hoped that finally the Triumvirate was going to take a last-ditch stand,

*The Liberale Weekblad (Liberal Weekly) was the official organ of the Liberal party up to the time of the dissolution of all political groups.

only a few weeks had to pass to show them how mistaken they had been. After Seyss-Inquart's speech, for instance, with its significant parallel between the Austrian Fatherland Front and the Netherlands Union, the Triumvirate had written, "They whom we consider the enemies of our people will never succeed in breaking the inner resistance of our nation by force of words. We are *not* prepared to trade our liberty for friendship."

Those were, no doubt, courageous words. Union members who read them, felt new hope born within them; as long as Netherlanders dared to speak their minds so bluntly, the Germans could not fail to understand that they had achieved nothing, and never would achieve anything. Unfortunately, only two months later the same "Unie" wrote, "We know and appreciate that Reich's Commissioner Seyss-Inquart tries to make us partners in a Netherlands-German relationship, with full equality of rights. In other words, the people of Holland will take their place in the new Europe as a separate nation."

It was highly reprehensible to publish this sort of sycophantic drivel while the authors knew that every Hollander was acquainted with the inhuman treatment of hundreds of "prisoners," with the spiritual tyranny of the Nazi bosses, and with the shameless pillaging of the country and its resources. The people of the Netherlands could not accept such half-heartedness.

They had been grateful to the Netherlands Union for its rallying cry. In those first months following upon the general confusion of the war, the idea to unite, if possible stronger than ever before, had been materialized through the enterprise of the Triumvirate. That had been a great and a good work. But when the enemy began to show his true character and the abyss between him and the Dutch nation became ever wider, the Union lost its bearings. Its leaders allowed time to pass without changing their obsequious attitude to one of resolute refusal to be silent accomplices to German crimes. No longer could the Union be looked upon as the possible organizer of patriotic resistance against the Nazis.

Yet, the end of the Netherlands Union was closer at hand than its members suspected. It came as an immediate result of the Nazi onslaught on Russia, in June, 1941. Seyss-Inquart, addressing the Dutch on June 28, emphasized that the people of Holland should feel one with Germany in her fight against "the Bolsheviks." The next issue of "De Unie" came with a reply to this statement. The editors of the paper declared:

"Although we and the people of the Netherlands recognize in Communism one of our greatest enemies, it is at this moment impossible for us to take sides in the Russo-German conflict. Such a decision could only be made by our own authorities, and in full liberty of action . . . It is our deepest desire to grant to others what we consider our greatest treasure: freedom of conscience."

German retaliation came swiftly. If ever the Nazis had hoped that by leaving the Union movement unmolested, they might swing its leaders and their 800,000 followers gradually into line, they now realized how mistaken they had been. Consequently, a long series of "verbotens" was published. All the movement's posters, which had been freely displayed and pasted upon hoardings and walls, were promptly destroyed. "De Unie" was suspended and the display of Union membership badges forbidden under pain of heavy punishment.

Next the still existing, though impotent, political parties—seven of them—were suppressed, so that the only actively engaged political unit was the National Socialist movement, or N.S.B., under Mussert's leadership. Subsequently, all local offices of the Union, established with the purpose of supplying "social information," were closed down. Announcing this to their readers, the editors of "De Unie" said, "This bars us from all public work. More than before we must now rely upon life *within the family*, which still remains the inviolable center of national existence."

A neutral paper in Sweden, quoting Hermann Goering's "Essener National Zeitung," divulged that the Nazis' main reason for obstructing the Netherlands Union had been its refusal to participate in the crusade against bolshevism.

Despite all curtailments the Union continued to work as well as possible throughout the summer and autumn of 1941, even producing its weekly organ which, obviously, had been suppressed only temporarily. The paper now had a circulation of 750,000 copies—an unheard-of figure for the Netherlands, and never before attained by any daily or weekly. The fact that German vengeance began to feel its way towards the leaders of the Netherlands Union, did not impair its usual activities.

In August, Linthorst Homan was "honorably dismissed" from his post of Commissioner for the province of Groningen. As long as the Germans had hoped to use this man as a tool for establishing a "better understanding" with the Dutch, they had left him his official title. Now that these tactics had failed beyond the shadow of a doubt, and the Netherlands Union was virtually paralyzed, Linthorst Homan was no longer needed.

By the end of the year the Netherlands Union was forced into liquidation; all creditors were requested to file their claims before January 7, 1942. A while later, on April 1, 1942, the last remnants of public distinction still resting upon the shoulders of Linthorst Homan, were destroyed. He was "honorably dismissed" as Curator of Groningen University.

So came the end of the Netherlands Union. But one more thing had to be done. The influence of the Triumvirate was to be completely eradicated. Even the Germans found it hard, however, to formulate acceptable crimes against these three men who, on several occasions, had gone so far in their declaration of willingness to cooperate. For many months they awaited their chance. Then, some time in the beginning of 1943, the opportunity came.

With the execution of political "suspects" at a high, with acts of sabotage constantly on the increase, and with passive resistance slowly developing into preparations for active revolt, the Germans applied their intimidation method of arresting thousands of first-class citizens by way of hostages. Among them were the three members of the Netherlands Union triumvirate. Linthorst Homan, De Quay and Einthoven found themselves once more united —but this time in a German concentration camp.

There is no doubt that with their disappearance the last vestiges of activity on the part of the Union petered out. Nonetheless, when the history of those difficult occupation years is finally written, its author will have to admit that those three men succeeded in keeping alive the flame of hope in the hearts of Holland's people. However hesitant their attitude and however ambiguous some of their viewpoints may have been, their rallying cry was heard and understood by a vast number of their compatriots. They fought bravely for the maintenance of time-hallowed liberties and—even if they failed to achieve their lofty purposes—managed to ward off the danger of ruthless nazification, at a time when the Netherlands' power of resistance was at its lowest ebb.

12

YOUTH UNDER SIEGE

"Have we been able to make Dutch youth feel the National-Socialist way? It is quite clear the answer must be, no . . . Nine out of ten youths in Holland revile Nazism."

Volk en Vaderland, October 16, 1942.

"In many boarding schools a typical symptom of these times is the collaboration between students and teachers to harass members of the Nazi Youth Storm."

Volk en Vaderland, January 22, 1943.

Mussert's Nationaal-Socialistische Beweging has never been able to boast of greater popularity among Holland's youth than among its adults. The National Youth Storm, which came into being a few years before the invasion, counted its membership by the hundreds rather than by the thousands. And so, when the country found itself delivered into the hands of the Nazis, these "conquerors" soon discovered that there was a great deal of plowing and sowing to be done in the field of youth's conversion.

In sharp contrast with Germany, where from the cradle to the altar every child is steeped in Hitlerite wisdom, the children and adolescents of the Netherlands, in their overwhelming majority, were completely indifferent to the "great cause." Worse even, they showed a definite dislike and hatred for the idolization of the Germanic leaders. It seemed particularly hard for them to understand that Adolf Hitler was a "unique gift of God, far above all human criticism."

Soon after the invasion radio Hilversum started upon the thankless task of "educating" Holland's boys and girls. Following the well-known recipe, so often applied in the Reich, the Nazi mouthpieces began by trying to undermine the self-confidence of youth. They repeated time and again that "truly speaking, the world of your parents was not much good." Against this gloomy picture of parental failings and plutocratic foibles, they displayed a bright and tempting sketch of the "New Europe" in which everyone—but more particularly every young man and woman—would find important work to do.

As usual, the Germans preferred to employ Dutch stooges for these "inspiring" talks. And so, less than a year after the start of the occupation, they hauled before the Hilversum microphone a young N. S. B. poet by the name of Cor Wiegen, who endeavored to gladden the souls of his fellow idealists with the following self-revealing tirade:

"The unity of our people was partially destroyed by foreign wolves. We, Holland's youth, did not possess the strength to resist. We felt self-satisfied and smug; actually we were ill. The good physician who might have cured us was carefully kept away from us. We were encouraged to believe we could thrive only if we drank, danced and listened to jazz bands."

Another somewhat similar challenge came from one of the very few officiating N. S. B. ministers, the Reverend Ouwerkerk. "You of Holland's youth," said this peculiar clergyman, "fritter away your best years in sophisticated boredom. But youth is too good to deteriorate among the ruins of what proved insufficiently strong to resist the storms of revolution . . . Dare to be young! Open your hearts and minds to our new times! Form your own opinion, and leave it to the ladies of the back stairs and the politicians of the sidewalks to waste their time with useless prattle."

Often the speakers tried to scare their listeners into totalitarian activities. In an anxious voice, both suave and sympathetic, they expressed their concern for the boys and girls, the young men and young women who "in this revolutionary time sit back quietly, awaiting the course of events." They are lost, the speaker would exclaim. They get farther and farther behind, and finally there will come a moment in which they will fail to understand the world. "You should be eager to work; within you there should be a flaming desire for action. You must have eyes for the enormous changes that have come about. You must endeavor to understand them; you must try to keep pace with them. If necessary you must run fast. But above all—you must dare, and dare again."

The obvious conclusion of this wise, unselfish advice was that Holland's youth must without further delay sign up with the Nationaal-Socialistische Beweging . . . But when a month went by without the expected results, the Dutch Nazis changed their approach and this time tried to entice an older and more experienced type of people, namely those to whom the education of Holland's children was entrusted.

Under the guidance of Dr. R. van Genechten, N. S. B.'er and public prosecutor of The Hague, an Educators' Guild was founded which, with great ardor, started out to imbue as many teachers as possible with Nazi "ideals." The League of Netherlands Teachers, a long-established body of educational workers, was "coordinated" and became part of the nazified National Center of Trade Unions (N. V. V.).* Woudenberg, dictator of the N. V. V., swiftly nominated a party member to the post of President of the Educators' Guild.

The remaining teachers' associations, the Roman-Catholic, the Christian and the Netherlands Teachers' Societies, did not fail to see the danger of the situation. They realized that in unity alone lay their chance to postpone the final disbandment of their groups. Early in 1941 they established the General Netherlands League of Teachers (Algemeen Nederlandsch Onderwijzers-verbond). Thus the Nazi Educators' Guild found itself confronted by well-organized and firmly-closed ranks of militant men and women.

To understand better this absence of enthusiasm for Nazism among the teachers of occupied Holland, one should know that throughout the years of Hitler's growth, the vast majority of Dutch teaching personnel had been plainly and openly opposed to the new régime. Every one of them, but more particularly the teachers in denominational schools, had learned a bitter lesson from the experience of their colleagues in the Reich. They were fully alive to the fact that under Nazi rule there would no longer be freedom of word or thought. As to the teachers in so-called "neutral" schools, many of them belonged to the intellectual crust of the Social-Democratic Labor Party. Between them and Nazism precious little love was lost.

It was a gigantic task indeed which the Nazis had set themselves. The simplest solution might have been to dismiss Holland's teachers, one and all. However, this would not have improved the situation. From the circle of Dutch Nazi teachers nothing like the required number of substitutes could be culled. The only alternative would have been to close down practically all schools in the occupied country.

In those circumstances they tried to make the best of a bad

*See chapter 5—Labor's Downfall and Enslavement—page 101.

job. For not only did they find arrayed against them a strong army of capable teachers—who in subtle, often almost imperceptible ways, were able to strengthen the will-to-resist of their pupils—but the children themselves, educated in a strong attachment to democratic liberties, displayed no longing whatever for the blessings of Hitlerism.

As general obstructionism, both passive and active, grew throughout the entire country, youth followed the example of their elders. The adolescents were fully aware of what had happened to their fatherland; the younger and youngest sensed the true and tragic state of affairs. They saw that lightheartedness and joy had disappeared from their surroundings. They were told that the Queen and the princely family had been forced to leave the Netherlands and were staying in foreign countries. They wondered at the strange men in outlandish uniforms, speaking an incomprehensible language. And with all the spontaneity of a child's mind that does not think of ultimate results but lives for the moment only, these youthful patriots threw themselves into the battle against the occupying power and against the traitors of the N. S. B.

A few months of occupation sufficed to attune every one of their rhymes and jingles to the situation. They skipped and jumped to the accompaniment of the most heartfelt curses against Adolf Hitler and his "moffen" (Huns). For the Fuehrer himself they advised a ten-minute immersion in ice-cold water, with the assurance that this would "finish all this dreadful mess." The mildest description of N. S. B.'ers was that of "dirty traitors." Often, however, these words were replaced by action and the children of Dutch Nazis were constantly attacked.

In November, 1940, the tension in most public schools had become so great that the authorities found it necessary to nominate an "authorized person to maintain peace and order, and to prepare such measures as will be needed to develop our schools in accordance with the new interests of the Dutch people." The N. S. B. teacher who was appointed to this Herculean task was a certain Van Rossum who immediately, in a press interview, menaced the recalcitrants by stating: "I *hope* it will be possible to limit the number of dismissals." Next, the former Department of Education, Arts and Sciences was split in two and the Amsterdam professor Jan van Dam nominated to the post of Secretary-General of Education.* Culture and Public Enlightenment was made into a

*See chapter 2—In The German Web—page 46.

separate Department, under the guidance of Dr. T. Goedewaagen.

All this had happened before the start of the winter of 1940. Only a few days after Van Dam's appointment, he broadcast a long speech composed of nothing but complaints. He began by trying to explain a measure which dated back to shortly after the capitulation. At that time the Germans had confiscated all school-books, without exception, purportedly to examine them for possible anti-National Socialist utterances. Ever since this requisitioning thousands of schools had been without the necessary text-books. Obviously, the Germans had found it a rather lengthy and embarrassing task to read through all this material. Here and there certain changes had already been announced, however, such as the elimination of the "Song of Hope" from the songbooks of the religious schools, because it expressed confidence in the ultimate conversion of the Jewish people.

It had also been made public that children's reading books in which such phrases occurred as "On the Queen's birthday everyone wears an orange ribbon," had been thrown into the German incinerators. The most ludicrous example of this lust to destroy was the case of a simple reading book in which the unsuspecting author, completely unaware of the future appearance on the historic scene of an Adolf Hitler and a Hermann Goering, had written the highly "subversive" sentence, *"Herman throws Adolf into the water."*

Now professor Van Dam tried to make it clear that the requisitioning and the destruction of those books by no means proved that they had been "forbidden." According to him they had only been "temporarily taken out of circulation. Every separate book will be restored to its rightful owner, unless it is found to contain passages which must be considered insulting to the German people and their leaders."

After this revelation the Nazi besought the teachers of Holland to "educate their pupils as citizens capable of attuning themselves harmoniously to the new world." For this elevated purpose they should "even neglect their own personal feelings and principles." Finally he addressed the students of Holland who only a few days previously had clearly demonstrated their abhorrence of the introduction of the first anti-Jewish measures.* With becoming modesty he exclaimed, "Closing your universities not only means that you are deprived of the privilege to sit at our feet . . . , but it will greatly harm and retard your intellectual development."

*See chapter 10—Slaughter of the Innocents—page 215.

Toward mid-December, 1940, all pupils, whether in schools or universities, were forbidden to display insignia or emblems. In the spring of 1941 this prohibition was extended to the wearing of uniforms. Yet, though it might be possible to forbid students the public display of their feelings, such sentiments could not be changed with the same ease. Night after night they sang patriotic songs in their clubrooms and even in the streets. Vengeance followed swiftly with the dissolution of all students' clubs, both at Leyden and Delft. Their clubrooms were seized and several students, together with a professor, arrested. In order to replace the ousted Jewish professors quite a number of German teachers appeared in the University classrooms—to the unconcealed dislike and fury of the patriotic students.

Around the middle of February, 1941, the Germans introduced the numerus clausus for Jewish students which—of course—met with the complete approval of professor Van Dam. With a show of great magnanimity he announced, however, that he had obtained "special permission" for a number of Jewish students who would get the opportunity to complete their studies. He did not add that this leniency would, in any case, fail to change the purposeless future awaiting these men. And the worthy professor continued:

"I must emphasize the desirability of peace and order in our universities. This week something regrettable happened in Leyden. A few fools, or malevolents, posted a kind of ultimatum claiming reopening of the University. Everyone will realize that this is about the worst way to achieve that purpose."

March, 1941, was almost past before the occupation authorities decided that the recalcitrant students had been sufficiently punished, at least for the time being. They announced that the Presidents and the Boards of Curators had been authorized to send students home, and even to close the Universities for no more than ten days at a time. Following swiftly upon the publication of this measure came the announcement that the Technical University of Delft would be reopened, but that "even the slightest incident will be sufficient to justify the severest measures. If necessary, and under certain circumstances, the University will be permanently closed."

On similar conditions Leyden University was reopened during the early part of May—but only to offer last year's students the chance to take their final examinations. Little interest was shown in the methods these young men and women had applied to prepare themselves without the assistance of their teachers. As a matter of fact, they had been forced to finish their studies with the sole help of textbooks, and some assistance from older students.

Both in Leyden and Delft the Presidents and Curators of the Universities resigned en bloc; they did not wish to accept the dictatorial powers which the Nazis were trying to lay upon their shoulders. The one unfavorable exception was the University of Groningen, in the north of the country. Here an N. S. B.'er, professor H. M. de Burlet, was President and this man gladly collaborated with the occupying authorities.

The Dutch Nazis openly rejoiced whenever a loyal professor resigned or was dismissed, as such an occurrence might give them another chance to fill a much-coveted post. Unhappily, among this herd of traitors there were only few intellectuals and so, to their profound chagrin, it often proved impossible to fill a vacant place from their ranks.

Besides, the method worked too slowly to their liking. In July, 1941, the Dutch Nazis therefore founded a "Society for the furtherance of National-Socialism." This foundation appointed Attorney-General Dr. R. van Genechten to special professor of Political Economy at Leyden. At the same time Secretary-General T. Goedewaagen, head of the Department of Culture and Public Enlightenment, was elevated to the rank of professor of "New Philosophy." Without loss of time this elated "scholar" announced in a radio interview that he would devote a goodly portion of his time to the teaching of the philosophy of blood relationships . . .

Only a few days later a third Nazi became professor. He was Dr. H. Krekel, a one-time journalist for liberal papers who had turned to Nazism long before the invasion. As soon as the Germans attained authority, he was made chief editor of the former liberal weekly "Haagsche Post" and simultaneously became a member of the N. S. B. Now his job was to be that of professor extraordinary of historical philosophy.

Unfortunately, the three gentlemen never delivered their inaugural speeches. Before that auspicious day the University of Leyden was once more closed by the Germans. Fresh outbursts of protests and other "irregularities"—as the invaders called them—had been the cause of this second close-down, which came in October, 1941.

On August 16, 1941, Reich's Commissioner Seyss-Inquart decreed that the authority of the Board of Curators of both Leyden and Delft Universities be transferred to the Presidents of those Boards. They, in their turn, would be placed under the supervision of the Department of Education which would appoint a Board of Curators of four members, for each of the two universities.

He also announced that it would still be possible to pass certain examinations, provided they took place before November 20. As from November 1, 1941, students preparing for their finals were permitted to transfer to the Universities of Amsterdam, Utrecht and Groningen—but all of these were already overcrowded. It was therefore decided that they would also be "admitted" to German universities.

This was, obviously, a new attempt to convert Netherlands' intellectual youths by removing them from the influence of their own liberal teachers. The new ruling intended to bring them under the leadership of Nazi demagogues; and as a further inducement to come to Germany the students were told that Dutch diplomas and degrees would be valid in the Reich, while German titles would henceforth hold good in the Netherlands.

*

Around this time the ambitious Van Genechten had a grandiose vision: he would change Leyden into a purely National-Socialist university. He discussed his plans at length at a gathering of the National-Socialist Students' Front, held at Utrecht around the middle of November, 1941.

Pointing out that the students of Leyden had been obliged to go to other universities while their teachers were "stumbling along the streets like dazed old men," or "abusing their free hours to produce secret pamphlets and similar filth," Van Genechten exclaimed, "Leyden, the academy imbued with politics, has now been closed. But there is a hope that before the year is out this phoenix will arise from his ashes as a new and purely 'folkish'* university. Leyden will then be a political university, truly serving the entire nation. The students will have to live up to the spirit inherent in a young university. They will have to submit themselves to the physical drill which will be required of everyone—students, teachers and professors alike." (Thunderous applause.)

*"Folkish" is a literal translation of the German word "Volkische," meaning "nationalistic on a strongly racial basis."

Two days later Van Genechten had himself interviewed by the A. N. P., the nazified Press Bureau, so as to express his satisfaction that "the hornets' nest had been cleaned out." He volunteered the additional information that at the folkish university of his creation all students were to be "of the purest aryan blood."

But alas . . . ! professor Jan van Dam, Secretary-General of the Department of Education, completely disagreed with his colleague in regard to the latter's exalted plans. Employing the same means as Van Genechten, he staged an interview with the A. N. P., in which he flatly contradicted everything Van Genechten had said concerning Leyden University. He would never dream, he shouted vehemently, of treating Leyden University as a "different" institution. No attempt would be made to change it into the folkish university Van Genechten had described. "This may be considered at a later date," Van Dam continued vaguely. "As to the information that professors will be obliged to participate in athletics and gymnastics, this is mere nonsense. I shall be satisfied if the Leyden professors show a little interest in physical culture."

Finally he denied the truth of Van Genechten's allegation that there had been examination swindles in which professors had "simply dragged their pupils through every difficulty." "If such a thing had really happened," Van Dam concluded, "those graduates would never have been allowed to enjoy the rights attached to their ill-gotten degrees."

In sharp contrast with Van Genechten's revolutionary plans, Van Dam stressed the regulation which had been published a few months previously, that students whose parents were not in the occupied country, could complete their courses throughout 1941 and 1942 without the payment of college fees. They would be permitted to sign I.O.U.'s, on condition, however, that they could prove their lack of funds resulted from prevailing war conditions.

*

From the beginning of the occupation the students of the Netherlands have played an important part in various underground movements. Eager to take the greatest risks, enthusiastic and resourceful, they never before deserved the epithet of "spes patriae" so much as since the invasion. They presented a united front against all efforts to nazify the university systems, and the Germans have been well aware of the dynamic power of these youngsters.

If closing down their schools of learning did not suffice,

other and severer methods must be applied. The first decree of this kind came in April, 1942, when all students between 18 and 24 were ordered to register with the German-instituted Labor Bureaus, for work inside the Reich. Thus an obligatory Labor Service grew out of the so-called Reconstruction Service.*

During 1941 some people had been inclined to believe that the Reconstruction Service "meant well." But at the end of the second occupation year it had become clear beyond doubt that the main purpose of this institution was to teach Holland's youth the principles of National-Socialism. Consequently, the success of the Labor Service fell far short of Nazi expectations. It had been hoped that the majority of 400,000 Dutch youths between the ages of 17 and 23 would register voluntarily, for their half-year's service in one of nineteen labor camps. But towards the end of January, 1942, the grand total of such volunteers had not quite reached the 6,000 mark.

This was too deep a humiliation; the occupying power could not tolerate it. And for this reason came the announcement that no student could enter a university if he had not been a Labor Service man. Besides, anyone wishing to become a Civil Servant after January, 1943, would be obliged to fulfill his Labor Service duties first. For those already in the employ of city, province or state, slightly different measures were taken. All employees between the ages of 18 and 21 must "do" six months Labor Service or be promptly dismissed, while any 17 year old had to serve his full year in a labor camp. Without this preliminary he would not even be allowed to enter a secondary school or a technical college. Naturally, the Universities would also be closed to him. In addition, the Secretary-General for General Affairs received the power to call into the Service all men within the age limit who "are not usefully employed, or unemployed, or who have not had a regular school or vocational training."

The response of Holland's students remained feeble, nonetheless. And only a few months after the introduction of the compulsory Labor Service a proclamation signed by prominent Netherlands intellectuals was secretly circulated throughout the country. They appealed to the students to "think of your future, and continue to refuse cooperation with the Nazi Labor Service."

By that time even the Germans no longer tried to pretend that the Service was a Reconstruction movement. Nazi "big shots"

*See chapter 1—The Debacle—Self-Reliance Regained—page 15.

came from Germany to witness special demonstrations of a purely military character. In one camp 400 N. S. B.'ers were "specially trained" for semi-military work on the eastern front.

The underground appeal to the students was not made in vain. The youngsters discovered many ways in which to escape, at least temporarily, from the hated Labor Service. Several of them developed a rather curious, unexpected interest in certain irrelevant subjects, thus prolonging their studies and postponing their final examinations. There was a veritable run on technical colleges, particularly Delft, and in many Dutch businesses the owners' sons were appointed co-managers. Hundreds of students ignored summonses to appear before Nazi doctors in connection with the Service. For this offense some of them were promptly sent to jail for periods up to two months.

In further retaliation, the German authorities tightened their grip upon Holland's university life. During the summer of 1942 they announced that even those who had completed their year's term of Labor Service were no longer at liberty to choose their university. Henceforth all applicants would have to go through a provisional examination at Utrecht University, after which they would be informed where to study. Only a comparatively small number of them were finally allowed entrance to a university.

But former students of Leyden University were inexorably barred. The only exceptions made were for those who had studied theology, natural science and philosophy. They, one and all, were referred to Amsterdam University. In any case, the courses for freshmen were postponed till November 1, to make sure that everyone falling under the compulsory Labor Service regulations had been found and sent to a camp. In stands to reason that this constant harassing of Netherlands' students and the interference with their activities, had entirely changed the old and rather pleasant concepts of a student's life.

In January, 1943, a Netherlands undergraduate escaped from the occupied country and reached England. He told of frequent German threats to close the University of Utrecht at which he had studied. Often students were suspended for having displayed their anti-Nazi sentiments too openly. Right up to the autumn of 1942 students' newspapers managed to subsist, though always severely censored by the enemy. Despite this rigid control, the editor of a Utrecht undergraduate paper managed for quite some time to publish Allied reviews of war events. He did this by placing official German reports side by side with news "from unofficial sources"—obviously the London and Boston radio. And invariably he made it a point to express his amazement at the "errors" which so frequently crept into the unofficial news, as compared with the official German war bulletins . . . The same daring youth published a memorial column for two young freshmen executed by the Nazis; in this article he paid a high tribute to the victims "who have given their lives for their Queen and country."

Out of 4,500 students at Utrecht University, there were only twenty who joined the Dutch Nazi party. They were completely boycotted and led a miserable, secluded existence. The students never missed an opportunity to show their disgust of Nazism. One of their law professors, after having adopted an executive post in the Nazi-established Culture Chamber, entered a classroom for his usual lecture. As one man the students remained seated, contrary to the venerated Dutch tradition demanding that students stand when their professor enters, in token of their respect for him.

After the shooting of several Dutch Nazis,* the German authorities hastily organized a "purge of saboteurs and terrorists" who, they seemed to think, were to be found in numbers at Holland's universities and high schools. Thousands of youths between the ages of 18 and 25, many of them students, were arrested. In Delft and Amsterdam alone six hundred students were reported apprehended in the streets and in their homes. They were held in prison for nearly a month. Then the Germans released them, but not before they had signed a "solemn declaration of obedience," in which they undertook to obey the laws, decrees and regulations enforced in the occupied Netherlands.**

The same expression of the will to obey was required of all other students, but only a very small percentage of Holland's 18,000 studying youths responded. Numbers of them went into hiding and others simply ignored the appeal of professor Jan van Dam, the Dutch Nazi Secretary-General of Education, to sign the declaration before the deadline of April 10. Even the professor's plea that the students would not be bound "for their lifetime" but only for the duration of the war, did not make an im-

*See chapter 8—Unholy Crusades—page 164.

**The declaration read as follows: "The undersigned, ..., born .... at ...., hereby solemnly declares that he will obey, in honor and in conscience, the laws, ordinances and other measures in force in the occupied Netherlands territory and that he will refrain from every act directed against the German Reich, the German Army or the Netherlands authorities. Also that he will abstain from such behavior and activities as would in the present circumstances endanger the public order at his university."

pression upon them. University education under the Nazis had become so much of a farce, anyhow, that the threat of excluding them from all universities no longer carried the power to subdue.

Whether they signed the declaration or not, they would in any event be eligible for Labor Service. Seyss-Inquart had made it clear that the Service was obligatory for every youth, and on February 28 Dutch Nazi "leader" Anton Mussert had reiterated this message, adding that as far as students were concerned even those who passed their finals must go and work in Germany for at least one year. This announcement was immediately confirmed by Commissar-General Fritz Schmidt,* the notorious Commissar for Special Services, who threatened to apply force to anyone "failing to *volunteer* to do his bit for Germany's total war effort."

When the collaboration of Netherlands' students remained conspicuous by its absence, the Germans thought of a different way to "get at them." The Boards of all universities and colleges were convoked to a meeting in which professor Van Dam informed them that Germany was in need of 8,000 Dutch Labor students and that the immediate cooperation of those present at the meeting was imperative. With the exception of the Nazi President of Groningen University,** all educators refused to collaborate; they would have nothing to do with the selection of their pupils for the Labor draft. During the ensuing weeks college and university life came to an almost complete standstill; it was no doubt due to this firm attitude of the educators that the Germans decided to liberate the thousands of young Dutch students imprisoned after the February attacks on members of Mussert's party.

Soon enough the Nazi authorities found out that many hundreds of students had accepted any kind of employment, in the towns as well as on farms. To round up these men Rauter, the dreaded German Commissioner for Public Safety, decreed that from May 3, 1943, no Dutch employer could keep in his service any student who had attended either a high school or a university during the current year and had not completed his studies. Violations of this order were to be punished with imprisonment up to six months and payment of fines up to 2,000 guilders (about $1,080), apart from the fact that "severest police measures would be taken against the offenders."

But even this new measure failed to help; and now the Germans announced the permanent closing of all denominational uni-

*Schmidt was "accidentally" killed while on a trip in France (June, 1943).
**See page 254.

versities.* Students of Catholic, Calvinist and other religious universities were told to apply to state universities if they wished to continue their courses.

On May 17 Goering's "Essener National Zeitung" reported that 4,000 Netherlands students had arrived in Germany and were "employed on vital work." Obviously, this was the first result of a further German decree, which ordered all men who had attended Dutch universities during 1942 and 1943 to report for Labor purposes to the Commander of the SS divisions in their district. Offenders against this new command were menaced with imprisonment in hard labor camps, and parents or guardians of such "criminals" were to be held personally responsible for the appearance of their sons or wards at the registration centers.

It was another drastic Nazi move in their efforts to ruin the lives of thousands of Holland's most promising youngsters. Yet—even this measure, coming after three years of oppression, will prove quite inadequate to stamp out the brave resistance of the students. The closing of their universities, which was expected to weaken their opposition, strengthened it instead. Holland's students know many ways in which to harass the enemy; the Nazis will find it well-nigh impossible to paralyze their well-organized underground work. They never slackened in their efforts to protect their intellectual heritage against the brute force of Nazism. When the long-expected allied invasion of the European Continent becomes a reality at last, the students of the Netherlands will no doubt play a most important part in the conclusive ousting of the enemy from every inch of Dutch soil.

*

Their unwholesome interest in the affairs of Holland's students did not prevent the Germans and their Dutch Nazi accomplices from thinking out and applying numerous changes in the teaching of young children. In April, 1941, a rule was published that affected both primary and secondary schools. As from the tenth of that month the appointment of every new teacher was exclusively placed into the hands of professor Jan van Dam, the Nazi Secretary-General for Education. Municipal councils or school boards were to submit a nomination list to him with no more than three names for each vacancy. Van Dam was free to choose one of the nominees, or to reject the slate in its entirety. The intention was obvious; whilst a semblance of neutrality would

*See chapter 9—"A Mighty Fortress"—page 207.

be retained, only N. S. B.'ers were henceforth to be chosen as teachers of Holland's children.

That this measure drew indignant protests from all classes, did not disturb the Nazis at all. It disquieted them much more to see how many parents took their children out of high schools and lyceums, particularly the denominational institutions. Only a few weeks after the introduction of the new rule, the Reformed Lyceum of Amsterdam had lost so many pupils that it was forced to close its gates.

Despite this opposition professor Van Dam blithely continued to work out further changes. In July, 1941, he announced that the curriculum of the preparatory, secondary and high schools had been "brought up to date." In other words, it had been placed in line with Hitler's New Order. Increased time was given to physical culture and to the teaching of German. French was relegated to a secondary place; no time was reserved for it in the elementary schools.

Everything was to be done to imbue the children with the spirit of the "New Times." Commissar-General Wimmer, to whom is entrusted the care of the entire educational system, declared in a meeting of German-Nazi teachers, which was held in the province of Limburg, "If we can't get the parents, we will win over the children. Perhaps we will find it possible to approach the adults through them. The better teacher you are, the more you will be able to do in this respect."

Shortly afterwards, Van Dam made another public appearance in which he announced further changes and "adjustments." He stressed that Reich's Commissioner Seyss-Inquart had endowed him with special powers to "advise denominational schools regarding their teaching program and the material they are to use." This, of course, in connection with the changes necessitated by the European situation. Any religious school unwilling to accept the Nazi conditions, would lose its claim to state subsidies, and run the risk of being closed, "as its internal peace and order will no longer be guaranteed."

With the advent of the new winter semester the teaching of German would get a preferred position for both seventh and eighth year pupils. The language of the Fuehrer would be on their school-program no less than three times each week. "This," Van Dam explained, "will promote contact and friendly intercourse between the Dutch and their German brothers, and make it possible for them to go to Germany if they cannot find employment at home."

But the last of his announcements was by far the most significant and ominous. "An interesting experiment will be made," Van Dam disclosed, "by establishing a Dutch duplicate of the German-Nazi Political Institute which trains selected youths to become the country's Fuehrers." In Holland the institute would be called "Nederlandsche Instelling Voor Volksche Opvoeding" (Netherlands Institute for Folkish Education), and be known by the initials NIVO. The school would be established near Arnhem, and its avowed aim was to create a new "Nazi aristocracy" which would eventually provide the material for a governing class. Candidates would be "Germanic, strong and healthy boys between the ages of 12 and 18." Quite appropriately a former sanitarium for nervous disorders was turned into the NIVO boarding school, so that among teachers as well as students many were sure to feel very much at home, right from the start . . .

"Storm," the organ of the Dutch Nazi SS, mentioned as the most important task of this folkish education "the development of thoroughly healthy bodies." It expected the bulk of the pupils to hail from the farmers' districts as there, the paper said, "the best folkish blood has been preserved."

To begin with, forty students between the ages of 12 and 18 were chosen from among no less than 580 applicants. They all wore uniforms and were promised diplomas admitting them to a university upon the completion of their school term. A few months afterwards these future aristocrats were called upon to continue their training in Germany itself. Subsequently, they departed for the Reich where they were incorporated in the Langemark School.

For a couple of months Van Dam had no further new plans to offer; he was hard at work on the practical application of his various "reforms." But on October 3, 1941, he burst into verbiage once more. Writing in Mussert's weekly Volk en Vaderland, he announced that political discussion had been forbidden in schools, and he continued, "What is the use of all disciplinary educational measures if at home the children hear nothing but broadcasts in Dutch from England and the United States? They listen to coarse language, incitement to murder and hymns of hate which come from London and are designed to poison their minds, in true Jewish fashion."

It was a repetition of the old lament regarding the indifference of Holland's youth to the blessings of the New Order. Time and again Nazis, both German and Dutch, exhausted themselves reproaching these youngsters that they were "indifferent, or negatively disposed." Generally the peroration to such speeches was the menace that when the New Order would at last be fully established, such "negative elements" would not escape their adequate punishment!

In December Van Dam admitted during the course of a radio interview that his plans for the reorganization of the school system "were not progressing very rapidly." What had been done was that the requirements for certain examinations were somewhat relaxed. But this was not so much due to Van Dam's reformatory spirit as to the scarcity of fuel which had greatly cut the number of available schools. Many school buildings had been requisitioned, and studying at home became more and more difficult because of the lack of coal. Insufficient nourishment, too, contributed its share, impairing the activities of very many students. Finally, school terms had to be shortened to allow pupils to fulfill their Labor Service duties.

Despite all this, the Nazi professor was still of good cheer, assuring his interviewers that "by the end of the next year" a definite revision of the entire educational system would have materialized. His first step towards that goal was made in January, 1942, when he obtained Seyss-Inquart's signature to a decree which placed teachers and professors completely in his power. For one thing, he could transfer them to other institutions if—as in the case of Leyden University—their school was closed down. He could dismiss them, too, without a retaining salary (wachtgeld) if they exercised their duties in a manner "detrimental to the fruitful development of Dutch education." Should they nevertheless persist in teaching privately, they would be punished with a maximum of two years' imprisonment or an unlimited fine, or both. Similar punishment was held out to the responsible heads of schools or private institutions accepting their services.

A special official was appointed to deal with such dismissals and this man, the N. S. B.'er Dr. G. D. Noordijk, began by ousting the head inspector for three provinces, those of Gelderland, Brabant and Limburg, all three of them containing an important Catholic element. The vacancy was filled by the leader of the so-called Roman-Catholic section of Mussert's N. S. B. Five days after his appointment this renegade convoked a meeting of the seventeen inspectors who were to work under his leadership. "I have always found neutrality in teaching quite impossible," he said. "And as a National-Socialist I feel obliged, before God and my conscience, to see that the 400,000 pupils in my district are educated to become men and women who will assist in obtaining for our country the place it deserves in the New Europe."

The inspectors' answer was as concise as it was clear. Sixteen out of seventeen refused to have anything to do with their Nazi "boss," and left him to his own devices.

*

The Catholics have been foremost amongst those who set out to obstruct the introduction of nazified education. Only physical force was able to stop their efforts to protect the tuition of Holland's Catholic youth. Whenever the nazified Department of Education issued a circular which the Catholics considered in contradiction to their principles, they referred it straightway to their waste-paper baskets. When an N. S. B.'er was elevated to the rank of delegate of a Catholic teachers' organization, not a single member remained. When the Nederlandsche Landstand* co-ordinated Catholic agricultural tuition, protest meetings were held at the agricultural schools of Venlo and Roermond, in Limburg province, which provided the occupying power with "very good reasons" for their close-down.

In March, 1942, Van Dam ordered all school principals to grant permission to members of the various Dutch Nazi youth organizations to exhibit Youth Storm posters, both inside the schools and on their outer walls. To a great extent this order was ignored; not a single Catholic school obeyed it.

In the end the new inspector for Gelderland, Brabant and Limburg stated crestfallenly in a letter printed by Mussert's Volk en Vaderland, "The teacher does not understand the new times and he passes this misunderstanding on to his pupils. But I *demand* cooperation. Spineless neutrality is the same as resistance and sabotage."

He and his colleagues might reiterate *ad infinitum* their firm decision to nazify Dutch youth, the results remained most disappointing. For some time they expected that N. S. B. children, if judiciously placed among "recalcitrant" pupils, might exercise a great influence "to the good." Alas! those stooges were annoyed

*See chapter 6—Plight of The Peasants—page 122.

and pestered instead. They were plagued with the persistence and ingenuity which are youth's very own. Often they found the tires of their bicycles punctured, and it became quite a habit to pay a fine if accidentally the name of a Nazi pupil was mentioned. They were "sent to Coventry" in the most complete meaning of the adage. They formed a small circle of outcasts, untouchables.

From time to time the "Stormmeeuw," monthly organ of the National Youth Storm, would contain bitter effusions on the situation in public schools. It is worth-while quoting one of them at length:

"It is Monday morning and a few early pupils enter our school," the story went. "As usual they discuss Russian, British and American successes and the splendid tactics of the Allies for which *the others* are falling so easily. It is very strange that none of the teachers seem to notice the tricolor insignia some of the pupils are wearing on their lapels . . . Now two boys are approaching, one of whom wears the Youth Storm uniform while the other proudly displays the emblem of the Youth Stormers. Immediately some of the teachers begin to smile and others whisper something that sounds like 'those b . . . .'

When these boys enter the classroom there is a sudden silence. As if by magic all the clamor and chatter dies down. But this only lasts some seconds. Then there are volleys of unfriendly remarks, from all sides. You can distinguish such words as 'rascals,' 'traitors,' 'you wait till our time comes'—and many other choice remarks which get lost in the general upheaval. Now the bell rings; the class grows more or less quiet.

When the teacher enters he feels at once that 'something is up.' Then he perceives the boy in uniform . . . He blanches and says in a hoarse, strangled kind of voice: 'Quiet, everybody.' He sits down, stony-faced; then he summons the Youth Stormer before the class. There the boy stands, the eyes of everyone glued upon him in unconcealed contempt. The teacher thumbs his book long and carefully. At last he finds a 'tough' question for the Youth Stormer to answer, but the boy remains silent.

'Don't you know the answer?', the teacher asks harshly.

'No sir,' is the firm reply of the Youth Stormer.

And then the teacher, in a tone of utter astonishment, 'What . . . . you don't know *that?* I thought you people in uniform knew *everything.*' (Homeric laughter.) 'Well—you may sit down . . .'

Soon afterwards the geography hour begins. A girl who is

to point out Dutch Guiana on the map, hesitates. She shrugs her shoulders when the teacher questions her as to where Surinam may be located. And now the teacher-oracle says joyfully, 'But, my dear girl, don't you know that our Allies . . . I beg your pardon, our *former* Allies, are helping us to protect that territory?' And the entire class yells gleefully, 'Yes, sir. Of course, we know that!'

The next victim is the Youth Stormer with the party emblem. He is to indicate a small island with a long-forgotten name, but he doesn't know it. Indignantly the teacher announces that he fails to understand how 'someone in *modern politics* has so poor a knowledge of geography.'

The class is roaring with approving laughter; but still greater fun is to come. During the English session—the last of the morning—the teacher orders the class to write in their copybooks, 'The greatest man in the world was . . . . ' He stops his dictation, and from several sides blithe voices make suggestions: 'Roosevelt!' . . . , 'Churchill!' . . . , 'Stalin!' . . . The teacher smiles encouragingly; then he puts up his hand and says quietly, 'No . . . no . . . ; Edison!'

The bell starts ringing; it is lunch time. What a pity—the fun is over. But at home everyone of those pupils will narrate the whole story—and not without the necessary embellishments and additions."

The fate of N. S. B. teachers was little better. They had to cope with strongly united, obstreperous groups. It is no exaggeration to say that many of them became neurotics under the constant stress of fighting the hatred and loathing of scores of patriotic children.

The children of Holland never displayed a sign of fear. They organized country-wide demonstrations, such as appearing in mourning on days of national commemoration. They never failed to discover new methods to show both the occupying powers and their helpers, the Dutch Nazis, what they thought of them.

That they succeeded is best proved by statements coming from an unsuspected source: the Nazis themselves. In the fall of 1942 Volk en Vaderland carried an article in which it answered the question: "Have we been able to make Dutch youth feel the National-Socialist way?" The reply was "Quite clearly, *no*. The vast majority despises us with an unreasoned dislike. At home those children are made to listen to the enemy radio while religious teachers tell them that 'Nazism is a weapon of Satan.' "

About this time a broadcaster over the Berlin radio had some bitter words to say on the retardative influence of Dutch parents on their children. "Hundreds of thousands of boys and girls in the Netherlands," this mouthpiece of Joseph Goebbels asserted, "desire nothing more ardently than to join the National Youth Storm. But their shortsighted parents prevent them from doing so, and those people are wholeheartedly assisted by priests, teachers and political agitators . . . The State should take this matter in hand and protect these brave, eager boys and girls who are ready to risk everything for their ideals."

But the children of Holland were not in need of such dangerous "protection." True enough, they were brave and eager—but in a rather different way. Perhaps the extent of their courage can be best gauged by what happened during the great sabotage trial, staged against seventy school children of Haarlem in the late autumn of 1940. They had established an "anti-National-Socialist organization" and valiantly tried to destroy communication cables of the German Army. Also, they had drawn up a long list of Dutch traitors who in good time were to be "liquidated." Finally, they had taken provisional measures to destroy Nazi gas supplies, motor cars and soldiers' barracks by fire.

When the "trial" closed, three minor boys had been sent to jail for 3½ years each, and several more were sentenced to shorter periods of imprisonment. Doubtlessly the most awe-inspiring moment was when the Prosecutor of the German Military Court addressed the "chief" suspect, with the insinuating question: "Now, who told you children to do these things?" The boy answered quietly, "No one. We acted of our free will and on our own convictions."

This proud reply evidently seemed to confuse the Nazi. And no wonder; youth in his own country was not allowed to possess a free will or personal convictions . . .

During three years of occupation—eleven hundred days of suppression and tyranny—the Germans have not advanced a single step toward the desired "coordination" of Holland's youth. All along the line, even in the field of sport, they have met with fierce resistance. Nazi efforts to absorb free Dutch youth organizations into the Youth Storm have foundered completely. The Socialist Youth League, A. J. C., disbanded on its own accord. The Netherlands Center of Youth Shelters refused to bar Jewish children, and was subsequently placed under the directorship of an

N. S. B.'er. The Boy Scout and Girl Scout movements, which had been equally unwilling to accept the doubtful honor of becoming a part of the Youth Storm, were dissolved during the summer of 1941.

In their persecution of these children the Germans went so far that at one time they arrested a group of 120 of them, on the charge of "having encamped as a Club." Another "suspicious" camp, somewhere in the province of Gelderland, was attacked by German policemen because the campers "had insulted them in the rudest possible manner." During this act of Nazi bravery a sixteen year old boy was seriously wounded.

Fifteen months after the invasion, in August, 1941, the Nazi Youth Storm counted 14,000 members. A year later that total had increased by one thousand—all of them between 10 and 18. Together they represented 1½% of all Dutch children and adolescents between those ages. In other words, there were about ninety-eight loyal boys and girls in Holland to every Nazi Youth Stormer.

One of the tasks of the Youth Storm was "to protect Nazi children" against the hatred of patriotic schoolmates. That sounded good; but most of the time the Youth Stormers have had their hands full defending themselves. Their cycle tours and marches were so often disturbed by the energetic attacks of loyalist children that finally the burgomasters of a number of cities addressed a "special warning" to the youngsters in their communities against continued molestation of Youth Stormers.

In January, 1942, the Nationale Dagblad, in its habitual list of complaints regarding the attitude of Holland's patriots, spoke with unusual fury of what had recently happened in a North Brabant village. The house inhabited by an N. S. B.'er had been constantly smeared with chalk; one morning the front door could not be opened. It had been sealed completely with a generous layer of cement . . .

The son of this N. S. B.'er was an active member of the Youth Storm. Unfortunately, wherever he showed himself in his resplendent uniform, he was thoroughly beaten up by the other village boys. This was intolerable, the Nationale Dagblad whined. "But the worst happened only a few days ago," the paper continued, "when the Youth Stormer was waylaid just outside his village and made to topple from his bicycle. The poor boy broke his leg."

This sort of thing is a daily occurrence among the children

of the Netherlands after three years of occupation. Where once youngsters were healthily unaware of politics and played their little games, or had their insignificant quarrels, Nazism has brought about deep and irreconcilable hatred. Youth is constantly challenged by the obnoxious parades of uniformed Nazi disciples. It is goaded into hard-handed protestations by the smug superciliousness of Youth Stormers who feel themselves the privileged offspring of a conquering tribe.

In the steadfast refusal of Holland's loyal children to enter the fold of Nazi regimentation, in their scorn for promises of a marvelous New Order which would be theirs exclusively, lies the greatest hope for a comparatively swift rehabilitation of the Netherlands. Despite the occupation and all German terror, the children of a democratic nation follow staunchly in the footsteps of their unyielding, liberty-loving parents.

During three years of suppression many surface changes have come about in the occupied territory. There is no denying that. Basically, however, things are as sound as they could be; the soul of the people has not changed. And thus Hitler's attack on the youth of the Netherlands will ultimately prove to be just another lost battle—a strife as costly and useless as Anton Mussert's efforts to convert the broad-minded, tolerant mass of his fellow countrymen into mean-spirited, bigoted adherents to the disastrous precepts of the great, God-given Fuehrer.

13

"KULTUR" INFUSIONS

" 'What does the paper say about it?' should mean 'what has our people got to say?' That, in turn, means, 'what does the National-Socialist movement have to say?' "

Secretary-General T. Goedewaagen, in a speech at Bussum, March 5, 1942.

"It would be a real Godsend if at the present moment our radio fans were not allowed to listen to anything but set, approved programs."

Volk en Vaderland, May 29, 1942.

It was a shrewd decision the Germans took when, immediately following the invasion, they announced that the press of the Netherlands would not be placed under censorship. On the contrary, all papers were "invited" to publish a special notice to the effect that they were free to print what they liked. It was an astute move to keep alive at least some of the confidence the Dutch had thus far put in the integrity of their newspapers. Had the press been subjected to the eagle-eye of a Nazi censor, the majority of Hollanders would no doubt have thought and said: "You can't believe a word." Now the press was still "free"; nothing had changed . . .

How ardently would the Germans have liked the people of Holland to believe this! But the Dutch were a sound nation, also spiritually, and they did not fail to observe what this nazi version of "freedom of the press" really meant. Well-known journalists, men who for years on end had contributed their share to the objective enlightenment of their compatriots, were peremptorily dismissed—to make place for a completely new variety of writers. These were recruited from National-Socialist organizations; scores of them soon occupied the vacant chairs of experienced, reliable and democratic-thinking newspapermen.

It did not take the Nazis long to find out that their "generous gesture" had not deceived the paper-reading public. From that moment they threw all further caution to the winds, and hurried the completion of their journalistic "change-over." The reorganization of the largest and best equipped of Holland's news agencies, the ANP, (Algemeen Nederlandsch Persbureau) took place in the space of a single day, everyone of the "new" men being a staunch adherent to the principles of Nazism. Now that the main source was poisoned, it was obvious that henceforth the news could hardly be expected to be true and wholesome.

The "purge" of the ANP happened only a few weeks after the occupation; from then on, right up to the present time, the Germans, assiduously helped by the disciples of their stooge Anton Mussert, have done all they could to pour out over Holland an endless stream of written and spoken propaganda. It commenced with what the Nazis fondly described as "psychological talks." The speaker took his listeners or readers into his confidence, talked down to them in a forgiving, fatherly sort of way, emphasizing that it was too silly, really, to remain stubborn and inactive in a time of turbulence and sweeping reforms.

It was, undeniably, a very commendable method; people less sure of themselves than the average Dutchman, might easily have fallen for it. Somewhere in those articles or speeches there usually was an appeal to remember the splendid characteristics of the audience's ancestry: ". . . Are we the same people who have given the world an admiral like Michiel de Ruyter, or fearless men like Jan van Schaffelaer and Van Speyck?* Are we no longer brave enough to take our future into our own hands? Must others do everything for us? Or are we still capable of reform on our own initiative?"

Another frequently applied method was to try and undermine the unpleasantly conspicuous self-confidence on which the Dutch prided themselves. The Nazi propagandists tried to ridicule it, make it look as if this self-confidence was a rather idiotic desire to go down in history as "martyrs for a great cause." "This is not only a strange phenomenon," the Nazi speakers used to say, "but it also is an unmistakable symptom of a diseased mind. Those 'self-confident' people have no convictions at all; they are led by a fixed idea. They yearn to play the role of martyrs . . . If only someone would come to search their homes, to arrest them and lead them to a dark dungeon, replete with mediaeval instruments of torture. If only they would be dragged before a row of mean-

*Jan van Schaffelaer, the fifteenth century Army leader who sacrificed himself by jumping to his death from the Tower of Barneveld (a township in the province of Gelderland), to save his battalion from annihilation. Van Speyck was a Navy Commander of the Netherlands who during the war with Belgium, in 1831, set fire to the powder kegs aboard his ship, rather than surrender to his enemies.

spirited judges, so that they could raise their heads in proud defiance, fully aware of the grim smile that would hover around their firmly-closed mouths . . ."

Both in the press and on the radio such terms as "Germanic brotherhood," "people's community," and "Volksgenosse" were frequently used. But it was exactly this indiscriminate and insidious repetition of "brotherly" names that aroused the ire of the Dutch. They resented being called the "folkish comrades" of the Germans. Huns were Huns—and between them and the people of the Netherlands no link of race or blood could possibly exist.

After some months of this the German Propaganda Bureau began to realize that neither radio Hilversum nor the combined press of the Netherlands had made the slightest inroad upon the obstinate Hollanders. A change of attitude was highly necessary—and it came. If these stiff-necked Dutch refused to listen to the "call of the blood," if racial parentage was nothing to them, they might perhaps feel more inclined to give serious consideration to the soft-spoken words of one of their fellow countrymen.

To this purpose an old hand in international journalism was ordered to come to Hilversum. He was a Hollander by the name of Max Blokzijl, a man of 56, who many years previously gained considerable success on the cabaret stages of the country where he, together with a colleague, made his appearance as a roving minstrel. It had begun with a reportage for the Amsterdam "Algemeen Handelsblad" on the life of ambulant street musicians. For six weeks Blokzijl and his fellow artist Pisuisse followed a route throughout the country, playing their guitars, singing on street corners and in village barns, and closely observing the reaction of their multifarious audiences. Their experiences, sometimes humorous, sometimes bitter, were published in a popularly-written book which was widely read. Soon afterwards Blokzijl and Pisuisse started a Cabaret, to bring to the people of Holland the true rendering of their own "Songs of Life." Together they travelled the country for many years; but at last came the parting of their ways.

Soon after the end of his histrionic successes, Blokzijl left Holland to become Berlin correspondent of the Algemeen Handelsblad. He retained this position till the invasion, and developed a great variety of Teutonic interests. He had married a German woman, had many influential German friends, and became president of the Berlin branch of the Foreign Press Association. His "letters" appeared regularly in the Handelsblad, and as a rule they were examples of good journalism. But ever since the growth of the Nazi idea—and particularly after the advent of Adolf Hitler to power—Blokzijl led a very extraordinary kind of journalistic double life. While in his regular contributions to the Handelsblad he adopted a critical, and at times even outspokenly unfriendly, attitude towards Nazism, he also produced a veritable stream of "Berlin Letters" which were published in a considerable number of provincial dailies in Holland. In these contributions, written under the pseudonym of "Roland," Blokzijl eagerly endeavored to defend Nazi ideologies and to break down the well-founded or intuitive resistance against Hitlerism which—even then—was prevalent among the majority of Netherlanders.

*

From the beginning of his arrival in Hilversum, Blokzijl proved to be one of the most astute radio propagandists on the Nazi payroll. He can without exaggeration be labeled as one of the enemy's most important accomplices, of greater value—and far more dangerous—than Anton Mussert. In striking contrast with the bulk of Nazi speakers, Max Blokzijl adopted a quietly persuasive tone. He avoided carefully the hysterical ravings and the staccato repetition of commonplace slogans which other propagandists had unanimously adopted to convince their listeners that Hitler and his followers "are always right." Indeed, Blokzijl was entirely different. He was a real find for the Germans, a man of histrionic talent, well versed in the art of addressing crowds of all kinds.

It is quite an experience to listen to him. Almost always his voice sounds jovial; he knows how to create an atmosphere that makes you think of a "wise old uncle" talking to you across the after-dinner table. He does not call his opponents names; he prefers to use a biting, cutting sarcasm, all his own. When he praises the achievements of Nazism, his eulogies remain discreet. He has a sense of humor and a ready wit. If he wishes, he can be both ironical and benignly admonishing; nonetheless, he remains a fatherly, kind-eyed sort of adviser who "means ever so well." He discusses at leisure the manifold problems besieging the Dutch Nazis. He is very modest indeed. He never misses his chance to say—in a by-the-way fashion but impressive enough—"Of course, I am not an educator or a lawyer"—or whatever profession presupposes the knowledge which he is on the point of imparting.

These qualities, so unlike the peculiarities of the average N. S. B. propagandist, were the cause of much confusion, particularly during the first few months of Blokzijl's broadcasts. Many of his listeners, in the occupied Netherlands as well as outside of it, did not quite know what to make of him. For one thing, he seemed rather eager to quote examples—most of them very striking and convincing—of the lack of popularity of Mussert's party. Over and again he spent valuable radio time quoting from sheaves of letters written to him by disappointed Mussert men. On one occasion he stated that he had received tens of thousands of such letters, most of them agreeing with his opinions, some with constructive criticism, ten percent anonymous and of a critical nature, and "five percent of such contents as clearly betray the criminal make-up of the writers." Some time during 1942 he promised to publish a book of these letters. This actually appeared many months later, and Blokzijl made it a habit to quote liberally from it whenever he seemed short of material. In several broadcasts he admitted that Nazism, despite the most frantic efforts, had failed to get a hold on the vast majority of Hollanders.

In the light of such tactics it did not seem altogether unjustified if some people asked themselves, "How can a Nazi, in the pay of the German authorities, talk in this way without being sent to jail? This man provides the patriots and the Dutch authorities abroad with first-class material to prove the nature of the uphill struggle of Hitlerism in the occupied territory."

But these questioners failed to understand that the real propaganda value of Blokzijl's speeches lay exactly in the tone he employed and in the subjects he dealt with. He was not trying to gain new members for Mussert's party, nor was he endeavoring to lure into the Nazi fold the most unyielding of Holland's loyal sons and daughters.

Blokzijl addressed a different audience—the middle-of-the roaders, individuals who under favorable circumstances are not unwilling to take certain risks for the sake of justice, but who are never too sure of themselves. They belong to the not inconsiderable group of hesitants, of "possible converts." They are not ready to join the Hitler movement because they admit that there is much in it which palls upon any decent being. On the other hand, they are prepared to arrive at some sort of compromise by following the line of least resistance. The longer the occupation lasts and the more they suffer from the material hardships which have followed in the wake of the German invasion, the oftener they are inclined to consider whether, after all, it might not be better to halt both passive and active resistance against the enemy, and sit back to await the course of events.

At night directly after dinner—and a none too satisfactory repast it is these days!—the friendly, quiet, persuasive voice of Max Blokzijl addresses them. He speaks to them as he would to old acquaintances. He tells them of the Germany he knows so well because he lived there for so many years. He mentions the fresh piles of letters received that day from listeners "who do not always agree with me." He makes little of the war and jeers, gently and ever so politely, at the "optimists" who expected England to invade "last autumn," or "last winter" . . .

In the demonstrative manner of a self-assured college professor he endeavors to make it clear that "the revolution which is now taking place, has nothing to do with the course of the war. War or peace, it is a social metamorphosis which had to come about and which must be completed. So, why continue to obstruct it?" Discreetly he disagrees with and scolds some of the vilest practices and antics of Nazi "hot heads." But he adds forgivingly, "Those are the unavoidable excrescences of our exciting and spectacular times."

He is out to sow discord, doubt and uncertainty. Slowly but surely he tries to undermine the will to resist in all those who are not self-confident. He does his best to make them understand that he is not airing his own and, of course, insignificant opinions. He is merely "the mouthpiece of countless thousands who approach me every day." He likes his listeners to believe that in reality the majority of their compatriots think as he does. Only, they are not as yet willing to admit it aloud . . . "But," says Max Blokzijl between the lines of every one of his talks, "those willing and prepared to fight the blessings of Nazism to the bitter end, are astoundingly few. You can take my word for that!"

It is not due to his lack of ardor or a paucity of approach that this man, after two and a half years of frequent talks, has not achieved greater success. He is, indeed, a most dangerous tool of Nazism, the more so as he doubtlessly *means* what he says. He is not a charlatan, one of the many opportunists who gladly accept German money and a chance of material improvement in exchange for an occasional half hour of hypocritical babbling. He has his own way of putting things. True enough, the material for his speeches is often provided by others but what he makes of it is a typical creation of Blokzijl, the journalist. It is flavored with his own views, expressed with the facility of an excellent stylist who knows how to say things without becoming a bore, or without ever repeating himself.

He is the "change of nourishment that whets the appetite," and Goebbels' Propaganda Bureau well understood this. In the desert of bragging and menacing, shouting and intimidation which is presented most of the time by the controlled Dutch radio, Blokzijl's talks are a sort of oasis, by contrast refreshing to look at—but exceedingly poisonous for the unheeding.

This strange fellow, once a worshipper of the Bohemian life and the unconventional, has turned into a true believer in Nazi regimentation, the "iron fist" that kills all individuality and turns people into will-less robots. In true Germanic fashion, he now adores everything signifying clock-work regularity and rigorous order: trains leaving and arriving to the second, no strikes of any kind, overwhelming military parades, mass demonstrations, the crowd subjected to one indomitable will . . . He saw the growth of Nazism and was dazzled by it into blind admiration for the Hitler slogan, *"There must be order."* He witnessed the militarization of Germany's youth—and it irked him to think that unbridled urchins could still play their pranks in Amsterdam's streets.

Since February, 1941 he has generously contributed his deadly share in the German efforts to kill the love of individual freedom innate in almost every Hollander. Were it not that through their underground movements and the untiring effort of Netherlands authorities abroad the people of Holland remained fully aware of the actual trend of world affairs, Max Blokzijl might well have made the thousands of converts he had hoped for. He is not afraid of airing untruths, nor does he shrink from exaggeration. He often betrays that his love of the stage is far from dead. He frequently changes the inflection of his voice. Now it sounds warm and generous, sympathetic and paternal, then again it grows cold and sneering, critical or disdainful. But he mostly gives his talks the ring of faith and true belief—even when it is obvious that a man of his intelligence must surely realize the hollowness of his own assertions. One only has to think of his enthusiasm during the early part of Hitler's fateful attack on Russia,* his repeated jubila-

*See chapter 8—Unholy Crusades—page 171.

tions about the "complete annihilation of the Soviet armies," and his prophecies concerning an early end to all Russian resistance.

But when the course of events glaringly belies his predictions, Blokzijl is not one whit put out. In April, 1942, after the terrible winter experiences of the German Army on the plains of Russia, he informed his public quietly and smilingly, "I feel fine today —because I know that the Axis will have crushed all opposition before this year is out. We will have brought the war to a triumphant close!"

The well-chosen, ofttimes parliamentary language of this competent renegade is the sugar coating on the bitter pill of constantly recurring Nazi barbarities. His Mephistophelian mannerisms are out to hypnotize the weaker elements among the Dutch into a comfortable slumber of complacency. And even if the results of his treacherous work have not come up to scratch, there is no denying that among many of the less critical, the venomous seeds of his upside-down reasoning have come to germination. Most of those plants will no doubt be destroyed by the coming storm of Holland's liberation. Whatever fragments there will be left, must be weeded out with patience—but thoroughly and relentlessly.

*

It was not mere accident that in November, 1940, only a few months after the capitulation, the former Department of Education, Arts and Sciences was cut into two sections. One of these was henceforth to be known as the Department of Education and Sciences headed by the Nazi professor Jan van Dam. The other, the Department of Culture and Public Enlightenment, was placed under the guidance of Dr. T. Goedewaagen. Each of these two nazified scholars had a clearly outlined task: while the former was to enslave the spirt of the schools and universities,* it would be the latter's duty to subjugate the press, the radio, and the liberal arts.

Whatever reproach might be made to either department because of a lack of tangible results, it certainly is not that of too puny an investment. Money seemed of no consequence; it was spent freely whenever there seemed a chance to approach the unruly Hollanders closely enough to inject some unadulterated Nazi poison. To this purpose Goedewaagen had more strings to his bow than the saturation of press and radio with Nazi ideas. He also headed a special section known as "the Department of Active

*See chapter 12—Youth Under Siege—page 252.

Enlightenment" whose task it was to plaster the whole of Holland full of Nazi posters, from time to time. Every community throughout the country had to cooperate by putting at the disposal of this remarkably active body as much free posting space as it might desire. In turn the walls and billboards of the Netherlands were "decorated" with a large variety of appeals to Dutch workmen inviting them to "come to Germany—and see the world," with invitations to join the N. S. B. or the Nazi-instituted Guilds, or with the garish bills that told the startled people of Holland how the "refugee"-Government in London had "bartered away the colonial possessions of Curaçao and Surinam" . . . Scores of color presses and quite a little army of draftsmen were kept busy producing fresh material for these graphic displays.

But the Department of Active Enlightenment had other duties besides. It published numerous periodicals for gratis delivery throughout the country, even when hundreds of dailies and weeklies had ceased to appear because of the alleged paper scarcity. They bore the most fantastic names, such as *Blockade, Victory, Order* or *Future,* and every conceivable thing was done to popularize these propaganda products, including the offer of money prizes for "best answers" to some "instructive" quiz.

The absence of immediate success could not discourage the Nazis. They tried out one kind of propaganda after the other, always hoping to hit upon the right method of influencing Dutch public opinion. Throughout 1940 and 1941, for instance, there was a constant "exchange" of Netherlands' and Nazi art. Special exhibitions were organized, such as an ambitious German book show which was presented under the name, "The German Book Of This Moment." No one less than little Dr. Goebbels himself came over to inaugurate this exhibition. And the splendid news he brought! More than 2,000 of the exhibited Nazi treasures were to remain in Holland's libraries, as a present of the Reich to its "Germanic cousins" . . .

Nazi poets and writers were rushed from Germany to Holland by the dozen, to address miserably small audiences made up of Germans living in Holland and complemented with a handful of Dutch Nazis. In Amsterdam a special exhibition took place of Westphalian art; for the distinction of harboring these treasures only the famous Rijksmuseum was considered good enough. Seyss-Inquart and his wife arranged a grand reception for the Nazi artists on the "requisitioned" Clingendael estate, and carried the insult so far that they had a few Dutch "converts" execute what was announced as 'typical dances of old Holland.' At the height of this memorable festival, Mrs. Seyss-Inquart—and with her several other wives of Germans high up in the Nazi hierarchy—demonstrated their noble intentions of sisterhood towards the Dutch by dancing with the members of the "old Holland" dance group who trampled around in wooden shoes, and were disguised as fishermen from beautiful Volendam.

In October, 1941, there was a Poets' Congress in the German city of Weimar, at which two Dutch Nazi "poets" represented Holland's creative artists. In the same month the little town of Osnabrueck, in northwestern Germany, was favored with a large-scale show of modern Dutch paintings, practically all of them the products of completely unknown Nazi geniuses. A similar exhibition was arranged in the spring of 1942, this time with the purpose of going on a long tour of the entire Reich. Among the thirty-five "prominent artists" who were publicized as contributors to this collection, there were only two or three who had ever been heard of before by Holland's connoisseurs.

But all these gatherings and art shows were mere sidelines. Goedewaagen's remarkable talent was destined to present the world with the benefits of his greatest creation, that of the Netherlands Culture Chamber. After a careful study of the activities of the Nazi "Kulturkammer" in Germany, the Secretary for Culture and Public Enlightenment announced in November, 1941 that soon the Reich's Commissioner would establish a Culture Chamber for the Netherlands. In fact, his prophecy was borne out almost immediately, because on November 25 Seyss-Inquart's decree to this effect was published.

The Culture Chamber was to embrace all people working in the plastic arts, architecture, music, literature, the theatre, motion pictures and the press. Each profession was to have its own guild, but all guilds were to belong to the Chamber whose prime duty was described as the "furtherance of Holland's culture in the light of its responsibility towards the Commonwealth of Peoples." Even if its meaning was not very clear, the phrase sounded good, anyhow.

To the President of the Culture Chamber full authority was given to refuse the acceptance of members if, in his judgment, these applicants "did not appear to possess the reliability or fitness required for the type of work in which they are engaged." Naturally, no Jew could ever hope to qualify for membership, while it was equally impossible for an "aryan" to continue work in any one of the named professions without joining the Culture Chamber. His failure to join the institution was declared punishable with fines as high as 5,000 guilders, or about $2,700.

During the next few months Goedewaagen was blithely engaged in nominating presidents, vice-presidents, directors-general and leaders of the various Guilds. Obviously, the appointees were almost exclusively members of, or sympathizers with, Mussert's movement. These nominations afforded loyal Hollanders a marvelous opportunity to find out who exactly in the world of art were traitors to their country. They also presented them with a chance to see long-standing suspicions confirmed. For example, Willem Mengelberg—the famous conductor of the Concertgebouw Orchestra whose Nazi leanings had long been known—accepted with alacrity his appointment as a member of the "Culture Council," an advisory body of twenty carefully-selected Nazis, at the complete disposal of the otherwise omnipotent leader of the Chamber.

On the same list of traitors could be found the name of a famous art connoisseur, Dr. D. Hannema, director of the world-renowned Booymans Museum at Rotterdam. Among others who had fallen for the advantages of a Nazi-protected artist's life were the young composer Henk Badings, of whose work competent critics had said many good things in pre-Nazi days, and the aged painter H. F. Boot of Haarlem, a quaint eccentric whose chief diversions had thus far been the production of not altogether unmeritorious still-lives and the "artistic" neglect of an ancient studio, covered with the grime and dust of years.

The inauguration of this hand-picked Culture Council was too significant an event to go by unnoticed. In the middle of February, 1942 the Council was officially installed by the Reich's Commissioner; and the conclusion of his and various other long-winded speeches was that "the voice of the Netherlands' people is at last adequately represented by a Culture Council." But one of the eloquent speakers admitted wistfully that "a few whom I would have liked to see here, too" were conspicuous by their absence. It sounded suspiciously like praise-in-disguise for the leading artists who had obstinately refused to have anything to do with Goedewaagen's ideas on the furtherance of culture. The majority of Holland's creative artists remained adamant. Goedewaagen himself confirmed this when, almost a year later—in January, 1943—he boasted that the artists who had thus far refused to join the membership, would not fail to meet with adequate punishment. The Chamber's strict control of all artists' material—including canvases, paints and the necessaries for sculpture—enabled it to grant the use of these materials only to *worthy* members of the organization. "Registrations have increased since we started to distribute artists' materials to our members," the great "reformer" exclaimed. But in the same breath he admitted that many of these new members had registered under protest only, declaring that "there is no choice left to us."

Before the second occupation year came to its close, Holland had been enriched with a Physicians' Guild, a Chamber of Apothecaries, a Dentists' Guild and even a Chamber of Veterinaries. It stands to reason that each of these organizations was headed by an N. S. B.'er; it was made equally clear that no one could avoid becoming a member if he was at all interested in retaining his means of livelihood.

One of the most serious consequences of this Teutonic urge to return to the mediaeval guild system was that it tried to do away with the physician's oath of secrecy. Its rescission was demanded because of "the need of publicity, to protect or to maintain rights of greater value than the rights of secrecy." There was, of course, no mention that it would be left completely to the competency of the Nazis to judge in every separate instance which of the "rights" would be of the greatest value. Besides, the doctor would from now on have to supervise the sanguineous and racial "qualities" of the coming generation. As the president of the Physicians' Chamber, Dr. Croin,* revealed during the inaugural meeting of his organization, "the physician must not only act as a healer but he must also advise his patients in the most important act of their lives, namely the selection of a partner for the process of reproduction . . ."

However grandiloquent this phraseology, the Physicians' Chamber never amounted to much. It was reported as late as April, 1943 that 4,000 Netherlands doctors, or about 97% of all Dutch physicians, rather than joining the Nazi institution, relinquished their titles but continued to practise. A local Haarlem paper revealed that the medical men in that city had covered with adhesive tape the word "Dr." on their professional nameplates.

*He resigned in March, 1943 and was succeeded by a well-known surgeon of Haarlem, Dr. Christian Goette who had been known as an admirer of Hitlerism before the invasion.

The Germans tried to derail the opposition by the simple announcement that every licensed practitioner was automatically a member of the Guild. Subsequently demands were sent out to all new "members" to furnish a mass of personal data, and two photographs. Soon the Chamber's offices were flooded with replies . . ., but unhappily for the guild leader, the majority of forms was sent back blank. Even those who finally accepted membership in the Physicians' Guild, continued to resent very strongly the interference with their professional code by German authorities, or Dutch-Nazi delegates.

Towards the end of April, 1943, when protest strikes broke out in every part of the country, the Germans ordered large numbers of Hollanders to stand guard over objects that might be sabotaged. Quite a number of those were ailing people, unfit for guard duty—and their doctors did not hesitate to confirm this by providing them with the necessary certificates. In retaliation, the Nazi authorities placed several doctors under "detention." The immediate answer came in the form of a general physicians' strike. After preliminary discussions all doctors suspended their office hours, accepting only the most urgent cases for treatment. Other cases were referred to the sadly over-burdened municipal authorities, and every would-be patient was informed that undue interference by the authorities prevented the doctors from giving medical assistance.

In another instance, a doctor was jailed because he refused to violate the medical code of secrecy by providing a layman with information about one of his patients. Without delay the other doctors in the town posted the following notice on their doors: "No consulting hours. A colleague was imprisoned because he rightfully refused to inform an unauthorized outsider on the nature of the illness of one of his patients. We will not resume our practice as long as this illegal detention lasts."

In these and several similar cases the Nazis were compelled to release their prisoners—simply because the joint action of the doctors left huge sections of the country without direly-needed physicians' help.

Writing in the March, 1943 issue of a Netherlands underground paper, a doctor gave a clear description of these Nazi efforts to force Holland's medical men into the strait jacket of a well-supervised guild. "But the members of my profession," the writer concluded, "will stick to their guns. Our oath orders us to be loyal to our patients and to our people. But it also forbids us to practise abroad. Therefore, we will not go to Germany where the enemy has sacrificed his own doctors to an exhausting war, and where general health conditions cry to heaven."

*

Gradually and persistently Goedewaagen's Department of Culture and Public Enlightenment tried to influence every cultural movement in the occupied country. Foremost among these were the press and the radio. If the German authorities had been inordinately proud of their decision not to install a Nazi press censorship, Goedewaagen saw to it that from the first of July, 1941, every paper published regularly a complete list of its responsible department heads, with their home addresses. For one thing, this would greatly facilitate the work of the Gestapo . . . ; but the measure was chiefly taken by way of warning to journalists of too much independence, editorial writers who daringly defied all German rules and continued to speak their minds whenever there were good reasons for this.

Apart from this indirect check on the activities of Holland's newspapermen, there were the more direct results of the "Camp for Journalists" into which the ancient castle of *De Cannenburgh,* near Vaassen, in Gelderland province, had been turned. Every week twenty-five newspapermen were given free transportation to the Camp, where quite a good deal of time was devoted to marching and trotting. The place was run on strictly Nazi lines, with regimentation and discipline as its leading principles. It was forbidden to use any other form of address than that of "campmate."

Campers were awakened by trumpet calls. They had to participate in daily drill and were obliged to attend the ceremony of hoisting the flag, during which their eyes must be "kept right." All other activities were patterned on German military exercises and "enjoyed" in groups.

The remainder of the day was spent with such "practical jokes" as throwing recalcitrant campmates—who had been too vociferous on the subject of their individual ideas on liberty—into a mud-filled pool. A witness of this diversion described it in glowing and enthusiastic terms, and concluded: "We laughed till the tears ran down our cheeks."

There were lectures, too. The N. S. B.'er-journalist Wouter Hulsteyn wound up each perfect day with "a serious and instructive talk on the high moral attitude of the Netherlands press under the New Order." These speeches were particularly appropriate coming from the mouth of an individual who in pre-Nazi days had gained country-wide notoriety because of his "law suits" against De Telegraaf, and by his swindling practices. This scribbler without talent or principles had once been the intimate friend and associate of Jewish newspapermen and publishers. With no trouble at all he had now turned into an ardent servant and admirer of Hitler and Mussert. His anti-Semitism was, if anything, even more virulent and fanatical than theirs.

In the autumn of 1941 Goedewaagen set out upon a thorough purge of recalcitrant and less desirable publications. Scarcity of newsprint was a splendid excuse; and so 53 out of a total of 140 dailies disappeared, in the company of 520 out of 650 bi-weeklies and other periodicals. The dailies and weeklies of the Socialist *Arbeiderspers* at Amsterdam—foremost amongst them "Het Volk," which was printed simultaneously in seven different centers of the country—were entirely nazified. There now remained only three large-scale circulation papers of liberal tendencies: the Algemeen Handelsblad and De Telegraaf of Amsterdam, and the Nieuwe Rotterdamsche Courant of Rotterdam. They all were swiftly coordinated. The larger portion of 4,000 trade papers and club organs of all kinds was simultaneously suppressed and a stipulation was made to the effect that towns below a specified inhabitants-total could only have one daily newssheet.

Journalists of the old régime were dismissed; the most fearless among them, such as the chief-editor of the Algemeen Handelsblad, D. J. von Balluseck, found themselves accused of subversive action, and transported to a concentration camp. In their places came members of the N. S. B., whose performance had not thus far betrayed outstanding journalistic capacities. But the Nazis were determined to eclipse all loyal newspapermen; it kept them busy throughout the winter of 1941-1942. Yet, in February, 1942 Mussert's weekly, Volk en Vaderland, still felt compelled to print the following bitter tirade against its Hitler-hating colleagues:

"We are not blind, dear colleagues, to be sure. We see full well that by the use of ambiguous headlines you try to repeat your old game of 'meeting the thinking public halfway' . . . You publish insignificant news items, only to have the apology of 'no space left' when you are requested to print an article on the genuine problems of our days."*

In the beginning of November, 1942 further reductions in the size of nearly all Dutch newspapers were announced. They came only a few weeks after the enemy had published a decree (September 1) forbidding the regular publication of all papers thus far issued by the Netherlands Reformed and Calvinist Churches. Some exceptions to this rule were promised; exemptions would be given in writing to "certain publishers" . . . But in subsequent months this promise was conveniently forgotten.**

The head of the Dutch Press Guild, Johan Huyts, editor of the Nieuwe Rotterdamsche Courant of which in pre-war years he had been a staff member, wrote an article in which he assured his readers that the remaining newspapers would from now on adapt themselves to the new political structure of the Netherlands, "a task which is greatly simplified by the dissolution of all political parties except the Nationaal-Socialistische Beweging. The press," he announced dramatically, "is evolving toward National-Socialism and the new restrictive measures will greatly help to improve the economic status of all remaining publications." And he concluded with the insinuation: "it will enable them to free their reading matter of the influence of special interest groups." Even then non-Nazi journalists had evidently not yet been eradicated, for Huyts told them that "they would have to make their choice and stop opposing the New Order. It is about time," he added prophetically, "for them to realize that Holland is going through a period of evolution prior to adopting a full-fledged National-Socialist régime."

Soon afterwards several papers—foremost among them the Catholic "Tijd" of Amsterdam—announced that they had been instructed to limit the total of their pages to 20 each week. De Telegraaf of Amsterdam was slightly more favored and could use a maximum of 30 pages per week. But the German-language paper, Deutsche Zeitung in den Niederlanden, which has appeared

*The case of the editor of Het Vaderland, The Hague, was a splendid example of this. The Germans had ordered the Dutch press to print excerpts from a Churchill speech, together with a biting Nazi commentary. The Hague journalist obeyed the order, but he used his own initiative for the headline which he based on a quotation from Churchill's speech. Thus the paper appeared with a boldface, three-column caption: "*England Wins The War.*" This was followed by a line of very small type: "Says Churchill." The editor was promptly arrested and fined $13,500 for his ingenuity.

**It was not the first Nazi attack upon the religious press. At the close of 1941 the Germans had suppressed "Pniël", a weekly for Christian families, which had been founded half a century earlier by the Rev. Dr. J. H. Gunning, a clergyman whose religious and literary writings earned him great renown. Even at that time the paper shortage was held responsible.

in the occupied country ever since the beginning of the occupation, continued to be as bulky as ever.

Some ingenious editors tried to circumvent the restrictive measures by using a much smaller type, and by reducing the amount of white space between the lines. That this detracted from the readability of their papers was of small importance. Very few loyal Netherlanders read them anyhow, and those who did accepted them merely as a means of comparison between German propaganda lies and the reliable broadcasts from London's BBC or Radio Orange. An official of the Amsterdam municipality, Registrar Douwes, expressed the thoughts of millions of his compatriots when he remarked of the "co-ordinated" newspapers, "They consist of 75% lies and 25% information as to where you can get your ration cards . . ."

Nonetheless, there were occasions on which the Dutch suddenly showed great interest in their daily press. When, for example, the colossal German defeat on the Russian front could no longer be concealed and the army communiqués with their admission of considerable setbacks became ever-gloomier reading, an unprecedented demand for newspapers was experienced.

Volk en Vaderland summed up the situation very succinctly when, in a February number of 1943, it complained of "patriotic arm-chair strategists who have suddenly developed a suspicious affection for the German Army communiqués, believing their contents as never before . . . The news from the Russian front," the writer wailed, "makes these people cry, 'All goes well.' They are willing to pay as much as two and a half guilders ($1.35) for a paper with unfavorable reports from Russia."

*

Indeed, the whole country had been thirsting for good, but even more for reliable news, ever since the Nazis tried to place their seal upon all Dutch information services. Immediately underground pamphlets and broadsheets had begun to appear, first mimeographed, soon afterwards printed. "Forbidden" pictures, particularly photographs of members of the royal house, were produced in their thousands and distributed all over the land. They were closely followed by the first issues of the clandestine newspaper "Vrij Nederland" (Free Netherlands) which now, after three years of oppression, still appears with the greatest regularity.

The Nazis might do what they liked to stamp out these "evils"—nothing helped. Secret newssheets, well-edited and written in excellent Dutch—which proved that the best Dutch minds contributed to their production—never ceased to reach the masses in quite a variety of ways. They would be stealthily deposited in the letterboxes during the nightly blackout hours, despite the curfew imposed upon every citizen; or they would be delivered from house to house in sealed envelopes, through the kind intermediary of . . . the postal authorities. As all addresses were handwritten—for which countless patriots gladly ran not inconsiderable risks—and as the Germans had found it impracticable to censor the huge volume of home mail, there was little they could do to stop this.

As time went by, the number and size of the underground newspapers increased, even though "Vrij Nederland" until this day has remained the most important of them all. There were "Uit de woestijn" (Out of the desert), "De Oranjekrant" (Orange Journal) "Trouw" (Faith) and "Het Parool" (The Password) which carried the motto *"True to God until death"*—a quotation from Holland's national anthem. Each copy of these newssheets, going from hand to hand, reached at least a score of readers. Reliable informants have often confirmed that a single issue of any underground paper was read by a minimum of 100,000 people.

As a rule the editorial staffs of these publications proved to be very well informed. They often predicted coming Nazi measures several days before they were announced; and once they described in detail a meeting of the N. S. B., the Nationaal-Socialistische Beweging, in which plans had been drawn up and discussed at length for the campaign against Van Rappard's party, the N. S. N. A. P., which culminated in its disbandment.*

There also existed an underground paper for the 18,000 odd students of the Netherlands. It appeared under the name of "De Geus" (The Sea Beggar), a title of honor, reverting to the heroic days of the 16th century in which large groups of Hollanders opposed, and ultimately overthrew, the Spanish tyrants who dominated them. "De Geus" formed a link between the pupils of all Netherlands universities, encouraging and instructing them in their fearless obstructionist work, or advising them how to counteract every new Nazi attempt to curtail their freedoms still further and influence their opinions.

---

*See chapter 8—Unholy Crusades—page 155.

1e JAARGANG No. 8	Ja, zij zullen Zich vervullen Deze tijden van geluk.	Deez' ellenden Gaan volenden En verpletterd wordt het juk.	20 JULI 1943

ONZE STRIJD OM INDIË.

Wanneer iets ons duidelijk maakt dat het een daad van goed Staatsbeleid is geweest van onze Koningin om in Mei 1940 naar Engeland te gaan, dan is het wel de discussie, die er in de geallieerde landen en met name in de Vereenigde Staten van Noord-Amerika plaats vond over de toekomst van Indië.

De Koningin heeft dat reeds terstond na haar komst in Engeland zoo aangeduid. De reden dat Zij het lot van Haar volk in het bezette gebied niet kon deelen, was dat er voor Haar gedurende den oorlog een taak was weggelegd, die verband hield met het feit, dat Nederland overzeesche gebiedsdeelen had, die Zij gedurende den oorlog niet aan hun lot kon overlaten. Dit was in het belang van die gebiedsdeelen zelf, en in het belang van ons volk en ons rijk als geheel. Het Koninkrijk der Nederlanden, verspreid als het is over vier werelddeelen, moest gedurende den oorlog, in den raad der volkeren, telkens als het zou gaan over zaken, die de toekomst van dat rijk als geheel of van een zijner deelen raken, zich kunnen doen hooren en dan vooral en het liefst door zijn meest competente stem.

* * *

Wij weten dat men in de wereld over het algemeen niet vanzelf aan zijn recht komt. Dat recht moet bepleit worden. Daarom zijn wij zoo dankbaar dat wij op het oogenblik in onze Koningin onze pleitbezorgster hebben.

In Amerika is men er zich van bewust dat zeer belangrijke bijdragen voor de herovering van Nederlandsch-Indië moeten komen van de zijde der Vereenigde Staten. Dit heeft tot gevolg dat men aldaar, met een naieve toepassing van de leus: Wie betaalt, beheert, zich begeven heeft in een zekere vrijmoedige discussie over de toekomst en de toekomstige status van Nederlandsch-Indië.

„Mannen zooals Wendell Wilkie" (Roosevelts tegencandidaat voor het Presidentschap bij de laatste verkiezingen), zoo lezen we in „Vrij Nederland" (Londen) van 6 Februari 1943, „bepleitten het denkbeeld om geheel Indië tot een soort pupil van de vereenigde volken te maken, zijn onmetelijke voorraden petroleum, tin en rubber vrij ter beschikking van de gansche wereld te stellen en de geheele opbrengst van Indië's hulpbronnen aan te wenden voor Indië's eigen gezondheid, eigen opvoeding, en voor Indië's ontwikkeling tot zelfregeering".

De verwerkelijking van dit plan van Wilkie zou in feite beteekenen de ontbinding van den band Nederland—Indië, zooals wij die sinds eeuwen hebben gekend en de oplossing van het Koninkrijk der Nederlanden, gelijk dit in art. 1 onzer Grondwet is omschreven.

* * *

Onze Koningin heeft in deze discussie ingegrepen door een Regeeringsverklaring over de toekomstige compositie van het Koninkrijk der Nederlanden, later gevolgd door Haar eerste reis naar Amerika, Haar toespraak tot het Amerikaansche Congres en meerdere redevoeringen.

De hoofdinhoud, immers het hoofddoel van die redevoeringen was de betuiging: Daar is, verspreid over vier werelddeelen, **één ondeelbaar Koninkrijk der Nederlanden**. De Koningin heeft den aard en de ontwikkelingslijn van dat Koninkrijk, den samenhang van zijn deelen, beschreven op een wijze, dat Zij in de Amerikaansche pers over het algemeen veel bijval ontmoette waardoor de denkbeelden van Wilkie op den achtergrond zijn geraakt.

Wij zullen op den juridischen aard van den samenhang van Nederland en Indië hier niet diep ingaan. Naar onze meening is de staatkundige ontwikkeling van Indië nog niet zoo ver gevorderd en is met name de staatkundige en sociologische structuur van Indië nog niet in die mate uitgegroeid dat Indië zonder meer als een gelijkberechtigd partner van Nederland in het rijksverband kan worden beschouwd. Voorshands moet men die gelijkberechtigdheid blijven zien als een gelijkberechtigdheid in wording.

Van veel meer belang is thans het hoofdpunt: het integrale behoud van ons rijk. Het feit dat men in Amerika de vraag kan stellen, zooals het daar in een tijdschrift geschiedde: Moet Koningin Wilhelmina Haar Rijk teruggegeven worden? moet ons doen begrijpen dat er hier meer noodig is dan alleen de staatkundige wijsheid van onze Koningin, dan het bepleiten van ons recht. Dat recht moet bevochten worden.

* * *

Wanneer men in Amerika zegt: Moet Indië aan Nederland worden teruggegeven? dan moeten wij daar niet met „ja" op antwoorden, maar dan moet heel Nederland zeggen: Er kan geen sprake zijn van een teruggeven van Indië door Amerika of Engeland aan Nederland; er kan alleen sprake zijn van de herovering van Nederlandsch-Indië op Japan.

Dat is alleen het heele probleem en daarmee is het opgelost ook.

De zaak moet zoo gezien worden: Tengevolge van den aanval van Japan zijn de Philippijnen, Malakka, Oost-Indië en Birma gelijkelijk tijdelijk verloren gegaan. In de verdediging van deze gebieden heeft Nederland met leger, vloot en luchtmacht, vooral met de beide laatste, belangrijke bijdragen geleverd. Nederland heeft zich oogenblikkelijk solidair verklaard toen Engeland en Amerika aangevallen werden. De Nederlandsch-Indische luchtmacht met name heeft krachtig meegedaan aan de verdediging van Malakka en Singapore. De Nederlandsche vloot is (ten deele) ondergegaan in de verdediging van Indië en van Australië.

THE UNDERGROUND PRESS . . .
Front page of an issue of *Trouw* (Loyalty). The text discusses the coming battle to liberate the Netherlands East Indies.

VRIJ NEDERLAND

NEDERLAND ORANJE

5 MEI 1943

3e JAARGANG No. 9

AAN ONZE LEZERS....

blad, de „Oranjekrant" (welks inhoud wij nooit konden appercieeren) vindt altijd weer ruimte Engeland in zijn scheldpartijen te betrekken.

Laten we nuchter zijn en vooral enkele feiten duidelijk vaststellen.

Geen enkel volk is uit liefde tot en verantwoordelijkheid voor andere volken in den oorlog gegaan. Hadden Rusland en Amerika en de kleine naties hun taak begrepen en dat allen tegelijk en op tijd gedaan, dan zou Duitschland reeds thans verslagen zijn.

HET PAROOL

No. 51

5 APRIL 1943

VRIJ ONVERVEERD

DE ORGANISATIE VAN HET VERZET.

DE ORANJEKRANT

(VIVERE MILITARE EST)

JAARGANG

Verschijnt

DE VRIJE STEM

3e Serie No. 2

Maart 1943

IK SLA DE TROM....

Ik sla de trom en dreun de droomers wakker.
Wie droomt verraad zijn vrouw, zijn kind, zijn makker;
Geen eerlijk man kan zich gelukkig voelen
als zijn gelijken, die het goed bedoelen
en nooit hun stuggen nek hebben gebogen,
door liederlijke landsknechten bespogen,
getrapt, geslagen worden totterdood
WORDT WAKKER, WANT DE NOOD IS GROOT.

Ik sla de trom, het is geen tijd voor zingen,

IN MEMORIAM.

Vrijdag 5 Febr. '43 was een zware dag in de bevrijdingsstrijd van het zwaar beproefde Vaderland.

Vanuit een Kriegswehrmachtsgefängnis te Utrecht werden niet minder dan 19 door de Duitse krijgsraden ter dood veroordeelde Nederlanders geëxecuteerd. Zij waren uit allerlei processen bijeengebracht om het vonnis aan hen te voltrekken. Zij waren van zeer uiteenlopende leeftijden en kwamen uit zeer verschillende maatschappelijke standen en beroepen.

In het aangezicht van de majesteit van de Dood,

... AND ITS FAR-REACHING INFLUENCE

Front pages of the four most important Underground newspapers. *Vrij Nederland,* now in its fourth year, is the oldest of all; *Het Parool* has a particularly wide distribution.

The remaining underground newspapers rendered similar services to their readers. They printed warnings against many a Gestapo trick, they provided a complete manual for successful sabotage, and prescribed the best policy to adopt in every fresh dilemma. When, for example, the Nazis introduced their Culture Chamber and its dependent guilds, it was the underground press which advised, "Do not buy or read books by writers belonging to the Nazi Literary Guild." When the Germans requisitioned all metals, including silver, copper and bronze coins in circulation, the underground press explained how things could best be hidden. These papers also revealed the horrifying details of life and death in Nazi-instituted concentration and labor camps and made it a point to print excellent biographical notes on some of the "gentlemen" who called themselves Dutch Nazis and were serving their Germanic brothers to the best of their ability. Often the secret press urged the population to follow closely the instructions of their government in London, reaching them via Radio Orange.

It was unavoidable that the frantic search of the Gestapo hounds for the editors and printers of underground sheets sometimes yielded results. During three years of Nazi occupation many a man has faced the German firing squad because of his "crime" of printing or distributing "enemy news," and many more have been sent to prisons and camps, with sentences ranging from 3 to 15 years.

Only a few of these victims managed to escape from Nazi jails and reach allied territory. One of them, describing the interrogation methods of suspects applied by the Gestapo, told of the barbaric tortures through which he and others had gone. If the Gestapo believed that a suspect was withholding important details, such as the name and whereabouts of an underground group leader, they would place his feet in a tub of water which was slowly brought to boiling point. Or, if the questioning was taking place in a winter month, they would compel the suspect to undress completely and place him on a chair in the prison courtyard. Here, surrounded by warmly-dressed Gestapo men, he was "third-degreed" as long as he could stand it. He was shouted at, and beaten, bullied and whipped. If he fainted, hot drinks were poured down his throat till he revived and the interrogation could be resumed. But if these and other treatments did not yield the desired results, the torturers would proceed to tear out their victim's fingernails, or "make him ripe for a confession" with the help of dazzling floodlights, shining straight into his eyes.

Yet the men and women—and even the hundreds of children who played their part in the quick distribution of underground newspapers—have never been deterred by the thought of the dreadful things that might be done to them should they be caught. Reliable underground information has become a first necessity in a country gagged and bound by its enemies. Far from obstructing the regular appearance of underground pamphlets by the relentless persecution of those who worked for them, the Nazis have only achieved that the people of Holland now rely unquestionably upon the advice and warnings of their clandestine press. It tells them the truth about events in- and outside Holland; and on special occasions it even provides them with extra editions—such as the one distributed shortly after the birth of Princess Juliana's third daughter. A four-page paper, illustrated with the portraits and coats of arms of Princess Juliana and Prince Bernhard, appeared under the appropriate title of "Oranjebode" (The Orange Messenger). Its contents were soon devoured by untold millions, not only in the occupied country but also abroad!

More than once the forbidden newssheets revealed in full the most secret Nazi orders handed out to the "uncensored" press of the Netherlands—thus spoiling Goebbels' little game and making it clear that not a trace remained of its former freedom.

At certain times, when events of great magnitude justified this, special appeals were rapidly printed and circulated. From the swiftness of their appearance and distribution it was obvious that the underground movement had grown into maturity, and was splendidly organized. When, in July, 1942, the first groups of helpless Jews were deported to Poland, a message was flashed to all patriots beseeching them to launch a protest against the perpetration of this barbarity.* The Germans, obviously astounded at the speed with which the call-to-arms had made the round, accused the Catholic and Protestant Churches of having collaborated in its distribution. Neither the underground press nor the Churches deigned to reply. It was too stupid a statement to contradict. In the underground movement neither religious adherences nor social status have ever made the slightest difference. People of all classes, urged by the same intense desire to be of service to their compatriots

*See chapter 10—Slaughter Of The Innocents—page 225.

and to harm the Nazis, continue to contradict the German propaganda lies and to uphold the morale of the nation till the country will regain its independence and rid itself of its enemies.

*

At the time of the invasion Holland possessed two powerful radio broadcasting stations which covered the entire country. There were, besides, a couple of short-wave stations (at Kootwijk and Eindhoven), beaming regular programs to the overseas territories in Asia. The "home" stations were both located in Hilversum; between them they covered the needs of the various religious and political groups, which by common consent had made arrangements to use a reasonable share each of the available broadcasting time.

When the Hitler hordes occupied the country, this working method remained in force; but because of the immediate "co-ordination" of all radio news and speeches, it underwent certain comparatively slight changes. For a few more months the various broadcasting companies were allowed to continue with the regular distribution of their musical programs and all other items of a non-political nature. Strange as it seemed, these programs could even be concluded in the usual way, with the playing of the national anthem. The only sweeping change was that no music of Jewish composers would be allowed to "poison" an unsuspecting public of Dutch listeners.

But in November, 1940, as soon as Goedewaagen headed the Department of Culture and Public Enlightenment, it was announced that a special delegate had been nominated for the "centralization" of all radio broadcasts. This man, an engineer by the name of Dubois, had not been known as an adherent of Nazism; and when shortly after his appointment he came to the microphone to explain what "radio centralization" really meant, he tried to confirm his "neutrality" by saying suavely: "The answer to this question is that as heretofore our programs will have something to offer to everybody. They will also fully maintain our religious liberties and endeavor to do justice to the various religious currents within our nation—just as before . . ."

It sounded very strange that centralization appeared necessary when there was nothing to change . . . The Dutch became suspicious; and rightly so. For only a couple of months later, in January, 1941, the truth came out. Delegate Dubois once more addressed his fellow countrymen, to tell them that the various broadcasting companies would be discontinued, and replaced by *one* State Broadcasting Company. What the Roman Catholics, the Protestants and Social Democrats had constructed through years of hard work, was completely wiped out by the enemy. The radio public fully understood the enormity of the catastrophe—even though the Nazi delegate mumbled some reassuring phrases about "maintaining our cultural heritage" and "the radio will continue to be a true mirror of all that lives and grows inside our beloved country."

On March 9, 1941, the *Nederlandsche Omroep* (Netherlands Broadcasting Company) came on the air for the first time, and three days later Seyss-Inquart decreed the installation of the *"Rijks-radio Omroep"* (State Radio), which automatically replaced the various broadcasting companies, and killed the publication of their program weeklies. All radio literature appearing henceforth would be completely "coordinated"; its publishers would be obliged to print without charge "all articles, photographs and drawings obtained from the Department of Culture and Public Enlightenment, and display them in such way as the Department may deem necessary."

That was the end of this "centralizer's" duty; on May 1, 1941, Dubois disappeared from the radio world. There were no further broadcasting stations to be "centralized." Dr. Herweyer, a district leader of Mussert's N. S. B. in the city of The Hague, became Director-General of the entire nazified broadcasting system.

The News Service of the nazified radio was entrusted to a separate body which, of course, showed an almost pathetic adoration for every report from German sources. Its newscasters and announcers were exclusively members of Mussert's Nationaal-Socialistische Beweging. The service also provided regular talks, many of which were destined for special groups, such as Holland's peasantry, or the poorer elements among the people of Amsterdam, the so-called "Jordaners." A lot of time was spent, besides, on full-fledged Nazi "blood and soil" broadcasts for which the services of experienced German propagandists were frequently solicited.

Another special section went by the purely Teutonic name of *Staatspolitieke Dienst* (State Political Service). It took care of all official ceremonies; it was, for example, the duty of this branch to broadcast such world-shaking events as the departure of Dutch Nazi volunteers for the Russian front. And throughout this medley of hopelessly ineffective propaganda, there ran a red thread of obscene platitudes and anti-Semitic jokes.

The first result of the various drastic changes was, of course, an enormous increase in the quantity of broadcasted propaganda material. There came an endless stream of martial sound, and much on-the-spot reportage of Nazi demonstrations. It was accompanied with a deterioration of the high standards which had marked the musical and general entertainment programs of the Netherlands radio.

Before long there was definite evidence that the Dutch public declined with thanks the honor of spending its time listening to the nazified programs. Hundreds of thousands who did not possess a receiving set of their own had been subscribers to one of the eight hundred "radio leased wire services"—private enterprises which possessed their own relaying stations. These companies installed amplifiers in the homes of their clients, thus enabling them to listen in to a choice of two or three major programs each day. Now that the radio had been robbed of its last vestiges of liberty, the number of "distribution" clients decreased by leaps and bounds. Towards the end of August, 1941 there remained only 225,000, out of an original total of nearly 450,000.

Until the advent of the Nazis, listening to any program was gratis enjoyment for every Netherlander in the possession of a radio set. Voluntarily, however, almost every listener contributed a few guilders per year to his favorite broadcasting station, thus helping it to defray the cost of bringing high-class diversion.*

As from December, 1940 every owner of a radio was forced to register his apparatus with the Postal authorities and pay a yearly tax of nine guilders, or $5.00, to the State. On May 1, 1942 this was increased to 12 guilders, or $6.65, per year. Gradually several further restrictions were introduced, the most significant among them being a decree of January 1, 1941, by which the various weekly radio journals were discontinued. They were to be replaced by one single paper, under the editorship of a Mussert man. As to the radio distribution centers, by the middle of June, 1941,

*Commercial advertising was not allowed on the Dutch radio. No program could, therefore, be sponsored. The broadcasting stations had to subsist on the voluntary contributions of their listeners, increased by the proceeds of their weekly program journals. The latter carried huge quantities of expensive advertising, however, which well turned the scales. The AVRO, most important non-sectarian broadcasting company, had for example been able to build a splendid studio in Hilversum, which brought first-class entertainment on a most generous scale. But despite the lavish sums spent on the composition of those programs, the AVRO had managed to form a reserve fund of *several million guilders!*

all eight hundred of them had been confiscated and placed under the supervision of the nazified Postal Department.

It is not difficult to answer the question why, in such circumstances, the majority of loyal Dutchmen were still prepared to pay their registration fees. It was the only means to hear the *real* radio, the forbidden broadcasts from the BBC and Radio Orange in London, and from Station WRUL in Boston. The offerings of the German invaders consisted largely of nasal sounds and loud music, rarely interlarded with something more enjoyable. The "artists" and "musicians" now let loose upon the public, were mainly N. S. B.'ers of whose artistry the world had thus far been blissfully ignorant. There was such paucity of material that the Germans were finally constrained to organize a contest for a radio play. The official closing date was fixed at October 15, 1941, but the interest shown to earn the prize of 300 guilders was so pitifully small that the period was extended several times. The final upshot of this extraordinary "appeal" was that in May, 1942, no winner had as yet been announced . . .

The people of Holland had neither time nor inclination to bother about "improving" the Nazi-sponsored programs. And if, at a fixed hour every afternoon, they could be found listening tensely to certain broadcasters, those were not announcing from Hilversum I or II, but from London or Boston. With the wistful sense of humor that proved to be one of their saving graces, the Dutch soon told each other that "every evening towards 7 p.m., the whole of Holland is caught by a *cold wave*"—no matter how hot the day had been. For at that hour the doors and windows of every house or apartment inhabited by loyal Netherlanders were hermetically shut—so as not to miss a single word of what the newscasters in faraway allied countries were saying.

Whenever occupied Holland was confronted with a new outburst of Nazi fanaticism, making itself felt through new and ever more stringent measures, its people relied upon the voices from abroad to explain the true portent of these Nazi decrees and—in many cases—to indicate the means of counteracting them. Not always did they agree with the standpoint of the broadcasters; there were many instances in which the counsel given was heatedly disputed. But this was merely a healthy expression of the Dutchman's ineradicable liberty to criticize, to put his opinions against those of his government.

On countless occasions, however, the Dutch have listened breathlessly and unitedly to voices reaching them through the ether from England or the western hemisphere. That was when their Queen or Princess Juliana addressed them, and in simple, heartfelt language made them realize how their difficulties and sufferings were those of the House of Orange, how their fight to regain lost liberties was the fight of their royal leader, and her government.

With bitter hatred the Germans have repeatedly admitted that the influence of the "London refugees" upon the loyal people inside Holland is very great indeed. Not only did they threaten the Dutch with heavy punishment in case of continued "obedience to the criminal instigators abroad," they also carried out their menaces. Scores of Netherlanders have lost their lives because they demonstrated their loyalty to Queen and Government, and lived up to the orders reaching them via the "forbidden" radio.

When in the last days of April, 1943 the Nazis, no longer able to hide their nervosity in view of the coming Allied invasion, ordered the immediate re-imprisonment of nearly four hundred thousand soldiers who during the summer of 1940 had been liberated by the great, magnanimous Fuehrer, the short-wave radio gave the signal for a country-wide protest. In many places it assumed the size of a full-fledged revolt.

No better acknowledgement could have been desired of the immense influence emanating from London, than the subsequent panicky decree of May 13, 1943, in which Seyss-Inquart confiscated all radio receivers, amplifiers and other accessories, an estimated total of about one million sets. Outdoor aerials were not confiscated but their removal within three months was made compulsory. Radio wholesale and retail dealers were to register their stocks. Exempt from these rules were, of course, all Germans and every "Hollander" belonging to the acolytes of Anton Mussert.

The Dutch were obviously getting out of hand. And even if the requisitioning of all radios would prevent the Nazi Propaganda Bureau from continuing its frantic conversion work on anything like the usual scale, it would also make it a good deal more difficult for loyal Hollanders to keep in touch with the only trustworthy sources of news and advice. But it stands to reason that Seyss-Inquart's command was not forthwith obeyed. Early in June, 1943 he repeated his order, reiterating the habitual threats of incarceration and death for every trespasser.

In the course of the next few weeks thousands of radio sets were delivered to the enemy. Yet, it may well turn out to be a disheartening task for the Germans to try and find many new and usable radios among the sacrificed lot. During three years' evasion of tyrannical decrees the Dutch have learned how to hide the things their enemies covet most.

As heretofore the voices from London and Boston will continue to be their guides. Less people will hear the actual broadcasts, but as many—if not more—will remain well-informed by word of mouth of what happens in the free, Allied world. They will follow the Nazi adverses in and outside Europe; they will be fully prepared for the moment in which the Allied armies invade the European continent, to start upon the gigantic task of cleaning it from the Hitler scourge.

*

In the realms of the plastic arts, the theatre, the films, music and literature the Culture Chamber disturbed and changed as much as it could. There were constant attacks, in print and speech, on the "decadent civilization" displayed in the works of such modern Dutch painters as Jan Sluyters, Jan Hoowij, Willem van Konijnenburg, or Mattheus Wiegman. In contrast, Nazi artists were protected and pushed without limit. But the unfortunate truth was that their exhibitions attracted no attention outside the Nazi membership. It was highly vexatious for Goedewaagen and his friends to discover that the swiftly increasing demand for works of art rarely embraced the creations of their protégés.

As to the theatre, Goedewaagen ordered the foundation of a special Dramatist's Bureau, under leadership of the N. S. B.'er Jaap van Kersbergen who was also appointed to an important post in the newly-formed Netherlands Broadcasting Company. This man made the startling discovery that among the tremendous repertoire of the Netherlands' stage there was practically nothing worth showing. Most plays were "either written or produced by Jews or homosexuals"... Consequently, this noble reformer saw himself obliged to organize a contest offering every play-writing Netherlander a chance to see his masterpiece selected for presentation to his compatriots. The jury consisted of Van Kersbergen—and no one else; he announced that the prize was to go to him or her who would "appear to be an asset to our stage, in a purely 'folkish'* spirit." The name of the winner was supposed to be published by October, 1941—but at that time not one word about the contest appeared in the press. Instead the matter was dropped—and never referred to again.

It was well-known that most of Holland's actors and actresses were fierce anti-Nazis, and when in February, 1942 it was decreed that everyone connected with the stage would forthwith have to join the Theater Guild, only about twenty people obeyed. Huge sums had been collected to support those who because of their refusal would become idle.

But the Nazis did not relish the idea of presenting the nation with "folkish" plays through the medium of twenty actors and actresses . . . The directors of the various Dutch theatrical companies were summoned to The Hague, and told that every recalcitrant actor would be looked upon as a saboteur and transported posthaste to a concentration camp. Even then many Dutch stage people refused to submit; they preferred to go into hiding. Soon afterwards it became known that the country's best elocutionist, Charlotte Koehler, had actually been transported to a Nazi camp because at the close of her last public appearance she had taken leave of her wildly applauding audience by waving an orange-colored handkerchief.

Apart from the legitimate stage, there were around 4,000 amateur theatrical associations, distributed throughout the Netherlands. In March, 1942, the Germans ordered them, one and all, to join the Culture Chamber, with the subsequent obligation to submit every line of their plays to the Culture Department's censorship. The result was that most amateur companies disbanded voluntarily. It brought to a temporary halt one of the most beloved pastimes of Holland's working and middle classes—a pastime dating back to the gay and prosperous days of the seventeenth century, and the unrivalled genius of Gerbrand Adriaenszoon Bredero.

In the film world, too, the Nazi occupation caused drastic changes. As Dutch movie studios never contributed greatly to the country's needs, there had been a constant demand for British, French and American products. This was emphatically discouraged, even when France had been conquered and America still was neutral. Only films made in the occupied territory or in the Reich

*See chapter 12—Youth Under Siege—page 255.

were allowed. Movies "likely to disturb the public order and safety" were banned, as were also excluded all films which the authorities considered "contrary to the national requirements, or against the educational spirit of our time."

The main fare of Holland's movie theatres would henceforth be a mixture of German "New Timers"—exceptionally tasteless and senseless products—and films *of educational value.* It stands to reason that the latter were the purest Nazi propaganda; but to avoid possible refusals to include this kind of trash, Goedewaagen decreed that the showing of any film could be made obligatory "on account of its outstanding informative, educational or cultural value." The first to fall under this heading was the anti-Semitic movie, "The Eternal Jew" (*Der ewige Jude*). This distinguished example of Teutonic Kultur was shown in every nook and corner of the occupied territory throughout a period of many months. Before the end of 1941 it was followed by another great creation, "With Germany For A New Europe."

The weekly newsreel, now exclusively glorifying Nazi invincibility, was run after the feature presentation, so that it was an easy matter for omnipresent Nazi spies to ascertain who among the audience made it a habit to leave the cinema before the newsreel came on.

The censorship of all films was entrusted to a one-time would-be producer, a certain G. J. Teunissen who was made president of a State Film Board. This man whose career had been marked by mediocre productions as well as several outright "flops," also replaced the president of the Netherlands Cinema League, and was chosen to lead the Film Guild. Soon after his installation Teunissen convoked a meeting of film producers and agents, to treat his audience to the joyful message that "at last the film industry in Holland had been completely freed of all Jewish influence." In January, 1943, the gentleman was reported to employ four assistants; between them these five censors replace the sixty who used to scan films in Holland before the invasion.

The worst blunder they made was, beyond doubt, when they passed a German film based upon the life of Rembrandt, the immortal Master. Under the direction of Hans Steinhoff a number of German actors distorted the facts of Rembrandt's life to such a degree that even Mussert's acolytes, despite their oath to admire everything Teutonic, could not help showing some displeasure.

Rembrandt had been pictured as a senile old man, and the nazified press protested vehemently, declaring that "the film was filled with anachronisms and factual errors." The life of the great painter had been turned into a banal enumeration of sordid love affairs. Above all, it was a desperate attempt to "prove" that Rembrandt, far from being Dutch, was a "Germanic" painter and a protagonist of German culture. So crude and ineffective a piece of propaganda this film turned out to be, that it was soon withdrawn from circulation.

Obviously, the stultifying influence of the Culture Chamber was also felt in musical circles. "Jewish" music as well as Jewish interpreters had been banned right from the start of the occupation. But now English, American, Russian and Polish composers were also "verboten," with the sole exception of Chopin's works. All music programs were subject to censorship, and as only Willem Mengelberg remained of the erstwhile array of famous conductors, the Department of Culture and Public Enlightenment encouraged young musicians to be trained at the expense of the State for second conductor, to lead the smaller symphonic orchestras. Composers willing to cooperate with the Nazis, received generous grants and promises of further support. In September, 1941, no less than nineteen such nazified musicians were enjoying the benefits of their masters' protection; foremost among them was the N. S. B.'er Henk Badings.

But far from filling the concert halls, as once they used to be filled to capacity whenever a famous conductor or soloist was to appear, Nazi meddling resulted in a swiftly decreasing number of concert-goers. To begin with, Jewish music lovers were barred; and the "aryan" audiences showed remarkably little anxiety to go to concerts conducted by Nazis, or in which Nazi-sponsored soloists were to elevate their souls. The Amsterdam Concertgebouw —before the invasion one of Holland's chief music centers—lost more than two-thirds of its membership within one occupation year. Mengelberg had fallen into disgrace and was shunned by all loyal Hollanders. There was an occasion on which a Mengelberg performance attracted so few listeners that, at the last moment, the Nazis hastily commandeered numbers of German citizens and followers of Mussert to fill the hall!

In the winter of 1941-2 the amateur choral and musical societies were fused, and made into one organization. They were not obliged to join the Culture Chamber; apparently Goedewaagen had learned a lesson from his unfortunate experience with the theatrical societies. Nonetheless, in the spring of 1942 the Department of Culture was very much annoyed by the fact that many choral societies "do not as yet send their programs to our Department long in advance of their performances." In an effort at "friendly" explanation the announcement stated, "those data are required to draw up our statistics and reviews." But the real meaning of the Department's anxiety to approve all music could not be concealed for long. "There are musical pieces," said Goedewaagen, "which may be considered undesirable. For that reason some numbers must be struck from all amateur programs." To give the Department plenty of time for this useful work, it was made obligatory to send in program schedules eight weeks before presentation, through the intermediary of the local mayor or police chief. The announcement concluded on a note of persuasion. "Large orchestras and musical societies have long practised this good habit," it said . . .

In spite of such efforts to "tame" Dutch musicians, professional and amateur, these people never failed to seize an opportunity to demonstrate their anti-Nazi sentiments. In July, 1942 the anti-Semitic weekly, De Misthoorn (The Foghorn), complained bitterly that "those men and women do not understand our New Times." As an example the pamphlet quoted the fact that the Arnhem Symphonic Orchestra took a particular pleasure in honoring Jewish musicians. When the orchestra leader fell ill, a Jewish first violinist—once a well-known player in the Berlin Philharmonic Orchestra—took his place. The famous Dutch pianist Willem Andriessen was soloist, and at the end of the concert the audience gave both him and the Jewish first violinist a tremendous ovation.

Half a year later the nazified press reported the case of an organist who on the occasion of a well-known educator's funeral played both the severely-forbidden "Andante" by Mendelssohn and the "Wilhelmus," the country's national anthem. An organist of a small town in the province of Brabant was accused of playing the British anthem, "God Save The King," at almost every service. The Germans arrested him—but they were forced to let him go when he proved that though the tune he played was, perhaps, similar to the British anthem, it really belonged to an old Netherlands folksong: *"O, Dearest Place On Earth."*

This musical sabotage continues subtly, both in city and village. The Nationale Dagblad of January 22, 1943, reported choking with indignation that a woman teacher at The Hague had her pupils sing songs of Mendelssohn. "That teacher has the temerity to tell her pupils, 'Children, this song is written by Mendelssohn, a Jewish gentleman. His works may not be performed at present—so we shall sing them' . . . She also teaches the children Negro spirituals such as *'I Got A Robe'* and *'Peter, Go Ring Those Bells.'* "

In the southern province of Limburg musical activity used to be traditional. "But now," an organizer of Nazi musical festivals complained in the Nationale Dagblad late in May, 1943, "they have come to a practical standstill. I travel across the whole province and talk to people. I ask them 'What is the matter with you? Why don't you collaborate? You have decent halls now, instruments and money to pay a good conductor—things you never used to have. All that is available; yet, you go on strike and refuse to play at our festivals . . . Many Limburgers," he concluded by way of a rather naïve discovery, "seem still unfriendly to the Culture Chamber, its aims and its work."

*

As in the case of the daily and periodical press, Goedewaagen used the splendid excuse of paper shortage to curtail the publication of new books. Not only was it necessary to submit each new manuscript to the Culture Chamber but it was the obvious intention to grant paper lots only for such books as were written by "thoroughly reliable" authors. The creators of Holland's real literature were, therefore, driven underground; they simply stopped writing, rather than bend to Goedewaagen's distorted interpretation of culture.

The few who sold themselves outright to the enemy were adequately rewarded. The prize of *Master of Netherlands Literature* was, for example, granted to the Nazi writer, Jan H. Eekhout for his book "Mirande." Only a few months later, however, the Master was accused of plagiarism when the literary critic of the Nazi weekly, Volk en Vaderland, revealed that the plot for Eekhout's latest book, "Pastoor Poncke," had almost entirely been lifted from a German novel. Immediately the literary critic of the Nationale Dagblad—strangely enough a close colleague of the accuser—set out to defend Eekhout. He retorted with the enlightening but somewhat startling declaration that "folkish literature cannot be bothered with demands for originality. The writers of our New Order are in too much of a hurry for that."

But even if the production of good literature became well-nigh impossible, the Germans could not with the same ease change Dutch predilection for good books. They might ban all works with an anti-German tenor or with expressions considered "insulting to Nazi ideals," it remained perforce a rather half-hearted sort of measure, as thousands of circulating libraries, all over the Netherlands, kept most of those works unperturbedly on their shelves. They had a good excuse. The owners of circulating libraries could hardly be expected to know the contents of every book they had in stock. And thus the German threat to hold these owners personally responsible if forbidden literature were found in their establishments, failed to work out.

Finally, the Department of Culture and Public Enlightenment provided the book trade with long lists of works to be removed from circulation. In December, 1941 one hundred and twenty books were placed on the forbidden list. Among them were works by world-renowned Dutch and German authors, such as Hendrik Willem van Loon, Maurits Dekker, Anton den Doolaart, Andreas Latzko, Erich Maria Remarque (author of "All Quiet On The Western Front"), Joseph Roth, Thomas Mann, Vicki Baum, Leon Feuchtwanger, Emil Ludwig, Franz Werfel, Arthur Schnitzler and even the American writer, John Gunther.

The longer the occupation lasted, the greater became the demand for books based upon the rich history of the Netherlands. The masses, virtually robbed of their usual diversions, had taken to reading and asked for stories eulogizing their country's greatest moments. The brave struggle against Spanish domination, in the sixteenth and seventeenth centuries, and its ultimate victory, provided endless chances for comparison with present sufferings; and so a veritable rush ensued on this kind of literature.

Patriotic readers showed no interest whatever in the much-advertised Nazi prize books. Rather than accept the trash which German propagandists tried to foist upon them, they preferred to wait for months until they could borrow a copy of "Holland's Glorie" (Holland's Glory) by Jan de Hartog, or "Het Wilhelmus," a short, effectively-written story by Leonhard Huizinga.

To counteract this popularity, the Nazis put almost insurmountable obstacles in the way of reprinting these successful books.

Paper was always to be had for Nazi publications, but permission to reprint other works was very difficult to obtain. From time to time remainders of various paper lots would grudgingly be released to certain publishers, and it became a common practice to bring out reprints on paper of various qualities, or varying color shades.

Few foreign books reached the country; even the well-known German "cheap editions," such as the Tauchnitz, were scarce. English novels could still be had from stock, and there were no restrictions on the sale of French books. The great difficulty was, however, to get them. Dutch importers received only a few copies of each new French book. The book trade was therefore obliged to contact French publishers direct—but generally without results.

When in December, 1941 the United States entered the war, the Nazis immediately decreed that all American authors were henceforth forbidden, with the sole exception of the American "classics"—that is, writers who had died before the end of 1904. This hasty ruling led to a rather comic situation. Most booksellers and owners of lending libraries were not quite sure whether an author was English or American. Of course, there was a comparatively short list of outstanding writers whose American nationality was not in doubt, but against this there were scores of others whose works remained for sale or hire simply because their nationality was "uncertain." It was July, 1942 before the Germans decided to publish a long, official list of those whom they considered American writers. Among them were many whom even the best informed in the book trade had thus far considered English.

The publication of this black list was another blow to the reading public of the Netherlands. Hundreds of volumes which had been in brisk demand, innocent stories without the slightest reference to Nazism, were suddenly withdrawn from circulation.

Parallel with the deterioration of the book market ran the disintegration of Holland's many illustrated periodicals. Several of the popular weeklies were forced out of existence, or placed under "trusted" Nazi editorship. The results were practically alike, as very few Hollanders spent their money on nazified magazines. Besides, even those periodicals which obeyed every German order, ran the risk of being suddenly suspended—sometimes for weeks on end.

A striking example was the case of "De Prins," a family weekly appearing regularly since 1900. One day the editor of this rather colorless and perfectly innocuous paper received a new portrait of Seyss-Inquart, with the command that it must be included in the week's issue. However, the paper was on the point of going to press and as no other space was available, the picture of the Reich's Commissioner appeared on the last page but one, right over a large advertisement for some commodity. This "humiliation" so upset the Nazis that "De Prins" did not appear again for six consecutive weeks.

By the autumn of 1942 several more periodicals had been disbanded "because of paper shortage." Among them were many of the better literary monthlies; but the best known of them, "Groot Nederland," still managed to survive. Its editors tried very hard to maintain both its original character and the necessary neutrality—even after several of their regular contributors had been punished for non-conformity to the rules of Goedewaagen's Culture Chamber.

In view of the ever-decreasing number of Dutch magazines, the demand for French and English language publications grew steadily; but the offering was so small that even back issues were eagerly bought. There was a particular interest in old copies of American periodicals, such as the National Geographic Magazine. The few available issues, dating back to 1939 or earlier, found eager buyers who, in their turn, were sure of a ready market after they had enjoyed their magazine from cover to cover.

*

However much the German tyrants endeavored to infuse their "Kultur" into the life of Holland, they never did more than scratch the surface. The real, deep-seated culture of the Netherlands, the free and true Dutch spirit, could not be contaminated by their "reforms in the folkish sense." Rather, it grew and widened under oppression and restrictions. If, for example, the divine solace of music was not acceptable from Willem Mengelberg, the traitor, it could always be had in the privacy of one's living room. Amateur concerts, once a favorite pastime of music-loving Holland, now became a part of social life—to such extent that musical instruments were sold in heretofore unknown quantities.

Libraries could surely be purged, but it was still possible to keep in one's own bookcases the master works of all times, next to the best of Holland's own literature. And even the books in which certain Germans had pronounced judgment on the nefarious Nazi system, could still be kept and read within the home. Exhibitions glorifying the New Order were rarely visited by loyal Hollanders; but these same obstinate people would spend hours and hours bent over some illustrated book on the 17th century Masters.

Holland's culture was retiring within itself. Temporarily ousted from public life, it met with greater admiration and warmer enthusiasm in the family circle, the Church and the classroom than ever before. *There* was, and still is, gathered the spiritual power which will help restore the Netherlands, once the Department of Culture and Public Enlightenment has disappeared—together with its disreputable miracle worker, Dr. Goedewaagen.

14

CHARITY AT PISTOL POINT

"Our Winter Help is a sign of the transition from the capitalistic-democratic period to the era of National-Socialism."

Mussert, in Volk en Vaderland, November 22, 1940.

"I have been trudging along all day, in the dripping rain. Success? . . . , the results are enough to make you cry! Plenty of doors remain locked—though you *know* the people are home. But who vexes me most is the maid who says placidly: 'Oh no—my madam doesn't give to the Winter Help.' "

Voluntary collector in the Nationale Dagblad, October 14, 1941.

In Nazi Germany the *Winterhilfe,* or Winter Help, is an institution whose task it is to gather everywhere and in every way, the enormous amounts needed to support the poor who—so it seems—are more numerous than ever in the ten year old National-Socialist State. It is called "a charitable movement," but this is merely a name; in reality it has nothing in common with the expression of true social feeling. It is a propaganda unit with a double purpose. On the one hand, it is to create an impression of social unity among the nation while, on the other, it must discover means by which to mulct the people and obtain the colossal amounts for charity which otherwise would have to be paid from State resources.

Within the Reich the results have been so satisfactory that the Nazis insisted upon the introduction of the Winter Help in Holland as soon as their administrative machinery was more or less in working order. But they had not been quick enough to prevent the spontaneous organization of a collection—in the early days of July, 1940—for the benefit of war victims. That street collection yielded no less than two and a half million guilders, or approximately one and a half million dollars. But by the end of August the Germans were far enough advanced with their own plans to forbid all further public collections. And in October the people of the Netherlands were treated to a Seyss-Inquart decree which proclaimed the foundation of the *Winter Help-Holland.*

Without further delay the new-fangled "charitable institution" set up its publicity campaign. The country was divided into a number of districts, and the recently appointed director of the Winter Help, a thus far unknown man by the name of Piek, criss-crossed the land to form Committees everywhere. Walls and billboards throughout Holland were covered with posters . . . which were as rapidly torn down again by loyal citizens. Soon the organizing Director, in his various press conferences, saw himself obliged to confess that "the real intentions of our Winter Help are not as yet understood." And he had to admit that many people refused to have anything to do with the Winter Help because they thought "that all the money we collect will go to Germany." Of course, he refuted "this slanderous allegation," and he had particularly bitter things to say about the wait-and-see attitude of the masses.

As time went by, the publicity campaign adopted a tone of great urgency. Authorities of all kinds were brought before the Hilversum radio to broadcast their approval. Huge advertisements appeared regularly in practically every newspaper. Local committees organized meetings in which the disappointingly small audiences were warmly advised to "contribute in accordance with your means," so as to prevent that "many will go hungry and get into even greater difficulties during the coming winter."

At last the long-announced first street collection took place. It yielded about 20% of the proceeds of the spontaneously organized July campaign. Altogether the half-million guilder mark was barely surpassed. Even though the Germans, and with them their Dutch-Nazi helpers, refused to see it—*that* was Holland's final judgment on the activities of the Winter Help. Business firms and private companies might be forced to contribute "generous gifts," Seyss-Inquart might indulge in public magnanimity and donate a hundred thousand guilders obviously stolen from Dutch public funds, the Netherlands' nation could not be goaded into supporting the movement.

But the Nazis were not discouraged; before the end of 1940 they organized a second collection—with even more disastrous results. Director Piek felt bitterly disappointed. To his closest associates he complained of the "fantastic stories and calumnies which make the work of our organization unnecessarily difficult."

Where street collections had proved of so little avail, the director—probably at the advice of his German instructors—decided to change the program and send Winter Help representatives to collect from door to door. Every donor was to sign his name on a list so that, Piek evidently hoped, most people would not dare to refuse, out of fear that it might harm them not to be mentioned. It was a charmingly simple form of blackmail, and the tension with which director Piek and his helpers awaited the results of the third collection, at the end of January, 1941, can be easily understood.

Alas! in spite of their efforts at intimidation, the Winter Help organizers were in for the cruelest disappointment. The totals gathered this time in no way equalled those of December. The 800,000 inhabitants of Amsterdam, for example, contributed altogether less than 17,000 guilders, or around two Dutch cents per capita.

From month to month the proceeds of these collections decreased no matter whether they were held in the streets, or from door to door. By March, 1941, it was decided to go around with lists on which the names and addresses of all inhabitants had already been placed, so that a refusal to contribute became an open and personal demonstration against the occupation authorities. Triumphantly the local director of the Amsterdam Winter Help cried, "We shall go from door to door, and will only consider our work well-done when every apartment in every house has given us a contribution."

But even this immoral pressure failed to produce the expected results. During four months of ceaseless collecting and at the expense of costly advertising in press and radio, the Winter Help gathered approximately three million guilders—or only 20% more than the July collection had yielded in one day. It was no good denying facts any longer: the Winter Help had "failed to appeal to the imagination and the charitable instincts of the masses."

Whilst further collections were, all the same, being organized, the various directors and their helpers never ceased complaining of the "obstructionist policies" which prevented them from making their work a success. Director Piek revealed that "underground action such as the posting of anonymous pamphlets with insulting contents for the leaders of the Winter Help" was rife. "When we try to tell the people that the proceeds of our collections will benefit our indigent compatriots in their entirety, our posters are besmirched, or torn down. This is a crime committed against our needy citizens . . ."

*

If only a few hundred—or even a few thousand—had refused to give to the Winter Help despite the fact that their names were mentioned on the collection lists, the Nazis might have been able to take vengeance. But it was impossible to retaliate when millions not only failed to contribute but also used strong language to describe their opinion of the "voluntary collectors." There were many who declared they *might* have given something if they had not found their names mentioned on the lists. This they considered a form of duress—and they definitely refused to be charitable at pistol point.

The results of the 1941-spring collections were so bad that, in order to save face, Seyss-Inquart announced he himself had contributed no less than half a million guilders, or about $270,000, to the Winter Help-Amsterdam, "from funds at his disposal." As only a couple of months earlier the city of Amsterdam had been condemned to pay a fine of fifteen million guilders, because of its spontaneous anti-Nazi strikes,* there was little doubt as to the sources of Seyss-Inquart's generosity.

In vain did the Winter Help organizers try to arrive at some form of cooperation with other charitable institutions. They also endeavored to influence the church collections, but the churches unanimously refused to send Seyss-Inquart as much as a copy of their collection plans. In the end the Germans could no longer contain themselves. Seeing their charitable intentions so "grievously misinterpreted" and their desire to support Holland's needy misconstrued as "just another way to rob the Netherlands' nation," they decreed that as from May 15, 1941, the "uncooperative—if not obstructionist—attitude of the various religious and nonsectarian organizations must make place for indubitable complacency." Otherwise, the edict said, a ban might be announced on all collections, or arrangements might well be made to resort to obligatory contributions to the Winter Help.

Naturally, this menace did not work out at all; no one could ever compel the Dutch to give their money to institutions they distrusted. On the other hand, no one could prevent them from forming temporary organizations—if need be underground—to

*See chapter 11—A Rallying Cry—page 244.

bring relief wherever this might be needed. When, for example, the Nazis staged a Winter Help collection at the Amsterdam Stock Exchange hardly anybody contributed. But it was a forceful lesson for the Nazi collectors to see how a veritable rain of coins and paper money came down upon the representatives of a Christian charitable institution, and on collectors for the "Joodsche Invalide": a Jewish organization which, in pre-invasion years, had done exemplary work for the care of the aged and the sick.

As usual, the Germans were slow in learning their lesson. And when the time came for the autumn campaign, they worked out a fantastic program, the chief merit of which was a remarkable display of stagey effects and empty hullabaloo.

In various towns knights-in-armor were to carry shields adorned with the coats of arms of the provinces concerned. Pages, heralds, and lancers, all dressed in mediaeval costumes, would form part of the processions, and military bands were to play "stimulating tunes" in half a dozen of the more densely populated districts. In Amsterdam a red omnibus would be parked near the Amstel River to receive donations from the passers-by and a decorated boat, its passengers dressed up to resemble the great 17th century naval hero, Admiral Michiel de Ruyter and his entourage, was to travel around the city on a motor lorry. The collectors would invariably be pretty Dutch girls in native costumes; and everywhere loudspeakers would blare forth songs and speeches applauding the Winter Help campaign.

On the surface, the results of the ensuing collections seemed to justify all this noise and clatter. During October The Hague alone gathered nearly $300,000 for "the good purpose." The newspapers who brought this information omitted, however, to mention that every important business house, throughout the country, had—literally speaking—been blackmailed into contributing important sums. Nazi burgomasters, for example, had intimated that firms in their community which forgot to contribute to the Winter Help, would no longer be considered worthy of furnishing their towns with supplies.

The general results of the country-wide campaign were so little satisfactory that Winter Help director Piek, using the radio for this purpose, besought the obstinate Dutch to change their minds and give generously, so that a total of at least ten million guilders would be reached. "It will be the greatest disgrace in the history of our country if the Winter Help fails to succeed," he cried. And he concluded by threatening anyone "spreading the dastardly rumor that the money goes to Germany" with "adequate measures, to be taken by the competent authorities." Repeatedly the Deutsche Zeitung in den Niederlanden, a German language paper appearing in the Netherlands, endeavored to bolster up Mr. Piek's assertions that most of the money would be used for charitable purposes inside Holland. But it stands to reason that such "explanations" could hardly convince the vast majority of the Dutch nation.

More and more Dutch Nazi mayors came to the rescue. Some of them threatened to discharge those officials whose name did not appear on the lists of "voluntary" contributors to the Winter Help. The burgomaster of Oldenzaal, a small town near the German border, distributed a circular among his municipal employees, in which he chided those among them who were "waiting to see from which direction the wind blows or who are paying lip service only to the occupying power, without the necessary inner conviction." In his opinion the entire staff of the town should join the Mussert party; all policemen should become a part of the N. S. B. Legal Front (Rechtsfront) and all workers within his community should join the Nazified Center of Trade Unions. Naturally, an immediate result of this wholesale change-over would be phenomenal contributions to the Winter Help!

But in spite of such frantic, ofttimes naïve attempts at conversion, the Winter Help collectors continued to meet with the most disheartening lack of enthusiasm among the masses. In Amsterdam a whole street, inhabited by prosperous people, gave the house-to-house collector a total of . . . 75 Dutch cents, or approximately 40c. Only a few days before Christmas, 1941, the press was instructed to publish another general appeal to "give freely because of the coming holidays. Political bitterness and disunity are destroying our national strength," said this urgent appeal, "and this at a time when unity is more necessary than ever. Dissension affects the whole of public life—also the Winter Help campaign which is exclusively aimed at alleviating the bitter distress now reigning in thousands of Netherlands' homes."

*

The second occupation winter was so hard that for many of the poorest there was no choice; they *had* to apply to the Winter Help for support. Immediately patriots in every corner of the country organized neighborly help drives, with the purpose of decreasing as much as possible the number of those forced to accept charity from the invaders and their accomplices. Hundreds of families pledged themselves to assist one another. They arranged aid parties and technical work units whose task it was to provide shelter and give economic assistance, especially in cases where the breadwinner of a family was imprisoned by the Nazis or, so as to escape German revenge, had been forced to go into hiding. All the same, the Germans proudly revealed that during the first year of the Winter Help's existence six million guilders had been expended on the support of the poor. But even if this figure were true—and there were no data whatever to support the bare statement—it compared very unfavorably with the average twelve million guilders per year which pre-invasion Holland devoted to charitable purposes.

The Nazis saw it clearly: to save the Winter Help from an ignominious end it would be necessary to change it, ever so carefully and warily, from an institution of volunteer workers to part of the official Nazi administration. A first step toward this aim was made in January, 1942, with the stipulation that all unemployed in need of clothing, shoes and cover were henceforth to apply to the Winter Help. Also, thousands of people who, owing to the scarcity of food and fuel, had been obliged to go to the Central Kitchens for their daily nourishment, were informed that from now on they would have to show a form signed by the district head of the so-called Nederlandsche Volksdienst (*Netherlands People's Service*), an N. S. B. institution working in close cooperation with the Winter Help.* As in practically every instance the district heads of the People's Service were Mussert men, it was the obvious intention to appease, first of all, the hunger of true believers in Adolf Hitler, and of his Dutch disciples.

In close imitation of the German example, the Winter Help also organized "one course meals" and "comradely evenings" with variety shows of the "highly amusing"—because strongly anti-Semitic—cabaret of the N. S. B. The main purpose of these enjoyable gatherings was to win more proselytes who could be used for the none too pleasant task of house-to-house collecting. The plans for Amsterdam called for no less than 10,000 of them who, between them, would cover the six hundred "blocks" into which the city had been sub-divided. By the end of February, 1942, only eight hundred of such volunteers had been registered . . . , and

*See chapter 10—Slaughter of the Innocents—page 233; also page 316.

even the ninety district heads needed to carry out the grandiose plan, failed to apply.

During the periodic "one course dinners" the speakers made it a hard and fast rule to complain of the general attitude of the Dutch. One of them, airing his indignation in an Amsterdam meeting, came to the conclusion that "the people of Holland have sunk low; they have lost their self-respect, their honor and their pride." He urged his fellow Winter Help workers to "march like Storm Troopers" and feel themselves like "goose-stepping Nazi soldiers, giving their all to the Winter Help cause."

But the volunteer collectors still met with a great deal of sarcasm and general unwillingness to contribute. "People sneer at them," complained Max Blokzijl in one of his radio talks during 1941. "It makes your blood boil to hear of the 'practical jokes' that are played upon them. For instance, there are people living on the third or fourth floor of an apartment house who answer the collector's call: 'Winter Help' with a friendly, 'Just come up, will you?' When the collectors have climbed the stairs* and arrive out of breath at their destination, there is no one to be seen, and no reply to their ringing or calling. Others again *do* answer, but they only say—with an expression of feigned surprise—'Winter Help? O, I didn't get that . . . No—we don't give to Winter Help.' "

The southern provinces of Brabant and Limburg, mainly Catholic, were if possible even more inflexible in their attitude towards the Winter Help than the rest of the country. But everywhere the organizers met with the same unwillingness to appreciate their charitable intentions. Directors of hospitals generally prevented Winter Help collectors from entering their institutions, "because it would disturb the rest of the patients." This the Nazis felt as a grave injustice; but it was worse still that large banks and business firms gradually reduced the amounts of their contributions. In the second occupation year their "gifts" diminished by half, and one of them—the important Rotterdamsche Bankvereeniging—gave nothing at all. This caused a wild outburst on the part of Meinoud M. Rost van Tonningen, Nazi-appointed head of the Netherlands Bank, who described that lack of generosity as "a scandalous affair which the directors of the Rotterdamsche Bankvereeniging will have to pay for dearly." If by that time there had

*Many laborers in Holland's biggest cities live in large apartment houses of three, or more stories. There are no elevators in these buildings, stairs in common use leading from floor to floor.

still been a single Netherlander willing to believe that the Winter Help actually relied upon the voluntary gifts of the people, Rost van Tonningen's emotional outburst would have proved its compulsory character to him.

Next followed a series of sweepstakes and lotteries with high prizes—gambling in the crudest form, a brutal speculation on the misery of millions. The first of these comprised six million lots; no less than one million guilders was to be reserved for the winners. In all big towns special booths were built for the sale of tickets and 1,200 salesmen, together with 2,500 lottery agents, were busily engaged in the same noble work. Processions were formed, headed by blaring bands; and only a few days after the start of the campaign, Winter Help headquarters patted themselves on the back with the triumphant announcement that the results were "enormous" and that the organization of the lottery had proved how well they "understood popular psychology."

But these jubilations came a little too early. Only a few weeks later the sale of lucky tickets had fallen off considerably, an average of only 18,000 per week being placed. At this rate it would have taken almost six years to dispose of the total of six million tickets. Finally, the Winter Help directors decided to make an end to it. A certain number of high prizes had actually been paid but the authorities carefully abstained from informing the public of the net results . They only announced that the "valuable experience" just gathered would doubtlessly lead to the organization of a similar lottery during the summer of 1942.

Meanwhile, the blackmail methods which the Winter Help had so consistently applied, were by no means discarded. It was no unusual experience for businesses and other commercial enterprises to read in the morning papers that the Nazi Winter Help "had received with thanks" their gift of 400, 500 or a thousand guilders. No need to emphasize that such an announcement was the first intimation these people had of their own charity! . . . There was, however, no misinterpreting the hint. They must give something substantial, and forthwith. A refusal would be explained as anti-Nazi action, with due punishment to follow.

Apart from these disproportionate "gifts," the average amounts contributed to the work of the Winter Help tell a story in themselves. The regularly published lists of contributions were divided into a section for gifts below and another for gifts above one hundred guilders. It was a remarkable thing that most voluntary contributions remained below the hundred guilders' mark and, as the months went by, grew smaller and smaller. The total for the four last months of 1941 was only one-fifth of what had been gathered during the spring of 1941, when the Winter Help acquired its first experience in blackmailing the Dutch. During the months of January-May, 1942, only 14% was obtained of the totals collected a year before.

Apparently still convinced that success would follow in the wake of "improved methods," the Nazis tried several new ways of stimulating public generosity. In quick tempo their collectors offered all kinds of emblems in exchange for a gift. Now they would be traffic pins or coats of arms. Then again the pins would bear reproductions of historical figures or take the shape of spring flowers. Winter Help organizer Piek travelled the country from one end to the other addressing hastily-convoked meetings of N. S. B.'ers and sympathizers. These he assured "before God and my conscience" that his only purpose was the well-being of the Netherlands people. Not one single cent of the collected money would go to Germany and the N. S. B. was not to receive one-quarter of the entire proceeds, as had been authoritatively revealed by the free London Radio Orange.

During 1942 the Nazis discontinued the publication of collection results. They were satisfied to announce that a Winter Help campaign had been "completely successful," or that the proceeds had been "considerably better." Figures were no longer revealed and certainly not in cases where the Winter Help authorities could not hide the truth and had to admit that the collected totals were "very much less than last year."

From time to time the flippant Nazi weekly Volk en Vaderland, however, would reveal the truth by divulging, in a strongly irritated tone and with great indignation, that collectors for the Winter Help relief were still being treated "like dirt." In the late autumn of 1942 the paper talked of one volunteer who had called on 38 people, all of whom pretended not to be at home. On that same day he had lost seven out of twenty-six old contributors and gained only two new ones. Altogether, his harvest had been . . . two guilders and sixty cents, or about $1.40. "It would have been more profitable for this man if he had stayed at home and put ten guilders in the collection box himself," the Volk en Vaderland editor exclaimed.

Another collector who had stationed himself near the Utrecht railroad works where at least a hundred employees were bound to pass in a short time, did not get a single contribution from them. Policemen in the same city had shown themselves "just as stingy." And of all the inhabitants of Utrecht the well-to-do classes were chronicled as having given the least and behaved the worst.

The organ of the Dutch Nazi Storm Troopers "Storm" had made an "interesting discovery," namely that collectors in N. S. B. uniforms brought in from four to five times as much as their non-uniformed colleagues. "Evidently," the paper concluded, "force might do a great deal to increase the rate of contributions." This threat was repeated shortly afterwards in an announcement printed by the Amsterdam newspapers. The item gave a detailed description of a carefully-kept card index which would henceforth be used as a check on everyone's willingness, or refusal, to contribute to the Nazi relief fund.

There were many other forms of coercion, such as the sending of letters to municipal employees. They were informed that, as many people "did not dare to contribute to the Winter Help because they feared the contempt of their friends," it had been decided to assume that no employee would object to sacrificing one half per cent of his yearly salary for that purpose. "If this assumption is wrong, however, your refusal must be upheld by a good explanation," the circular concluded menacingly.

*

In the face of the bad reception given to the German Winter Help, Mussert and his followers decided to start a charitable movement of their own. With the approval of Seyss-Inquart they founded the *Nederlandsche Volksdienst,* or Netherlands People's Service, in July, 1941. Its purpose was vaguely described as "the care of all Netherlanders, from a viewpoint of the people's welfare —and other similar purposes." But if the description of its aim was devoid of all new thought, the People's Service turned out to be even less original in its activities. It worked out an intricate plan which sub-divided every city and town into "districts" and every district into a number of "blocks," each with its own responsible leaders. It was the old German system again, a colorless imitation of the *National-Sozialistische Volkswohlfahrt.*

Long before the invasion Holland had known such aid societies as the Green Cross, the White Cross and the White-Yellow Cross, all of which had brought assistance and solace to the impecunious sick. These splendid associations, however, were promptly accused of "taking their instructions from the other side of the Channel" and given the choice to either disband or become a part of the People's Service. Most of them preferred the former, and finally the People's Service mainly concerned itself with the worries of N. S. B.'ers, and their families. It sent a few hundred N. S. B. children to Germany, after having provided them with miniature swastika flags. It made arrangements for a number of neurotic N. S. B. women to spend some weeks in the country; and it even showed its kindly feelings towards the aged by buying and furnishing a "Home for Aged Ladies" in the village of Dieren, near Arnhem. But despite this thoughtful program, and although its membership cost only one guilder per year, the organizing Mussertmen, nearly twelve months after the innovation of their People's Service, admitted reluctantly that "far too few have joined our Volksdienst."

Obstruction to this Dutch-Nazi benevolent society was, beyond doubt, best organized among the Dutch Catholics. The Bishop of Roermond, Mgr. Lemmens, circularized the clergy with a message in which he expressed his fear that "the Netherlands People's Service, considering the mentality of its leaders, will doubtlessly try to propagandize ideologies among us which we, as Catholics, cannot accept." How well this advice was understood appeared shortly afterwards. In November, 1941, the R. A. F. came over the southern city of Maastricht and caused fairly heavy casualties and damage to private property, while bombing military targets. But not a single Catholic applied to the People's Service for support. Instead they one and all went to the Aid Society which their Bishop had organized.

*

Millions of loyal Netherlanders will have nothing to do with the charity forced upon them by their enemies—but this does not mean that they have lost their proverbial capacity for doing good and assisting the needy. On the contrary, never before have Hollanders given so freely and on so large a scale for the sake of helping their fellowmen. The only difference is that they refuse all contact with Nazi go-betweens. Instead, the churches—Protestant as well as Catholic—are playing a preponderant part in distributing support, in kind and money, wherever this is needed.

Closely collaborating with them are innumerable underground organizations, making weekly collections for succour to compatriots in distress. Victims of German tyranny, relatives of people who have lost their lives in the fight for Queen and country, receive effective help. Never yet have the funds available for these and many other charitable purposes, been exhausted.

No greater compliment could be paid to the Netherlands spirit of sacrifice under Nazi oppression than was contained in the discouraged utterance of a disillusioned Winter Help collector of Maastricht, only a few months ago. "It's no good trying," this Nazi said crestfallenly. "During four days of house-to-house visits I have not succeeded in collecting anything like the amount any priest in this city can get together in four minutes—or less!"

15

TRAGEDY IN THE FAR EAST

"The greater the number of Netherlanders who will give up their passive attitude (toward Nazism), the better the chance that Berlin, at the end of the war, will put itself out successfully for the sake of our Empire."

N. S. B. propagandist Jan Hollander, on February 16, 1942.

"The Netherlands from now on must find its salvation in assisting in the development of Europe, and giving all its energy to the colonization of West Russia."

Deutsche Zeitung in den Niederlanden, March, 1942, after the fall of Bandung.

Seldom have the people of Holland displayed so intense an interest in their East Indies' territory, far away in the southwestern Pacific, than after the occupation of the motherland by the Nazis. They realized with pride that—even if fate had ordained that, for the moment, they play a losing role in Europe—their struggle for liberation was forcefully supported in the overseas Archipelago. For there, more than seventy million fellow-Netherlanders did all they could to help beat the German tyrants, and at the same time prepared themselves to ward off any possible attack on the independence of their three thousand tropical islands.

Throughout the Netherlands the demand for literature on the East Indies increased rapidly; the general thirst for knowledge regarding the rich territories in Asia proved almost unquenchable. Books on the history and development of the Indies were devoured and immense interest was displayed in lectures on Indian subjects. Official bodies normally occupied with matters concerning the colonies in the East, continued to function as if the connections with Asia had not temporarily been cut.

Indeed—only a small part of the Kingdom of the Netherlands had been forced to capitulate. There still were the Indies—East as well as West—free Dutch territory under the leadership of Queen Wilhelmina and her government.

Quite naturally, therefore, the people of Holland followed the political developments in the Far East with profound interest. They felt by intuition that the attitude of their government in London, and of its representatives in the Indies, was firm and undaunted, although far removed from any challenge or rash act. There was great confidence in the Governor-General, Jonkheer Dr. A. W. L. Tjarda van Starkenborgh Stachouwer, and in his advisers, more particularly in the person of Dr. Hubertus J. van Mook, who at that moment headed the Economic Department of the East Indies' Government.

When in June, 1941, the long-standing economic negotiations with Japan came to a somewhat sudden close, this did not particularly upset the people in Holland. On the contrary, an immediate and favorable reaction on the Stock Exchange was experienced when soon afterwards it became clear that commercial relationships with Japan would continue on a "normal" footing. Let it not be thought, however, that this conviction gave the burghers of occupied Holland a false sense of security; they were, in their majority, by no means unaware of the precarious situation in the southwestern Pacific. It was well-known that Japan would not recoil from aggression if she thought this necessary to further her imperialistic policies. Besides, in a speech pronounced on July 30, 1941, Queen Wilhelmina had addressed her people to tell them that she and her advisers, in constant collaboration with the British and American governments, were closely following the development of events in the Far East.

"Aggressive measures are never to be feared from the side of the Netherlands Government," the Queen said. "But that government is and remains decided to accept the challenge if our Far Eastern territory were to be menaced by force of arms. If, in connection with the geographic situation of the Netherlands East Indies, circumstances would make this necessary, we would certainly accept the war forced upon us, and together with our Allies we would fight the enemy." A few months afterwards, these words were borne out to the letter. The political attitude of the Netherlands government could hardly have been affirmed in a clearer or more concise way.

During the latter part of the summer and the autumn of 1941 the tension in the Far East increased slowly but unmistakably. The Nipponese occupation of Indo-China, the appearance of the ultra-aggressive Tojo Cabinet—these were unquestionable signs of serious trouble looming ahead. Moreover, in October, the German press launched a fierce campaign against the Netherlands Indies. Its government was advised to "free itself from the nefarious policies of England and America," and the nazified Dutch press was scrupulously abused to support this "altruistic" advice and to sow discord between the Indies and its possible Allies.

When only a couple of months before the Japanese invasion of the Archipelago, the head of the Indies' defense forces, Lieutenant-General G. J. Berenschot, was killed in an airplane accident near Bandung, the Algemeen Handelsblad, of Amsterdam, openly accused the British Secret Service of having staged this mishap. Shortly afterwards, in the first days of December, the Queen complied with a request from her Governor-General to leave Dr. Van Mook—who had recently been appointed Colonial Minister—in the Indies rather than allow him to start out for London, the temporary seat of the Netherlands Government. This was immediately "explained" in typical Nazi fashion. The sudden resolve to leave the new Minister in Batavia was, said the Nazi press, irrefutable proof of "tension and discord" among the rulers of the Indies and the government in London. "This 'government,' " the report of Goebbels' Propaganda Bureau continued, "has now become the completely will-less instrument of Great Britain's imperial politics."

But only two days later the world was to receive the most conclusive evidence of the unity existing between Batavia and London. On Sunday evening, December 7, around 10 p.m. Netherlands' time, the message flashed around the globe that Japan had attacked both British and American territory and that—so it seemed—Pearl Harbor had been mercilessly bombed. The incredible had happened! Japan's military clique had dared to challenge the mightiest power on earth. War had come to the Pacific.

Not for a moment did the Netherlands government hesitate. Japan's plans were an open book to her. She knew that the Nipponese would try to keep the East Indies neutral, so as to subjugate the islands with greater ease after obviating the possibility of having to grapple with mighty allies of the Dutch. It was a line of action the Japanese had learned from their western "brothers," the Nazis. "One by one"—exactly as Hitler broke up and subjugated most of the European continent.

Immediately the Netherlands Cabinet convened and Queen Wilhelmina signed a declaration of war on the Japanese. At 3 a.m., in the night from Sunday to Monday, it was announced that the

Kingdom of the Netherlands—although its own Asiatic territory had not as yet been attacked—considered itself in a state of war with Japan. It was splendid evidence of daring statesmanship; it showed an attitude which in England and in the United States met with the greatest sympathy.

The first reaction in occupied Holland was not unfavorable, though many Stock Exchange quotations dropped. The news that the United States had now completely entered into the war, which came almost simultaneously with the first reports of Hitler's retreat in Russia, caused a wave of optimism. At that moment the Dutch did not realize that Japan's offensive power had been greatly underrated and that the democracies, out there in the Far East, were facing a mighty, shrewd and well-prepared opponent. On the evening of December 8, 1941, Premier Pieter S. Gerbrandy, broadcasting via Radio Orange, acquainted his listeners with the exact wording of the Queen's proclamation.

"Neither the safety of our territory in the East, nor the link which binds us to our British allies, nor the very special relations existing between the Netherlands and the United States allow our government to remain an idle observer. The Kingdom of the Netherlands considers itself at war with Japan because the aggression—which intends to eliminate one by one those countries desiring the peace—must and shall be crushed by closely allied nations. Now that our friends, the Americans and the English, are attacked, the Kingdom of the Netherlands places all its defense powers and its resources at the disposal of our mutual warfare . . . The Netherlands did not hesitate to defend itself immediately and with courage when it was wantonly attacked in Europe; neither will our Indies waver now that a similar attack is threatening us in Asia."

The next day the Prime Minister broadcast a further explanation to the declaration of war, in which he questioned his listeners, "Is there a single person among you who would not have accused the Netherlands government of lack of faith if for only one minute it had resolved to stand aside and await the course of events? And if among you there should be some, some very few, who would be inclined to reason opportunistically and say, 'All right—but we ourselves were not attacked as yet,' then I would ask these people: 'Do you really believe that a callous attack on Singapore and the Philippines, made without any previous declaration of war, does not betray a desire of the enemy to come down with the same lightning speed on Sourabaya, or Balikpapan?' "

In this way the Netherlands government, thanks to the radio, was able to motivate its political decisions in the face of the entire Netherlands people. It was something to be truly grateful for, because simultaneously the enemy mobilized all its available strength for a full-scale offensive on the morale and self-reliance of the Dutch at home. As the news from the Russian front became worse, the Germans devoted the largest headlines in all newspapers to Japanese reports of almost continuous victories.

On the 10th of December, 1941, the Nationale Dagblad jubilated in excessively large type, "Three-quarters Of Entire American Fleet Annihilated." Through the falsification of texts and the tendentious cutting of radio news broadcast by the Batavia "N.i.r.o.m." radio, the Nazis endeavored to create the impression that confusion and dissension were rife in Batavia. The short-wave sender "Phohi" at Eindhoven, in North Brabant province, was used by the occupation authorities to broadcast to the Indies and repeat tirelessly, day after day, that the declaration of war on Japan had been utterly uncalled for. On New Year's Eve it attempted to give the Dutch a chance to direct greetings to their relatives in the Indies—a very cleverly conceived detail of the psychological warfare. Unhappily for the organizers, this broadcast never took place, as the Indies had made it clear that its reception would not in the least be appreciated.

*

The economic reverberations of the war in the Far East were not as good. During the months of June, July and August, 1941, the rates of eighty leading Indies' stocks had undergone colossal increases—some of them more than 35%. By the beginning of December some quotations had increased far above 60% as compared with the rates quoted in the spring of 1941. But almost immediately after the fatal December 7 all gains made during the previous eleven months were lost. The Stock Exchange realized that even if the Indies could be held, the damage done to several of the most important plantations and oil fields would be such that maintenance of the high rates thus far quoted would be completely unjustified. Some stocks dropped by more than 50%, and the average losses represented 30 to 40% of the quotations on December 6, 1941. When the news came through of Japanese landings on Tarakan and other outlying islands of the Archipelago, many oil shares lost all attraction for the investing world, and before the middle of February things began to look very bad indeed.

Steadily approaching through the Malayan jungles, the Japanese had nearly reached Singapore. With pride and admiration the Netherlanders at home had followed the brave feats of the "indomitable Dutch," as President Roosevelt had named the boys from Holland and the Indies who fought the Japs wherever they could find them. To read and hear of the fearless exploits of Dutch submarines and the Netherlands East Indies' Air Force made the subjugated Hollanders almost happy. This was the true, proverbial Dutch spirit, a revival of the courage and daring so often displayed by their ancestors in former centuries. When during the last days of January, 1942, the news came through of the battle of the Macassar Straits, in which the Japanese lost no less than 32 ships, people congratulated one another in the streets. The fierce fight put up in the Indies was experienced at home as a splendid answer to repeated Nazi claims of invincibility. Things were made none too easy for the Nazis of the East!

Then came the fall of Singapore and directly afterwards the first landings of the Japanese invaders near Palembang, on the east coast of southern Sumatra. And with these colossal adverses came the realization of the truth. Suddenly the occupied country understood the mortal peril in which Java, most important island of all with a population of 45 million souls, found itself. In only seven days Singapore, until recently considered an impregnable bastion, had fallen to the enemy. How much longer would Java be able to hold out? Would the Allies be in a position to send adequate assistance, and would it come in time?

These doubts and fears were promptly capitalized by Nazi propagandists. While the situation in the Indies grew more and more desperate, Mussert's followers began to sneer at the credulity of their "misguided compatriots." "Where *are* your Allies?" the Nazi propaganda asked. "Are they going to leave the Indies in the lurch as they forsook Holland? All right—General Wavell has made Java his headquarters . . . ; but does this mean that more Allied divisions have arrived in his wake? No—there is no hope left to beat the Japanese." And every one of these spiteful effusions concluded with a reiteration of Mussert's "prophecy," made on December 14, 1941: that the Indies could not be held.

This cunning pro-Axis talk naturally irked the vast majority of loyal Hollanders. They rebelled against fate which rewarded with defeat the courage and integrity of their Government to declare war upon Japan as soon as the Allies had been attacked.

To blight the people's mood still further, Anton Mussert's *Volk en Vaderland,* eagerly reacting to a mere rumor distributed by the Japanese radio, and stating that in the battle of the Java Sea all Dutch cruisers had been sunk, published flaming protests against the "senseless sacrifices" made by London, Batavia and other scapegoats. Much later, when it became known that in the Java Sea battle only the *Java* and the *De Ruyter* had been lost, the Nazi weekly pounced upon this opportunity to deliver another lecture, completely ignoring the fact that it had already written off the entire fleet of Netherlands' cruisers some time previously . . .

During the second half of February, 1942, the Nipponese inexorably closed their ring around the Java bastion. From Palembang they penetrated towards the southern tip of Sumatra. They made landings on the south coast of Borneo and Celebes. They took the famous isle of Bali. The Dutch fleet stationed at Sourabaya and Tandjung Priok, reinforced by British and American units, had no chance of escape. The struggle for Java proper was on. In that last week of February the Government in London broadcast an appeal to all Dutch churches and to all Netherlanders, wherever they might be, to "think particularly of the Indies in their prayers" on Sunday, March 1. The response was overwhelming. That Sunday morning the churches of Holland were fuller than ever, and the urgency of the people's prayers became even greater because of the news that the Japanese had made successful landings in three places along the northern coast of Java.

There was deep dismay in the hearts of all loyal Hollanders, but particularly great was the agony of those thousands of families whose relatives were living in the Indies. That same night the heavy losses of the Dutch fleet were announced, and on the next day Prime Minister Gerbrandy, in London, addressed his countrymen in simple but heartfelt words. On Tuesday night, March 3, Lieutenant-Admiral J. T. Furstner, the Navy Minister, used Radio Orange to read a message from the Queen, informing her people under German domination that a start would be made immediately with the reconstruction of the severely damaged fleet.

Meanwhile, in Java, the comparatively small Dutch army was bravely facing immensely superior forces. The air fleet, insignificant in number after its sacrifices over the Malayan mainland, but tremendous in its decision to die fighting, challenged the enemy wherever it could. But every fragment of bad news, each advance of the Japanese, was duly used by the Nazi propagandists. When

General Wavell left Java, the Germans hastened to comment that the "rats were scurrying off the sinking ship." When it became known that the Governor-General would not allow a single European, with the exception of a handful of government officials, to leave the Indies, Radio Berlin commented scornfully, "But the English will be allowed to quit . . . We leave it to the people of Holland to pronounce judgment on this attitude of their 'Allies.' "

The news from the Far East left no further room for optimism; an early end to the struggle for Java was now to be expected. This, then, was the moment to emphasize how tenaciously the Indies had been defended, even after a large part of the Air Force had been lost in a vain effort to help the British stem the furious attack on Singapore. In the early morning hours of March 8, 1942, a government representative addressed the downcast people of Holland and said:

"Our compatriots on the other side of the globe have done much more than keep high the honor of the Netherlands. They have confirmed the inalienable rights of white as well as colored Dutchmen in these territories. We have fought shoulder to shoulder with our Indonesian friends; we have won and lost battles with them. The white inhabitants of the Indies never left their domiciles, thus proving to the world that we Netherlanders—no matter race or color—are inextricably bound up with our Indies' territory." That same evening Bandung capitulated. The official radio station in the beleaguered mountain city broadcast its last message: "We are now shutting down. Goodbye until better times. Long live the Queen" . . . The Netherlands East Indies was lost; all over its magnificent isles swarmed the little yellow men from the north.

*

It was exceedingly difficult for the Dutch to accept the inevitable and replace a natural enough sentiment of bitter disappointment with trust in the future. It took extraordinary courage to face realities squarely.

"Let us not," said Queen Wilhelmina in an address on Sunday, March 15, "be so downcast by the terrible events that have befallen our Commonwealth, that we forget how every ounce of strength will be needed for our ultimate purpose: Victory . . . I am fully convinced that in the future, with the forceful assistance of our Allies, we shall defeat the enemy in Europe as well as in Asia."

There is ample evidence that these quiet words, spoken in a

tone of utter reliance, greatly heartened the people at home. And even when Anton Mussert besought the Dutch "to wake up at last from your stupor of misplaced and abused confidence" there was not a single patriotic Netherlander who chimed in with him. Neither he nor the sly, sarcastic sneers of the renegade journalist Max Blokzijl, could make the Hollanders lose trust in their Queen and her government.

Particularly fierce were the attacks upon the Governor-General of the Indies; the mildest description pictured him as the "sickly fruit of the old oak tree of the Tjarda's." Simultaneously the N. S. B. published complete Honor Lists of comrades interned in the Indies since December 8, 1941. The impression was created that shortly it would be possible to contact friends and relatives in the occupied Archipelago through the kind intermediary of those honorable gentlemen. But despite the fact that Mussert himself asserted he had "pleaded for this in influential circles," nothing ever came of it.

Economically the fall of the Indies resulted in a further drop of Stock Exchange quotations. But after the first shock these quotes recuperated swiftly and throughout 1942 the rates for Netherlands Indies' shares gained remarkably. Better than anything else this proved the unshakeable confidence of Dutch investors in the ultimate liberation of the colonies. Amsterdam Rubber shares, for example, quoted 328 on the day before the capitulation of Bandung and dropped to 110 soon after March 8. But two months later they had recovered to 185—and very much the same picture could be observed with regard to most of the other important Netherlands East Indies' stocks. Evidently, all Nazi efforts to undermine Dutch confidence in the rehabilitation of the Indies remained fruitless.

And after all—neither the Germans nor Mussert's N. S. B.'ers could expect much better. What did they have to offer the Dutch? The return of the Netherlands Indies? That would be expecting rather too much from Japan. In fact, the Dutch Nazis received a crystal-clear hint from their German bosses not to speak of the future of the Indies. For though there was every reason to believe that the Germans did not particularly relish the fact that their "dear allies," the Japanese, had grabbed the Archipelago, they could do nothing much about it as long as the Tripartite Pact remained in force. Silence was, therefore, the password—a particularly painful affair for Mussert who as late as November 3,

1941, had dramatically exclaimed in his Nationale Dagblad: "The Indies loose from Holland? Never. Netherlands' rights in the East and West will be completely maintained!"

And so the only thing left to do for the N. S. B. was to stage a modest blackmail campaign which tried to make the Dutch believe that Berlin "might be able to do something for us in the long run," if only the whole of Holland would turn National-Socialist. A little later the Nationale Dagblad, replying to letters which had expressed astonishment at Mussert's resigned attitude, contended that the Indies "had asked for the trouble we have witnessed by declaring war upon Japan. What will happen after the war nobody knows as yet," the article concluded lamely, in rather striking contrast to the fierce contention of a few months ago, that the Indies could never be taken away from the Netherlands.

Finally the occupying authorities prescribed an even more complete silence. Not a word was to be said or written any more on the subject of the Indies. It was lost—and the people of Holland would do well to concentrate upon the possibilities inside Hitler's New Europe. When in June, 1942, the Netherlands East Company was formed and Meinoud M. Rost van Tonningen appointed its president, it soon transpired that one of the Company's main tasks would be to convince the Dutch that their enterprise and colonization power might be most profitably applied in the occupied areas of White Russia, and the Baltic States. It would still mean "going East," the Nazi propagandists emphasized with a quaint sense of twisted humor. "Hollanders will be able to live very prosperously on the most fertile soil of Europe," a German spokesman told the Dutch. But their response remained so pitifully small, despite subsequent measures to enforce wholesale emigration to the "promised land," that towards the end of May, 1943, the East Company was about to be liquidated, and was kept alive only through the interest certain German industrialists began to show in the project.

All the Company had thus far achieved was the transportation of a few thousand N. S. B.'ers and some unemployed loyal workmen to the devastated regions of Letland where they lived in gigantic barracks and vainly tried to get used to the desolate country, its strange tongue and its barren soil. Even the fact that Netherlands corporations formerly active in the Indies were induced to "contribute enthusiastically" from their capitals, so as to support the Nazi plans for Dutch colonization in parts of eastern

Europe, had not turned the venture into a success. Perhaps the discouraging reports on living conditions which from time to time appeared in the newspapers, despite all German censorship, contributed to this failure. During August, 1942, for instance, the Riga correspondent of the Nieuwe Rotterdamsche Courant wrote in his paper, "The living standard of Lithuania is so much lower than that of Holland that it is inconceivable Dutch truck gardeners will be able to gain a decent livelihood in that country. Other regions which have been frequently mentioned for the settlement of Hollanders are poor, neglected and deteriorated districts where the war has caused immense destruction." In conclusion the writer reported that for the next few years it would be impossible for farmers settling in these regions to "work on their own account. For the time being those Dutchmen can only work as wage earners for Germans" . . .

*

There is no denying that the occupied motherland would have derived immense moral support from a more protracted fight against the Japanese aggressors. The battle for the Indies lasted too short a time, despite the heroic resistance of Europeans and Indonesians alike. Many Netherlanders felt bitter about the lack of real support given by Holland's allies, but they also admitted that not enough had been done by the Dutch themselves. There was little reason to reproach others when Holland had not seen fit to build up adequate defense forces for the protection of the immensely rich Archipelago. The fleet had been too small, the army by no means adequate to fight off attacks in force, the air corps was hardly more than a promising nucleus.

But worst of all was the loss of contact with tens of thousands of sons and daughters, brothers and sisters. The agony of not knowing their fate was hardest to bear of all. Were they imprisoned by the Japanese? Had they been killed in the repeated bombing attacks on Java's largest cities? What was the fate of Netherlands women and children delivered into the power of the vengeful Nipponese?

There only remained a quiet conviction that the sacrifices of today would ultimately yield their fruit. True, the moral support and uplift derived from the knowledge that the Indies were free and working hard to expedite the liberation of the homeland, were gone. But there still was an active government, led by a dauntless Queen. There still were many fleet units left, and in the mighty Merchant Marine the country still wielded a powerful weapon. Besides, there were new armies being moulded in Canada and England. And in the United States hundreds of flyers, escaped from the Indies, were training diligently and enthusiastically for a quick come-back in the southwestern Pacific.

These certainties have helped the Dutch to forget their initial disappointments. They made it possible for them to ignore all Nazi propaganda and never give way to panicky impulses—even in those days when the news from the Far East grew blacker by the hour.

During that period a reporter for Goering's Essener National Zeitung visited the town of Haarlem, near Amsterdam. In the center of the city loudspeakers were bellowing forth the most alarming news items; and the Nazi journalist evidently expected to find the place seething with excitement and despair. "Instead," he wrote, "it seemed as if the loudspeakers sent their news into empty space. Nothing betrayed that the people standing about or passing along were shaken by the depressing reports from the Far East."

Obviously, this self-control was partly artificial; no patriotic Hollander would publicly display his disappointment and grief, thus "affording solace" to the enemy. But it was also partly genuine. For the average Netherlands citizen never doubted the ultimate liberation of his homeland and the Indies, even though he realized that after the war a much-changed Holland and an equally changed Indies will be parts of a renewed Netherlands Kingdom.

16

TRIUMPH OF THE SPIRIT

It is very difficult to imagine oneself among the suppressed people of the Netherlands. A vivid imagination is needed to follow and to understand the thoughts and emotions of men and women fighting with all their might against a foreign tyrant. For even where on the surface things seem to run their usual course, unutterable suffering and fierce hatred reign supreme. The country has been robbed of its greatest asset, its liberty.

Liberty—invisible and inaudible, an intangible idea; yet its influence was omnipresent. It was the air in which the people of Holland thrived, the soil on which its liberal principles and ideologies flourished. Then came the invasion, and the unbearable stench of Nazi putrefaction poisoning the atmosphere. Suddenly liberty was transformed into a visible, audible, tangible something. What had been an unimportant, matter-of-fact ingredient of daily life became a yearning, a deeply hurting desire for freedom, a universal revolt against the heavy hand of the oppressor.

When some months after the invasion a nazified newspaper printed an editorial in which the writer said: "Our country has fought and it capitulated, but the entire struggle lasted so short a while that in many parts of Holland the people still do not realize it is over," this statement was basically true. If the war against the invading Huns had lasted many months, if there had been several fronts on which severe and bitter fighting took place, and if the subjugation of the Netherlands had been a matter of slow Nazi progress, there is no doubt that the nation, as a whole, would have been clearly aware of losing the struggle. The people would have witnessed a conglomeration of defeats. No doubt, their individual sufferings would have been greater, and the inevitability of final surrender would have loomed ahead as a terrible mechanized monster that could not be halted in its annihilating course.

But now the war was over almost before it had begun. As a natural result, it left little or no impression on large sections of the

Dutch. Only in those places where the fighting had been most severe, where towns and villages were bombed and destroyed and thousands of brave soldiers met their death, the horrifying reality of a German invasion had penetrated deeply into the people's soul. By the very swiftness of their *blitzkrieg* the Nazis had robbed themselves of the fruits of victory.

This explains why, after a short period of doubt and uncertainty, the Netherlanders were capable of facing their enemies unitedly. They were the same people of pre-invasion days, only far stronger and more conscious of their unassailable characteristics. With every new restrictive German measure the Hollanders became more aware of their strength and solidarity, and realized more clearly the vital importance of those privileges of which they were being deprived.

During those first months one German rule in particular brought home to the Dutch that they had lost their personal liberty. That was the limitation of their freedom of movement. Restrictive authority, especially the police, had never been very popular in the Netherlands. Now the German *Polizei,* both military and civil, did what the Dutch police had always avoided. It forced people to stay where they were, or told them *where* to go and *when*. Though in itself this decree, as well as many others, may seem rather insignificant, it was more than enough to heap upon the occupation authorities the smouldering hatred of the entire populace. These "small" measures—which were inevitably felt by every stratum of the nation—were sometimes more capable of fanning the fire of dislike and loathing than the most sweeping edicts of Reich's Commissioner Seyss-Inquart.

The introduction of curfew which kept every citizen indoors between midnight and four a.m., the blackouts which were rigorously adhered to in every nook and corner of the country, the lack of any public amusement—these and other similar regulations were felt as harsh and stupid attacks upon the personal freedom of the individual. Travelling, a favorite pastime of every Hollander, became a severely rationed commodity—not only for journeys abroad but also for trips within the country.

Another measure arousing the ire of every loyal Netherlander was the introduction of the so-called "personal identification card." From the first of March, 1941 every citizen above the age of 15 was obliged to carry this card on him in all circumstances—even when swimming or taking part in sports events. This registration, unprecedented in the history of the country, was looked upon as an injury, to which insult was added by the fact that every registered person had to pay a guilder for that doubtful distinction.

It is not in the nature of a Hollander to be registered, to be told that he *must* fill out cards and questionnaires, to be commanded about and barked at. Pre-invasion Holland was proudly aware of the fact that it belonged to the least-regimented states of western Europe—yet exemplary order ruled throughout the ranks of the people. Now, suddenly, the average Dutchman found himself treated as a patient in a sanitarium. His day was arranged for him. He was told what to do with every hour, when to get up, what to eat, when to go to bed. But he did not feel in need of this strict régime. All he desired was to be left alone, to regulate his life in accordance with his own ideas.

At every turn of the road the Germans were bound to irritate the Dutch with their ukases and circulars. The more they insisted upon having things done a certain way, the more the people of Holland itched to do them exactly in the opposite manner. The Nazis had hardly settled down before they disbanded all Freemason Lodges and organized public exhibitions against the Freemason movement. But the large majority of the Dutch were perfectly aware of its innocence, and stared with astonishment at the stream of Nazi destruction let loose upon these useful institutions.

The next victims of Nazi interference were various Christian, theosophical and other religious or semi-religious movements. Even the harmless Esperanto clubs were no longer allowed to gather for the study of Zamenhof's artificial world language. The list of "forbidden" Societies and Leagues grew by the day; the Oxford Group—being described as the "latest form of Freemasonry, presenting itself under cover of religion"—was also prohibited.

Indignation was general; the inanity of these indiscriminate disbandments, the lack of any logical grounds for them, the prejudice and superstition which generally seemed to be the only reasons for still more "verbotens"—all this was too much for the level-headed Dutch.

To the Germans such an attitude came as a complete and most unpleasant surprise. "At home" the incontestable finality of a Nazi command was never disputed. It was hard for them to understand that the people of another country—and that a subjugated land in the bargain—dared to voice their disagreement with the rules and regulations imposed upon them by an invincible Nazi hierarchy. Their Teutonic impotence to gauge the character of a foreign nation, prevented the Nazis from discovering that this was *not* the way to "convert" the Dutch.

When next they introduced special German Courts to deal severely with trespasses upon their edicts, they gave further evidence of their inability to get on with the average citizen of the Netherlands. For the slightest misdemeanors "culprits" were punished so disproportionately that it often seemed as if the officiating judges had lost their minds completely. Imprisonment, and fines far beyond their means were showered upon hundreds of accused; and at least one highly-irritated German judge declared that the possession of an anti-Nazi poem—which he described as "subversive literature"—should be punished with death.

Long before the end of the first occupation year, it was clear that the Nazis, unwilling or incapable of basing their regime on some measure of understanding of the Dutch people, had made up their minds to replace right with might. From day to day the forms in which their tyranny expressed itself, became severer and farther-reaching. The road of Nazi "justice" led rapidly from persecution of the individual to the incarceration of large groups.

This began in July, 1940 when one hundred thirty Netherlanders, among them several intellectuals, were transported to a German concentration camp because, the Nazis declared, "numerous Germans have been interned by the government of the Netherlands Indies." In the ensuing months more hostages were sent to the dreaded Buchenwalde camp, including many women and children. In the dark of the night people were hauled from their beds, packed into buses and carried away to some unknown destination. Generally the relatives of the "chosen" received their first news from the deported in the form of a bill for transportation charges. Among the interned were professors, members of the disbanded Parliament, a former Minister, journalists and the sons of two Netherlands Cabinet members—boys who had never been politically active. Their imprisonment was the lowest form of spiritual blackmail, aimed at their fathers; it remained, of course, unsuccessful.

Yet—while this was going on and while the tyrannical nature of the Nazi occupation could hardly be doubted by anyone in his right senses, the Germans still endeavored to keep up the pretense of not looking down upon the Dutch but rather, considering them their friends and "brothers of the blood." The military, from the highest officer to the common soldier, behaved correctly and showed remarkable respect for women and children. They were the peons used to carry the screen which was to hide from public view the relentless cruelty of the Nazi bosses.

*

The preceding chapters have made it clear that these crude and, therefore, typically-German tactics failed to work out in every respect. Instead, the general disdain and hatred for the Nazis increased steadily. These were not sentiments born from a feeling of inferiority. The Hollanders were well aware of their immense superiority over the herds of goose-stepping automatons which had settled down upon their land, and tried to rule over them.

Whatever the Germans did to "strengthen the links between the people of Holland and the occupying forces," the outcome was invariably contrary to the intention. When in December, 1940 the ban on dancing was lifted, very few people visited the quickly reopened ballrooms, simply because they had no desire to mingle with the German officers and soldiers. With the exception of a small number of young, untutored girls, the women of Holland paid no attention to the occupation troops. The more frequently the Germans repeated that they had freed the Netherlands from the "yoke of the English, the Jews and the Freemasons," the more they were jeered at and despised. Nazi soldiers billeted with Dutch citizens had so bad a time that in the end the Nazi authorities were compelled to discontinue this quartering system.

But the soldiers remained well aware of the general mood. They knew the bitter jokes that were being cracked at their expense—particularly during those autumn months of 1940 in which the invasion of England was expected any day . . . but never came off. Along the protracted Dutch coastline thousands of men were constantly trained in the rapid loading and unloading of tanks and guns. Flat-bottomed Rhine barges were requisitioned by the hundreds, and the press and radio worked overtime to spread the news that "it" might begin at any minute. But alas! It soon became evident that the invasion idea was petering out ingloriously. It is difficult to describe how intensely the people of Holland rejoiced in this fact. They felt it as a personal victory over the enemy, and their sentiments were expressed in a wide range of jokes, such as the one about the German officer who, upon entering a streetcar drenched by the pouring rain, was greeted by the conductor with the astonished remark: "What? Are you back already?". . .

Wherever they went, the German soldiers were keenly aware of mocking eyes and significant smiles. It was one of the many forms of passive resistance which during the first year of the occupation played so important a part in the struggle against the invader. To mention only a few other manifestations: there was the habit of naming newborn babies after members of the House of Orange; the enthusiastic welcome given to the "new greeting" of *Ozo,* the initials of "Oranje zal Overwinnen" (Orange Shall Conquer); the "V" sign stealthily given with the help of the index and third finger of the left hand; an empty frame in which only a few days previously the picture of Queen Wilhelmina had been displayed and which had now been replaced by a large label, *"Temporarily Absent."* Besides, there were the doggerels that went from mouth to mouth, such as this:

"I crave for the day
Upon which the last Hun,
Without *Sieg,* without *Heil,*
To the devil will run."

And finally, there was the chain letter, quickly moving from home to home and rectifying the "erroneous" information of the Nazi-gagged radio.

Another form of passive resistance was the so-called "slow down" sabotage, rampant throughout Dutch industry. All work would only benefit the German war machine; so why hurry, or try to maintain the high standard which distinguished most of Holland's industries before the invasion? Even if it was impossible to refuse all labor in behalf of the enemy, it always seemed feasible to slow down—and the 1941-42 production figures of the Limburg coal mines provide glaring evidence of the disastrous results for the invaders.

As the period of German domination lengthened, Dutch resistance became more calculated and wary. The people learned countless ways in which to annoy and hinder the usurpers. After the strikes of February, 1941 which coincided with the first roundups of innocent Jewish youngsters, sabotage rapidly increased. There were attacks on German guards; communication cables were cut and mysterious fires broke out in a number of factories. The Germans retaliated with colossal fines, varying between a million and two and a half million guilders, to be paid by comparatively small communities. With this came the threat that innocent hostages would be executed if the actual perpetrators of acts of sabotage could not be traced. At the same time, measures were taken to allow for the swift replacement of municipal authorities with German or Dutch Nazi "Commissars." To make sure of a good start, a number of loyal mayors were forced to resign for the benefit of Nazi successors.

Meanwhile the military courts were busily engaged pronouncing death sentences. Intricate and startling "plots" were suddenly discovered all over the country and there was much loose talk of a "secret organization," headed by a certain Colonel Verdun. From two or three at a time, the number of executed grew to a dozen, eighteen, twenty-four. Before the first year of German tyranny had passed, several hundred Hollanders had been shot and countless more transported to the Nazi torture camps.

On the tenth of May, 1941 all Netherlands newspapers were compelled to publish a German ordinance which filled the cup of petty tyranny to overflowing. "It is the emphatic wish of the German authorities," said the order, "that on this day everything in the nature of a demonstration must be unconditionally avoided. This also includes ceremonies at war memorials, and other gatherings in memory of those fallen in the war, collections in behalf of war victims, etc. It is also strictly forbidden to march in closed formation, or in any other group form, for the purpose of laying wreaths on military graves."

But despite this prohibition there was an endless pilgrimage to the graves of those who lost their lives both in the war and in the bombings of Rotterdam, Rhenen and Middelburg.

The first year of suppression had passed—but not so the war against the Hun. It was waged with undiminished ferocity and with full awareness that many more men and women would have to pay with their lives for obstructing the Nazi monster.

*

During three years of German suppression, Orange has become more than a symbol to the people of the Netherlands. Though, like the red, white and blue of the Dutch flag, it recalls memories of the happy country Holland was before the Nazi attack of 1940, it intensifies to an almost unbearable degree the desire for speedy liberation. But Orange also is a mighty force, playing an active part in Dutch resistance. There is no doubt, for example, that the radio addresses of Queen Wilhelmina were among the most important events of the second occupation year. Whenever Radio Orange announced a speech of the Queen, the entire country knew of it in record time, and more than a million radio sets were tuned to London. Young and old, peasants, dockworkers, clerks, shopkeepers and artisans in eleven hundred different towns and villages listened to the voice of *their* Queen, that firm, decisive voice which expressed so clearly the common will to victory and the preparedness to sacrifice.

There was unity between the people and their Queen. All those who stood in the front ranks of the battle, the tens of thousands of underground saboteurs, the clergy, teachers and students, agreed that Queen Wilhelmina fully understood their war and the dangers it entailed. The voice that reached them from across the Channel was that of a wise, inspiring woman. Her word was law—perhaps even more so than before the coming of the enemy.

When in the beginning of May, 1942 no less than seventy-two loyal Dutchmen were executed in one day, the Queen urged her subjects to be more careful than ever in speech and writing, and she besought them not to revolt as yet, so as not to spoil their chances for the future. Whatever disappointment there had been in the first days of the occupation because the Queen and her Government left the invaded country, during this second year of German tyranny the Hollanders fully realized and appreciated the wisdom of that departure. They now experienced the benefits of the untiring energy, sharp insight and limitless responsibility of their Queen, and they understood that, had Queen Wilhelmina remained inside Holland, she would at best have been a helpless prisoner of war.

How important the person of the Queen had become in the hearts of practically all Netherlanders was obvious from the growing coarseness with which the Germans attacked her. After the invasion of Russia, the Queen had placed herself and her government squarely behind the Soviets; in revenge Seyss-Inquart ordered promptly that the portraits of living members of the royal family were to be eliminated from all public buildings, throughout the Netherlands.

In September, 1941 the Queen said in a radio broadcast: "The archenemy of mankind, Adolf Hitler, has tried to annihilate us. Not only has he usurped our country and bereft it of its liberty, not only have his hordes looted it and delivered our people to famine, he has also tried to rob it of its most sacred possessions by crushing its very soul. But in this he has not succeeded. On the contrary—after more than a year of suppression Holland is and feels more invincible than ever."

A few weeks later, the following "statement" of the Reich's Commissioner was released:

"Wilhelmina of Orange-Nassau, having learned nothing from the course of events, stubbornly adheres to the Bolshevist-capitalistic front and thereby places herself outside the commonwealth of the New Europe. She calls the Head and the defense forces of the Greater German Reich the most astounding names. From the distance, and quite irresponsibly, she goads the people of Holland into a desire for sabotage and brute force against the occupying power. She incites them to actions which will only result in the harshest retaliation. At the order of the Reich's Commissioner, the Commissary-General for Public Safety has therefore stipulated that all possessions within the occupied territory, of the living members of the House of Orange-Nassau are to be confiscated. They will be devoted to purposes of public utility, in so far as they will not be requisitioned by the occupying power for the duration of the war."

Without delay the various royal palaces were plundered. The use of names of the members of the House of Orange-Nassau was strictly prohibited to economic and non-economic associations and institutions, as was the display of pictures "which might indicate contact with the House of Orange-Nassau." Yet, almost half a year later it was necessary for the Nazis to repeat this ban. Obviously, the majority of the people had given little attention to the strict orders of the Reich's Commissioner.

And so Orange became an active force and, at the same time, a flaming symbol in the national struggle for liberty. Besides, during the second occupation year the authority of the Netherlands Government in London grew visibly. To arrive at this greater confidence, many psychological obstacles had had to be cleared. The government was, after all, "in safety" and "talking was easy, on the other side of the water." Moreover, it was composed of representatives of the political parties which many Hollanders, rightly or wrongly, held responsible for all shortcomings. Among them was not a single great national leader, a figure comparable to Churchill or Roosevelt. Some members of the cabinet had been severely criticized even during the time they ruled a free Netherlands. Besides, it had made a rather unpleasant impression on the people of subjugated Holland that their government was very slow in recognizing the Soviet Union. Finally, not all Ministers were capable of moving the thousands who risked their lives in listening to Radio Orange to such a degree as could their Queen. Sometimes their speeches had left a bitter taste of indecisiveness and a certain lack of perseverance.

But such criticism, justified or not, by no means attacked the principle of full recognition of the government. All Dutch patriots agreed that the country's leaders had acted well in shifting their headquarters temporarily to London. They appreciated the forceful radio talks of their Prime Minister. They were pleased when the Cabinet was reinforced with Dr. van Mook. And the authority of the government was, if anything, increased by the manifold and violent attacks made upon it by the Germans and the leaders of Mussert's party. The text of "Juggernaut Over Holland," a most enlightening, forcefully-written book by Foreign Minister Eelco N. van Kleffens, was smuggled into the Netherlands, duplicated and eagerly read. Hundreds of thousands of workers listened breathlessly to a first-of-May speech by the Social Democrat leader, J. W. Albarda; his good and simple words gave them courage to continue their bitter fight. In short, London was looked upon for directives in almost every phase of the struggle against the German despots. The unasked question of the Dutch was, "Tell us what to do! We, inside our country, are strictly separated from one another; it is hard for us to decide. You in London know more than we. Instruct us how to act, what to do to support the Allied cause."

And indeed, during the second and third occupation years the government—by means of the radio—made it a rule to advise and to direct in almost every one of the many crises. Most important among these were the matter of forced labor, the extermination of Holland's Jewish minority, the effort to shanghai thousands of students for work inside the Reich, and the vain attempts to compel Holland's physicians to exercise their profession in accordance with the disgusting, inhuman concepts of Nazism.

In every one of those instances the government prescribed the attitude of all loyal Hollanders under the heel of the German oppressors. And to the utter dismay of the Huns, that advice from London was followed to the letter, so that both the press and all

INVASION JITTERS AND NAZI VANDALISM

To ward off the coming Allied invasion, the Germans have blasted a wide path through the heart of The Hague; (*top, left*:) a tank trap in the center of the new town; (*right*:) the Scheveningen Pier before it was blasted; (*bottom*:) the white areas are completely demolished streets and squares.

INVASION JITTERS AND NAZI VANDALISM

(*top:*) Two views of the Roman Catholic Church dedicated to the Blessed Martyrs of Gorinchem, showing various stages of its demolition by the Nazis; (*bottom:*) the home of former Prime Minister Hendrik Colijn is demolished to the last stone.

Nazi mouthpieces were ultimately obliged to admit how tremendous was the influence and the authoritative power of "that clique of emigrés and Jews in London."

They exhausted themselves in finding terms adequate to describe their feelings toward those Dutchmen on the other side of the Channel whose success in upsetting their plans was so unquestionable. "Sadistic Jews," "lackeys of Churchill," "radio heroes speaking from their shelters" and "microphone slaves" were some of the mildest epithets flung into the ether daily via the patient Hilversum sender. The cool and concise comments on the events of the day, reaching almost all of Holland via Radio Orange, particularly infuriated the Germans. What sense was there in ladling out generous portions of first-class German propaganda if this was immediately counteracted by the quiet and factual reports of the London broadcasters? It was galling—particularly in those sad days of the spring of 1942 when the news from the Russian front grew more ominous by the hour, and the bulk of loyal Hollanders showed no interest whatever in the most inspiring radio talks on the coming annihilation of Bolshevism . . .

*

Even if the reverses of the Allied forces in the southwestern Pacific together with the spectacular success of General Rommel in Libya were hardly fit to inspire much joy in the hearts of Dutch patriots, they never wavered—but they freely criticized, and expressed their disappointment. Yet, they continued to look to the British Allies who would, somehow, overcome their present difficulties and find the road to ultimate victory. There were many ways in which to demonstrate this unshaken confidence; some of them were small, others important but all of them highly significant. It required a firm decision and uncommon courage, for example, to name a newly-born child "Winston" after the British Prime Minister, or to entrust to the Red Cross food parcels for British prisoners of war. Such acts, however trifling in themselves, were an open challenge to the enemy.

But even more dangerous was the prompt assistance given to members of the R.A.F. who had been forced down while on their constant flights across the country. Scores of men and women have paid dearly, some of them with their lives, for the help extended to English flyers. Here, too, terrorism never worked out. The appearance of British planes in Holland's skies was invariably the cause of wild enthusiasm. If, on account of bad weather conditions, the regular air parade did not take place for two or three consecutive days, the people became restless and irritable.

The Germans had no doubt hoped that this sympathy for the "enemy" would swiftly change into hot resentment, and even hatred, on the very day they were to stage their first bombardment of targets inside the Netherlands. Once again they were sadly mistaken.

It would be ridiculous to say that the Hollanders "enjoyed" these heavy attacks on their cities and villages. However accurate the bombing, there were bound to be a certain number of civilian casualties. In a few instances, such as the bombardment of Eindhoven in December, 1942 and the attacks on Rotterdam of October, 1941 and February, 1943 there were many dead; hundreds of families lost one or more of their members. But as long as the raids yielded the results that were expected of them, the sorely-tried citizens of Holland's towns were willing to bear this additional suffering. They understood that victory could not be won without it.

Compared with the acceptance of such great risks, it was of little consequence to give up the many pleasures that had been a routine part of pre-invasion existence. To leave the beautiful beaches and the dunes along Holland's west coast to the enemy, so that he might quietly construct his defenses against a possible invasion, was by no means easy. To be driven out of their homes because the German authorities decided to clear a wide belt between the North Sea and the inner defenses of the country, was certainly no less hard to bear. To be transported "elsewhere" like will-less cattle, to be lodged in rough encampments on the barren sands of the Veluwe, in the very heart of Gelderland province, without means of subsistence and virtually robbed of all material possessions, was unsettling and degrading enough. But these hardships were of small significance if compared to the importance of giving effective help to the Allies, both through assisting their stranded air men and by means of ever-extending sabotage-campaigns.

Sabotage was a completely spontaneous action; it hardly ever required special provocation. It simply was a *must*—the only thing within the reach of almost anybody, to help expedite the coming of liberation. Going slow, throwing the administrative set-up of the Huns into confusion, thwarting and plaguing them—

all this became an absolute necessity. Tales of new sabotage methods made the round like wildfire; the younger laborers in particular threw themselves full of enthusiasm into the task of sabotaging the enemy. Of course, this was a dangerous game—but what was the value of a human life if its sacrifice could bring the day of ultimate reckoning somewhat nearer?

The German authorities were exceedingly irritated by the way in which their blackout rules were constantly infringed upon, throughout Holland. In several towns they threatened to cut off the electric supply entirely. In one month's time no less than 900 summonses were served by the Rotterdam police and during April, 1942, numerous trespassers against the blackout rules were arrested at The Hague and kept in jail for a full night.

During the ensuing months the Nazis issued several decrees to eradicate sabotage once and for all, in several of its forms. Imprisonment for terms up to five years and a fine not exceeding fifty thousand guilders (or about $27,500) were held out to those who dared to "produce, distribute or keep in stock anti-German pamphlets, reproductions or other similar objects." Next, the carrying of all firearms and other weapons was prohibited. Exemptions would only be made for people "whose reliability cannot be questioned—and then only in cases of the most urgent necessity." To make sure that no arms had been hidden, all Netherlands officers were once more ordered to relinquish their weapons before the middle of August, 1941.

During the autumn, in the face of increasing sabotage, the Germans introduced the death penalty for "every action which aims at, or may cause the endangering of, public order or the safety of public life." It stands to reason that under this vague description could be ranged any misdemeanor which in the eyes of the Nazi tyrants was serious enough to be paid for with a human life. Any "criminal" over the age of 16 could be condemned to death; and the horror of this new decree was further increased by a proclamation from the Director-General of Police which held out rewards up to one thousand guilders to anyone providing the occupation authorities with the names of saboteurs.

When sabotage became rampant, despite the harshest measures, the Germans appointed "voluntary citizen guards" whose task it was to watch over objects of military importance which might be the "target for tonight" of the ever-active saboteurs. It stands to reason that the voluntary part of these nightly watches was nonsensical; in reality, the Nazis purposely picked out many old and sick people to help perform these unpleasant nocturnal duties.

In the collieries of south Limburg sabotage soon became part of the miners' daily task; and even after the incarceration of several leaders there was no noticeable improvement. When the prisoners were finally released as good-for-nothing unemployed and returned to their places of habitation, they were welcomed with a wealth of flowers. Their fellow-citizens had gathered very considerable sums of money for their subsistence.

In the agricultural districts, the peasantry sabotaged the crops of their opponents. The Dutch Nazis who had been put at the helm of several institutions, never ceased complaining—now because of the non-delivery of artificial manure, then again because several dairy farmers had allowed huge supplies of milk to go sour rather than deliver them to the German authorities.

Next to these and many similar forms of unconcealed sabotage, there developed underground another forceful struggle against the enemy. The secret press began to extend its influence; it reached practically the entire loyal population.

As sabotage increased, so grew the number of executions. If during the first occupation year only a few score victims had fallen, between May, 1941 and May, 1942 that number had multiplied many times until it was topped by the wholesale murder of 96 patriots whose only crime had been their love for Queen and country. Among them were many officers of the Netherlands Army and Navy, accused of having broken their pledge not to take up arms against the German Reich.

Immediately following this hecatomb came the order addressed to all former officers of the Netherlands Army up to the age of 56, to register. More than 2,000 men obeyed the command and were promptly incarcerated. They were transported to German prison camps, and little or nothing has been heard of them since.

That springtime was a time of sore trials. There were nearly a hundred victims of the Nazi execution squads; more than 2,000 former officers were re-interned and—to crown it all—nearly 500 hostages were taken, picked from the most representative ranks of the populace. But even these developments could not intimidate the Dutch. On the contrary, their common sufferings transformed the people into one huge, closely-knit family which knew that many more sacrifices would be required in the holy struggle for liberation.

Nonetheless, they had learned a great deal. No longer was resistance seen as a dangerous "game" of unorganized daredevils. The terrible retaliation of the Nazis had demonstrated conclusively that they were vile opponents who would not recoil from any form of revenge. The executions, the capturing of hostages and the introduction of ever-stricter regulations made the Dutch very wary. From now on the greatest care and circumspection would be necessary in the relentless fight against the invaders.

Thus, during the third year of Germany's domination over the Netherlands, the underground movement grew by leaps and bounds and became organized to a degree where it was able to regulate the general methods of opposition, and lead them into the most advisable channels.

There was no choice. To yield to the satanic enemy under the stress of unemployment or hunger, to fall victim to his blackmailing methods and stand aside from the battle of resistance was, of course, excluded. It was equally useless—but far more dangerous—to await an early invasion by the Allies and postpone all subversive action until then. The people of Holland realized to the full that every individual had to contribute his share to the struggle for freedom.

Above all, it was necessary to hold on to the spiritual values which, throughout a history of centuries, had moulded the Netherlands character. The Spaniards in the 15th and 16th centuries, the French under Napoleon had tried in vain to crush Dutch pride and kill the nation's innate love of independence. Where those oppressors had failed, the Germans stood no better chance to succeed.

As the third year of occupation ran towards its close, several of Mussert's acolytes were killed. Those "executions" were as many irrefutable indications that the normally quiet, peace-loving Dutch would, if need be, take the lives of their adversaries rather than bear the ignominy of their degrading activities in the service of the enemy. Several members of the new-fangled "Secretariat" were murdered or severely wounded* and those who remained surrounded themselves, quavering with fear, with heavily-armed Storm Troopers' guards. Nonetheless, on June 3, 1943 news came through that another member of the Secretariat had fallen.

*Dr. H. Reydon who was severely wounded on February 10 when patriots shot him at The Hague (see chapter 8—Unholy Crusades—page 164) died on August 24, 1943 as a result of this attack.

He was Folkert E. Posthuma, one time Minister of Agriculture.

As time went by, entire sections of the population united to throw themselves into the war against the Huns. First came the students, then the physicians. It was of no consequence to the strength of these revolts whether some of the participants paid with their liberty—or even with their lives—for their resolute action. They were the only possible answers to the enemy's temerity, the only way to show him that his attacks upon the nation were bound to remain unsuccessful, no matter where and how they were to be launched. No opportunity was ever left unused to give the Germans repeated and unmistakable proof of the hatred and loathing every loyal Hollander fosters for them.

And thus the murmur of resistance is gradually changing into the harsh clamor of armed attack. As the Allied position improves and the chances of a conclusive Nazi victory become unlikely, the day of liberation grows into something almost tangible. The gray haze of desperate longing for freedom lost makes place for the certainty of driving out and annihilating the enemy. It matters little whether another few months, another year or even longer, will have to pass before the country is cleansed of the scourge that fell upon it early on the morning of May 10, 1940.

Through the tortures of these years the spirit of the Dutch has, if anything, been purified and strengthened. In their common vicissitudes people of all ranks have found one another. Standing together they have shown the enemy their mettle; together they will oust him for all time. And the rousing welcome they will give their Queen when she returns to her impoverished country, will usher in a new era of liberty, tolerance and steady progress. In many ways that era will doubtlessly surpass the centuries of humanitarianism and enlightenment which made the Netherlands worthy of a prominent place among the most civilized nations of Europe.

APPENDIX I

The typewritten text of the letter General Winkelman addressed to his officers informing them of what had actually happened before the destruction of Rotterdam's center by the Germans is reproduced on the opposite page. In translation it reads as follows:

Commander-in-Chief of Land & Sea Forces

G.H.Q. June 27, 1940

Subject:
Speech of the Reich's Commissioner
Seyss-Inquart

On the occasion of his visit to Rotterdam, Reich's Commissioner Dr. Seyss-Inquart has delivered a speech in which—according to press reports—he has said that the destruction of Rotterdam was our own fault. The Commissioner added that this was not meant as a reproach to the Dutch commanders because as a result of the absence of leadership the decisive powers of those commanders were impaired.

This representation is against the true facts so that I have been compelled to lodge a protest with Dr. Seyss-Inquart against his speech. In this document I have informed that authority that the fact that our Government (and rightly so) had placed itself in safety, had no detrimental influence whatever on the capacity of Dutch commanders to make their decisions. I have, moreover, stated that it was not our fault that Rotterdam was subjected to a bombardment. As you will doubtlessly be interested to know the actual facts, I give you hereafter the details which supported my protest.

On May 14 at 10:30 a.m. the Commander of Rotterdam, Colonel Scharroo, received a written message. This was an ultimatum to stop the defense immediately, as otherwise the severest measures would be taken against the town. The ultimatum expired within two hours; the answer therefore had to be sent before 12:30 p.m. As the letter was unsigned and as therefore the possibility of a mystification was not excluded, I answered immediately in writing that a similar proposal could only be taken into consideration if it had been duly authenticated and signed by an authorized commander.

That answer arrived at 12:15 p.m.—in other words, a *quarter of an hour before the ultimatum lapsed*—at its destination: the Noordereiland near the Koningsbrug (the north island near Kingsbridge). The Netherlands Captain Bakker, however, was forced to wait in that spot with the German Major von Choltitz until 12:35 p.m. for the arrival of German generals.

At 1:20 p.m. a new ultimatum—this time duly signed—was handed to Captain Bakker for a period of three more hours.

With this ultimatum Captain Bakker, in the company of two German officers, returned to the Netherlands Commander.

Meantime, when at 1:20 p.m. the German flying squad was approaching, a red signal was fired, at the order of the German Lieutenant-General Schmidt. This, according to a German explanation, was a sign that bombardment should not take place. And the same thing was repeated at 1:25 p.m. near the second bridgehead of the Willembrug, at the order of one of the two Germans who accompanied Captain Bakker. Despite these warnings the bombardment began at 1:30.

It is clear from the above that if the Germans truly intended to avoid the bombardment, the arrangements they made to achieve their purpose failed. In no circumstances can the damage done to Rotterdam be ascribed to a lessened decisiveness of Dutch authorities.

As it is impossible to publish this contradiction through the press, I have thought it fit to free the Dutch defense forces in this manner from the blemish fastened to them: that they should have been the cause of Rotterdam's tragic fate.

The General Commander-in-Chief of Land
and Sea Forces
(was signed:) H. G. Winkelman

Opperbevelhebber van Land- & Zeemacht.　　　　Afschrift.　　　　A.H.K. 27 Juni 1940.

Onderwerp: Rede van den Rijkscommissaris Dr. Seys Inquart.

Ter gelegenheid van zijn bezoek aan Rotterdam heeft de Rijkscommissaris Dr. Seys Inquart een rede gehouden, waarin hij blijkens in de pers verschenen verslagen o.m. heeft medegedeeld, dat de vernietiging van een deel van Rotterdam aan onze eigen schuld te wijten zou zijn. De Rijkscommissaris voegde er aan toe dat dit niet bedoeld was als verwijt aan de Nederlandsche bevelhebbers, omdat tengevolge van de afwezigheid van de leiding de besluitvaardigheid van deze bevelhebbers zou zijn geremd.
Deze voorstelling van zaken is in strijd met de feiten, zooals deze zich in werkelijkheid hebben voorgedaan, zoodat ik mij genoodzaakt heb gezien bij Dr. Seys Inquart een protest tegen zijn rede in te dienen. Daarbij heb ik deze autoriteit medegedeeld, dat het feit dat de Regeering zich-terecht-in veiligheid had gesteld, van geen nadeeligen invloed op de vaardigheid tot het nemen van besluiten bij de Nederlandsche bevelhebbers is geweest. Voorts heb ik gezegd, dat het niet onze schuld is geweest dat Rotterdam werd gebombardeerd. Daar het U ongetwijfeld belang zal inboezemen hoe de ware toedracht ten deze is geweest, geef ik U hieronder de bijzonderheden, waarmede ik mijn protest heb gestaafd.
Op 14 Mei te 10.30 ontving de commandant in Rotterdam, Kolonel Scharroo een schriftelijk stuk, behelzende een ultimatum om de verdediging onmiddellijk te staken, daar anders de scherpste maatregelen tegen de stad zouden worden genomen.
De tijdsduur van dit ultimatum bedroeg 2 uren. Het antwoord moest dus uiterlijk om 12.30 zijn ingekomen. Daar de brief niet onderteekend was en dus de mogelijkheid van mystificatie niet uitgesloten was, heb ik per ommegaande schriftelijk doen weten, dat een dergelijk voorstel alleen dan in overweging kon worden genomen, indien het behoorlijk gewaarmerkt en door een bevoegden commandant zou zijn onderteekend.
Dit antwoord was om 12.15 dus <u>een kwartier vóór het verstrijken van den termijn</u> te bestemder plaatse: <u>Noordereiland nabij Koningsbrug aangekomen.</u>
De Nederlandsche kapitein Bakker heeft daar echter met een Duitschen overste von Choltitz tot 12.35 moeten wachten op de aankomst van Duitsche generaals. Om 13.20 is aan kapitein Bakker een nieuw, thans behoorlijk onderteekend ultimatum, met een geldigheidsduur van 3 uren, overhandigd.
Hiermede is genoomde kapitein in gezelschap van twee Duitsche officieren naarden Nederlandschen Commandant teruggekeerd.
Intusschen was om 13.20 bij de nadering van het Duitsche vliegtuigeskader op last van den Duitschen Luitenant Generaal Schmidt een roode seinpatroon afgeschoten (vlg. Duitsche verklaring als teeken, dat het bombardement niet moest worden uitgevoerd) en om 13.25 werd dit bij het Zuidelijke bruggehoofd van den Willemsbrug in opdracht van een der beide Duitschers, die kapitein Bakker vergezelden, herhaald. Desniettegenstaande is het bombardement om 13.30 begonnen.
Uit het vorenstaande blijkt, dat, indien de Duitschers het voornemen hebben gehad het bombardement niet te doen doorgaan, de hunnerzijds daartoe getroffen regeling gefaald heeft en dat de aan Rotterdam toegebrachte schade in géén geval te wijten is aan mindere besluitvaardigheid van Nederlandsche zijde. Daar het niet mogelijk is deze weerlegging door middel van de pers bekend te stellen heb ik gemeend langs dezen schriftelijken weg de Nederlandsche weermacht te moeten bevrijden van de ten onrechte op haar geworpen blaam, dat zij de oorzaak van Rotterdams noodlot zou zijn geweest.

De Genreal, Opperbevelhebber Land- & Zeemacht,

w.g. Winkelman.

GENERAL WINKELMAN'S CIRCULAR

This is the actual text of General Winkelman's letter to his officers regarding the bombing of Rotterdam (for complete translation of text see Appendix I).

BEKENDMAKING

De Wehrmachtbefehlshaber in den Niederlanden, General der Flieger Fr. Christiansen, maakt het volgende bekend:

Na de capitulatie van het Nederlandsche leger in Mei 1940 heeft de Führer en opperbevelhebber van de Duitsche weermacht bevel gegeven tot onmiddellijke invrijheidstelling van de Nederlandsche soldaten uit de krijgsgevangenschap. Deze maatregel werd vanzelfsprekend genomen op voorwaarde, dat de Nederlandsche officieren en manschappen deze grootmoedige handelwijze met een dienovereenkomstige houding ten aanzien van de Duitsche bezettende macht zouden beantwoorden. Een groot gedeelte van hen heeft aan deze verwachting voldaan; in vele gevallen is echter onder invloed van onverantwoordelijke ophitsers een tegenovergestelde ontwikkeling gevolgd.

Reeds in Mei 1942 moesten derhalve de voormalige beroepsofficieren opnieuw in krijgsgevangenschap worden weggevoerd. De Duitsche weermacht heeft sindsdien bijna een vol jaar laten verstrijken in de verwachting, dat deze duidelijke waarschuwing zou worden verstaan. In feite hebben echter afzonderlijke leden van het voormalige Nederlandsche leger door hun vijandig gedrag telkens opnieuw het vertrouwen, dat bij hun vrijlating in hen werd gesteld, geschonden. Dit misbruik van een volkomen vrijwillig teruggeschonken vrijheid wordt thans niet langer meer geduld.

De Wehrmachtbefehlshaber in den Niederlanden beveelt derhalve, dat de leden van het voormalige Nederlandsche leger terstond opnieuw in krijgsgevangenschap worden weggevoerd. Hij zal de betrokken personen in de dagbladpers tot persoonlijke aanmelding oproepen. Wie aan den oproep van den Wehrmachtbefehlshaber geen gevolg geeft of tracht, zich op andere wijze aan de krijgsgevangenschap te onttrekken, moet op de strengste maatregelen rekenen. Dit geldt eveneens voor personen, die de betrokkenen bij dergelijke pogingen ondersteunen. Allen, die thans in krijgsgevangenschap moeten terugkeeren, hebben dit uitsluitend aan de ophitsers te danken, die door hun misdadig gedrag dezen maatregel noodzakelijk maakten.

PROCLAMATIE

Officieren en soldaten van het Nederlandsche Leger!

DE NEDERLANDSCHE REGEERING neemt met diepe verontwaardiging kennis van den laatsten maatregel van den vijand, waarbij hij het Nederlandsche Leger in krijgsgevangenschap roept.

Zij waarschuwt de menschen met nadruk tegen het gehoor geven aan dien oproep!

Hij, die zich desondanks toch meldt bedenke, dat hij daarmede den vijand dient, zijn gezin zonder bescherming laat en zijn leven in gevaar brengt. ***Wij zijn in oorlog met Duitschland. Dat bewijzen de laatste maatregelen opnieuw. Wie in oorlog zich aanmeldt voor krijgsgevangenschap is een lafaard.***

Er is maar één manier om krijgsgevangen te worden, en dat is: dat de vijand U gevangen neemt. Ieder goed soldaat zorgt in den *oorlog* dat de vijand hem *niet* kan vangen.

Het geheele Nederlandsche volk zal hiertoe moeten samenwerken.

Ongetwijfeld zal de vijand trachten, door middel van politie- en andere Nederlandsche opsporingsorganen, met geweld zijn oogmerken te bereiken. Geen ambtenaar werke hieraan mee!

Niemand verleene op eenige wijze medewerking aan den vijand.

De bevrijding is nabij.

Leve de Koningin *Leve het Vaderland!*

Wie gaat, pleegt landverraad!

Vermenigvuldig en geef snel door!

IMPRISONMENT OF GENERAL WINKELMAN

(*top:*) The General (second from right) is seen in the company of several Dutch officers, at the entrance to a German prison camp; (*bottom, left:*) Air Gen. Christiansen's Order for immediate registration of all members of the former Netherlands army (May, 1943); (*right:*) underground pamphlet exhorting every former soldier, in the name of the Netherlands Government, to go into hiding.

APPENDIX II

THE PEACE COURTS IN ACTION

The best way to understand the "justice" dealt out by the Nazi-established Peace Courts, is to compare their sentences for patriots accused of insulting or attacking members of the National-Socialist movement with convictions pronounced on Dutch-Nazis guilty of aggression against loyal Netherlanders.

Each of the five Peace Courts that had been established in Amsterdam, Arnhem, 's-Hertogenbosch, The Hague and Leeuwarden* consisted of only one member, known as the Judge of the Peace. He was to pronounce sentence unassisted; appeal remained, however, possible. To this purpose a special Court of three members was installed at The Hague, with the Attorney-General of The Hague Court, the rabid N. S. B.'er Van Genechten, functioning as its General Prosecutor. From his decisions no further appeal was possible. The High Court of Justice which had always been the last instance to which any citizen accused of a crime could take recourse, was simply ignored. More than that, a special stipulation was made that all "inadequate" sentences for political misdemeanors committed between the beginning of the invasion and the establishment of the Peace Courts, could be revised.

This shameless chicanery infuriated the Netherlands people so much that twice in quick succession the Nazis were forced to "elucidate" the new measure. To justify Van Genechten's interpretation of Netherlands criminal law, the press and radio announced that the slight punishment thus far requested by the ordinary Courts against people "insulting members of the N. S. B. in the most grievous way, generally by calling them traitors," had virtually been insult heaped upon injury . . .

---

*On August 16, 1941

Late in November, 1941 the Nazis were still trying to explain. But in the meantime the Peace Courts had been exceedingly busy. They had, first of all, "revised" the sentences pronounced upon members of the Dutch police and military forces who in the invasion days of 1940 had opened fire on members of the N. S. B. guilty of treasonable acts, and killed ten of them. Some who had been acquitted by loyal judges, were now condemned to five, ten and even fifteen years in jail. By way of special grace one such verdict was changed to incarceration in a sanitarium for the mentally diseased. Finally Van Genechten went so far as to demand the death penalty for an Army Captain charged with having shot to death a brother of Anton Mussert. Their belated blood lust thus placated, the Peace Courts began to pour out the vials of their wrath upon the smaller fry.

For calling an N. S. B.'er a traitor, a citizen of the village of Maasland was sentenced to a fine of twenty guilders and a week in prison. A 17 year old high school pupil from Hillegersberg, a Rotterdam suburb, had to pay 250 guilders for the same "crime." Others were sent to jail on similar charges for periods varying from two weeks to two months. In every case the accused were also sentenced to pay considerable fines.

A most remarkable instance was that of a policeman who had fired his gun at a Dutch Storm Trooper while he was busily "beating up a citizen, probably because the man walked in his way." As soon as the police officer interfered, however, the Storm Trooper and several of his comrades attacked him with bludgeons, knives and daggers. As a reward for his dutiful behavior the policeman was sent to prison for two weeks. In the summing-up this loyal civil servant was told that the "police must not interfere as hitherto in such cases. Within certain limits they must leave these utterances of revolutionary tension alone" . . .

The other Peace Judges did not stay behind. One of them sent a provincial teacher to prison for a month because the man had said, "Thanks to the N. S. B. we are now left without butter or meat." In Breda, a young girl was imprisoned for ten days because she had dared to say "traitor" to a passing N. S. B.'er. A similar fate was reserved for a nineteen year old girl of Bergen-op-Zoom who had flung the same epithet at the head of a former friend whom she saw passing by on the arm of a German officer. A courageous Catholic lady of 70 took offense at the challenging attitude of her National-Socialist neighbor who came to her door and provoked passers-by. "There she is again, that traitor," the aged lady had exclaimed. The judge, having pity on her because of her age, made her pay fifty guilders' fine and volunteered the remark that it was strange to find so many Roman Catholics amongst those accused of insulting N. S. B.'ers.

An Amsterdam bookbinder refused to accept a copy of Volk en Vaderland from a door-to-door canvasser. The enterprising Nazi lady thereupon smacked the man in the face who in his turn called her "a dirty cad." The judge sent the man to prison for two months; as to the canvasser, there was no punishment for her. Parallel to this ran the case of a patriot from Nieuwerkerk. He had torn a Nazi newspaper to pieces when it was "offered" to him by an N. S. B.'er. The fragments he had thrown in the canvasser's face while saying: "Thank you. I have no need of toilet paper." Two weeks in jail. A Rotterdam house-painter came to blows with an N. S. B.'er and apparently had the better of it. Doubtlessly his victory was worth all of the thirty-five guilders the Peace Judge made him pay.

A man from Utrecht had been rash enough to say to fellow travelers in a train, "All Netherlanders are decent except the N. S. B.'ers." This heartfelt opinion cost him a twenty-five guilders' fine. A Rotterdam laborer had given the following advice to a truck driver working for the German Army: "Why don't you go to Russia? I'm not afraid of your uniform; it won't be long before we get you and hang you." He was given two weeks in jail to think it over.

A sixty year old bookkeeper of the same city saw a number of uniformed Storm Troopers strutting past. Indignantly, the man had shouted, "Look at that scum. *We* may not wear anything orange but *they* run around in their uniforms!" Eight days in jail.

An eighteen year old boy had torn an N. S. B. flag from a bicycle. Five days in prison. A railroad worker who had witnessed how some Storm Troopers beat up a loyal Dutchman, had broken the windows of an N. S. B.'er's home in retaliation. Twenty days in jail or a fine of forty guilders. Another laborer had "ostentatiously" spat against the window of a house inhabited by a Mussert acolyte who had made disparaging remarks on the Netherlands Army. A fine of fifteen guilders, or six days' imprisonment.

*

And now for a few sentences pronounced by the same judges on members of the National-Socialist movement. A taxi-driver at The Hague who, working with a group of Storm Troopers had completely ruined a shop in the center of the town and beaten the shopkeeper mercilessly, was given four months in prison.

Three other Storm Troop heroes attacked a solitary merchant and beat him unconscious. This amusement came to sixty guilders among the three of them. Another black shirt had slapped a laborer who—so he said—had turned away his face when the N. S. B. flag was carried past. Small fine. Another member of Mussert's movement had beaten an asthmatic youth whom he accused of coughing "purposely and significantly" while passing him. Ten guilders' fine.

Five Storm Troopers of Zwolle battered the furniture of a coffeehouse to smithereens because the bartender refused to sell them more drinks. One was acquitted; the others were sentenced to pay a fifteen guilders' fine each. A Storm Trooper from Nijmegen paid with one month imprisonment for the following list of trespasses: Beating up a shopkeeper because of anti-Nazi utterances. Maltreating an office clerk who had made the "V" sign with his fingers; the man was ill for ten weeks. Hitting two boys with his leather belt and repeatedly insulting members of the police force. The Peace Judge, passing sentence upon this noble soul, drew particular attention to "all the good this man has done for the N. S. B." He even persuaded the fellow to ask for pardon and assured him, "I shall advise favorably."

A woman and her daughter had freely insulted several neighbors, calling them "filthy Communists, rabble and scum." To their defense they advanced that since the invasion "they don't leave us alone in our street." The sympathetic judge made them pay one fine of five guilders. An N. S. B.'er had attacked the head of a school who prevented him from distributing Nazi leaflets among the pupils. He had beaten the man so severely that a concussion of the brain ensued. Fined to pay fifteen guilders.

In July, 1941 members of the Youth Storm endeavored to paste streamers and posters for the Nazi movement on the house-walls of Zandvoort's burgomaster. This official quietly requested them to go. When one of the youngsters pushed the man aside, he slapped him. The Youth Stormers went away to fetch assistance and the local Commander of the Storm Troops ordered two of his patrols to arrest the burgomaster. Those gentlemen thereupon entered the Mayor's home through one of its windows. When the burgomaster's wife ran to the telephone to call the police, a Storm Trooper approached her and threatened to hit her with a chair. This was the signal for a general fracas during which the burgomaster was floored. The Storm Troopers sat on him until the police arrived and threw them out. The Peace Judge, pronouncing the opinion that "the Storm Troopers have a useful and beautiful task to fulfill," punished only one of the culprits, the patrol leader. He was sent to jail for three months.

However incomplete, this resumé provides a clear picture of the type of justice now prevailing in a country which gave the world such men of law as Hugo Grotius, Asser, Meyers and Van Vollenhove.

APPENDIX III

The complete text of the letter of the Catholic churches as read from the chancels on Sunday, February 21, 1943 follows:

"Beloved Faithful:

"The bitter suffering and anguished worry under whose weight so many are stooped, in consequence of the severe measures taken, especially in these recent times, by the occupation authorities, urge us to write to you and to convey our sense of common participation.

"We are filled with the deepest compassion for the numberless persons called upon to bear such great and bitter sufferings. But we would fail in our duty if we did not publicly raise our voice against the injustice to which so large a part of our people is being subjected. In this we are following that path indicated to us by Our Holy Father, the Pope, who in his latest Christmas message, among other things, declared:

> " 'The Church would be untrue to herself, ceasing to be a mother, if she turned a deaf ear to her children's anguished cries, which reach her from every class of the human family. She does not intend to take sides for either of the particular forms in which the several peoples and States strive to solve the gigantic problems of domestic order or international collaboration, as long as these forms conform to the Law of God. But, on the other hand, as the "Pillar and Ground of Truth" and guardian, by the will of God and the mandate of Christ, of the natural and supernatural order, the Church cannot renounce her right to proclaim to her sons and to the whole world the unchanging basic laws, saving them from every perversion, obfuscation, corruption, false interpretation and error.'

"Therefore, with other important church groups, we have directed to the Reich's Commissioner the following letter:

" 'The Protestant churches and the Roman Catholic Church in Holland feel compelled to write once more to you, Herr Reich's Commissioner, with profound seriousness. On many occasions already they have directed to you grave complaints against the mounting injustice with which the Dutch people are being treated, which is a matter that also affects profoundly the churches themselves.

JUSTICE, MERCY AND LIBERTY

" 'As they told you, they, by the calling imposed upon them in the Name of Christ, have made their voice heard also when principles rooted in the Gospel were impugned in public life. They pointed out particularly those principles which constitute the foundations of the public Christian life of our people; namely, Justice, Mercy and Liberty in their relation to human life.

" 'They must bear witness to the fact that the heads of Governments, too, are subject to the Law of God, and have the obligation of abstaining from acts that are prohibited by that Law. The churches would fail in their responsibility if they neglected to admonish the heads of Governments for the sins committed by them in the exercise of their power or neglected to forewarn them by reminding them of the severity of the judgment of God.

" 'The churches already have denounced the increasing lack of justice; the persecution and execution of Jewish fellow-citizens; the imposition of a conception of life and of the world that is contradictory to the Gospel of Jesus Christ; forced labor service as an institution of National Socialist education; the violation of the freedom of Christian instruction; the imposition of forced labor in Germany on Dutch workers; the execution of hostages; the arrest and imprisonment of many persons, among them ecclesiastical dignitaries, under such conditions that a very considerable number already have had to make the sacrifice of their lives in concentration camps.

" 'Now, to all this, is added the hunting down—as if they were slaves—and the arrest and deportation of thousands of young people.

" 'In all these actions the Divine Law has been violated in increasing measure.

PREACH AGAINST HATE

" 'The churches preach against hate and the spirit of vengeance in the heart of our people, and raise their voice against manifestations of these vices. According to the Word of God no one can be his own judge. But in the same measure, the churches also have the duty, by their calling, to preach this word of God: "Obey God rather than men." This function serves as the norm in all conflicts of conscience, even for those arising from the measures in question. By virtue of Divine Law, no one may offer the slightest collaboration to acts of injustice, because, in so doing, he shares the guilt of the injustice itself.

" 'Herr Reich's Commissioner, it is in obedience to the Lord that the Churches are obliged to address this letter to you: they pray that God may lead you in His way, that you may restore the right so grievously violated in the exercise of your power.'

"Thus far our collective letter to the Reich's Commissioner.

"Beloved Faithful, in the midst of all the injustice and anguish you have suffered, our sympathy goes out in a very special manner to the young forcibly taken from their homes, to the Jews and to our brethren of the Catholic Faith who are of Jewish descent, who are exposed to so great suffering. Furthermore, we are profoundly grieved by the fact that, for the execution of the measures taken against these two categories of persons, the collaboration of our own fellow-citizens, such as those in public authority, State employees and the directors of institutions, has been demanded.

"Beloved Brethren, we are aware in how serious a conflict the consciences of the persons involved find themselves. Therefore, to remove any doubt and uncertainty you may entertain on this point, we declare most emphatically that collaboration in this matter is forbidden in conscience.

RECOURSE TO PRAYER

"If refusal to collaborate should demand sacrifices of you, be strong and constant in the conviction that you are doing your duty before God and man.

"Beloved Brethren, we have not physical force at our disposal. All the more, therefore, we exhort you to adopt that means which, everything considered, is infallible, that is, suppliant prayer that God may hasten to take pity on us and upon the world.

"This our Joint Pastoral is to be read in the usual manner at all scheduled Masses on Septuagesima Sunday, February 21, in all churches and chapels having a permanent rector and within our ecclesiastical province.

"Given at Utrecht, February 17, 1943."

The Joint Pastoral is signed by the Most Rev. John De Jong, Archbishop of Utrecht; the Most Rev. Peter Adrian William Hopmans, Bishop of Breda; the Most Rev. William Lemmens, Bishop of Roermond; the Most Rev. John Peter Huibers, Bishop of Haarlem, and Bishop Mussaerts, Coadjutor of 's-Hertogenbosch.

*

Here follows a synopsis of the letter of protest—almost identical to the above pastoral message—emanating from the United Reformed Churches of the Netherlands. It was read from the pulpit of every Protestant Church throughout the country on Sunday, February 21, 1943:

"Events of the last weeks have compelled the churches to speak to their congregations. It is the task of the church to raise its voice even in public matters, protesting when principles rooted in the Gospel are violated. The church therefore repeatedly lodged serious complaints with the occupying power regarding measures constituting specific violations of the principles on which the Christian life of the Netherlands people is based, namely, justice, charity, and freedom of conscience.

"The church would be neglecting its duty if it failed to impress on the authorities that they too are subject to Divine Law. It therefore had drawn the attention of the occupying power to increasing lawlessness, the persecution unto death of Jewish fellow citizens, the fact that an outlook flagrantly violating the Gospel of Christ is forced upon the people, the compulsory Labor Service as a Nazi educational institution, forced labor of Netherlands workers in Germany, the killing of hostages, and the imprisonment of numerous Netherlands subjects including church dignitaries, so that an alarming number have already lost their lives in concentration camps.

"In view of the latest developments, the church now raises its voice against the acts of hunting, rounding up and carrying off thousands of youths.

"On the other hand the church feels bound to issue an emphatic warning against hatred and feelings of revenge in the hearts of the Netherlands people. According to the word of God, no one may take the law in his own hands.

"It is also the church's duty to preach the word of God, saying God must be obeyed above men. This word is a guide in all conflicts of conscience including those created by measures now being taken. It forbids cooperation in unjust deeds. Cooperation renders the participant an accomplice in injustice.

"The churches desire to bring these matters again to the notice of the Reich's Commissioner.

"They pray God that the occupying power and the Netherlands people may find the way to justice and to obedience to His word."

*

The complete text of the pastoral letter regarding the registration of some 400,000 demobilized soldiers, for re-internment in German camps and for slave labor in the Reich,* follows. It was read from the chancels of all Catholic churches on Sunday, May 16, 1943.

"Ever heavier trials visit the country. A world outlook which is diametrically opposed to Christianity has been forced upon our people these last three years. In every sphere Nazism attempts to extend its influence and take the lead.

"Although Nazism remains the powerful master of the situation here, the spiritual power of resistance of the overwhelming majority of the Netherlands people is unbroken. This fills us with great consolation and faith in the future. Despite all suppression of those differently-minded and the bait of various material advantages, the Netherlands people will never become nazist if we remain but loyal to our ancestral faith.

"There is strength in faith. But, our beloved faithful, although we have no fears about your faith, yet we are filled with deep care and compassion through the calamities which have struck our people and through the worse calamities still threatening.

"We do not speak of the privations experienced by man and which threaten to assume the character of a lack of the most necessary. Greater still is the suffering caused by deportation and forced employment abroad. How many families have been torn asunder? How much spiritual distress is thus suffered? To how many moral dangers are tens of thousands exposed from all sides? How many joys of living are being destroyed? We are also thinking of those who built up their own enterprises in many years of exertion and now see themselves threatened with destruction.

---

*See Chapter 13—"Kultur" Infusions—page 295.

"The limit has been reached. All able-bodied men who can be spared at all will be fetched away. This is deportation on a scale such as the Christian world has never known. For that we must return to the times of Babylonian exile when God's people were carried away to exile, causing the prophet Jeremiah to exclaim, 'Ploratus et ululatus multus,'—'Lamentation is heard in Ramah, loud weeping and crying, Rachel weeping for her sons.' (Jeremiah 31:15)

"Not only the deportation shocks us, but also the horrible injustice which is contrary to all human and divine laws.

"As shepherds of your souls we may not be silent on what is being done to our people. Posterity would consider it our eternal shame if we viewed this injustice silently. The bishops' task is to stand for the right and to condemn wrong as wrong, otherwise they would fall short of their duty.

"If ever there was a nation which did not want war it was the Netherlands nation. We were unprepared and only defended our country when it was attacked. We had to do this because it was our duty and because our country was dear to us. Though our country is small, our love for it is as great as any people's for theirs. Now our country is not only usurped, but a large part of the population is being carried away forcibly. Men must work for their enemy.

"At first it was said that Netherlanders must work abroad because there was no work for them here. Now they must work for Germany to assure a German victory, as explicitly stated.

"Here comes for us a conflict of conscience. According to the Fourth Commandment, we must honor and love our country and make sacrifices for it. Now we not only may do nothing for our country, but we are even forced, under threat of heavy punishment, to help the enemy.

"Herein especially lies the injustice done to us and against which we raise our voice. True, it is being presented as though it was all Christians' duty to fight against Bolshevism, but this is only a catchword. Those really desiring to fight 'Godless Bolshevism,' so sharply condemned by the Pope, must not suppress Christianity with all manner of means as is done by Nazism, which does not persecute Christianity bloodily, but saps its vitality instead.

"The Nazis in power do not shrink even from preventing the Church from exercising care for the souls of her own children.

When the employment of Netherlands workers in Germany was extended widely, endless negotiations took place with the proper authorities to obtain consent for Dutch priests to accompany them to the border in order to look after the religious interests of Catholic Netherlands workers.

"In vain. The negotiations were fruitless.

"No, the only power for fighting Communism is not Nazism, but Christianity. For 'Nobody may lay any other foundation than that which has been laid, which is Christ.' (Corinthians 1:3-11)

"In a previous pastoral letter we have already stated, 'We do not possess means of force. But we entreat you to take refuge in God and to search your inner hearts.'

"Our people as such has not yet prayed in this awful time as it ought. If you do that, God will help you. This is not a phrase, but an unfailing promise of God Himself.

"The Holy Father in this tragic hour dedicates the Holy Church and the entire world to the Immaculate Heart of Mary and rouses us in this month of May to crusade and prayer. This is our last remedy.

"May the Virgin Mother and the Mother of Charity help us.

"The Archbishop of Utrecht,
"The Bishop of Breda,
"The Bishop of Haarlem,
"The Bishop of Roermond,
"The Bishop of 's-Hertogenbosch."

*

On the same date and subject a message was read by the Protestant clergymen of Holland. Some highlights follow:

"The sight of our suffering people fills our hearts with burning pain. The General Synod of the Netherlands Reformed Church therefore calls for communal prayer.

"Numberless people have been plunged into the deepest need by the measures announced since April. The misery among relatives of the victims, the anxiety and tension which we have had to bear since the beginning of May, the grief of families whose student sons have been deported or whose fathers, sons and brothers will shortly be called up for involuntary service, has deadened our souls. On every one of us presses heavily the burden of what we feel to be crying injustice.

"However much we may exert ourselves to assist each other in this great misery, yet we feel our impotence and the lack of justice.

"As a church we must in the midst of all the need prevailing in and around us pray, maybe learn anew to pray. In this prayer we must confess our sins, the sins of our people and of our church.

"But we must also beseech Him Who is almighty and just, mercy-bringing and merciful, Who has pity on us in His court, Who was and is and always will be Our Saviour, that we may have a part in the Holy Ghost Which may fill our hearts with the sighs which we cannot speak. Let us not stop calling upon Him Who is the Father of Jesus. Who is willing to give us everything, upon Him, Who punishes in order to bless, Who takes in order to give, Who kills in order to revive.

"We shall not have peace if we do not seek the future in Him Who says, 'Fear none of those things which thou shalt suffer. Be thou faithful unto death and I will give thee a crown of life.' "

*

Shortly afterwards it became known that the Nazis had introduced sterilization practices in Holland. For this purpose several hundred Jews were brought back from the "sifting center" of Westerbork in the province of Drente and operated upon in a recently evacuated institute for aged and ailing Jews, "De Joodsche Invalide" at Amsterdam. The marriages of these unfortunate men with "aryan" wives had been childless. In protest against these barbarities, the leaders of the nine religious bodies existing in the Netherlands (the Netherlands Reformed Church, the Roman Catholic Church, the three Calvinist Churches, the Mennonite Church, the Remonstrant Congregation and both Evangelical-Lutheran Churches) signed the following letter which was forwarded to Reich's Commissioner Seyss-Inquart:

"After many happenings in the years of occupation which have caused the Christian churches of the Netherlands to feel forced to complain to Your Excellency, notably regarding the question of Jewish citizens, there now occurs something so terrible that we cannot desist from addressing these words to Your Excellency in the name of the Lord.

"We have already complained about several acts on the part of the occupying power which clash with the spiritual principles of our people, which has at least attempted, since its birth, to live with its government in accordance with God's word.

"Now a beginning has been made with the sterilization of members of so-called mixed marriages. But God, Who created heaven and earth and Whose commandment applies to all men and to Whom Your Excellency also must give account one day, told men, 'Be fruitful and multiply.' (Genesis 28)

"Sterilization constitutes physical and spiritual mutilation directly at variance with the divine commandment that we shall not dishonor, hate, wound or kill our neighbors. Sterilization constitutes a violation of divine commandment as well as of human rights.

"It is the last consequence of an anti-christian racial doctrine which destroys nations, and of a self-exaltation without bounds. It represents a view of the world and of life which undermines real Christian and human existence, making it ultimately impossible.

"You, Your Excellency, are the prominent, *de facto* highest political authority in the Netherlands. As things are, you are entrusted with the maintenance of law and order in the country. You are entrusted with this not only by the Fuehrer of the German Reich, but also through inscrutable dispensations by that God Whom the Christian church proclaims on earth.

"To you apply, exactly as to all other men, and to you especially because you happen to be placed in this high office, the commandments of this Lord and Judge of the entire earth. Therefore, the Christian churches of the Netherlands are ordered by God, and in accordance with His word, to say to Your Excellency:

"It is the duty of Your Excellency to stop the shameful practice of sterilization. We do not have illusions. We are well aware that we can hardly expect that Your Excellency will heed the voice of the church, which is the voice of the gospel and which is the voice of God. But what we cannot expect as human beings we dare to hope for because of our faith in Christ.

"The living God has the power to convert and change also Your Excellency's heart. For that we also ask God, for the good of Your Excellency and for our suffering people.

"P. de Bruyn, President, and H. J. Dyckmeester, Deputy Secretary, Netherlands Reformed Church,
"J. de Jong, Archbishop, the Roman Catholic Church,
"A. L. Rutgers, the Calvinist Churches,
"G. W. van Deth, the Calvinist Churches in the Restored Union,
"H. Janssen, the Christian Calvinist Church,
"F. Kleyn, the Remonstrant Brotherhood,
"S. N. B. Halbertsma, the Baptist Society,
"H. Grottendieck, the Evangelical Lutheran Church,
"W. J. F. Meiners, the Restored Evangelical Lutheran Church."

Bibliography

The following list comprises the most important books on events in the Netherlands since May, 1940. Besides, countless articles on the same subject have appeared in newspapers and periodicals.

ALBRAND, MARTHA. *No Surrender.* Boston, Little, Brown and Co., 1942.

ASHTON, H. S. *The Netherlands at War.* London, George Routledge and Sons, 1941; pp. 98-113.

BEELAERTS VAN BLOKLAND, FRANS. *The Five Days of Holland.* Washington, 1940.

BEERS, A. C. VAN. *Queen Wilhelmina's Country.* London, The Rolls House Publishing Company, 1943.

BOISOT. *De Wedergeboorte van het Koninkrijk.* London, Netherland Publishing Company, 1943.

BOVENE, G. A. VAN and ROOSDORP, C. J. *Wij Varen Voort—Historische Feiten en Uitspraken vlak voor en na den 10 Mei 1940.* Batavia, G. Kolff & Co., 1941 [?]

CARSE, R. *The Unconquered.* New York, National Travel Club, 1942; pp. 32-50.

CLARK, GEORGE N. *Holland and the War.* Oxford, Clarendon Press, 1941.

COLTON, O. A. *Can the Nazis Beat the Dutch?* 1943.

DUKER, ABRAHAM G. *Governments-in-exile on Jewish Rights.* New York, The American Jewish Committee, 1942.

EINZIG, PAUL. *Europe in Chains.* Harmondsworth, Middlesex, Penguin Books, 1940; p. 73.

EINZIG, PAUL. *Hitler's "New Order" in Europe.* London, Macmillan, 1941; p. 87.

Europe under Hitler, in Prospect and in Practice. London, Royal Institute of International Affairs, 1941.

Europe under the Nazi Scourge. London, Times Publishing Co., 1941; pp. 78-82.

FRANKS, H. GEORGE. *Holland Afloat.* London, Netherland Publishing Co., 1942.

GASTEL, G. VAN. *Netherlands Industry under German Pressure.* (In: Netherlands Trade Review, October, 1942; p. 14.)

HARSCH, JOSEPH C. *Pattern of Conquest.* New York, Doubleday, Doran and Co., 1941.

HARTOG, JAN DE. *Hollands Glorie.* London, The Netherland Publishing Co., 1941.

HEIDE, DIRK VAN DER. *My Sister and I, the Diary of a Dutch Boy Refugee.* New York, Harcourt, Brace and Co., 1941.

HOFER. *Wij Strijden met de Teekenstift (1939-1940).* Batavia, G. Kolff, 1940.

INTER-ALLIED INFORMATION COMMITTEE. *Axis (The) System of Hostages.* Conditions in Occupied Territories, No. 1. London, His Majesty's Stationery Office, 1941; pp. 9-10.

INTER-ALLIED INFORMATION COMMITTEE. *Rationing under Axis Rule.* Conditions in Occupied Territories, No. 2. 1942.

INTER-ALLIED INFORMATION COMMITTEE. *Religious Persecution.* Conditions in Occupied Territories, No. 3. 1942.

JONG, L. DE. *Holland Fights the Nazis.* London, Lindsay Drummond, 1941.

JONG, L. DE. *Je Maintiendrai.* Part I. London, Netherland Publishing Co., 1941.

JONG, L. DE. *Je Maintiendrai.* Part II. London, Netherland Publishing Co., 1942.

KEEP, M. H. *It Happened There.* Garden City, N. Y., Country Life Press Association, 1940.

Keep your Pity for the Weak. New York, Netherlands Information Bureau, 1943.

KLEFFENS, EELCO N. VAN. *Juggernaut over Holland.* New York, Columbia University Press, 1941.

KOTSCHNIG, WALTER M. *Slaves Need no Leaders.* New York, London, Toronto, Oxford University Press, 1943; pp. 68-80.

MALONEY, JOHN. *Let There Be Mercy: The Odyssey of a Red Cross Man.* Garden City, N. Y., Doubleday, Doran and Co., 1941; pp. 205-219.

MAUGHAM, VISCOUNT. *Lies as Allies or Hitler at War.* London, Toronto, New York, Oxford University Press, 1941; pp. 44-45.

Mein Kampf in Holland; or, Straight from the Horse's Mouth. New York, Netherlands Information Bureau, 1943.

Netherlands News, Vols. 1-7. New York, Netherlands Information Bureau.

OLIVEIRA, M. DE. *A Epopeia de Armada Holandesa.* Lisbon, A. M. Pereira, 1943.

PAASSEN, PIERRE VAN. *That Day Alone.* New York, The Dial Press, 1941; pp. 223-274.

Press, Dutch. List of Dutch Newspapers; Their Tendencies before and after the Invasion. London, Dutch Government Press Service, 1941.

REVEILLE, THOMAS. *The Spoil of Europe.* New York, W. W. Norton and Co., 1941.

RICE, EDWARD JR. *Three Years of War.* New York, Dell Publishing Co., 1942; pp. 38-39.

RIESS, CURT. *Underground Europe.* New York, The Dial Press, 1942; pp. 95-116.

Sixth Column, The. New York, Alliance Book Corporation, 1942. Chapter V, "Holland" by Dr. N. A. C. Slotemaker de Bruine; pp. 143-183.

SOMEREN, LIESJE VAN. *Escape from Holland.* London, Herbert Jenkins, 1942.

STRABOLGI, LORD. *Campaign in the Netherlands.* London, 1940.

TABORI, PAUL. *A Wreath for Europe.* New York, Ives Washburn, 1942; pp. 253-264.

TER KUHLE, E. *Ik Denk aan Rotterdam.* Batavia, G. Kolff and Co., 1941.

VOS, NICO C. *Nederland, mijn Nederland.* Amsterdam, Scheltens & Giltay, 1940.

Vrij Nederland. (Weekly for Netherlanders) 7 Park Lane, London, W. 1. Netherland Publishing Co.

WHITE, MARION. *If We Should Fail.* New York, M. S. Mill Co., 1942.

Wij Varen. Op 12 Mei 1940 met de "Johan de Witt" van Amsterdam naar Batavia via Kaap de Goede Hoop. Batavia, G. Kolff and Co., 1940 [?]; pp. 14-55.

Wilt U de Waarheid Weten? Berlin, Hauptabteilung für Volksaufklärung und Propaganda, 1940.

Index

(*The page references in italics refer to the Appendices*)

ACTIVE ENLIGHTENMENT, DEPT. OF, work of the, 278

Actors, anti-Nazi attitude of, 297; imprisonment of an actress, 297; ordered to join Culture Chamber, 297

Administrative system, Nazi - in occupied Holland, 31, 42

Advertising, commercial - and Dutch radio programs, 293

Agrarian Front, formation of the Nazi, 110; horticulturists' unwillingness to join the, 120; rebaptized "Nederlandsche Landstand," 124; Catholics warned not to join the, 194

Agricultural Schools, *see* Schools

Agriculture, upswing in, 72

Aid societies, several - disbanded, 317

Air force, in action against Japanese, 324; new Dutch - built up in U. S. A., 330

A. J. C., *see* Socialist Youth League

Albarda, Social-Democrat leader J. W., -'s radio speeches popular, 340

Aldermen, resignation of many, 142

Algemeen Handelsblad, Amsterdam daily, "co-ordination" of the, 285

Algemeen Nederlandsch Persbureau, nazification of the, 272

Allies, efforts of - to help in defense of Java, 324; bitterness about lack of help from, 329

Amateur theater, must join Culture Chamber, 297

Ambulance, Nazi, difficulties in "donating" - to troops in Russia, 172

American, banned - authors officially listed, 303

Amsterdam, city of, situation of German refugees in, 5; protest strike against ceiling prices, 81; restrictions on Jewish butchers, 212; Jewish merchants banned from public markets, 212; Dutch Nazis march provocatively through -'s Jewish quarter, 216; more - Jews rounded up, 219; special - ghettos harbor Jews from all Holland, 223; first round-up of Jews for deportation, 228; Reformed Lyceum closes down, 262; excels in refusing support to Winter Help campaigns, 311

Amsterdam, University of, open to theology, natural science and philosophy students, 258

A. N. P., *see* Algemeen Nederlandsch Persbureau

Anthems, national, used to "obstruct" Nazis, 300

Anti-Catholic, propaganda via Hilversum radio, 197; action of Nazis, 205, 206

Anti-Jewish, *see* Jewish, and Antisemitism

Anti-parliamentary, attitude of the Netherlands Union, 237

Antiques, boom in demand for, 69

Anti-Russian, - propaganda, 168

Anti-semitism (-ic) of Mussert, 25; Seyss-Inquart on -, 40; obligatory showing of - films, 221, 298; cabaret of the N.S.B., 312

Arable land, *see* Land

Arbeiderspers, *see* Volk, Het

Archbishop, De Jongh (of Utrecht) heavily fined, 206

Army, new - formed in Canada, England, 330; all former - officers to register, 344

Army of Occupation, size of, 41; problem of feeding the, 73

Arnhem, city of, Symphonic Orchestra of - accused of philo-semitism, 300

Art(s), boom in - collecting, 69; subjugation of the liberal, 278; Nazis organize - exhibitions, 279; Modern Dutch - exhibited in Germany, 280; - materials controlled by Culture Chamber, 282; increased demand for works of -, 296; plastic - under Nazi rule, 296

Art dealers, in unexpected places, 69
Artists, Nazi, reception for - organized by Seyss-Inquart, 279
"Aryanization", method of - of Jewish businesses, 222
Atrocities, against Dutch Jews, 229
Atrocity tales, - regarding Soviet Russia, 168
Austria, Dutch children to - movement, 18
Authors, loyal - stop producing, 301; Nazi - distinguished, 301; works of various - banned, 302; banned - officially listed, 303
Authors, German Nazi - give lectures in Holland, 279
AVRO, broadcasting company, non-secretarian in pre-invasion days, 293

BADINGS, HENK, composer - turns Nazi, 281; accepts German support, 299
Bali, island of, taken by Japanese, 325
Balluseck, D. J. von, imprisonment of -, chief editor Algemeen Handelsblad, 285
Baltic states, colonization in - urged by Nazis, 328
Bandung, N. E. I., capitulation of -, 326
Battle (s), of the Macassar Straits, 324; of the Java Sea, 325
Baum, Vicki, books by - forbidden, 302
BBC, London, interesting broadcasts of the, 287, 294
Bedcover, scarcity of, 82
Beer, rationing of, 86
Berenschot, Lt.-General G. J., killed in accident, 321
Bernhard, Prince, *see* Prince Bernhard
Bible Study Groups, formation of, 198, 199
Bishop, J. H. G. Lemmens, of Roermond, deprived of part of residence, 206
Blackmail, Nazis apply - for Winter Help purposes, 308, 310, 314
Black market, industrialists forced to - practices, 57; - for cycles and cycle tires, 65; development of - in foodstuffs, 67*ff*; punishment for - offenders, 70, 71; - for bread, 77; - for eggs, 78; - for meat, 78; - for potatoes, 79; - for poultry, 79; - for fruit, 80; - for vegetables, 80; - for cigars and cigarettes, 85; - for horses, 114; - for horticultural produce, 121; - for milk, 121; - for suckling pigs, 121
Blackout (s), rigorously adhered to, 332; constant trespasses of - rules, 343
Blitzkrieg, too swift to bring Germans full benefits, 332
Blockade, British - cause of lack of fodder, 115
"Blockade," Nazi periodical, 279
Blokzijl, Max, propagandist for Nazism, 44; - on requisitioning of metals, 61; - exhorts Dutch to help fight bolshevism, 169; becomes editor of "De Standaard," Amsterdam, 202; biographical sketch of -, 273*ff*; activities in Nazi service, 274
"Blood and Race" theory, application of the -, 32
Blood donors, Jews cannot be, 216
Boening, Dr., German - to shanghai Dutch laborers, 96
Bolshevism, "threat of -" propaganda, 167
Bombing (s), German - of Rotterdam, *347*; reaction of Dutch to allied, 342
Book (s), theological - destroyed, 206; Germany makes "gift" of 2000 - to Holland, 279; Nazis organize show of German, 279; publishing under Nazi regime, 301; some forbidden, 302; difficulty to reprint, 303; foreign - few in number, 303
Boot, H. F., Haarlem, painter - turns Nazi, 281
Booymans Museum, Rotterdam, head of - turns Nazi, 281
Borneo, island of, Japanese forces land on, 325
Boy Scouts, *see* Scout movement
Brawls, underground leaders urge stop of - with Storm Troopers, 146
Bread, rationing of - introduced, 73
Bread-flour, poor quality of, 76
Bredero, Gerbrand Adriaenszoon, 297
British allies, Nazi campaign against, 24

Briton, Colonel, vi
Broadcasting, before the invasion, 291; State - company inaugurated, 292
Brucken Fock, Dr. Hans von, estimates cost of occupation army, 53
Buchenwalde, camp of, *see* Concentration camp (s)
Burgomasters, correspondence course for Nazi, 139; stormy investiture of several Nazi, 139, 140; Nazi - blackmail municipal staffs into supporting Winter Help, 311; loyal - ousted, 337
Burlet, N. H., professor -, Dean of Groningen University, cooperates with Nazis, 254
Business, "Aryanization" methods of Jewish -es, 222
Butter and fats, rationing of, 74

CABINET, personal - of Mussert appointed, 165
Camp, - life for Nazi journalists, 284
Canada, new army formed in, 330
Cannenburgh Castle, a "camp" for journalists, 284
Capital, all Jewish - concentrated in nazified Bank, 221
Capital punishment, *see* Dealth penalty
Capitulation, announcement of the, 1
Carnation, white - emblem of national allegiance, 26
Carp, Dr. J. H., heads "Secretariat of State" 165
Casualties, in Rotterdam, 10; announcement of - among Dutch Nazi volunteers prohibited, 183
Catholic (s), refusal to support the Winter Help, 313; obstruct N.S.B. -instituted "Nederlandsche Volksdienst," 317
Catholic bishops, protest against nazification of Catholic Trade Unions, 105
Catholic church (es), refuse rites for Dutch Nazis killed in action, 182, 193; persecution of the - in Germany, 187; join Protestants in protest-interview with Seyss-Inquart, 190; pre-invasion denunciation of National-Socialism, 193; episcopal letter against National-Socialism, 193; pastoral letter of Nov. 10, 1940, 193; members of the - cannot support the N.S.B., 194; on strained terms with N.S.B., 194; Lenten Letter of Feb. 22, 1942, on attitude of Catholic labor, 195; complete text of pastoral letters of the, *354, 358*
Catholic newspapers, suppressed, 205
Catholic Press Bureau, leader of - killed in concentration camp, 207
Catholic Trade Unions, nazification of all, 104
Catholic University of Nijmegen, assailed by Nazis, 207; under German control, 207
Catholic workers, refuse to join Nazified trade unions, 195
Catholic youth movements, *see* Youth movements, Catholic
Cattle herd, reduction of the, 114, 117, 118
Cattle markets, Jews forbidden entrance to, 221
Ceiling prices, on fruit and vegetables, 80; protest strike against, 81
Celebes, island of, Japanese make landings on the, 325
Censorship, absence of - on press, 271; on plays and songs, 297
Central Agricultural Organizations, oppose Nazi Agrarian Front, 110
Ceremonies, on May 10, 1941, severely restricted, 337
Chain letter, as a means of passive resistance, 336
Charity, *see* Winter Help
Chickens, *see* Poultry
Children, *see also* Schoolchildren; sent "vacationing" in Austria, 18; Jewish - to go to special schools, 221; Jewish - barred from youth shelters, 268; help distribute underground newssheets, 290
Choral societies, amateur - "co-ordinated," 299
Christian, National - Trade Unions, nazification of the, 104
Christiansen, Nazi Air Force General Friedrich, heads occupation troops, 42
Church, *see also* Catholic, Protestant, Reformed

Church collections, restrictions on, 204; prohibition of, 205

Church(es), attendance of - increases, 186; accused of distributing underground newssheets, 290; refuse to cooperate in Winter Help work, 309; distribute support to needy, 317; nine leading - protest unanimously against sterilization of Jews, *361*

Cigarettes, rationing of, 85

Cigars, rationing of, 85

Citizen(s), to stand guard against sabotage, 343

Civil servants, Reformed churches protest against ousting of Jewish, 188

Civil service, extension of the, 72; - closed to Jews, 212; all Jews eliminated from, 213; entrants to and members of the - must do Labor Service duties, 257

Clergy, brave attitude of Holland's, 199

Clergymen, rounded up and arrested, 206

Cleveringa, Rudolph Pabus, Dean of Leyden University, defends ousted Jews, 214; taken to German concentration camp, 216

Clingendael, castle of, used by Seyss-Inquart, 279

Clothing, rationing of, 81, 82; collection of warm - for Germans on eastern front, 173

Coal, *see* Fuel

Coffee, rationing of, 76

Coins, introduction of zinc, 61

"Cold Wave", listening to forbidden radio called, 294

Colijn, Dr. Hendrikus - sent to concentration camp, 201; spokesman of joint political groups, 235; disavows the Netherlands Union, 239

Collections, Nazis restrict - in Protestant churches, 204; public - for victimized German Jews, 211; public money - forbidden except for Winter Help, 306; poor results of street - for Winter Help, 307

Collectors, efforts to find voluntary Winter Help, 312

College fees, *see* Students

Colleges, denominational, *see* Denominational Universities

Colonization, Dutch - of White Russia and Baltic States, 328

Commemoration, restrictions on - of invasion day, 337

Communist Party, disbanding of the, 100

Composer(s), young - Henk Badings turns Nazi, 281; accepts German support, 299

Concentration camp(s), Jews sent to - of Buchenwalde, 219; groups of Dutch prisoners sent to German, 334

Concertgebouw, Amsterdam, monster meeting in the, 39

Concertgebouw Orchestra, *see* Mengelberg, Willem

Concerts, great increase in amateur, 304

Confessional Colleges, *see* Denominational Universities

Confessional Schools, *see* Denominational Schools

Confessional Trade Unions, *see* Trade Unions, Catholic; Trade Unions, Protestant

Congress, poets' - at Weimar, 280

Contagious diseases, *see* Diseases

"Coordination", swift - of trades, 47, 48

Cost of living, rise of the, 60

Costa, Mendes da, famous Dutch-Jewish sculptor, 209

Council, Jewish, *see* Jewish Council

Courts, German Peace, sentences of the, *349*

Courts, military, death sentences of German, 337

Cover, warm, collection of - for Germans fighting in Russia, 173

Cream, only on doctor's prescription, 74

Crop(s), sabotage to - of N.S.B. farmers, 344

Cross, Dutch patriots display the - as a "token" of recognition, 203

Cruiser(s), *see* Fleet

Culture and Public Enlightenment, Dept. of, *see* Goedewaagen

Culture Chamber, *see* Netherlands Culture Chamber

Culture Circle, Catholics warned not to join the Nazi, 194

Culture Council, installation of Nazi, 281; names of some members of the, 281

Curfew, special - for Jews, 230; introduction of, 332

Cycle(s), black market in - and cycle tires, 65; contest for substitute cycle tires, 65; scarcity of - tires, 65; theft of - tires, 65; requisitioning of, 66

Cycle-taxi(s), replace motor cars, 64

DAM, Professor Jan van, appointed Secretary-General of Education, 46, 251, 278; assails Van Genechten on Leyden University changes, 256; to appoint all new teachers, 261; changes school curriculums, 262; rules fate of all teachers, 264

Dancing, ban on - lifted, 335

David, Star of, *see* Star

Death penalty, for black market offenders, 71; asked by German military courts, 337

Death rate, rise of the, 87

Declaration of obedience, *see* Obedience

Dekker Maurits, books by - forbidden, 302

Delft, Technical College of, mass protest against ousting of Jews, 213; closed by Nazis, 216; reopened, 253; students' clubs dissolved, 253; Deans and Curators resign en bloc, 254

Den Helder, naval base of, R. A. F. attack on, 19

Denominational schools, influence of - curtailed, 205; children leave - because of N.S.B. teachers, 262; threatened with loss of State subsidy, 262

Denominational Trade Unions, *see* Trade Unions, Catholic; Trade Unions, Protestant

Denominational Universities, activities of - curtailed, 205; closing of, 260

Deportation, wholesale - of foreign Jews resident in Holland, 192; mass - of Dutch Jews rumored, 225; - en masse begins, 226; changes in - system, 229; denounced by Churches, *355*, *359*

Deutsche Zeitung in den Niederlanden, appears in full size, despite paper shortage, 286

Diseases, contagious, increase of, 87

Doctors, *see* Physicians

Doggerel(s), sample of anti-Nazi, 336

Domination, Spanish, *see* Spanish domination

Doolaart, Anton den, books by - forbidden, 302

Drama, Nazi contest for best Netherlands, 296

Dutch Nazis, march provocatively through Amsterdam's Jewish district, 216

Dutch SS, *see* Standarte Westland

EAST COMPANY, *see* Netherlands East Company

East Indies, *see* Netherlands East Indies

Economic Collaboration, National Committee for -, 47

Economic conditions, in invaded country, i

Economic Front, Nazi - established, 138

Economic Organizing Committee, 48

Economic, pillage of Holland, 51*ff*; results in Holland of Far Eastern war, 323

Education, Arts and Sciences, *see* Dam, Professor Jan van

Education, Nazi - of youth, 248; Dept. of - divided in two, 251, 278; drastic changes in school curriculums, 262; Dutch Nazi youths to be trained as Fuehrers, 263; inspectors ousted, 264; Jan van Dam rules fate of all teachers, 264; Catholics oppose nazified, 265

Educators' Guild, founding of Nazi, 250

Eekhout, Jan H., Nazi author - distinguished, 301

Eggs, rationing of, 74

Eindhoven, city of, Allied bombing of, 342

Einthoven, L., co-founder of the Netherlands Union, 236; sent to concentration camp, 247

Electricity, rationing of, 83

England, new Dutch army formed in, 330; invasion of, 335
Enschedé, town of, Nazi terror in textiles center of, 219
Esperanto, groups disbanded, 333
"Eternal Jew, The", obligatory showing of anti-semitic film, 221, 298
Evacuation, hardships of, 342
Executions, swift increase of, 337; reach high total, 344
Exemptions, from forced labor law for Jews, 231
Exhibitions, *see* Art (s)
Exports and Imports, central service for - regulating all international trade, 57

FACHGRUPPEN, *see* Guilds
Farmers, opposition of the, 109; official Nazi -Journal published, 124; sabotage crops of N.S.B.'ers, 344
Farmers' Wives, League of, *see* League of Farmers' Wives
Farm horses, requisitioning of, 114
Farmhouses, destruction of, 12; repair of war-destroyed, 63
Farm land, sale of - restricted, 112
Farm labor, depletion of, 114
Farm machinery, scarcity of, 114
Fertilizers, looting of indispensable, 113
Feuchtwanger, Leon, books by - forbidden, 302
Film (s), forced showing of anti-semitic, 221, 298; all foreign - banned, except German, 297; drastic changes in showing of, 297; Nazi newsreels, 298; censorship on - instituted, 298; Nazi - on life of Rembrandt, 298
Film Board, State, Nazi heads the, 298
Film Guild, Nazi - at work, 298
Finances, decline of Holland's, 57*ff*
Fine (s), Nazis impose colossal - on various cities, 337
Fire arms, army officers must relinquish, 343
Fischboeck, Dr. Hans von, Commissar-General for Finance, 44
Fish, high prices of, 79
Flag, Dutch, symbolic value of the, 337
Fleet, Dutch cruiser - reported annihilated, 325; at Sourabaya and Tandjung Priok caught in trap, 325; suffers heavy losses, 325
Flyers, Dutch, new - force formed in U. S. A., 330
Fodder, lack of, 115; requisitioning of, 118
"Fog Horn, The," *see* "Misthoorn, De"
Folksongs, used to obstruct Nazis, 300
Foodstuffs, State Bureau for the distribution of, 49
Forbidden radio, *see* Radio
Forced labor, in Germany, 92, 93; for deported Jews, 230; exemptions from the - laws, 231; denounced by Churches, *355, 357*
Foreign trade, no longer dependent, 57
Freemason movement, disbanded, 333
"Fuehrer (s)", training of Dutch Nazi youths as, 263
Fuel, rationing of, 82; scarcity of, 83, 264; miners apply "slowdown" tactics, 336; sabotage in mines increases, 344
"Future," Nazi periodical, 279

GAS, shortage of, 63; rationing of heating, 83
Geelkerken, C. van, deputy N.S.B. leader, Head Stormer of the National Youth Storm, 148; gets place in Secretariat of State, 163
Genechten, Professor Robert van, gets place in Secretariat of State, 163; founds Educators' Guild, 250; appointed special professor at Leyden, 254; suggests transform Leyden into National-Socialist University, 255
Generators, wood - for automobiles, 63
Gentiles, not to enter domestic employment of Jews, 216; extend help to persecuted Jews, 218; disobey anti-Jewish edicts, 220; protest against institution of the "Jewish Star", 224; assist persecuted Jews till end, 232
Gerbrandy, Pieter S., Prime Minister of the Netherlands, foreword by, i; Nazi campaign against, 23; Nazi characterization of, 158; broadcasts explanation of declaration of war on Japan, 322

German Army, suffers defeats in Russia, 171; accepts volunteers of "related Nordic groups", 174
German Courts, introduction of special, 334
German lauguage, *see* Language (s)
German motorized transport division, N.S.B.'ers serve in the, 175
German-Russo war, *see* Soviet Russia
German teachers, in Delft and Leyden Universities, 253
German Universities, *see* Universities
Gestapo, iv; hunts and tortures men of the underground press, 289
"Geus, De", students' underground paper, 288
Ghettos, Jews from all over Holland lodged in Amsterdam, 223; Dutch Jews in the - of Poland, 229
Girl Scouts, *see* Scout movement
Goebbels, Dr. Joseph, inaugurates German Book exhibition, 279
Goedewaagen, Prof. T., becomes professor at Utrecht University, 163; heads Dept. of Culture and Public Enlightenment, 251, 278; appointed professor of "New Philosophy" at Leyden University, 254; subjugates press, radio and liberal arts, 278; announces foundation of Culture Chamber, 280; organizes same, 281; purges Netherlands periodical press, 285
Gold, privately-owned - requisitioned, 54
Gold reserves, of Netherlands Bank taken by Nazis, 54
Government, legal Dutch, prayer for the - and for the Royal House, 200
Government, Netherlands, growing authority of - in London, 339; gives directives in crises, 340
Governmental apparatus, Nazis set up their, 31
Governor-General of N. E. I., *see* Stachhouwer
Gravemeyer, Dr. K. H. E., Secretary Netherlands Reformed Church, imprisoned, 205; released and rearrested, 206; second release, 206
Green Cross, Aid Society disbanded, 316
Green Police, 7; rounds up Jewish "hostages," 228; rules Dutch people, 332
Groningen Agricultural Association, disbands, 124
Groningen, province of, J. Linthorst Homan dismissed as Commissioner for, 246
Groningen, University of, J. Linthorst Homan ousted as Curator of, 247; President of - cooperates with Nazis, 254; President of the - helps Nazis get students for labor in Germany, 260
"Groot Nederland", *see* Periodicals
Gruene Polizei, *see* Green Police
Guards, Voluntary citizen - against sabotage, 343
Guiana, Dutch, discussed at school, 267
Guilds, resuscitation of the, 31; Nazis try to organize agrarian, 111; poster appeal to workers to join the Nazi, 279; all - to join Culture Chamber, 280
Gunther, John, books by - forbidden, 302

"HAAGSCHE POST," weekly - gets Nazi editor, 254
Haarlem, city of, sabotage trial against - children, 268; how - reacted to fall of Indies, 330
Hague, city of The -, *see* The Hague
"Hall of the Knights", *see* Ridderzaal
Handelsblad, *see* Algemeen Handelsblad
Hannema, Dr. D., head of Rotterdam "Booymans Museum," turns Nazi, 281
Hartog, Jan de, success of historical novel by, 302
Health, swift deterioration of public, 87
Heijermans, Herman, Dutch-Jewish playwright and short story writer, 209
Helder, town of Den, *see* Den Helder
Herweyer, Dr. W. A., head of the nazified radio gets place in Mussert's "Personal Cabinet," 165, 292
Hess, Rudolph, vi
Het Volk, *see* Volk, Het
High Court of Justice, Nazis ignore the, *349*
Hilversum, *see* Radio Hilversum

Historical, novel by Jan de Hartog a great success, 302
History, Netherlands, Nazi misstatements concerning the, 33; clergy uses parables from, 200
Hitler, Adolf, "enlightening" pamphlet on, 37; -'s principles for the German attitude toward Holland, 153
Hoeben, Dr. Hein, Catholic journalist - dies in concentration camp, 207
"Holland's Glorie," *see* Hartog, Jan de
Homes, *see* Houses
Hoowij, Jan, "decadent" art of, 296
Horses, *see* Farm horses
Horticulture, post-invasion status of Dutch, 118
Hostages, sent to German concentration camps, 334; threatened with execution, 337; more - taken, 344
House of Orange, love for - increases, 23; demonstrations in favor of the - forbidden, 29; prayers for the - maintained, 199; political leaders emphasize fealty to the, 235; babies named after members of the, 336; possessions of members of - confiscated, 339
Houses, destruction of, 63
Housing situation, problem of housing Rotterdam refugees, 11
Huizinga, Leonhard, success of short novel by, 302
Hulsteyn, Wouter, renegade journalist - lecturer in "camp for newspapermen," 285
Human hair, use of, 62
Huyts, Johan, head of Nazi Press Guild, 286
Hygiene, endangered through lack of soap, 76

IDENTIFICATION CARD, introduction of the Personal, 332
Illegal slaughter, punishments for, 78
Indies, *see* Netherlands East Indies
Indies, West, *see* Netherlands West Indies
Indo-China, occupied by Japanese, 320
Industry, Dutch - "loaded" with Nazi orders, 55
Interest rate, lowered on German loans, 54
Inundation, draining of inundated lands, 10
Invasion, course of the, 2, 3, 5; Nazi *White Book* on the - of Holland, 16; allied - of the European Continent, 41; battles lasted too short a time, 331; Nazi preparation for - of England, 335
Israels, Josef, Jewish painter, 209

JANKE, WILLY, head of Nazi press department, 44
Japan, aggression by - expected, 320; pre-war commercial relations with, 320; at war with Netherlands, 321; effect in Holland of declaration of war on, 321; Prime Minister Gerbrandy explains declaration of war on, 322; loses many ships in battles with Dutch, 324; -'s position and the Tripartite pact, 327
Java, island of, attacks and landings on, 324, 325; fighting on the, 325; capitulates to Japanese, 326
Java Sea, battle of the, 325
Jewish, Reformed Churches protest ouster of - Civil Servants, 188; joint protest of Christian Churches on behalf of - Netherlanders, 191; all - elements to be eliminated, Commissar Schmidt announces, 192; world-famous - lawyers, 209; world-renowned - jurists, artists, 209; extent of anti - feeling, 210; first anti- - measures, 212; all - businesses registered, 213; new restrictions on - businesses, 217; dismissal of - musicians, 218; physicians to treat Jews only, 218; all - capital concentrated in nazified bank, 221; children to go to special schools, 221; -owned real estate registered, 221; 'aryanization" methods of - businesses, 222; - possessions sent to Germany as "voluntary gifts," 223; increase of - suicides, 225, 229; extermination of Dutch - life certain, 232; children barred from youth shelters, 268; banning of - music and musicians, 299; collection for - institute "Joodsche Invalide," 310; "Joodsche Invalide"

building used for sterilization of Jews, *361*
Jewish churches, attacks on, 218, 219
Jewish Council, powerlessness of the, 224; warns Jews to obey call to forced labor, 231
Jewish merchants, forbidden to sell in Amsterdam public markets, 212
"Jewish Star," wearing of - made compulsory, 223; gentiles protest against the, 224
Jews, persecution of the, iv; first round-up of Amsterdam, 38; deportation of foreign, 192; since the Napoleonic era, 209; during Queen Wilhelmina's reign, 210; barred from Amsterdam public markets, 212; ousted from Civil Service, 212, 213; barred from movie theatres, and concert halls, 216, 299; all - and half-Jews registered, 216; excluded as blood donors, 216; first physical attack upon Amsterdam, 216; may not employ gentile domestic labor, 216; barred from having radio sets, 217; young - rounded up in Amsterdam, 217; banned from Stock Exchanges, 218; excluded from hotels, boarding houses, public gardens, etc., 218; further round-up of Amsterdam, 219; banned from cattle markets, 221; sequestration of all arable land belonging to, 221; barred from public meetings, institutions, railroad stations, "Aryan" shops, etc., 222; denied telephone service, 222; professions closed to, 222; from all over Holland lodged in Amsterdam ghettos, 223; young - called for work in "Labor Camps," 223; mass deportation of - announced, 225; deportation begins, 226; deportation of Dutch - to Poland's ghettos, 229; deported - put to forced labor, 230; robbed of their homes, 230; forbidden to use unassigned public benches, 231; excluded from Culture Chamber, 281; underground press protests against deportation of, 290; persecution of - denounced by Churches, *355*, *357*; sterilization of, *361*
Jews, foreign - in Holland first deported, 228
Jews, German, Nazi persecution of, 210; help to persecuted, 210
Jongh, Archbishop J. de -'s pastoral letter against destruction of Trade Unions, 195; heavily fined, 206
Joodsche Invalide, *see* Jewish
"Joodsche Weekblad," warns readers to obey call to forced labor, 231
Journalist(s) "drilling" of Nazi, 284; among Dutch hostages, 334
"Joy and Labor" movement, initiated for nazified Dutch workers, 102
"Juggernaut over Holland," *see* Kleffens, Eelco N. van
Juliana, Princess, *see* Princess Juliana
Justice, Department of, N.S.B. enters the, 143
Justice, German, samples of, 334

KERSBERGEN, JAAP VAN, leader of Nazi Dramatists' Bureau, 296
Keyer, Dr. K., head Nazi Medical Front, gets place in "Secretariat of State," 165
Kitchens, Central, influence of the N.S.B. on the, 312
Kleffens, Foreign Minister Eelco N. van, Nazi campaign against, 23; attacked by Rost van Tonningen, 134; -'s book "Juggernaut over Holland" smuggled into occupied territory, 340
Koehler, Charlotte, imprisonment of actress, 297
Konijnenburg, Willem van, "decadent" art of, 296
Kraemer, Prof. Hendrik, famous theologian - arrested, 207
Krekel, Dr. H., appointed professor of historical philosophy at Leyden University, 254

LABOR, *see also* Laborers *and* Forced labor
Labor Bureaus, students must register with the, 257
Labor draft, 55
Laborer(s), dismissal of - forbidden, 12; prohibition to dismiss, 90; unemployed - sent to Germany, 92; conditions of Dutch - in Germany, 93, 98; shortage of - in the Reich,

94; nazified Dutch - get a "Joy and Labor" movement, 102; initiate slow-down campaign, 107; farm - sent to Reich, 114; poster appeal to - to "come to Germany," 279
Laborers, Catholic, refuse to join nazified Trade Unions, 195
Labor Exchanges, Germans appointed to head, 13; nazified, 45; activities of the - to send Dutch workers to Germany, 96, 97
Labor Front, replaces the N. V. V., 103
Labor Press, nazification of the, 101
Labor Service, former soldiers incorporated in the, 91; obligatory for Civil Servants, students, 257; military character of the, 258; obligatory for every youth, 260; school term shortened in favor of, 264
Land, sequestration of Jewish-owned arable, 221
Landstand, Nederlandsche, *see* Nederlandsche Landstand
Langemark School, Germany, Dutch Nazi youths sent to the, 263
Language (s), German - "preferred" for schools, 262
Lankenau, German Inspector-General, - of the Munich police force, appointed at The Hague, 144
Latzko, Andreas, books by - forbidden, 302
Law Front, Nazi - instituted, 138
League of Farmers' Wives, refuses collaboration with Agrarian Front, 123
League of Netherlands Teachers, "coordination" of the, 250
Legal Front, Nazi-instituted, 311
Legion, Volunteer - of the Netherlands, *see* Volunteer Legion
Lemmens, Mgr. J. H. G., bishop of Roermond, deprived of part of his residence, 206
Letland, Nazi "colonizing" efforts in, 328
Leyden, city of, clergyman uses story of -'s struggle against Spain, 200
Leyden University, protest against ouster of Jews, 214; closed by Nazis, 216; reopened, 253; students' clubs dissolved, 253; Deans and Curators resign en bloc, 254; Dr. H. Krekel appointed professor of Historical Philosophy at, 254; closed again, 254; T. Goedewaagen appointed professor of New Philosophy at, 254; Van Genechten appointed professor of Political Economy at, 254; to be a purely National-Socialist University, 255; dispute about change-over of, 256; former - pupils barred from study, 258
Liberty, loss of, 331
Libraries, Circulating - under Nazi regime, 301
Limburg, coal miners of -, apply "slow down" tactics, 336; sabotage in - mines increases, 344
Linthorst Homan, J., co-founder of Netherlands Union, 235; dismissed as Groningen province Commissioner, 246; ousted as Curator of Groningen University, 247; sent to concentration camp, 247
Lippman, Rosenthal & Co., Amsterdam bank of - appointed to "guard" all Jewish capital, 221
Liquor, rationing of, 86
Literature, *see* Authors
Lithuania, living conditions of "colonizers" in, 329
Loans, interest lowered on German, 54; government - under Nazi auspices, 59
Lodges, Freemason - disbanded, 333
Loon, Hendrik Willem van, "forbidden" author, 302
Loon, Dr. Johannes van, Dutch Nazi becomes President of Supreme Court, 143
Looting, in its various forms, 51*ff*
Lottery, public - to find money for unpopular Winter Help, 313
Louwes, S. L., head of National Rationing Board, 75
Ludwig, Emil, -'s books forbidden, 302
Luftwaffe, poem on the "mercy" of the, 20; Mussert brings homage to the, 26

"MAASBODE, DE," disbandment of, 205
Macassar Straits, battle of the, 324
Magazines, *see* Periodicals

Malnutrition, iv; effects of constant, 87
Manifest, joint - of political parties, 235
Mann, Thomas, books by - forbidden, 302
Marechaussée, *see* Police, State -
Margriet Francisca, Princess, special underground paper on birth of, 290
Markets, public - forbidden to Amsterdam Jews, 212
Mass deportation, *see* Deportation
Mauthausen (Austria), Young Amsterdam Jews killed in - sulphur mines, 217
Mayors, *see* Burgomasters
Meat, rationing of, 74, 78; illegal slaughter of, 78
Medical Front, Nazi - established, 138
Mengelberg, Professor Willem, conducts jubilee concert, 14; conductor - active in German "Joy and Labor" movement, 102; accepts post as member of Nazi Culture Council, 281; only remaining pre-invasion conductor, fallen into disgrace, 299
Merchant Marine, a powerful weapon, 330
Metals, requisitioning of, 60
Meyer, Arnold, National Front leader, suggests formation of a Dutch Legion, 175
Meyers, Eduard Maurits, professor, 209; defense of - by R. P. Cleveringa, 214
Middelburg, town of, destruction of, 12
Milk, rationing of, 74; only skimmed - available (Aug. 1941), 77
"Misthoorn, De," anti-Catholic utterances of the, 203; denounces doctors for help to Jews, 230; attacks Arnhem Symphonic Orchestra for "honoring Jewish musicians," 300
Mook, Dr. Hubertus J. van, confidence in, 320; attacked by nazified press, 321; appointed Colonial Minister, 321; popular in occupied Holland, 340
Motley, John Lothrop, i
Mueller, Frederik Ernst, Dutch Nazi - appointed burgomaster of Rotterdam, 140
Municipal Councils, deprived of authority, 141
Music, restrictions on "Jewish" and other, 299; used to sabotage, 300
Musical instruments, large sale of, 304
Musicians, strike of - in Limburg, 301
Mussert, Anton Adriaan, leader of the N.S.B., remains in hiding, 5; "Fuehrer" of the Nationaal-Socialistische Beweging, 24*ff* and *passim*; biographical sketch of, 128*ff*; disappointments and difficulties of, 136*ff*; sends birthday telegram to Hitler, 138; appointed Leader of the Netherlands' people, 153; is warned against responsibilities of people's "leadership," 159; assails German "imperialism," 162; forms a Secretariat of State, 163; appoints a Personal Cabinet, 165; opposes Seyffardt's Volunteer Legion, 176; urges enlistment in Volunteer Legion, 179; forms a "Territorial Guard," 185; death of a brother of, 350
Mussert movement, hatred for - increases, v
Mussert's Secretariat, members of - killed, 345

NATIONAAL JONGEREN VERBOND, *see* National Youth League
Nationaal-Socialistische Beweging, *see* N.S.B.
Nationaal-Socialistische Nederlandsche Arbeiders Partij, competes with N.S.B., 34; disbandment of the, 155, 161; N.S.B. campaign against the, 288
National Center of Trade Unions (N.V.V.), is nazified, 101; increased benefits offered to members of nazified, 106; Catholics warned not to join the, 194; comprises Teachers' League, 250
National Committee for Economic Collaboration, 47
National Front, *see* Meyer, Arnold
National Geographic Magazine, *see* Periodicals

National League of Civil Servants, Nazi - established, 139
National-Socialist Motorized Corps, Dutch SS men join the, 147
National-Socialist University, Leyden to be made into a, 255
National - Sozialistische Kraftfahrer Korps, *see* National-Socialist Motorized Corps
National Youth League, disbanded, 28
National Youth Storm, Nazi - expanding activities, 138; lack of interest in the, 148; size of - membership, 248
Nationale Dagblad, headed by Rost van Tonningen, 134; admits small N.S.B. membership, 166
Nazi Courts, division of the, 45
Nazi posters, throughout Holland, 279
Nazi Treasury Bills, introduced, 6; Germans insist on acceptance of, 13; payments made in, 52
Nazis, Dutch, occupy administrative posts, 43
Nazis, German - in Holland, Schmidt leader of all, 44
Nazis, spiritual tyranny of the, i
"Nederlandsche Gemeenschap," new political movement by name of, 235
Nederlandsche Landstand, takes place of Nazi Agrarian Front, 110; inauguration of the, 122; "leaders" for - branches appointed, 124
Nederlandsche Landwacht, *see* Territorial Guard
"Nederlandsche Omroep," Radio - inaugurated, 292
Nederlandsche Unie, 36; note on the, 160; foundation and main program points of, 236; "collaborationism" of the, 237; ambiguous attitude of the, 238, 243; condemns anti-semitism, 238; reaction of political parties to the, 239; rapid development of the, 241; Germans turn against the, 241; refuses co-operation with the N.S.B., 241; fails to develop political program, 242; flag of the - banned from display, 243; Germans tighten grip on the, 243; urges support of Nazi Winter Help, 244; disappoints Dutch people, 245; activities of the - hampered by Nazi restrictions, 246; refuses to side in German-Russo conflict, 246; forced into liquidation, 247
Nederlandsche Volksdienst, excludes Jews from benefits, 233; Dutch Nazi-instituted - cooperates with Winter Help, 312; purposes of the, 316; mainly concerned with N.S.B.'ers, 317; fiercely obstructed by Catholics, 317
Netherlands Bank, placed under German control, 50; Weekly Statement reveals condition, 58; first yearly report under Nazi regime, 58; headed by Rost van Tonningen, 135
Netherlands Broadcasting Company, *see* Nederlandsche Omroep
Netherlands Center of Youth Shelters, *see* Youth Shelters
Netherlands Commonwealth, *see* Nederlandsche Gemeenschap
Netherlands Culture Chamber, initiation of the, 280; obligatory membership of the, 280; leading artists refuse to join the, 281; controls all art materials, 282; underground press warns against the, 289; disturbing influences of the - on plastic arts, 296; exercises censorship on plays, songs, 297; stultifies musical life, 299; censors amateur musicals, 300
Netherlands East Company, reported on point of liquidation, 328; urges colonization of White Russia and Baltic States, 328
Netherlands East Indies, Nazis condemn - declaration of war on Japan, 158; increased interest in the, 319; Nazis prohibit discussion of Japanese-held, 328; loss of contact with relatives in the, 329; means of defense of the - too weak, 329; popular reaction to fall of the, 330
Netherlands Labor Front, *see* Labor Front
Netherlands Labor Service, *see* Labor Service
Netherlands literature, *see* Authors
Netherlands People's Service, *see* Nederlandsche Volksdienst

Netherlands Socialist Party, *see* Social Democratic Labor Party

Netherlands SS, displays greater activity, 138

Netherlands Union, *see* Nederlandsche Unie

Netherlands West Indies, American troops arrive in the, 158; Surinam discussed at school, 267; free Dutch territory, 319

Newspapers, *see also* Press; first appearance after invasion, 6; Dutch - abused to "prove" Soviet Russia is beaten, 171; no - censorship, 271; purge of periodical, 285; size of - reduced, 286

Newsreels, *see* Film(s)

News Service, Nazi - on radio, 292

Nijmegen, town of, (Catholic University of), *see* Catholic University

Nivo, *see* Political Institute

Notstandsbeihilfe, activities of the, 35

N.S.B. (Mussert Movement), members released after capitulation, 5; immediately after the capitulation, 25; competition from other Nat.-Soc. parties, 34; Holy Sacraments refused to Catholic members of the, 106, 194; farmers' opposition to the, 125; extracts from a diary of a farmer member of the, 126; foundation of the, 129; ingredients of - membership, 130; early history of the, 130*ff*; penetrates into the Magistracy, 143; gets into Dutch police force, 144; examples of popular loathing for members of the, 149*ff*, 248; tenth anniversary of the, 159; Seyss-Inquart declares - only tolerated political party, 160; commemorates eleventh anniversary, 163; gets a "Secretariat of State," 163; Nationale Dagblad admits - membership is small, 166; first thousand - members leave "to fight bolshevism," 180; creates organization to look after Volunteer Legion members on furlough, 184; on strained terms with Catholic churches, 195; leaders of the - condemn the Nederlandsche Unie, 242; unpopularity of the, 248; students demonstrate hatred for the, 258; more members of the - appointed to teachers' jobs, 262; children among patriotic pupils, 265; teachers strongly opposed by pupils, 266; poster appeal to laborers to join the, 279; growing - influence on public charity, 312; publishes "Honor Lists" of Quislings in the N. E. I., 327; crops of - farmers sabotaged, 344

N.S.B., party paper, *see* Nationale Dagblad

N.S.K.K., *see* German Motorized Transport Division

N.S.N.A.P., *see* Nationaal-Socialistische Nederlandsche Arbeiders Partij

Numerus clausus, for Jewish students, 216, 253

N.V.V., *see* National Center of Trade Unions

OBEDIENCE, declaration of, thousands of students refuse to sign - and go into hiding, 259; text of the, 259

Occupation Army, *see* Army of Occupation

Officers, Army, ordered to relinquish fire arms, 343; all former - registered, 344

"Official Journal," *see* Verordeningenblad

Oil wells, drilling of - in Overijsel, 63

Orange, as a symbol of liberty, 337, 339

Orange, Radio, London, *see* Radio Orange

"Oranjebode," special underground paper, 290

"Oranjekrant, De," underground paper, 288

"Order," Nazi periodical, 279

Oxford Group, disbanded, 333

Ozo, "new greeting" form, 336

PACIFIC WAR, *see* Netherlands East Indies

Painting, *see* Art(s)

Palaces, royal, looting of, 339

Palembang, N. E .I., Japanese landings near, 324

Parachutists, German - in action, 2

Parliament, Houses of, abolition of, 43
Parliament, Member(s) of, among Dutch hostages, 334
"Parool, Het," underground paper, 288
Pastoral letter(s), of February 21, 1943, 196; complete text of several, *354*
Pasture land, breaking-up of - made obligatory, 117, 121; farmers not interested in breaking-up of, 120
Peace Courts, installation of the, 151; sentences of the Nazi, *349*
Pearl Harbor, bombing of, 321
Peasants, farms for "racially pure," 112; sabotage crops of N.S.B.'ers, 344
Periodical(s), decay of - under Nazis, 303; rising demand for foreign, 304; monthly - survives, 304
Phipps, British Ambassador Sir Eric, attacked by Rost van Tonningen, 134
Physicians' Chamber, Nazis introduce a, 282
Physicians, Jewish - to treat Jews only, 218; gentile - try to help Jews, 230; refuse to join Nazi-instituted - Chamber, 282; general -' strike, 283; oppose Nazis "en bloc," 346
Pisuisse, *see* Blokzijl, Max
Plays, German censorship on, 297
"Pniël," weekly, suppressed, 286
Poets, Congress for Nazi - at Weimar, 280
Poets, German Nazi - speak in Holland, 279
Poland, Dutch Jews in the ghettos of, 229
Police, loyal members of the Dutch - force shot, 144; N.S.B. penetration into the Dutch - force, 144
Police, German, to supervise Dutch police forces, 42
Police, State (or Marechaussée), increase of the, 15
Political Institute, foundation of a German-Nazi, 263
Political leaders, emphasize faithfulness to royal house, 235
Political parties, completely paralyzed, 234
Political press, Netherlands Union publishes weekly, "De Unie," 238; "De Unie" reaches huge circulation total, 241, 246; monthly "Volk en Arbeid" prohibited, 241; canvassing with De Unie prohibited, 243
Political Service, State, *see* Staatspolitieke Dienst
Polizei, German Grüne, *see* Green Police
Pony-taxi(s), replace motor cars, 64
Pope Pius, Christmas message of, *354*
Posters, Nazi - throughout Holland, 279; Nazi - to boost Winter Help, 307
Posthuma, Folkert E., joins the Nazi party, 110; heads the "Production Control," 119; gets place in "Secretariat of State," 164; Nazi official - killed, 346
Posthuma Committee, for organizing agricultural production, 119
Potatoes, rationing of, 75, 76
Poultry, wholesale slaughter of, 115
Prayer, for Queen and legal government, 200
Press, *see also* Newspapers, *and* Religious, Political; suppression of Catholic newspapers, 205; daring students' paper at Utrecht, 258; Nazi influence on the, 284; purge of periodical, 285; regular publication of religious - forbidden, 285; part played by the underground, 288; growing power of the underground, 344
Press Bureau A.N.P., *see* Algemeen Nederlandsch Persbureau
Press, German, attacks rulers of the Netherlands East Indies, 321
Press Guild, Nazi - headed by renegade journalist, 286
Press, Netherlands, no censorship for the, 271; nazified - attacks rulers of the N. E. I., 321
Price ceiling, on all commodities, 6; on fruit and vegetables, 80; protest strike against, 81
Priests, salaries of - -teachers severely cut, 205
Prince, Bernhard's birthday (1940), start of open resistance, 26

Princess Juliana, Nazi's accuse - of "bartering" Surinam, 158; broadcasts of, 295
"Prins, De," weekly - banned for six weeks, 304
Prisoner (s), groups of Dutch - sent to German concentration camps, 334
Prisoners of war, return from Germany, 14
Production Control, introduction of - measures, 113, 119
Professions, various - closed to Jews, 222
Propaganda Bureau, German, various methods of the, 273
Propaganda, German, "builds up" Japanese victories in Pacific, 323
Propagandist (s), *see* Voorhoeve (Ernst); Blokzijl (Max)
Protest, joint Protestant and Catholic, 190; Seyss-Inquart replies to Catholic-Protestant, 191
Protestant Churches, degrading of the - in Germany, 187; protest to Secretaries-General, 189; join Catholics for protest-interview with Seyss-Inquart, 190; ignore order forbidding collections, 205; dignitaries of - sent to Nazi prisons, 208; denounce first anti-Jewish measures, 212; text of several protest letters of the, *357, 360*
Protestant newspapers, curtailed, 205
Provincial Assemblies, "reorganization" of, 141
Provincial Commissars, Nazi - in authority over all mayors, 141
Psychological talks, as part of Nazi propaganda, 272
Public health, *see* Health
Publishing, *see* Books
Punishment (s), disproportionate - by German Courts, 334

QUAY, PROFESSOR J. E. DE, co-founder of Netherlands Union, 235; sent to concentration camp, 247
Queen Emma, statue of - made center of national demonstration, 27
Queen Wilhelmina, speeches by, ii; campaign to vilify, 21; plan for her imprisonment, 22; demonstrations on -'s 60th birthday, 29; Nazis condemn -'s declaration of war on Japan, 158; Reformed Churches uphold authority of, 188; broadcasts of, 295, 338; declares war on Japan, 321; addresses people on fall of Indies, 326; exercises great influence, 338; -'s flight to England, 338; Germans increase attacks on, 338; portraits of - banned, 338; -'s possessions in occupied Holland confiscated, 339
Querido, Israel, Dutch-Jewish author, 209
Quislings, "honor lists" of - in the Indies, 327

RADIO, listening to "enemy" - forbidden, 28; head of the nazified, 165; Nazi news service on, 292; commercial sponsorship, 293; "leased wire" - services, 293; samples of Nazi - programs, 293, 294; "improvement" of Nazi - programs, 294; interest in "forbidden" foreign - broadcasts, 294; sets and equipment confiscated, 295
Radio Hilversum, in Nazi service, 273; before the invasion, 291; "centralization" of the, 291
Radio Orange, London, starts activities, 28; interest in - broadcasts, 287, 294; broadcasts Queen's speeches, 338
R. A. F., accused of bombing non-military targets, 19; growing sympathy for, 28; assistance to downed - men, 341
Railroad stations, barred to Jews, 222
Rape-seed, compulsory planting of, 117
Rappard, Dr. Van, *see also* Nationaal-Socialistische Nederlandsche Arbeiders Partij; -'s annexionist attitude, 155; bends down to Mussert, 160; -'s party fused with N.S.B., 161; rejoins German S.S., 161
Rationing, *see* under each separate commodity (bread, potatoes, etc.)
Rationing cards, suppression of unemployeds', 93
Rationing office (s), robbed, 70
Rations, for German citizens, 88
Rauter, Walter, General Commissary

of German Security Police, appointed, 43
Ravenswaay, C. van, placed in "Secretariat of State," 164; killed, 164
Real estate, Jewish - registered, 221; Jewish-owned - sold without owners' consent, 231
Rechtsfront, *see* Legal Front
Reconstruction Fund, forming of a, 9
Reconstruction problems, 12
Reconstruction Service, school Breda of the, 14; work of the, 15; creation of the, 90; develops into an obligatory labor service, 257
Reconstruction work, 62
Red Cross, gets parcels from Holland for British war prisoners, 341
Red Cross, German, poor results of a collection for the, 172
Reformed Churches, General Assembly of the - submits decisions to Seyss-Inquart, 187; protests against ousting of Jewish Civil Servants, 188; pastoral letter of September, 1941, 190; protest letter of the -, dated April 19, 1942, 191
Registration, of Jewish businesses, 212; of Jews and half-Jews, 216; of students with Labor Bureaus, 257; of former Army officers, 344; of demobilized soldiers denounced by Catholic Church, *358*
Reich's Commissioner, appointment of a, 6, 7
Reichskreditkassenscheine, see Nazi Treasury Bills
Relief, voluntarily - organizations, to obstruct Winter Help, 310
Religious newspaper(s), suspension of, 201; Nazis issue - weekly "Volk en Evangelie," 202; regular publication forbidden, 286
Remarque, Erich Maria, books by - forbidden, 302
Rembrandt, ludicrous Nazi film on, 298; a "Germanic" painter, 299
Requisitioning, of gasoline and transportation material, 6; of farm horses, 114; of cows, 116; of calves, 117
Resistance, first public demonstration, 26; forms of passive, 336; organization of, 345
Retaliation, on Dutch prisoners, 334; hostages to be shot in - for acts of sabotage, 337
Revival, religious, throughout the country, 199
Revolutionary Socialist Labor Party, disbanding of the, 100
Reydon, Dr. H., gets place in "Secretariat of State," 164; is seriously wounded, 164; Nazi - dies as result of assault, 345
Ridderzaal (Hall of the Knights), inauguration of Seyss-Inquart takes place in the - at The Hague, 8
Rijksmuseum, Amsterdam, exhibition of German art in the, 279
Rijsoord, capitulation signed in village of, 5
Ritual slaughter, *see* Slaughter
Roman-Catholic, *see* Catholic
Roosevelt, Franklin Delano, memorandum to - concerning fate of Jews, 229
Roskam, E. J., made "leader" of the Agrarian Front, 110; activities of - as Nederlandsche Landstand leader, 122; appoints "leaders" for Nederlandsche Landstand, 124; placed in Mussert's "Personal Cabinet," 165
Rostov, Dutch Nazis "help to conquer," 174
Rost van Tonningen, Meinoud M., received by Hitler, 36; appointed head of Netherlands Bank, 46; -'s first yearly report as head of the Netherlands Bank, 58; confers with Netherlands Socialist Party, 100; supervises newly-established Labor Front, 103; biographical sketch of, 133*ff*; heads Netherlands Bank, 135; gets place in "Secretariat of State," 164; heads the Netherlands East Company, 328
Roth, Joseph, books by - forbidden, 302
Rotterdam, city of, bombing and destruction of, 3; problem of reconstruction, 10; help to victims of bombing of, 35; allied bombings of, 342; German bombing of, *347*
Rotterdamsche Bankvereeniging, cuts out support of the Winter Help, 313

Rotterdamsche Courant, Nieuwe, "co-ordination" of the, 285; Johan Huyts, editor of the -, heads the Nazi Press Guild, 286
"Royal," nomenclature - changed into "National," 23
Royal House, *see* House of Orange
Royal Institute for the Marine, discontinued, 14
Ruiter, G. J., Dutch Nazi - appointed Director-General of Agriculture, 117
Russia, *see* Soviet Russia
Russo-German war, influence of the - on labor conditions in the Reich, 94
Royal Military Academy, Breda, discontinued, 14

SABOTAGE, increases, v; on farms owned by N.S.B.'ers, 125; trial against Haarlem children, 268; samples of musical, 300; rapid increase of, 336; "slow-down" campaigns, 336; hostages to be shot in retaliation for acts of, 337; new - methods, 343; harsh measures against, 343
St. Laurens church, Rotterdam, burning of the, 3
"Scales, The," *see* Waag, De
Schaffelaer, Jan van, 272
Scheltinga, Jonkheer D. Blocq van, heads Mussert's "Personal Cabinet," 165
Schmidt, Dr. Fritz, Commissary-General for Special Events, appointed, 44; supports the N.S.B., 135; announces Jews will be eliminated, 192; rails against Pastoral letter of February 21, 1943, 196; threatens any one not "volunteering" for Labor Service, 260
Schnitzler, Arthur, books by - forbidden, 302
Scholten, Professor, arrested, 208
Schoolbooks, *see* Textbooks
Schoolchildren, oppose Nazi rulers, 251; leave schools because of N.S.B. teachers, 262
Schools, special - for Jewish children, 221; anti-Nazi sentiments in the, 251; changes in - curriculums, 262; political discussion in schools disallowed, 263; affected by fuel scarcity, 264
Schools, agricultural, Catholic - closed down after protest against nazification, 265
Schools, confessional, *see* Denominational Schools
Schoorl concentration camp, gets first "load" of Jewish victims, 217
Schrieke, Prof. J. J., Nazi-appointed Secretary-General of Justice, 143
Scout movement, dissolved, 269; boy scouts persecuted, 269
Sculpture, *see* Art (s)
S.D.A.P., *see* Social Democratic Labor Party
Secretariat, Mussert's, several members of - killed, 345
Secret organization, "Colonel Verdun" supposed to head a, 337
Sentences, for black market offenders, 70, 71; of the Peace Courts, 151
Seyffardt, Lt.-General Hendrik A., gets place in Mussert's "Personal Cabinet," 165; suggests "donation" of an ambulance to Nazi troops in Russia, 172; forms Volunteer Legion, 176; pays sympathy calls to relatives of "Volunteer Legion" casualties, 183; is killed, 165, 185
Seyss-Inquart, Dr. Arthur, Reich's Commissioner for the occupied Netherlands, *passim*
Shares, *see also* Stock Exchange; registration of foreign, 54
Shoes, rationing of, 82
Shopping, restriction for Jews, 222
Shortwave radio, *see* Radio
Singapore, fall of, 324
Slaughter, ritual, for Dutch Jews prohibited, 212
"Slow down" campaigns, in industries and coal mines, 336
Sluyters, Jan, "decadent" art of, 296
Smuggling, of grain to Belgium, 122
Soap, lack of, 76
Social Democratic, radio speeches of - leader J. W. Albarda popular, 340
Social Democratic Labor Party, Rost van Tonningen confers with leaders of the, 100; "co-ordination" of the, 234; dissolution of the, 236; influence of the - during last fifty years,

130; many teachers belonged to membership of, 250
Social progress, during last half century, 130
Socialist Party, Nazi, *see* N.S.N.A.P.
Socialist Trade Unions, throttling of the, 101
Socialist Work Community, 34
Socialist Workers' Commonwealth, formation of the, 100
Socialist Youth League (A.J.C.), disbanded voluntarily, 268
Soldiers, re-imprisonment of, 295
Soldiers, German, hatred for, 335
Song of Hope, struck from students' textbooks, 252
Soviet Russia, Holland's reaction to bravery in defense of, 167; Nazis spread atrocity tales concerning war in, 168; Nazi propaganda efforts to convince Dutch - is beaten, 170; slow recognition of the, 340
Spanish domination, period of - in comparison with Nazi tyranny, 200
Speyck, Admiral Van, 272
Sponeck, General Von, Commander-in-Chief of German Air Division, ordered to take The Hague, 22
"Staatspolitieke Dienst," radio section, 292
Stachhouwer, Jhr. Dr. A. W. L. Tjarda van Starkenborgh, confidence in - as Governor-General of the N. E. I., 320; attacked by Nazi propagandists, 327
Stage, *see* Actors, Theater
"Standaard, De," Amsterdam, Colijn edits the Calvinist, 201; Max Blokzijl appointed editor of, 202
Standarte Westland, Dutch Nazi section of the S. S. - in action, 147; general loathing for men of the, 148; recruiting drive for the, 169; soldiers of the - have their baptism of fire, 174; incorporated in German SS "Viking" division, 174
Star of David, wearing of - made compulsory, 223; gentiles protest against the, 224
State Broadcasting Company, replaces pre-invasion radio companies, 291
State Museum, *see* Rijksmuseum
State radio, inaugurated, 292
Sterilization, Churches protest against - of Jews, *361*
Stock Exchange, boom on the -, owing to Nazi interests, 55; entrance to - denied to Jews, 218; shows further drop after fall of the N. E. I. but recuperates, 327; N. E. I. war and the Amsterdam, 322, 323
"Storm," monthly of the Dutch Nazi S. S., 147
Stormmeeuw, monthly of Youth Storm, cites instances of "persecution" at school, 266
Storm Troopers, Dutch Nazi - expand their activities, 138; become more aggressive, 144; general loathing for Dutch Nazi, 149; urged to join Volunteer Legion, 179; in German army service on east front, 181
Strike(s), Dutch patriots - because of first attack on Jews, 244; physicians' -, spring, 1943, 283; of Limburg musicians, 301; Amsterdam's heavy fine because of anti-Nazi, 309; of February, 1941, 336
Students, of Delft and Leyden protest against ouster of Jewish Civil Servants, 213*ff*; permitted to transfer to other Universities, 255; special arrangement regarding payment of college fees, 256; obliged to perform Labor Service before commencing study, 257; dodge Labor Service duties, 258; directed to certain universities, 258; arrested, 259; refuse to sign "declaration of obedience" and go into hiding, 259, 260; liberated, 260; at work in Germany, 261; food and fuel shortages affect work of, 264; underground paper for, 288; oppose Nazis "en masse," 346
Students, University - forbidden to wear insignia, emblems, or uniforms, 253
Students' clubs, dissolution of - at Delft and Leyden, 253
Students' Front, Nazi - established, 138; home of - at Utrecht destroyed by fire, 148
Study, affected by fuel scarcity, 264
Study clubs, Esperanto - disbanded, 333

Subjugation, disadvantages of rapid, 331
Submarines, Dutch - in action against Japanese, 324
Substitutes, for tea and coffee, 76
Suicides, increase of Jewish, 225, 229
Sumatra, Japanese land on, 325
Supreme Court, Nazi professor becomes President of the, 143
Surinam, *see* Netherlands West Indies
Synagogue(s), attack on - at The Hague, and elsewhere, 218, 219

TALKS, PSYCHOLOGICAL, as German propaganda, 272
Tauchnitz editions, *see* Books
Taxes, 59
Taxi(s), cycle - replace motorcars, 64
Tea, rationing of, 76
Teachers, salaries of priest-, severely cut, 205; "co-ordination" of the League of Netherlands, 250; political adherences of most, 250; German - in Delft and Leyden Universities, 253; new - to be appointed exclusively by Jan van Dam, 261; more N.S.B.'ers appointed, 262; completely governed by Jan van Dam, 264; N.S.B. - strongly opposed by pupils, 267
Teachers' Organization, Nazi - established, 138
Teachers' societies, united against Nazism, 250
Technical College, *see* Delft
"Telegraaf, De," questions Rost van Tonningen on Netherlands Bank Report, 58; "co-ordination" of the daily, 285
Telephone, service denied to Jews, 222
Territorial Guard, Mussert forms a, 185
Teunissen, G. J., heads Film Guild, 298; Nazi - made film-censor, 298
Textbooks, Nazis make changes in students', 252
Textiles, rationing of, 81; Nazi terror in - center of Enschedé, 219
Theater, Nazi influences on the, 296; amateur - suppressed, 297
The Hague, city of, rebels against bread rations, 77 ;attack on synagogue at, 218; Winter Help collections in, 310
Theologians, arrest of various, 207, 208
Theosophical movements, Nazis' interference with, 333
"Tijd, De," Catholic daily - allowed to appear, 205
Tobacco, attempts at "home-growing" of, 86
Token, Dutch display crosses as a - of patriotism, 203
Tolerance, Seyss-Inquart on, 40; religious - during Queen Wilhelmina's reign, 210
Tonningen, Meinoud M. Rost van, *see* Rost van Tonningen, Meinoud M.
Town management, Germans change system of - completely, 139*ff*
Trade papers, suppression of many, 285
Trade unions, all - placed under German control, 99
Trade Unions, Confessional, nazification of all, 104; "special conditions" offered to workers who remain members of the nazified, 107
Trade Unions, Roman Catholic, destruction of the, 195
Transportation, difficulties, 63
Travelling, severely restricted, 332
Travel, railroad - for Jews on permit only, 222
Treaty of Munster (1648), 32
Trees, stolen from roadside for fuel, 84
Tripartite Pact, embarrassing to Germans, 327
"Trouw," underground paper, 288
Truck gardeners, pressure upon, 119; difficulties of, 120
Tuition, *see* Schools

"UIT DE WOESTIJN," underground paper, 288
Ultimatum, German, sent to General Winkelman, 3
"Underdivers," Jewish, 225
Underground, leaflet urges assistance to Jews, 232; various - papers enumerated, 288; special - paper for students, 288; organizations support compatriots in distress, 318; growing power of the - press, 344; movement well organized, 345

Underground movement, urges stop to brawls with Storm Troopers, 146; students in the, 256
Unemployment, pre-war - in Germany, 89; figures for Holland, 90; Nazi methods to increase, 95
"Unie, De," organ of the Netherlands Union, 238; attains huge circulation figure, 241, 246; Germans prohibit canvassing with, 243; suspended, 246
Union, Netherlands, *see* Nederlandsche Unie
Unions, *see* Trade Unions
United States of America, new Dutch air force formed in Jackson, Miss., 330
Unity, growing - among Holland's churches, 198
University, Catholic, *see* Catholic University
Universities, authority of heads of - changed, 253, 255; diplomas and degrees of Dutch - valid in Germany, 255; students sent to Nazi-chosen, 258
Universities, denominational, *see* Denominational Universities
Universities, German, Dutch students permitted to transfer to, 255
Utrecht, University of, provisional exams given at, 258; students' newspaper subsists, 258; escaped undergraduate of - reveals situation, 258

"V" campaign, vi; applied in the churches, 202; "V" sign, a form of passive resistance, 336
Vaderland, Het, editor of - plays trick on Nazis, 286
Van der Veen, Y. G., socialist journalist - commits suicide, 101
Vegte, W. L. Z. van der, gets place in "Secretariat of State," 164
Verdun, Colonel, supposed head of a secret organization, 337
"Verordeningenblad" (Official Journal), 7, 45; first copy appears of, 9
"Victory," Nazi periodical, 279
Viking Division, *see* Standarte Westland
Vlissingen, Dr. Fentener van, 47
Volk, Het, socialist party paper - nazified, 101, 285
Volk en Arbeid, monthly - of the Netherlands Union prohibited, 241
Volk en Evangelie, Nazis issue religious weekly, 202
Volkdienst, *see* Nederlandsche Volksdienst
Volksche Opvoeding, *see* Political Institute
Volunteer Legion of the Netherlands, formed, 176; recruiting for the - a failure, 177; first and second contingent of - leave, 178, 179; disdain for "veterans" of the, 182; announcement of - casualties forbidden, 183; marriage formalities simplified for members of the, 183; N.S.B. creates organization to look after - members on furlough, 184
Volunteers, accepted for German army, but only of "related Nordic groups," 174
Voorhoeve, Ernst, Dutch Nazi propagandist - addresses Netherlands workers in Germany, 98; reveals N.S.B. propaganda blunders, 132; joins German troops to fight in Russia, 150; admits Protestant and Catholic leaders refuse to see him, 202; suggests cross-bearers should be molested, 204
"Vreugde en Arbeid" movement, *see* "Joy and Labor" movement
Vrij Nederland, underground paper, appears regularly, 287

W. A., *see* Storm Troopers
Waag, De, semi-fascist weekly, 46; publishes unfavorable comment on Anton Mussert, 138
Wages, ceiling on, 60
Walcheren, island of, capitulation of, 7
Wavell, General, leaves Java, 326
Weeklies, *see* Periodicals
Weer Afdeeling, *see* Storm Troopers
Welter, Charles J. I. M., Colonial Minister, visits the Netherlands Indies, 23
Werfel, Franz, books by - forbidden, 302

Westerbork, concentration camp at, 229, *361*
West Indies, Netherlands, *see* Netherlands West Indies
White Book, Berlin's - on invasion of Holland, 16
White Cross, Aid Society disbanded, 316
White Russia, colonization in - urged by Nazis, 328
White-Yellow Cross, Aid Society disbanded, 316
Wiegman, Mattheus, "decadent" art of, 296
Wilhelmina, Queen, *see* Queen Wilhelmina
"Wilhelmus Het," success of book, 302
William the Silent, statue of - made center of national demonstration, 27
Wimmer, Dr., General-Commissary for Law & Justice, 43
Winkelman, General, announces capitulation, 1; imprisoned, 15*ff*; letter about bombing of Rotterdam, *347*
Winter, 1941-42, severity of, iv
Winter Help, Nederlandsche Unie urges its members to support, 244; introduction in Holland, 306; in Germany, 306; various efforts to collect money for, 307; poor results in Amsterdam, 309; elaborate shows to support - collections, 310; extent of - during first year, 312; treatment of voluntary - collectors, 313, 315; resorts to sweepstakes and lotteries, 313; compulsory character of the, 314; significant collection figures, 315; civil servants forced to contribute to, 316; finds "abundant" support, 318
Wohltat, Dr., appointed Commissary to the Netherlands Bank, 50
Woltersom, H. L., heads Economic "organizing committee," 48; plans applied in Agrarian Front, 111
Wood, cut from privately-owned forests, for fuel, 84
Workers, *see* Laborers
Woudenberg, H. J., Dutch Nazi Labor Commissar, visits Netherlands labor camps in Reich, 97; Dutch Nazi - made head of nazified Center of Trade Unions, 101; made leader of the Labor Front, 103; nazified Socialist press on the person of, 104; placed in Mussert's "Personal Cabinet," 165; nominates a Nazi as President of the Educators' Guild, 250
WRUL, radio station, interest in broadcasts from, 294

YOUTH, -'s education to Nazism, 248
Youth movements, Catholic, disbanded, 105
Youth Shelters, Netherlands Center of - placed under Nazi leadership, 268
Youth Storm, monthly "Stormmeeuw" cites cases of Nazi children's "suffering" at school, 266; estimated membership, 269; constantly attacked, 269; members of the - fight Zandvoort mayor, *352*

ZANDVOORT, coastal resort of - bans Jews from public places, 218; burgomaster of - fights Youth Stormers, *352*
Zeeland, province of, fighting in, 5
Zuider Zee, reclamation of the, 123
"Zwarte Soldaat, De," weekly of Dutch Nazi S. S., describes their "activities," 145; announces Jewish life in Holland extinct, 231

Acknowledgment is due to the Netherlands Information Bureau, in New York, for many of the photographs reproduced in this book. The pictures of the Nazi invasion of the Netherlands have been reproduced from "Die Niederlande im Umbruch der Zeiten," published by the Germans in Holland during 1941.

EX LIBRIS
FATHERS' LIBRARY
BAY ST. LOUIS, MISS.
SOCIETATIS VERBI DIVINI

EX LIBRIS
FATHERS' LIBRARY
BAY ST. LOUIS, MISS.
SOCIETATIS VERBI DIVINI

EX LIBRIS
FATHERS' LIBRARY
BAY ST. LOUIS, MISS.
SOCIETATIS VERBI DIVINI

DAVID GLENN HUNT
MEMORIAL LIBRARY
GALVESTON COLLEGE

THE NETHERLANDS EAST INDIES
EQUATOR AND HAVE F

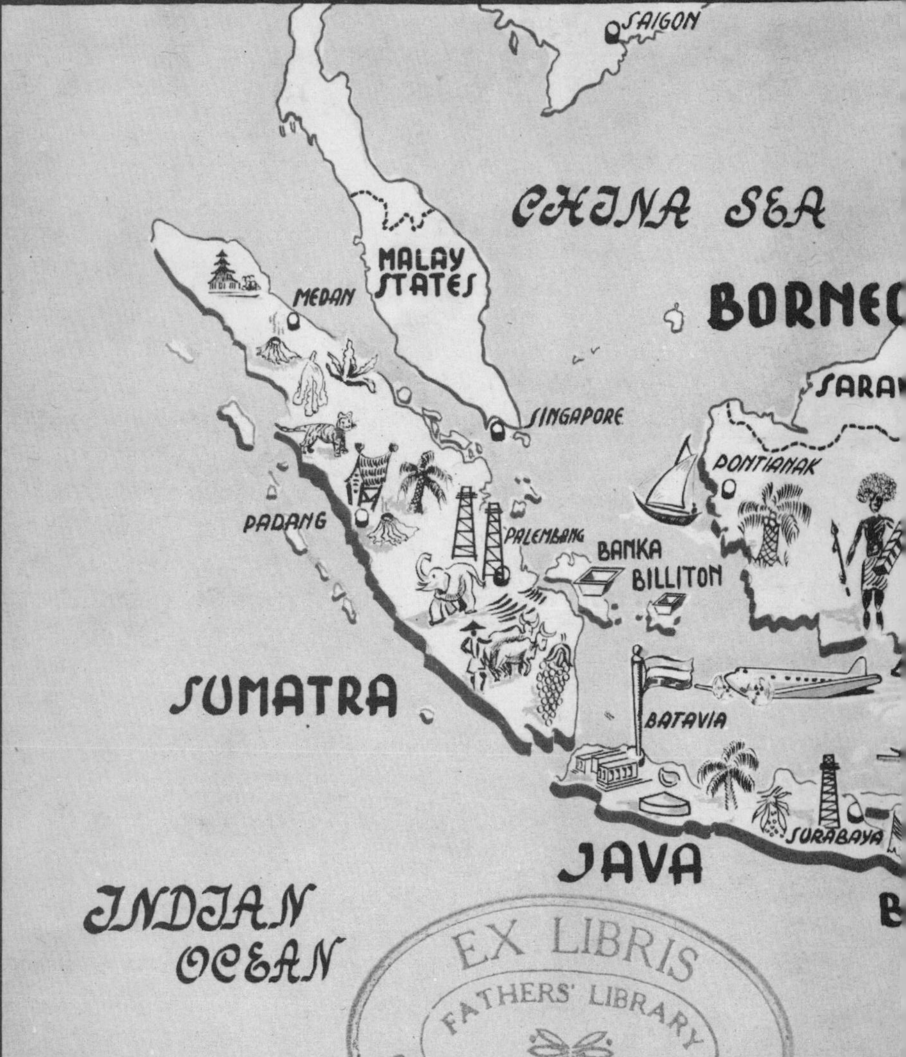

EX LIBRIS
FATHERS' LIBRARY
BAY ST. LOUIS, MISS.
SOCIETATIS VERBI DIVINI

PERCENTAGES OF WO

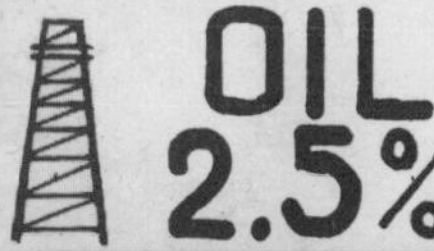